EC COMPETITION LAW

EC Competition Law

An Analytical Guide to the Leading Cases

Ariel Ezrachi

·HART·
PUBLISHING

OXFORD AND PORTLAND, OREGON
2008

Published in North America (US and Canada) by

Hart Publishing
c/o International Specialized Book Services
920 NE 58th Avenue, Suite 300
Portland, OR 97213-3786
USA
Tel: +1 503 287 3093 or toll-free: (1) 800 944 6190
Fax: +1 503 280 8832
E-mail: orders@isbs.com

Website: www.isbs.com

Hart Publishing, 16C Worcester Place, OX1 2JW
Telephone: +44 (0)1865 517530 Fax: +44 (0)1865 510710
E-mail: mail@hartpub.co.uk
Website: http://www.hartpub.co.uk

British Library Cataloguing in Publication Data

Data Available

ISBN: 978-1-84113-674-5

Typeset by Forewords, Oxon
Printed and bound in Great Britain by
TJ International Ltd, Padstow, Cornwall

The Nature of this Book

This book is designed as a working tool. It is a concise, highly practical guide to the leading cases which shape European competition law.

Cases in this book include judgments of the European Court of Justice and Court of First Instance as well as leading decisions of the European Commission. Reference is also made to a number of cases from the Unites States and from European Member States. The book covers over 250 cases, including the majority of cases that are taught in leading universities across Europe.

The book is divided into ten chapters, focusing in particular on Articles 81 and 82 EC and their public and private enforcement. A short introduction at the beginning of each chapter reviews the relevant regulations and guidelines and provides an analytical framework for the cases covered in the chapter. All case entries are accompanied by commentary which adds further context by, among other things, analysing the case in relation to other cases, regulations and guidelines.

In line with the functional approach at the heart of this book, case entries are concise. They include a mixture of quotes and summaries, extracting the main points of each case that are relevant to the chapter in which the case appears. The reader will not find long extracts from regulations or guidelines in this book. These are easily accessible in hard or electronic form.

References in decisions or judgments to the old numbering of the Treaty of Rome have been updated throughout this book to include the renumbering following the Treaty of Amsterdam. Thus, references in earlier cases to Articles 85, 86 and 90 EC are represented as Article 81 EC (ex 85 EC), Article 82 EC (ex 86 EC) and Article 86 EC (ex 90 EC).

Outline Contents

Contents

Table of Cases

Introductory Note

This Table of Cases is divided into four sections: Court of Justice, Court of First Instance, Commission and Other Cases (which contains all national court rulings and rulings by non-Community international/European courts). References such as '178–9' indicate (not necessarily continuous) discussion of a case across a range of pages. Page numbers in bold denote full discussion of the case in question.

Court of Justice

Court of First Instance

Commission

Other Cases

The Concept of Undertakings

The term 'undertaking' identifies the addressees of the European competition provisions. As such, it is central to the analysis of Article 81 EC, Article 82 EC and the European Merger Regulation, as only 'undertakings' may be subjected to these regulatory instruments.

The Functional Approach

The EC treaty is silent on the meaning of the term 'undertaking', leaving it to the European Courts to develop and establish its content and realm. To ensure the full effectiveness of the competition provisions the Courts adopted a functional approach, applying the term to entities engaged in economic activities regardless of their legal status and the way in which they are financed. This functional approach focuses on the commercial nature of activities and not on the type of entity engaged in them. Consequently, it may capture individuals, trade associations, partnerships, clubs, companies and public authorities. See for example:

IV/33.384 etc	FIFA – distribution of package tours during the 1990 World Cup	3

The Relativity of the Concept

The notion of undertaking is a relative one. The functional approach and the focus on activity rather than the form of entity may result in an entity being considered an undertaking when it engages in some activities but not when it engages in others. The relativity of the concept is most evident when considering activities carried out by non-profit-making organisations or public bodies. These entities may at times operate in their charitable or public capacity but may be considered as undertakings when they engage in commercial activities. The economic nature of an activity is often apparent when the entities offer goods and services in the marketplace and when the activity could, potentially, yield profits.

The following cases highlight the way in which the courts and Commission assessed the nature of activities:

C–41/90	*Höfner and Elsner v Macrotron GmbH*	4
C–364/92	*SAT Fluggesellschaft v Eurocontrol*	5
C–159/91 etc	*Poucet v Assurances Générales de France*	6
C–343/95	*Cali & Figli v Servizi ecologici porto di Genova SpA*	7
T–319/99	*FENIN v Commission* (CFI)	8
C–205/03	*FENIN v Commission* (ECJ)	9
C–309/99	*Wouters*	11
C–264/01 etc	*AOK-Bundesverband*	12

See also summary references to:

C–244/94	*Fédération Française des Sociétés d'Assurance*	6, 12
C–475/99	*Ambulanz Glöckner v Landkreis Sudwestpflaz*	7, 10
C–157/99	*Smits and Peerbooms*	9
1006/2/1/01	*BetterCare v The Director General of Fair Trading*	10
C–218/00	*Cisal di Battistello Venanzio & Co Sas*	13

Single Economic Entity

Moving away from the functional assessment of the activity, another question related to the term 'undertaking' is raised in the application of Article 81 EC. The Article applies to, among other things, agreements between undertakings. It therefore does not cover internal activities within an undertaking but only agreements between undertakings.

The concept of undertaking may encompass several legal entities or natural persons. Subsequently, the corporate principle of separate legal personality gives way in the area of competition law to the economic concept of undertaking. The scope given to the term undertakings may affect the application of competition laws to groups of companies. On one hand it may exclude agreements between separate legal entities within a single economic unit from the application of competition law and view them as an internal allocation of functions. On the other hand, it may link separate legal entities by viewing them as a single undertaking, thus holding the group of entities responsible for an anticompetitive activity carried out by one of them. See for example:

C–73/95 P	*Viho Europe BV v Commission*	14
IV/32.732	*IJsselcentrale and others*	15
C–189/02 P etc	*Dansk Rørindustri and others v Commission*	16
2003 WL 21236491	*Provimi Ltd v Aventis Animal Nutrition SA and others*	17
1072/1/1/06	*Sepia Logistics Ltd v OFT*	18

See also summary references to:

170/83	*Hydrotherm v Compact*	14
T–68/89 etc	*SIV and others v Commission*	14
22/71	*Beguelin Import Co v SAGL Import Export*	14
C–286/98	*Stora Kopparbergs Bergslag AB v Commission*	16
2002 WL 31413939	*Suretrack Rail Services Limited v Infraco JNP Limited*	18

FIFA – distribution of package tours during the 1990 World Cup Case IV/33.384 and IV/33.378 European Commission, [1992] OJ L 326/31	**Undertakings** Functional Approach

Facts

The European Commission considered a complaint regarding the ticket distribution system endorsed by the International Federation of Football Associations (FIFA) during the FIFA World Cup, held in Italy in 1990. The organisation of the event and the distribution of tickets were managed through a 'local organising committee' which was set up jointly by FIFA and the National Italian Football Association (FIGC). The ticket distribution system operated through various sport associations yet it included a restriction on sales to travel agencies. This restriction enabled the exclusive grant of the world wide distribution rights of tickets as part of package tours to an Italian joint venture '90 Tour Italia SpA'. This exclusivity arrangement prevented other travel agencies from offering combined package tours with tickets for the 1990 World Cup. In its decision the Commission considered the compatibility of the exclusive distribution agreement with Article 81 EC. A preliminary question concerned the nature of the entities involved and whether they constituted an undertaking within the meaning of Article 81 EC.

Decision

Any entity, regardless of its legal form, which engages in economic activity, constitutes an undertaking within the meaning of Articles 81 and 82 EC. An economic activity includes any activity, whether or not profit-making, that involves economic trade. (para 43)

The World Cup is indisputably a major sporting event yet it also involves activities of an economic nature. These activities include the sale of package tours comprising hotel accommodation, transport and sightseeing, the conclusion of contracts for advertising, the conclusion of television broadcasting contracts and more. (para 44)

FIFA is a federation of sports associations and accordingly carries out sports activities, yet it also carries out activities of an economic nature. These include, among other things, the conclusion of advertising contracts and television broadcasting rights which account for around 65 per cent of total World Cup revenue. Consequently, FIFA is an entity carrying on activities of an economic nature and constitutes an undertaking within the meaning of Article 81 EC. (paras 47–9)

Similarly, the National Italian Football Association (FIGC) carries on activities of an economic nature and is consequently an undertaking within the meaning of Article 81 EC. (paras 50–3)

The 'local organizing committee' was set up jointly by FIFA and the FIGC for the purpose of carrying on activities relating to the technical and logistical organisation of the World Cup and the establishment and implementation of the ticket distribution arrangements. The local organizing committee's revenue derived from, among other things, television rights, advertising rights and the sale of tickets. The exclusive rights granted to the Italian joint venture '90 Tour Italia' resulted in remuneration for the local organizing committee. Subsequently, the local organizing committee carried on activities of an economic nature and constituted an undertaking within the meaning of Article 81 EC.

Comment

Note that the fact that an organisation lacks profit motive or economic purpose does not in itself bring it outside the concept of undertakings.

On the functional approach, see also the following cases below (pages 4–13), which focus on the distinction between economic activity and public or charitable activities which fall outside the competition prohibitions.

Höfner and Elser v Macrotron GmbH
Case C–41/90
ECJ, [1991] ECR I–1979, [1993] 4 CMLR 306

Undertakings
The Relativity of the Concept
Employment Procurement

Facts

A preliminary reference to the ECJ by the German court seeking advice on, among other things, whether a monopoly of employment procurement granted to a public employment agency constituted an abuse of a dominant position within the meaning of Article 82 EC.

In its ruling the ECJ examined the exclusive rights in light of both Article 82 EC and Article 86 EC. The latter concerned the conditions that a Member State must observe when it grants special or exclusive rights. The former examines whether an undertaking abused its dominant position and thus required the ECJ to establish whether the public employment agency may be classified as an undertaking.

Held (on the concept of undertaking)

In the context of competition law, the concept of an undertaking encompasses every entity engaged in an economic activity, regardless of the legal status of the entity and the way in which it is financed. (para 21)

'The fact that employment procurement activities are normally entrusted to public agencies cannot affect the economic nature of such activities. Employment procurement has not always been, and is not necessarily, carried out by public entities. That finding applies in particular to executive recruitment.' (para 22)

It follows that an entity such as a public employment agency engaged in the business of employment procurement may be classified as an undertaking for the purpose of applying the Community competition rules. (paras 21–3)

Comment

In defining the scope of the Community rules on competition, the ECJ gave priority to considerations of an economic nature rather than to stricter classification of a legal entity. The functional benchmark relies on the nature of the activity rather than on the form of the entity. This functional approach widens the group of entities which may be classified as undertakings and thereby subjected to the competition provisions. These may include, among other things, individuals, trade associations, clubs, societies, partnerships and companies.

Examples of entities being found not to constitute an undertaking may be found below in Case C–364/92 *SAT v Eurocontrol* (page 5 below), Case C–159/91 etc *Poucet v Assurances Générales de France* (page 6 below), Case C–343/95 *Diego Cali & Figli Srl* (page 7 below), Case T–319/99 and C–205/03 *FENIN v Commission* (pages 8–9 below), and Cases C–264 /01 etc *AOK-Bundesverband* (page 11 below).

Note that the application of Article 82 EC to public bodies or undertakings entrusted with the operation of services of general economic interest may be limited by the provisions of Article 86(2) EC. Subsequently, a public employment agency such as the one in this case, which is classified as an undertaking, is subjected to the prohibition contained in Article 82 EC, so long as the application of that provision does not obstruct the performance of the particular task assigned to it. A Member State which has conferred an exclusive right to carry on that activity upon the public employment agency may be in breach of Article 86(1) EC where it creates a situation in which that agency cannot avoid infringing Article 82 EC. On the application and interpretation of Article 86 EC, see Chapter 9 'Competition Law and the State'.

SAT Fluggesellschaft mbH v Eurocontrol Case C–364/92 ECJ, [1994] ECR I–43	**Undertakings** The Relativity of the Concept Public Tasks

Facts

Eurocontrol is a regionally oriented international organisation which was founded by a multinational agreement between several Member States to strengthen cooperation between them in the field of air navigation and provide a common system for establishing and collecting route charges for flights within their airspace.

The dispute in question came before the Belgian court and concerned the refusal of the air navigation company SAT Fluggesellschaft mbH (SAT) to pay Eurocontrol the route charges for flights made between September 1981 and December 1985. SAT alleged, among other things, that the procedure followed by Eurocontrol in fixing variable rates for equivalent services constituted an abuse of a dominant position.

In a reference made by the Belgian 'Cour de cassation', the ECJ was asked whether Eurocontrol was an undertaking within the meaning of Articles 82 and 86 EC.

Held (on the concept of undertaking)

In Community competition law, the concept of an undertaking encompasses every entity engaged in an economic activity, regardless of the legal status of the entity and the way in which it is financed. Subsequently, in order to determine whether Eurocontrol's activities are those of an undertaking within the meaning of Articles 82 and 86 EC, it is necessary to establish the nature of those activities. (paras 18, 19)

The Convention establishing Eurocontrol outlines its tasks which are chiefly concerned with research, planning, coordination of national policies and the establishment and collection of route charges levied on users of airspace. Eurocontrol also provides air space control for the Benelux countries and the northern part of the Federal Republic of Germany from its Maastricht centre. For the purposes of such control, Eurocontrol is vested with rights and powers of coercion which derogate from ordinary law and which affect users of airspace. With respect to this operational exercise Eurocontrol is required to provide navigation control in that airspace for the benefit of any aircraft travelling through it, even where the owner of the aircraft has not paid the route charges owed to Eurocontrol. Finally, Eurocontrol's activities are financed by the contributions of the Member States which established it. (paras 20–6)

Eurocontrol carries out, on behalf of the Contracting States, tasks in the public interest aimed at contributing to the maintenance and improvement of air navigation safety. Eurocontrol's collection of route charges cannot be separated from its other activities. The charges are set by, and collected on behalf of, the Member States and are merely the consideration, payable by users, for the obligatory and exclusive use of air navigation control facilities and services. (paras 27–9)

'Taken as a whole, Eurocontrol's activities, by their nature, their aim and the rules to which they are subject, are connected with the exercise of powers relating to the control and supervision of air space which are typically those of a public authority. They are not of an economic nature justifying the application of the Treaty rules of competition.' (para 30)

Comment

Eurocontrol was found not to constitute an undertaking. The collection of the route charges was held by the ECJ to be inseparable from Eurocontrol's other activities, thus making its operation as a whole one that is connected with the performance of a public/state task.

Poucet v Assurances Générales de France	**Undertakings**
Joined cases C–159/91 and C–160/91	The Relativity of the Concept
ECJ, [1993] ECR I–637	Sickness Funds

Facts

Mr Poucet and Mr Pistre sought the annulment of orders served on them to pay social security contributions to French social security organisations which manage the sickness and maternity insurance scheme for self-employed persons in non-agricultural occupations. The proceedings, which took place in the French Tribunal des Affaires de Securité Sociale de l'Herault, were stayed while the French tribunal referred to the ECJ for a preliminary ruling two questions, one of them on whether an organization charged with managing a special social security scheme is an undertaking for the purposes of Articles 81 and 82 EC.

Held (on the concept of undertaking)

The social security systems at issue subject self-employed persons in non-agricultural occupations to compulsory social protection. They are intended to provide cover for all the persons to whom they apply against the risks of sickness, old age, death and invalidity, regardless of their financial status and their state of health at the time of affiliation. (paras 7–9)

The systems pursue a social objective and embody the principle of solidarity. The compulsory contribution to such system is indispensable for application of the principle of solidarity and entails paying statutory benefits which bear no relation to the amount of the contributions received. (paras 8–13)

The schemes at issue are entrusted by statute to social security funds whose activities are subject to control by the State. The funds thus cannot influence the amount of the contributions, the use of assets and the fixing of the level of benefits. (paras 14, 15)

The concept of an undertaking, within the meaning of Articles 81 and 82 EC, encompasses all entities engaged in an economic activity. It does not include, therefore, sickness funds and organisations involved in the management of the public social security system. These organisations fulfil a social function exclusively which is based on the principle of national solidarity and is entirely non-profit-making. Accordingly, the organisations to which this non-economic activity is entrusted are not undertakings. (paras 17–20)

Comment

Solidarity was used in this case as the benchmark which distinguishes between commercial and non-commercial activities. Its impact on the nature of the scheme was apparent at different levels: first, 'solidarity in time' in that the contributions paid by active workers were directly used to finance benefits paid to pensioners; secondly, 'financial solidarity', balancing the compulsory schemes in surplus and those in deficit; and thirdly 'solidarity in relation to the least well-off', who are entitled to certain minimum benefits even in the absence of adequate contributions paid by them. (See analysis by AG Tesauro in Case C–244/94 *Fédération Française des Sociétés d'Assurance v Ministère de l'Agriculture et de la Peche* [1995 ECR I–4013].)

Contrast the facts in *Poucet v Assurances Générales de France* with those in Case C–244/94 *Fédération Française des Sociétés d'Assurance*. There, the scheme in question was based on the principle of capitalisation and paid benefits to persons insured in proportion to their contributions and the financial results of the investments made by the insurance provider. The scheme established a direct link between the amount of contributions and the amount of benefits and followed the principle of solidarity only to a minimal extent, in so far as it provided for a limited balancing mechanism between insured persons.

Note references to both of these judgments in Case C–264/01 etc, *AOK-Bundesverband*, page 12 below.

Cali & Figli v Servizi ecologici porto di Genova SpA	**Undertakings**
Case C–343/95	The Relativity of the Concept
ECJ, [1997] ECR I–1547	Task of a Public Nature

Facts

A dispute between Cali & Figli and Servizi ecologici porto di Genova SpA (SEPG) regarding the payment to be made by Cali & Figli for preventive anti-pollution services performed by SEPG in the oil port of Genoa. The proceedings which took place in the Italian Tribunale di Genova were stayed while the Italian tribunal referred to the ECJ for a preliminary ruling several questions concerning the application of Article 82 EC, one of them being whether SEPG could qualify as an undertaking.

Held

'As regards the possible application of the competition rules of the Treaty, a distinction must be drawn between a situation where the State acts in the exercise of official authority and that where it carries on economic activities of an industrial or commercial nature by offering goods or services on the market (Case 118/85 *Commission v Italy* [1987] ECR 2599, paragraph 7).' (para 16)

'In that connection, it is of no importance that the State is acting directly through a body forming part of the State administration or by way of a body on which it has conferred special or exclusive rights …' (para 17)

'In order to make the distinction between the two situations referred to in paragraph 16 above, it is necessary to consider the nature of the activities carried on by the public undertaking or body on which the State has conferred special or exclusive rights (Case 118/85 *Commission v Italy*, cited above, paragraph 7).' (para 18)

SEPG activities are carried on under an exclusive concession granted to it by a public body. The anti-pollution surveillance for which SEPG was responsible in the oil port of Genoa is a task in the public interest which forms part of the essential functions of the State as regards protection of the environment in maritime areas. Such surveillance is connected by its nature, its aim and the rules to which it is subject with the exercise of powers relating to the protection of the environment which are typically those of a public authority. It is not of an economic nature justifying the application of the Treaty rules on competition. (paras 15, 22, 23)

Comment

Note that the public task in this case was performed by SEPG, which was not a state entity. Despite this, SEPG was held not to act as an undertaking as it exercised official authority. SEPG's position was not pertinent to the analysis since the public nature of the task performed was not questionable.

In many instances, doubts may be raised as to the public nature of the task performed. See for example Case C–475/99 *Ambulanz Glöckner* [2001] ECR I–8089 where health organisations, to which the public authorities delegated the task of providing the public ambulance service, were held to be undertakings. The court focused on the nature of the activity and noted that 'any activity consisting in offering goods and services on a given market is an economic activity' (para 19). It held that 'the medical aid organisations provide services, for remuneration from users, on the market for emergency transport services and patient transport services. Such activities have not always been, and are not necessarily, carried on by such organisations or by public authorities. … The provision of such services therefore constitutes an economic activity for the purposes of the application of the competition rules laid down by the Treaty' (para 20). The activities in question were carried on under market conditions, albeit facing limited competition. As such they resemble schemes operating under the principle of capitalisation (see for example Cases C–244/94, C–159/91 page 6 above) and are distinguishable from those operating under the principle of solidarity.

FENIN v Commission	**Undertakings**
Case T–319/99	The Relativity of the Concept
CFI, [2003] ECR II–357	Purchasing Goods

Facts

FENIN is an association of undertakings which markets medical goods and equipment used in Spanish hospitals. It submitted to the Commission a complaint alleging an abuse of a dominant position, within the meaning of Article 82 EC, by various bodies or organizations responsible for the operation of the Spanish national health system (SNS). The Commission rejected FENIN's complaint on the ground that the alleged bodies were not acting as undertakings when they purchased medical goods and equipment from the members of the association (Decision SG(99) D/7.040). FENIN launched an action for annulment.

Held (on the concept of undertaking)

It is a well established principle that the concept of an undertaking covers any entity engaged in an economic activity, regardless of its legal status and the way in which it is financed. (para 35)

Whereas the offering of goods and services on a given market were the characteristic feature of an economic activity, purchasing, as such, was not. Therefore, in deciding whether an activity is economic, it was incorrect to dissociate the activity of purchasing goods from their subsequent use. The nature of the purchasing activity had to be determined according to whether or not the subsequent use of the purchased goods amounted to an economic activity. (para 36)

'Consequently, an organisation which purchases goods – even in great quantity – not for the purpose of offering goods and services as part of an economic activity, but in order to use them in the context of a different activity, such as one of a purely social nature, does not act as an undertaking simply because it is a purchaser in a given market. Whilst an entity may wield very considerable economic power, even giving rise to a monopsony, it nevertheless remains the case that, if the activity for which that entity purchases goods is not an economic activity, it is not acting as an undertaking for the purposes of Community competition law and is therefore not subject to the prohibitions laid down in Articles 81(1) EC and 82 EC.' (para 37)

Consequently, SNS did not to act as an undertaking. This conclusion relies on SNS operating according to the principle of solidarity in that it was funded from social security contributions and other State funding and in that it provided services free of charge to its members on the basis of universal cover. Consequently SNS did not act as an undertaking when purchasing from FENIN. (paras 38–40)

Comment

FENIN challenged the Commission's reliance on Poucet and Pistre (page 6 above), arguing that whereas in Poucet and Pistre the question before the Court was whether such bodies acted as undertakings in their dealings with their members, in this case the question centred on whether SNS acted as undertaking when purchasing from third parties goods which they needed in order to provide services to their members. FENIN thus favoured a functional approach which focused on the nature of the activity rather than the nature of the body. Accordingly, FENIN deemed irrelevant the principle of solidarity relied upon in Poucet and Pistre. The CFI impliedly rejected this argument when in its decision it based its conclusion that SNS did not act as an undertaking on the fact that it operated according to the principle of solidarity.

The consequences of dual, public and private, characteristics were not explored in this case. FENIN argued that SNS, on occasion, provided private care in addition to State-sponsored healthcare and consequently in those circumstances should be regarded as an undertaking. The court did not decide on this point as it was not raised in the original complaint to the Commission.

FENIN v Commission	**Undertakings**
Case C–205/03P	The Relativity of the Concept
ECJ, [2006] ECR I–6295, [2006] 5 CMLR 7	Purchasing Goods

Facts

FENIN appealed against the judgment of the Court of First Instance (Case T–319/99 (page 8 above)) in which the CFI dismissed its action for annulment against the Commission's decision. In its appeal to the ECJ, FENIN alleged that the CFI misinterpreted the definition of 'undertaking' by either [1] wrongfully omitting to consider whether a purchasing activity is in itself an economic activity which may be dissociated from the service subsequently provided or, [2] failing to consider whether the provision of medical treatment, is itself economic in nature and therefore makes the purchasing activity an economic activity subject to the competition rules.

Held

FENIN's allegations, on which the second part of the plea is based, were not raised at first instance and are submitted for the first time at the appeal stage. 'It follows that the second part of the single plea relied on by FENIN must be dismissed as inadmissible.' (paras 22, 20–22)

With respect to the first part of the plea, the CFI rightly held in paragraph 36 of its judgment 'that it is the activity consisting in offering goods and services on a given market that is the characteristic feature of an economic activity (Case C–35/96 *Commission v Italy* [1998] ECR I–3851, paragraph 36).' (para 25)

The CFI rightly deduced that 'there is no need to dissociate the activity of purchasing goods from the subsequent use to which they are put in order to determine the nature of that purchasing activity, and that the nature of the purchasing activity must be determined according to whether or not the subsequent use of the purchased goods amounts to an economic activity.' (para 26)

FENIN's plea, according to which the purchasing activity of the SNS management bodies constitutes an economic activity in itself, must therefore be dismissed as unfounded. Appeal dismissed.

Comment

In his opinion AG Maduro provided an excellent overview of the concept of undertakings. The opinion is interesting, not the least since the AG proposed that the ECJ uphold the second part of the appeal and refer the case back to the CFI. AG Maduro was of the opinion that the CFI should have distinguished between SNS activities and roles. In this respect, the compulsory membership of a sickness or insurance fund should have been distinguished from the activity in this case, being that of the provision of healthcare. 'Accordingly, the degree of solidarity which exists in that sector must be assessed in the light of factors other than those which apply to the activity of a sickness or insurance fund' (paras 30, 31, 46, 47, AG opinion). 'In the present case, it does not appear that the activity of providing health care to its members carried on by the SNS is of a different kind from that which was carried on by the public hospitals in *Smits and Peerbooms* [Case C–157/99 [2001] ECR I–5473]. While it does not comprise only hospital care, it none the less includes such care. Similarly, if patients do not pay medical practitioners the amount owing in respect of treatment provided to them, those practitioners are nevertheless remunerated. However, in order to determine whether that activity should be subject to competition law, it is necessary to establish whether the State, with a view to adopting a policy of redistribution by entrusting that activity exclusively to State bodies which would be guided solely by considerations of solidarity, intended to exclude it from all market considerations' (para 52, AG opinion). 'The judgment under appeal shows that the SNS is obliged to guarantee universal cover to all its members free of charge. However, the Court of First Instance did not state whether the requirements of the market are entirely satisfied by public bodies or whether private organisations having the characteristics of an undertaking take part in it as well. The essential information for concluding that the activity of providing health care of the SNS is of a non-economic nature is therefore not available' (para 53, AG Opinion). 'In any event, were it to be concluded that the SNS carries on an economic activity, that would not call into question the social objectives pursued by the SNS, because such a conclusion does not preclude the implementation of the principle of solidarity, whether in relation to the method of financing by social security and other State contributions or in relation to the provision of services provided to members free of charge on the basis of universal cover. The application of competition law and a recognition that certain sectors must be subject to special rules are not mutually incompatible. On the contrary, the purpose of Article 86(2) EC is precisely to provide a basis for conferring exclusive rights on undertakings entrusted with the operation of services of general interest [Case C–475/99 *Ambulanz Glöckner* [2001] ECR I–8089]. The likely effects of making certain activities carried on by undertakings entrusted with the operation of services of general interest subject to competition law do not lead to a reduction in social protection any more than do those which arise from the application of the principle of freedom of movement to the health sector. In both cases, Community law seeks to incorporate principles of openness and transparency into health systems originally conceived on a national scale …' (para 55, AG Opinion). He concluded that the case should be referred back to the CFI 'for it to make the necessary findings in fact in order to determine whether public and private health sectors coexist in Spain or whether the solidarity which exists in the provision of free health care is predominant' (paras 54, 57, AG Opinion).

It is interesting to contrast the ECJ and CFI approach in *FENIN* with the judgment of the English Competition Commission Appeal Tribunal (CCAT) in *BetterCare v The Director General of Fair Trading* [Case No 1006/2/1/01 [2002] Competition Appeal Reports 299]. There, the CCAT considered an alleged abuse by a Trust which was entrusted, under the law, to provide nursing home and residential care services for elderly persons. The trust was accused by BetterCare, a UK provider of residential and nursing home care, of abusing its dominant position by forcing it to agree to unduly low prices. The CCAT considered whether the Trust may be considered as an undertaking and concluded that it was acting as an undertaking, both in the purchasing of services from BetterCare and the direct provision of elderly care by its own statutory homes. The CCAT decision differs from the European courts' approach in *FENIN* in terms of the test used to establish economic activity and the finding of solidarity. According to the CCAT, the decisive factor was the Trust being in a position to generate effects which the competition rules seek to prevent. The CCAT also distinguished the facts in BetterCare from those in previous European cases and found little to support the application of the principle of solidarity in this case.

In August 2004, the UK Office of Fair Trading (OFT) issued a Policy note 1/2004 on 'The Competition Act 1998 and Public Bodies' (OFT 443). According to the publication, 'Following the FENIN judgment, it is the OFT's view that, even if an entity is in a position to generate anti-competitive effects, it will not be an undertaking for the purposes of the competition rules if the subsequent related supply of the goods or services (for which the purchases are made) do not themselves constitute economic activities and the entity does not itself directly provide the services' (para 22, OFT 443). 'Although the subject matter of the FENIN case concerned services provided free to end users, it refers to Poucet & Pistre in reaching its conclusion that the SNS operates according to the principle of solidarity. The OFT's view is that the FENIN judgment is not restricted to cases where the services provided by the purchaser are free at point of use since this was not the case in Poucet & Pistre where members paid monthly contributions towards their cover. This means that if an entity pursues a non economic aim such as purchasing social care in order to provide care for those who cannot fully fund it themselves, i.e. the entity contributes to their care, the OFT will take the view that it is not engaged in economic activity and thus not acting as an undertaking provided that it does not provide these services directly itself. In the BetterCare II case for example, without such contribution from the State the vast majority of residents may not have been able to receive any care' (para 23, OFT 443).

Wouters v Algemene Raad van de Nederlandse Orde van Advocaten	**Undertakings**
Case C–309/99	Relative Concept
ECJ, [2002] ECR I-1577, [2002] 4 CMLR 27	

Facts

The case arose out of a dispute between Mr Wouters and the Dutch Bar which under its regulations prohibited its members from practising in full partnership with accountants. Mr Wouters argued that the prohibition is incompatible with Community rules on competition and freedom of establishment. The Dutch court referred the case to the ECJ asking, among other things, whether a regulation concerning partnerships between members of the Bar and other professionals is to be regarded as a decision taken by an association of undertakings within the meaning of Article 81(1) EC.

Held

'In order to establish whether a regulation such as the 1993 Regulation is to be regarded as a decision of an association of undertakings within the meaning of [Article 81(1) EC], the first matter to be considered is whether members of the Bar are undertakings for the purposes of Community competition law.' (para 45)

The concept of an undertaking covers any entity engaged in an economic activity, regardless of its legal status and the way in which it is financed. It is also settled case-law that any activity consisting of offering goods and services on a given market is an economic activity. Members of the Bar offer, for a fee, services in the form of legal assistance and bear the financial risks attached to the performance of those activities. That being so, members of the Bar carry on an economic activity and are undertakings for the purposes of Article 81 EC. The complexity and technical nature of the services they provide and the fact that the practice of their profession is regulated cannot alter that conclusion. (paras 46–9)

A second question is whether when it adopts a regulation concerning partnerships between members of the Bar and members of other professions, the Bar is to be regarded as an association of undertakings, or on the contrary, as a public authority. 'According to the case-law of the Court, the Treaty rules on competition do not apply to activity which, by its nature, its aim and the rules to which it is subject does not belong to the sphere of economic activity (see to that effect, Joined Cases C–159/91, C–160/91 *Poucet and Pistre* [1993] ECR I–637, paragraphs 18 and 19, concerning the management of the public social security system), or which is connected with the exercise of the powers of a public authority (see to that effect, Case C–364/92 *Sat Fluggesellschaft* [1994] ECR I–43, paragraph 30, concerning the control and supervision of air space, and Case C–343/95 *Diego Cali & Figli* [1997] ECR I–1547, paragraphs 22 and 23, concerning anti-pollution surveillance of the maritime environment).' (para 57)

The Netherlands Bar is not fulfilling a social function based on the principle of solidarity (unlike certain social security bodies (*Poucet and Pistre*)), nor does it exercise powers which are typically those of a public authority (*Sat Fluggesellschaft*). It acts as the regulatory body of a profession, the practice of which constitutes an economic activity. Its governing bodies are composed exclusively of members of the Bar elected solely by members of the profession. In addition, when it adopts measures such as the Regulation in question, the Bar is not required to do so by reference to specified public-interest criteria. Subsequently, the Netherlands Bar must be regarded as an association of undertakings within the meaning of Article 81(1) EC. (paras 58–64).

Comment

The Bar was held to be an association of undertakings when it adopts a regulation such as the 1993 Regulation which regulates the member's economic activities. Note, however, that the Bar was held not to constitute an undertaking or group of undertakings for the purposes of Article 82 EC, since it does not carry on any economic activity and because its members are not sufficiently linked to each other to be able adopt the same conduct and limit competition between them. (paras 112–14)

AOK-Bundesverband and others v Ichthyol-Gesellschaft Cordes	**Undertakings**
Joined Cases C–264, 306, 354 and 355/01	Relative Concept
ECJ, [2004] ECR I–2493, [2004] 4 CMLR 22	Sickness Funds

Facts

Reference from the German courts for a preliminary ruling, concerning the classification of German 'associations of sickness funds' as undertakings. According to the statutory health insurance scheme in Germany, employees are obliged, subject to some exceptions, to be insured by statutory sickness funds. These funds, which are governed by German law and financed through contributions levied on insured persons and their employers, based on their income, operate under the principle of solidarity. They compete, to a limited extent, with each other and with private funds when providing services to those people for whom insurance is voluntary. In the proceedings at the German courts the question arose whether these funds, when operating according to the law and set the maximum level of contribution for medicines and medical products are operating as undertakings.

Held

'The concept of an undertaking in competition law covers any entity engaged in economic activity, regardless of the legal status of the entity or the way in which it is financed (Case C–41/90 *Höfner and Elser* [1991] ECR I–1979, paragraph 21, and Case C–218/00 *Cisal* [2002] ECR I–691, paragraph 22).' (para 46)

'In the field of social security, the Court has held that certain bodies entrusted with the management of statutory health insurance and old-age insurance schemes pursue an exclusively social objective and do not engage in economic activity. The Court has found that to be so in the case of sickness funds which merely apply the law and cannot influence the amount of the contributions, the use of assets and the fixing of the level of benefits. Their activity, based on the principle of national solidarity, is entirely non-profit-making and the benefits paid are statutory benefits bearing no relation to the amount of the contributions (Joined Cases C–159/91 and C–160/91 *Poucet and Pistre* [1993] ECR I–637, paragraphs 15 and 18).' (para 47)

'The fact that the amount of benefits and of contributions was, in the last resort, fixed by the State led the Court to hold, similarly, that a body entrusted by law with a scheme providing insurance against accidents at work and occupational diseases, such as the Istituto nazionale per l'assicurazione contro gli infortuni sul lavoro (the Italian National Institute for Insurance against Accidents at Work), was not an undertaking for the purpose of the Treaty competition rules (see Cisal, cited above, paragraphs 43 to 46).' (para 48)

'On the other hand, other bodies managing statutory social security systems and displaying some of the characteristics referred to in paragraph 47 of the present judgment, namely being non-profit-making and engaging in activity of a social character which is subject to State rules that include solidarity requirements in particular, have been considered to be undertakings engaging in economic activity (see Case C–244/94 *Fédération française des sociétés d'assurance and others* [1995] ECR I–4013, paragraph 22, and Case C–67/96 *Albany* [1999] ECR I–5751, paragraphs 84 to 87).' (para 49)

'Thus, in *Fédération française des sociétés d'assurance and others*, at paragraph 17, the Court held that the body in question managing a supplementary old-age insurance scheme, engaged in an economic activity in competition with life assurance companies and that the persons concerned could opt for the solution which guaranteed the better investment. In paragraphs 81 and 84 of *Albany*, concerning a supplementary pension fund based on a system of compulsory affiliation and applying a solidarity mechanism for determination of the amount of contributions and the level of benefits, the Court noted however that the fund itself determined the amount of the contributions and benefits and operated in accordance with the principle of capitalisation. It deduced therefrom that such a fund engaged in an economic activity in competition with insurance companies.' (para 50)

Sickness funds in the German statutory health insurance scheme are involved in the management of the social security system and fulfil an exclusively non-profit making social function, which is founded on the principle of national solidarity. The funds are compelled by law to offer their members benefits which do not depend on the amount of the contributions. The funds are not in competition with one another or with private institutions as regards grant of the obligatory statutory benefits in respect of treatment or medicinal products which constitutes their main function. (paras 51–4)

'It follows from those characteristics that the sickness funds are similar to the bodies at issue in *Poucet* and *Pistre and Cisal* and that their activity must be regarded as being non-economic in nature.' Subsequently, the funds do not constitute undertakings within the meaning of Articles 81 EC and 82 EC. (paras 55, 57)

The latitude available to the sickness funds when setting the contribution rate and their freedom to engage in some competition with one another is meant to encourage the sickness funds to operate in accordance with principles of sound management and does not call this analysis into question. (para 56)

When the fund associations determine the fixed maximum amounts they merely perform an obligation which is imposed upon them by the law. This action is linked to the exclusively social objective of the sickness funds and does not constitute an activity of an economic nature. (paras 58–64)

Comment

In paragraph 58 the Court noted that there is a possibility that, 'besides their functions of an exclusively social nature within the framework of management of the German social security system, the sickness funds … engage in operations which have a purpose that is not social and is economic in nature. In that case the decisions which they would be led to adopt could perhaps be regarded as decisions of undertakings or of associations of undertakings.' The court then concluded that the fixing of maximum amounts in this particular case is linked to the social objectives of the funds (paras 58–64). The statement of principle is interesting as the court considered it possible for the funds to be classified as undertakings if they would engage in operations which are not social in nature.

Note that the ECJ judgment did not follow the opinion of Advocate General Jacobs. In his opinion, AG Jacobs stated that 'compulsory state social security schemes such as those at issue in *Cisal* [Case C–218/00 *Cisal di Battistello Venanzio & Co Sas v Istituto Nazionale Per L'Assicurazione Contro Gli Infortuni Sul Lavoro*, [2002] ECR I–691, [2002] 4 CMLR 24,] and *Poucet and Pistre* [Joined cases C–159/91 and C–160/91, page 6 above] are not classified as economic activities because they are incompatible, even in principle, with the possibility of a private undertaking carrying them on' (paras 30–2, AG opinion). 'By contrast, pension schemes which are funded through the administration of a capital fund, into which contributions are paid, and in which benefits are directly related to contributions, have been held in *FFSA* and *Albany* to be subject to the Community competition rules, despite the existence of certain elements of solidarity. In such schemes, the redistributive element is not such as to entail a suppression of the types of activity habitually provided by private insurance and pension companies, such as actuarial assessment and the management of investments.' (para 34, AG opinion). He subsequently distinguished between this case and *Cisal* and *Poucet and Pistre* as in the present case there was potential for the funds to compete with one another and with private undertakings in the provision of health insurance services, a fact which demonstrates that the system's redistributive element is not such as to preclude economic activity. He added that the fact that the level of benefits provided under a scheme is determined by law cannot in itself rule out the application of the competition rules. Given the existence of such competition, he concluded that EC competition rules should be applicable. In addition he concluded that the setting of fixed amounts, which is the alleged anti-competitive conduct, falls within the sphere of the economic activity which the sickness funds perform.

Viho Europe BV v Commission   **Undertakings**
Case C–73/95 P   Single Economic Unit
ECJ, [1996] ECR I–5457, [1997] 4 CMLR 419

Facts

Parker Pen Ltd operated a distribution system in Europe which was partially based on wholly owned subsidiaries. The sales and marketing activities of these subsidiaries were directed and controlled by Parker Pen. One of the main characteristics of the system was the prohibitions imposed on Parker Pen's subsidiaries from supplying Parker products to customers established in Member States other than that of the subsidiary.

Viho Europe BV challenged Parker's practice in a complaint to the European Commission alleging, among other things, that Parker infringed Article 81 EC by restricting the distribution of Parker products to allocated territories, consequently dividing the common market into national markets. The Commission rejected the complaint on the ground that Parker's subsidiary companies were wholly dependent on Parker Pen UK and enjoyed no real autonomy in determining their course of action. Subsequently the implementation of Parker's policies was regarded as a normal allocation of tasks within a group of undertakings which is not subjected to Article 81 EC.

Viho Europe BV appealed to the CFI for annulment of the Commission's decision. The CFI dismissed the appeal and held that in the absence of an agreement between economically independent entities, relations within an economic unit cannot amount to an agreement or concerted practice between undertakings which restricts competition within the meaning of Article 81 EC (Case T–102/92 *Viho v Commission* [1995] ECR II–17).

Viho appealed to the ECJ.

Held

'Parker and its fully owned subsidiaries form a single economic unit within which the subsidiaries do not enjoy real autonomy in determining their course of action in the market, but carry out the instructions issued to them by the parent company controlling them.' (para 16)

As the subsidiaries do not enjoy real autonomy in determining their course of action in the market, activities within the Parker unit, even if affecting the competitive position of third parties, cannot make Article 81 EC applicable. Such activities are unilateral and could in principle only fall under Article 82 EC if the conditions for its application were fulfilled. Appeal dismissed. (paras 17, 18)

Comment

Note the ECJ ruling in Case 170/83 *Hydrotherm v Compact*, [1984 ECR 2999], where it held that 'in competition law, the term "undertaking" must be understood as designating an economic unit for the purpose of the subject-matter of the agreement in question even if in law that economic unit consists of several persons, natural or legal' (para 11).

Also note the CFI judgment in Cases T–68/89, T–77/89 and T–78/89 *SIV and others v Commission*, [1992 ECR II–1403], where it was held that Article 81 EC refers only to relations between economic entities which are capable of competing with one another and does not cover agreements or concerted practices between undertakings belonging to the same economic unit (paragraph 357). See also the ECJ ruling in Case 22/71 *Beguelin Import Co v SAGL Import Export*, [1971] ECR 949, which focused on the lack of economic independence.

IJsselcentrale and others	**Undertakings**
Case IV/32.732	Single Economic Unit
European Commission, [1991] OJ L28/32	

Facts

The Commission considered a complaint which alleged that four electricity-generating companies in the Netherlands, and a joint venture (SEP) established by them to facilitate cooperation between the electricity generators, infringed Article 81 EC. As part of the assessment of the complaint the Commission considered the competitiveness of a cooperation agreement concluded between the four electricity companies and SEP. It especially focused on Article 21 of the cooperation agreement which prohibited the importation and exportation of electricity by undertakings other than SEP.

SEP argued that Article 81 EC is not applicable to the cooperation agreement as it was not concluded between independent undertakings. It submitted that the participating companies formed an economic unit, because they were components in 'one indivisible public electricity supply system'. Accordingly, Article 21 of the cooperation agreement secured an internal allocation of tasks within the group and is not subjected to competition laws.

Held

Article 81 EC 'is not concerned with agreements between undertakings belonging to the same group of companies, and having the status of parent company and subsidiary, if the undertakings form an economic unit within which the subsidiary has no real freedom to determine its course of action on the market, and if the agreements are concerned merely with the internal allocation of tasks as between the undertakings.' (para 23)

In this case, however, 'the four participants do not belong to a single group of companies. They are separate legal persons, and are not controlled by a single person, natural or legal. Each generating company determines its own conduct independently. … The fact that the generators all form part of one indivisible system of public supply changes nothing here. The distributors likewise form part of the same system, but there is no reason to suppose that they form an economic unit with the generators on that ground alone. Finally, it cannot be said that SEP itself forms an economic unit with one or more of the generating companies. SEP is a joint venture controlled by its parent companies together.' (para 24)

Comment

The Commission's finding that the companies do not form part of the same undertaking paved the way for the application of Article 81 EC to the agreements between them.

Note that SEP's argument raises an interesting question as to the level of control which would be deemed to deprive companies from 'real autonomy in determining their course of action in the market' (*Viho Europe BV v Commission*, page 14 above). Whereas in *Viho* the holding structure of the Parker Pen group gave rise to clear control and dependence, it is difficult to identify clearly which lower levels of control might suffice to bring different companies under the umbrella of a single undertaking. On this issue note references to *Sepia Logistics v OFT* and *Suretrack Rail Services Limited v Infraco JNP Limited*, page 18 below.

In merger cases control is defined by Article 3(2) of the Merger Regulation (Regulation (EC) No 139/2004) as the possibility of exercising decisive influence. The Commission Consolidated Jurisdictional Notice on the control of concentrations between undertakings (10 July 2007) elaborates on that concept. Note that the Merger Regulation benchmark for control; 'possible decisive influence', is lower than the Viho benchmark which requires 'actual control'. (See *Viho*, para 16, contrast with the Jurisdictional Notice, paras 23, 11–35.)

Dansk Rørindustri A/S and others v Commission	**Undertakings**
Joined Cases C–189, 205–8, 213/02 P	Single Economic Unit
ECJ, [2005] ECR I–5425	

Facts

Joined appeals on several CFI judgments in which the CFI dismissed the appellants' actions for annulment of Commission decisions in which various undertakings, and in particular certain of the appellants, were found to participate in a series of agreements and concerted practices within the meaning of Article 81(1) EC (Case IV/35.691/E-4 Pre-insulated pipes) ([1999] OJ L 24/1). One of the issues raised on appeal concerned the CFI finding that a group of companies constituted a single undertaking for the purpose of European competition law.

Held

'… the anti-competitive conduct of an undertaking can be attributed to another undertaking where it has not decided independently upon its own conduct on the market but carried out, in all material respects, the instructions given to it by that other undertaking, having regard in particular to the economic and legal links between them (see, in particular, Case C–294/98 P *Metsa-Serla and others v Commission* [2000] ECR I–10065, paragraph 27).' (para 117)

'It is true that the mere fact that the share capital of two separate commercial companies is held by the same person or the same family is insufficient, in itself, to establish that those companies are a single economic unit with the result that, under Community competition law, the actions of one company can be attributed to the other and that one can be held liable to pay the fine for the other (see Case C–196/99 P *Aristrain v Commission* [2003] ECR I–11005, paragraph 99).' (para 118)

In the present case the CFI did not infer the existence of the economic unit constituting the Henss/Isoplus group solely from the fact that the undertakings concerned were controlled from the viewpoint of their share capital by a single person, but considered a series of additional elements. These established that the companies were controlled by one individual who held key functions within the management boards of those companies and represented them in various meetings. (paras 119, 120)

'In those circumstances, the Court of First Instance cannot be criticised for having held, following an overall and, in principle, sovereign assessment of a range of facts, that the various undertakings constituting the Henss/Isoplus group must, for that purpose, be regarded as belonging to a single economic entity.' (para 130)

Comment

Note the ECJ decision in Case C–286/98 *Stora Kopparbergs Bergslags AB v Commission,* [2000] ECR I–9925, [2001] 4 CMLR 12. There, while dealing with a claim contesting the CFI finding that two entities formed one single undertaking, the Court noted that 'the fact that a subsidiary has separate legal personality is not sufficient to exclude the possibility of its conduct being imputed to the parent company, especially where the subsidiary does not independently decide its own conduct on the market, but carries out, in all material respects, the instructions given to it by the parent company (see, in particular, *ICI v Commission,* cited above, paragraphs 132 and 133); Case 52/69 *Geigy v Commission,* [1972] ECR 787, paragraph 44, and Case 6/72 *Europemballage and Continental Can v Commission,* [1973] ECR 215, paragraph 15).' (para 26)

Provimi Ltd v Aventis Animal Nutrition SA and others	**Undertakings**
2003 WL 21236491	Single Economic Unit
High Court (Queen's Bench Division), [2003] EWHC 961 (Comm)	

Facts

Following an investigation into the vitamin and pigment markets in Europe, the Commission found that various manufacturers of vitamins, among them F Hoffmann-La Roche and Aventis SA, had operated price-fixing and market-sharing cartels contrary to Article 81 EC (Commission decision in Case COMP/E-1/37.512 – Vitamins). The claimants, who had purchased vitamins from the Roche and Aventis groups during the existence of the cartels, brought proceedings in the English court for damages against a number of the cartel members and subsidiaries of the cartel members.

In the applications before the court, the defendants' aim was to strike out and/or set aside part of the proceedings. One of the issues raised by the applicants was that there is no infringement of Article 81 EC if the implementation of the agreement by the subsidiary company consisted simply of obeying the orders of the parent company to sell at cartel prices that have been agreed by the parent company without the knowledge of the subsidiary.

Held (on the concept of undertakings)

It is arguable that where two corporate entities are part of the same undertaking and one of those corporate entities has entered into a cartel agreement with a third independent undertaking, then if the first corporate entity, which was not part of the agreement and lacks knowledge of it, implements that infringing agreement, it is also infringing Article 81 EC. 'In my view it is arguable that it is not necessary to plead or prove any particular "concurrence of wills" between the two legal entities within Undertaking A. The EU competition law concept of an "undertaking" is that it is one economic unit. The legal entities that are a part of the one undertaking, by definition of the concept, have no independence of mind or action or will. They are to be regarded as all one. Therefore, so it seems to me, the mind and will of one legal entity is, for the purposes of Article 81, to be treated as the mind and will of the other entity. There is no question of having to "impute" the knowledge or will of one entity to another, because they are one and the same.' (para 31)

'In my view the fact that, in the Decision, the Commission identifies only one particular legal entity as the "infringing undertaking" does not detract from my conclusion. EU competition law has to bow to the practical fact that in national laws it is legal entities that exist; and it is legal entities that own the funds from which fines are paid. So particular entities need to be identified in order to enforce the Decision. But those practical considerations cannot determine a prior question which is whether, if one entity of an undertaking is an infringer by agreeing to fix prices, another entity that has implemented the same infringing agreement, is also an infringer.' (para 32)

Comment

Note that in this motion the court aimed to establish whether claims brought by the claimants were arguable. The weight attributed to the holding of the court should reflect this lower yardstick. Nonetheless, the court's reasoning in paragraph 31 is likely to facilitate future claims for damages.

The defendants in this case relied on the Viho case (page 14 above) and claimed that there is no infringement if the implementation of the agreement consists simply of obeying the orders of a parent company to sell at cartel prices that have been agreed by the parent. Mr Justice Aikens rejected this claim and distinguished between the cases. Whereas in *Viho* the court considered policies implemented within one economic entity, and thus held that Article 81 EC cannot be infringed, in *Provimi* the parent company dictated prices which were agreed in a cartel agreement between the parent company and another independent undertaking. (paras 26–8)

Sepia Logistics Ltd and another v Office of Fair Trading	**Undertakings**
Case No 1072/1/1/06	Single Economic Unit
Competition Appeal Tribunal, [2007] CAT 13	

Facts

Sepia Logistics Ltd (formerly known as Double Quick Supplyline Ltd (DQS)) appealed to the Competition Appeal Tribunal against a decision taken by the Office of Fair Trading (OFT) in which the OFT concluded that, together with a number of suppliers of aluminium double-glazing spacer bars, it participated in an anticompetitive agreement and/or concerted practice and infringed the Chapter I prohibition of the UK Competition Act 1998. The OFT decision addressed not only DQS but also its parent company, Precision Concepts Ltd (PC), on the basis that PC formed part of the same undertaking as DQS, and was equally liable for its participation in the infringement. On appeal, DQS and PC challenged, among other things, the OFT's conclusion that DQS and PC form part of the same undertaking.

Held

'… It is well established that an undertaking does not correspond to the commonly understood notion of a legal entity under, for example, English commercial or tax law; and that a single undertaking may comprise one or more legal or natural persons.' (para 70)

'The European Court of Justice (ECJ) in *Hydrotherm*, [Case 170/83 *Hydrotherm Gerätebau GmbH v Compact de Dott Ing Mario Andreoli & CSAS* [1984] ECR 2999, [1985] 3 CMLR 224] said at paragraph [11]: "In competition law, the term 'undertaking' must be understood as designating an economic unit for the purpose of the subject-matter of the agreement in question even if in law that economic unit consists of several persons, natural or legal."' (para 72)

Crucial to this question is the matter of control as highlighted in Case C–73/95 P *Viho v Commission*. The issue of control was also considered in Case C–286/98 *Stora Kopparbergs Bergslag AB*, where the ECJ held that the fact that a subsidiary has separate legal personality does not exclude the possibility of its conduct being imputed to the parent company, especially where it does not independently decide its own conduct on the market. Similarly, in Cases C–189/02 P etc *Dansk Rørindustri and others v European Commission*, the ECJ held that conduct of one undertaking can be attributed to a controlling undertaking. (paras 73–6)

In this case DQS was a wholly-owned subsidiary of PBM of which 80 per cent were held by SGH, which was a wholly-owned subsidiary of PC. PC therefore owned indirectly 80 per cent of the shares in DQS. Mr Sander, a director of both DQC and PC had direct involvement in the infringement. Subsequently, PC, through Mr Sander, was both aware of DQS' involvement in the infringement and capable of exercising control over DQS. (paras 77–80)

Comment

Note the English High Court of Justice (Chancery Division) decision in *Suretrack Rail Services Limited v Infraco JNP Limited*, [2002] WL 31413939, [2002] EWHC 1316 (Ch), where as part of an application for interim relief the Honourable Mr Justice Laddie commented that 'The fact that subsidiaries take their own decisions does not, of itself, indicate whether those subsidiaries are either independent of each other or independent of the parent. … If the fact that directors of a subsidiary take their own decisions and make their own assessment of the risks and profitability of the decisions from the viewpoint of that subsidiary were enough to prevent the subsidiary from being considered as part of a single economic unit for competition law purposes, then all subsidiaries would be treated as being separate undertakings' (para 18). Chapter I of the UK Competition Act 1998 was held not to be applicable as the three companies concerned were subsidiaries of the same parent company and subsequently an 'agreement between undertakings' did not exist.

Also note Case IV/32.732 *IJsselcentrale and others*, and the commentary on page 15 above.

2

Market Definition

Market Definition

The definition of the market is an important step in the identification of boundaries of competition between firms. The main purpose of market definition as laid down in the Commission Notice on the Definition of the Relevant Market for the Purposes of Community Competition Law (1997 OJ C 372) 'is to identify in a systematic way the competitive constraints that the undertakings involved face. The objective of defining a market in both its product and geographic dimension is to identify the actual competitors of the under-takings involved that are capable of constraining their behaviour and preventing them from behaving independently of an effective competitive pressure. It is from this perspective, that the market definition makes it possible, inter alia, to calculate market shares that would convey meaningful information regarding market power for the purpose of assessing dominance or for the purpose of applying Article 81 EC' (para 2).

The Commission Notice on the Definition of the Relevant Market provides valuable insight into the methodology applied by the Commission when defining the product and geographical markets. The product market is generally defined in the notice as one which 'comprises all those products and/or services which are regarded as interchangeable or substitutable by the consumer, by reason of the products' characteristics, their prices and their intended use' (para 7). The geographic market is defined in the notice as one which 'comprises the area in which the undertakings concerned are involved in the supply and demand of products or services, in which the conditions of competition are sufficiently homogeneous and which can be distinguished from neighbouring areas because the conditions of competition are appreciably different in those areas' (para 8).

The process of market definition is also referred to in some detail in the Commission's Guidelines on the Assessment of Horizontal Mergers ([2004] OJ C 31/5), and the Commission's Discussion Paper on the Application of Article 82 of the Treaty to Exclusionary Abuses (December 2005).

Although the process of market definition is primarily an economic exercise, European case law provides a useful reflection of the methodology used in the analysis. The following cases highlight various aspects of market definition.

Product and Geographical Markets

Market Definition in Article 82 EC Cases

The SSNIP test which is used to define the market is based on the assumption that prevailing prices on the market are competitive. However, in the context of Article 82 cases, it is often the case that the price on the market is likely to be above competitive levels. Failure to take this into account may give rise to the 'cellophane fallacy' and lead to the market being defined too widely. Consequently, in cases of dominance it is appropriate to rely on a wider range of methods to assess the market and eliminate false substitutes. See the Notice on Market Definition (paragraph 25) and the Commission's Discussion Paper on the Application of Article 82 of the Treaty to Exclusionary Abuses (December 2005) (paragraphs 11–19).

Barriers to Entry and Potential Competition

The methodology used to define the market primarily focuses on demand and supply substitutability. As such, it does not provide the complete picture of the competitive pressures faced by the undertakings. An analysis of the wider picture, including potential competition, is called for where the position of the undertakings involved in the relevant market raises concerns from a competition point of view. On potential competition and barriers to entry, see discussion in Chapter 5 below.

United Brands v Commission Case 27/76 ECJ, [1978] ECR 207, [1978] 1 CMLR 429	**Market Definition** Product and Geographical Markets

Facts

In a Commission decision United Brands was found to infringe Article 82 EC by abusing its dominant position in the market for bananas (IV/26.699 Chiquita). United Brands (UBC) appealed to the ECJ and challenged, among other things, the Commission's conclusions with respect to the market definition.

Held (on market definition)

'In order to determine whether UBC has a dominant position on the banana market it is necessary to define this market both from the standpoint of the product and from the geographic point of view.' (para 10)

'As far as the product market is concerned it is first of all necessary to ascertain whether, as the applicant maintains, bananas are an integral part of the fresh fruit market, because they are reasonably interchangeable by consumers with other kinds of fresh fruit such as apples, oranges, grapes, peaches, strawberries, etc. Or whether the relevant market consists solely of the banana market which includes both branded bananas and unlabelled bananas and is a market sufficiently homogeneous and distinct from the market of other fresh fruit.' (para 12)

'For the banana to be regarded as forming a market which is sufficiently differentiated from other fruit markets it must be possible for it to be singled out by such special features distinguishing it from other fruits that it is only to a limited extent interchangeable with them and is only exposed to their competition in a way that is hardly perceptible.' (para 22)

'The ripening of bananas takes place the whole year round without any season having to be taken into account. Throughout the year production exceeds demand and can satisfy it at any time. Owing to this particular feature the banana is a privileged fruit and its production and marketing can be adapted to the seasonal fluctuations of other fresh fruit which are known and can be computed.' (paras 23–5)

'There is no unavoidable seasonal substitution since the consumer can obtain this fruit all the year round. Since the banana is a fruit which is always available in sufficient quantities the question whether it can be replaced by other fruits must be determined over the whole of the year for the purpose of ascertaining the degree of competition between it and other fresh fruit.' (paras 26, 27)

'The studies of the banana market on the court's file show that on the latter market there is no significant long term cross-elasticity any more than – as has been mentioned – there is any seasonal substitutability in general between the banana and all the seasonal fruits, as this only exists between the banana and two fruits (peaches and table grapes) in one of the countries (west Germany) of the relevant geographic market.' (para 28)

'As far as concerns the two fruits available throughout the year (oranges and apples) the first are not interchangeable and in the case of the second there is only a relative degree of substitutability. This small degree of substitutability is accounted for by the specific features of the banana and all the factors which influence consumer choice.' (paras 29, 30)

'The banana has certain characteristics, appearance, taste, softness, seedlessness, easy handling, a constant level of production which enables it to satisfy the constant needs of an important section of the population consisting of the very young, the old and the sick.' (para 31)

'As far as prices are concerned two FAO studies show that the banana is only affected by the prices – falling prices – of other fruits (and only of peaches and table grapes) during the summer months and mainly in July and then by an amount not exceeding 20%. Although it cannot be denied that during these months and some weeks at the end of the year this product is exposed to competition from other fruits, the flexible way in which the volume of imports and their marketing on the relevant geographic market is adjusted means that the conditions of competition are extremely limited and that its price adapts without any serious difficulties to this situation where supplies of fruit are plentiful.' (paras 32, 33)

'It follows from all these considerations that a very large number of consumers having a constant need for bananas are not noticeably or even appreciably enticed away from the consumption of this product by the arrival of other fresh fruit on the market and that even the personal peak periods only affect it for a limited period of time and to a very limited extent from the point of view of substitutability.' (para 34)

Geographic market: the French, UK and Italian markets are organised nationally and subsequently display different market conditions. The effect of this is that UBC's bananas do not compete on equal terms with the other bananas sold in these states, which benefit from a preferential system. The Commission was right to exclude these three national markets from the geographic market under consideration. On the other hand, the Federal Republic of Germany, Denmark, Ireland and the Netherlands form an area that is sufficiently homogeneous to be considered in its entirety as one geographic market. (paras 36–57)

'It follows from all these considerations that the geographic market as determined by the Commission which constitutes a substantial part of the common market must be regarded as the relevant market for the purpose of determining whether the applicant may be in a dominant position.' (para 57)

Comment

The decision centres on the characteristics of bananas that single them out from other fruits (para 31). These unique features arguably indicate low substitutability. To prove substitutability one need not show that all customers would seek substitutions when faced with an increase in price, but that a sufficiently large number of customers would do so. It is therefore important to assess the size of the marginal consumer group which would react to a change in price. When this group is large enough the increase in price would be deemed unprofitable.

In paragraph 31 the Court commented that a large group which consists of the very young, the old and the sick especially values the special characteristics of bananas and is 'locked in' due to its inelastic demand. A similar statement is repeated on paragraph 34. Note, however, that in order to assess substitutability the analysis should have not centred on the 'captive consumers' but rather on whether a sufficient number of non-captive consumers would seek substitution when faced with an increase in price. If this marginal group is large enough, the increase in price would be unprofitable.

Examples of captive consumers may be found when considering the market for spare parts (Case 22/78 *Hugin v Commission* (page 29 below)), or the secondary market for computer games (COMP/35.587 *Nintendo* (page 31 below)).

Note that a monopolist may be able to isolate the captive group by using price discrimination, thus charging higher prices from those with inelastic demand. In this respect, note paragraph 43 of the Commission Notice on the Definition of the Relevant Market: 'The extent of the product market might be narrowed in the presence of distinct groups of customers. A distinct group of customers for the relevant product may constitute a narrower, distinct market when such a group could be subject to price discrimination. This will usually be the case when two conditions are met: (a) it is possible to identify clearly which group an individual customer belongs to at the moment of selling the relevant products to him, and (b) trade among customers or arbitrage by third parties should not be feasible.'

Note the ECJ's short reference to the absence of a temporal dimension to the market in question (paras 28–30). Evidence on seasonal changes to cross elasticity of demand was considered in the Commission investigation (IV/26.699 *Chiquita*) but not dealt with by the ECJ in its judgment.

Hoffmann-La Roche & Co v Commission	**Market Definition**
Case 85/76	Product and Geographical Markets
ECJ, [1979] ECR 461, [1979] 3 CMLR 211	

Facts

Hoffmann-La Roche (Roche) applied for the annulment of a Commission decision (IV/29.020 – *Vitamins*) which found Roche to have abused its dominant position in the market for vitamins A, B2, B3, B6, C, E and H. Roche challenged the Commission's decision on several points, including the definition of the market.

Held (on market definition)

'The contested Decision refers to bulk vitamins belonging to 13 groups. ... The Commission found that there was a dominant position in the case of seven of the eight groups of vitamins manufactured by Roche. ... The parties are agreed, on the one hand, that each of these groups has specific metabolizing functions and for this reason is not interchangeable with the others and, on the other hand, that in the case of the possible uses which these three groups have in common, namely for food, animal feed and for pharmaceutical purposes, the vitamins in question do not encounter the competition of other products.' (para 23)

The Commission considered that each group of vitamins constitutes a separate market. Roche accepted this point of view but argued that the C and E group of vitamins, as far as each of them is concerned, together with other products, form part of a wider market. (para 24)

'It is an established fact that vitamins c and e apart from their uses in the pharmaceutical industry and in food and animal feed ... are also sold, inter alia, as antioxidants, fermentation agents and additives ...' (para 25)

'If a product could be used for different purposes and if these different uses are in accordance with economic needs, which are themselves also different, there are good grounds for accepting that this product may, according to the circumstances, belong to separate markets which may present specific features which differ from the standpoint both of the structure and of the conditions of competition. However this finding does not justify the conclusion that such a product together with all the other products which can replace it as far as concerns the various uses to which it may be put and with which it may compete, forms one single market. The concept of the relevant market in fact implies that there can be effective competition between the products which form part of it and this presupposes that there is a sufficient degree of interchangeability between all the products forming part of the same market in so far as a specific use of such products is concerned. There was no such interchangeability, at any rate during the period under consideration, between all the vitamins of each of the groups c and e and all the products which, according to the circumstances, may be substituted for one or other of these groups of vitamins for technological uses which are themselves extremely varied.' (para 28)

'On the other hand there may be some doubt whether, for the purpose of delimit the respective markets of the c and e groups of vitamins, it is necessary to include all the vitamins of each of these groups in a market corresponding to that group, or whether, on the contrary, each of these groups must be placed in a separate market, one comprising vitamins for bio-nutritive use and the other vitamins for technological purposes.' (para 29)

Comment

Following the consideration of demand substitutability, each group of vitamins was held to constitute a separate market. Note that vitamins C and E could be used for different purposes, for some of which they did act as substitutes. Nonetheless, this limited substitution seemed insufficient to establish interchangeability.

Nederlandsche Banden Industrie Michelin v Commission	**Market Definition**
Case 322/81	Product and Geographical Markets
ECJ, [1983] ECR 3461, [1985] 1 CMLR 282	

Facts

Michelin NV, the Dutch subsidiary of the Michelin group, was responsible for the production and sale of Michelin tyres in the Netherlands. Michelin NV was found by the European Commission to abuse its dominant position on the market for new replacement tyres for lorries, buses and similar vehicles by operating anticompetitive target-based discount schemes (IV/29.491 *Michelin*). On appeal, Michlen NV challenged, among other things, the Commission's definition of the market.

Held (on market definition)

'The applicant claims that the definition of the relevant market on which the Commission based its Decision is too wide, inasmuch as in the eyes of the consumer different types and sizes of tyres for heavy vehicles are not interchangeable, and at the same time too narrow inasmuch as car and van tyres are excluded from it although they occupy similar positions on the market. …' (para 35)

'The Commission defends the definition of the relevant product market used in its Decision by pointing out that with a technically homogeneous product it is not possible to distinguish different markets depending on the dimensions, size or specific types of products: in that connection the elasticity of supply between different types and dimensions of tyre must be taken into account. On the other hand the criteria of interchangeability and elasticity of demand allow a distinction to be drawn between the market in tyres for heavy vehicles and the market in car tyres owing to the particular structure of demand, which, in the case of tyres for heavy vehicles, is characterized by the presence above all of experienced trade buyers.' (para 36)

'As the court has repeatedly emphasized … for the purposes of investigating the possible dominant position of an undertaking on a given market, the possibilities of competition must be judged in the context of the market comprising the totality of the products which, with respect to their characteristics, are particularly suitable for satisfying constant needs and are only to a limited extent interchangeable with other products. However, it must be noted that the determination of the relevant market is useful in assessing whether the undertaking concerned is in a position to prevent effective competition from being maintained and behaves to an appreciable extent independently of its competitors and customers and consumers. For this purpose, therefore, an examination limited to the objective characteristics only of the relevant products cannot be sufficient: the competitive conditions and the structure of supply and demand on the market must also be taken into consideration.' (para 37)

'Moreover, it was for that reason that the Commission and Michelin NV agreed that new, original-equipment tyres should not be taken into consideration in the assessment of market shares. Owing to the particular structure of demand for such tyres characterized by direct orders from car manufacturers, competition in this sphere is in fact governed by completely different factors and rules.' (para 38)

'As far as replacement tyres are concerned, the first point … is that at the user level there is no interchangeability between car and van tyres, on the one hand, and heavy-vehicle tyres on the other. Car and van tyres therefore have no influence at all on competition on the market in heavy-vehicle tyres.' (para 39)

'Furthermore, the structure of demand for each of those groups of products is different. Most buyers of heavy-vehicle tyres are trade users, particularly haulage undertakings, for whom, as the Commission explained, the purchase of replacement tyres represents an item of considerable expenditure and who constantly ask their tyre dealers for advice and for long-term specialized services adapted to their specific needs. On the other hand, for the average buyer of car or van tyres the purchase of tyres is an occasional event and even if the buyer operates a business he does not expect such specialized advice and service adapted to specific needs. Hence the sale of heavy-vehicle tyres requires a particularly specialized distribution network which is not the case with the distribution of car and van tyres.' (para 40)

'The final point which must be made is that there is no elasticity of supply between tyres for heavy vehicles and car tyres owing to significant differences in production techniques and in the plant and tools needed for their manufacture. The fact that time and considerable investment are required in order to modify production plant for the manufacture of light-vehicle tyres instead of heavy-vehicle tyres or vice versa means that there is no discernible relationship between the two categories of tyre enabling production to be adapted to demand on the market …' (para 41)

'The Commission rightly examined the structure of the market and demand primarily at the level of dealers to whom Michelin NV applied the practice in question. Michelin NV has itself stated, although in another context, that it was compelled to change its discount system to take account of the tendency towards specialization amongst its dealers, some of whom … no longer sold tyres for heavy vehicles and vans. This confirms the differences existing in the structure of demand between different groups of dealers.' (para 42)

The applicant also contends that the Commission arbitrarily excluded retreads from the relevant market while these offer consumers a genuine alternative as regards both quality and price. 'In this regard it must first be recalled that although the existence of a competitive relationship between two products does not presuppose complete interchangeability for a specific purpose, it is not a pre-condition for a finding that a dominant position exists in the case of a given product, that there should be a complete absence of competition from other partially interchangeable products as long as such competition does not affect the undertaking's ability to influence appreciably the conditions in which that competition may be exerted or at any rate to conduct itself to a large extent without having to take account of that competition and without suffering any adverse effects as a result of its attitude.' (paras 48, 46–52)

With respect to the geographic market definition, 'The Commission's allegation concerns Michelin NV's conduct towards tyre dealers and more particularly its discount policy. In this regard the commercial policy of the various subsidiaries of the groups competing at the European or even the world level is generally adapted to the specific conditions existing on each market. In practice dealers established in the Netherlands obtain their supplies only from suppliers operating in the Netherlands. The Commission was therefore right to take the view that the competition facing Michelin NV is mainly on the Netherlands market and that it is at that level that the objective conditions of competition are alike for traders.' (paras 26, 23–8)

Comment

The CFI confirmed the Commission's definition of the product market which stemmed from examination of substitutability at the dealer level. It also accepted the exclusion of retreads from the relevant market as these were only partially interchangeable (para 48). It explained that although Michelin 'produced calculations to show that the price and quality of retreads are comparable to those of new tyres and that a number of users do in fact consider the two groups of products interchangeable for their purposes, it has nevertheless admitted that in terms of safety and reliability a retread's value may be less than that of a new tyre and, what is more, the Commission has shown that a number of users have certain reservations, which may or may not be justified, regarding the use of a retread, particularly on a vehicle's front axle' (para 49, see further paras 50–2).

The Commission identified the Netherlands as the relevant geographical market. The CFI accepted this analysis. It noted that the Commission decision addressed Michelin NV which is active in the Netherlands (rather than the Michelin group as a whole) and its abusive discount policy and conduct in that country. The court noted that 'in practice dealers established in the Netherlands obtain their supplies only from suppliers operating in the Netherlands' (para 26). Several commentators argued that this reasoning overly focuses on the alleged abusive behaviour to define the geographical market, instead of on the conditions of competition and the national dealers' possible reaction to increase in price.

Note the similar market analysis in Michelin II (Commission Decision 2002/405/EC (2002 OJ L 143/1)), as well as the CFI judgment on appeal (Case T–203/01 *Michelin v Commission* [2003] ECR II–4071).

Facts

British Airways (BA) operated a range of target incentives which were offered to travel agents. These commission schemes had one notable feature in common: in each case meeting the targets for sales growth lead to an increase in the commission paid on all tickets sold by the travel agent, not just on the tickets sold after the target was reached. The Commission found that this practice amounted to an abuse of BA's dominant position (IV/D-2/34.780 Virgin/British Airways). For the purpose of establishing dominance, the Commission took the view that the relevant market was the UK market, comprised of the services which airlines purchase from travel agents for the purposes of marketing and distributing their airline tickets (recital 72). BA challenged that analysis by the Commission, arguing that even if it exists, the market for services supplied by travel agents to airlines cannot constitute the relevant product market in the circumstances of this case.

Held

'According to settled case-law (Case 322/81 *Michelin v Commission* [1983] ECR 3461, paragraph 37; Case T–65/96 *Kish Glass v Commission* [2000] ECR II–1885, paragraph 62, confirmed on appeal by order of the Court of Justice in Case C–241/00 P *Kish Glass v Commission* [2001] ECR I–7759), for the purposes of investigating the possible dominant position of an undertaking on a given product market, the possibilities of competition must be judged in the context of the market comprising the totality of the products or services which, with respect to their characteristics, are particularly suitable for satisfying constant needs and are only to a limited extent interchangeable with other products or services. Moreover, since the determination of the relevant market is useful in assessing whether the undertaking concerned is in a position to prevent effective competition from being maintained and behave to an appreciable extent independently of its competitors and, in this case, its service providers, an examination to that end cannot be limited to the objective characteristics only of the relevant services, but the competitive conditions and the structure of supply and demand on the market must also be taken into consideration.' (para 91)

'It is clear from BA's pleadings that it itself acknowledges the existence of an independent market for air travel agency services, since it states in … its application that travel agents themselves operate in a competitive market, competing with each other to provide the best possible service to their customers.' (para 92)

'In that regard, although travel agents act on behalf of the airlines, which assume all the risks and advantages connected with the transport service itself and which conclude contracts for transport directly with travellers, they nevertheless constitute independent intermediaries carrying on an independent business of providing services.' (para 93)

'As the Commission states in recital 31 of the contested decision, that specific business of travel agents consists, on the one hand, in advising potential travellers, reserving and issuing airline tickets, (and) collecting the price of the transport and remitting it to the airlines, and, on the other hand, in providing those airlines with advertising and commercial promotion services.' (para 94)

'In that regard, BA itself states that travel agents are and will remain, in the short term at least, a vital distribution channel for airlines, allowing them efficiently to sell seats on the flights they offer, and that there is a mutual dependence between travel agents and airlines which are not in themselves in a position to market their air transport services effectively. As BA has also stated, travel agents offer a wider range of air routes, departure times and arrival times than any airline could. Travel agents filter information concerning various flights for the benefit of travellers faced with the proliferation of different air transport fare structures, which arise from the real-time pricing systems operated by airlines.' (paras 95, 96)

'The Court therefore considers that the services of air travel agencies represent an economic activity for which, at the time of the contested decision, airlines could not substitute another form of distribution of their tickets, and that they therefore constitute a market for services distinct from the air transport market.' (para 100)

Article 82 EC applies 'both to undertakings whose possible dominant position is established, as in this case, in relation to their suppliers and to those which are capable of being in the same position in relation to their customers.' (para 101)

'BA cannot therefore validly argue that, in order to define the product market in question, with a view to assessing the effects on competition of the financial advantages which it allows to travel agents established in the United Kingdom, it is necessary to determine whether a single supplier of air transportation services on a particular route can profitably increase its prices. Such a parameter, which might be relevant in relation to each airline, is not of such a kind as to enable measurement of BA's economic strength in its capacity not as provider of air transport services but as purchaser of travel agency services, on all routes to and from United Kingdom airports, either in relation to all other airlines regarded in the same capacity as purchasers of air travel agency services or in relation to travel agents established in the United Kingdom.' (paras 103, 104)

The Commission did not make any error of assessment in defining the relevant product market. (para 107)

'As for the geographic market to be taken into consideration, consistent case-law shows that it may be defined as the territory in which all traders operate in the same or sufficiently homogeneous conditions of competition in so far as concerns specifically the relevant products or services, without it being necessary for those conditions to be perfectly homogeneous (Case T–83/91 *Tetra Pak v Commission* [1994] ECR II–755, paragraph 91, confirmed on appeal by judgment in Case C–333/94 P *Tetra Pak v Commission* (Tetra Pak II) [1996] ECR I–5951).' (para 108)

In the overwhelming majority of cases, travellers reserve airline tickets in their country of residence. Moreover, IATA's rules on the order of using the coupons in airline tickets prevent tickets sold outside the territory of the UK from being used for flights departing from UK airports. (paras 109, 110)

'Since the distribution of airline tickets takes place at national level, it follows that airlines normally purchase the services for distributing those tickets on a national basis, as is shown by the agreements signed to that end by BA with travel agents established in the United Kingdom.' (para 111)

'Contrary to what BA maintains, the fact that BA concludes global agreements with certain travel agents is not capable of establishing that the latter increasingly deal with airlines on the international level. As is shown in recital 20 of the contested decision, which BA has not challenged, those global agreements were signed with only three travel agents and only for the winter season 1992/1993. Moreover, those agreements were merely added to local agreements made in the countries concerned.' (para 115)

The Commission did not make any error of assessment in defining the relevant geographic market. (para 116)

Comment

Note how the product market definition stemmed from the market in which BA's alleged anticompetitive activity took place. Subsequently, in paragraphs 103 and 104 the CFI rejected BA's argument that the market should be defined based on whether a single supplier of air transportation services on a particular route can profitably increase its prices. The CFI noted that such approach would not allow measurement of BA's economic strength in its capacity as purchaser of travel agency services.

BA lodged an appeal against the CFI judgment. Appeal dismissed (Case C–95/04 P).

Mitsui/CVRD/Caemi	**Market Definition**
Case COMP/M.2420	One-way Product Substitution
European Commission, [2004] OJ L 92/50	

The Commission appraised under the European Merger Regulation a proposed acquisition of joint control of Caemi, a Brazilian iron ore mining company by CVRD and Mitsui, another Brazilian iron ore producer and a Japanese trading company, respectively. Following the Commission assessment the transaction was cleared subject to conditions.

As part of the assessment the Commission examined the market for the supply of iron ore. In doing so it considered the substitutability between DR lump and pellets, on the one hand, and BOF lump and pellets, on the other. It noted that 'this is a one-way substitution process: the latter are replaceable by the former but not vice versa, principally on account of the higher iron content and lower level of impurities of DR ore. However, in view of the higher price of DR iron ore, this substitutability of DR ore for BOF ore is of a theoretical nature' (para 134). Additionally, the Commission found there to be 'a one-way substitutability between DR lump and DR pellets, in that DR lump cannot replace DR pellets over a certain proportion of the burden (for technical reasons) but DR pellets can fully replace DR lump' (para 135). This provided indication for the existence of a market for 'DRI pellets' and a separate market for 'DR lump and pellets' (paras 136, 140).

Bertelsmann/Springer/JV	**Market Definition**
Case COMP/M.3178	One-way Geographical Substitution
European Commission, [2006] OJ L 61/17	

Following an appraisal under the European Merger Regulation, the Commission cleared the creation of the 'Rotogravure printing joint venture' by German media companies Bertelsmann AG and Axel Springer AG.

In its decision the Commission identified a distinct product market for high-volume rotogravure printing of magazines. With respect to the geographical market definition, the Commission noted that 'the structure of supply and demand for rotogravure printing services in Germany differs considerably from the situation in most other European countries. Owing to the large rotogravure printing capacity available in Germany which accounts for almost 50% of the total capacity installed in the EU, there are considerable exports of printing services, in particular to France and the UK. By contrast, German customers purchase rotogravure printing services abroad only to a rather limited extent. However, the number and volume of print jobs handled by foreign rotogravure printers for German customers varies among the different product markets described above' (para 59). This finding contributed to the conclusion that German consumers faced a domestic market consisting of German suppliers, and to the Commission noting the possibility that the market for magazines in other Member States might be wider and include Germany: 'As to the other countries, such as France and UK, the market investigation has shown that imports of rotogravure magazine printing services from Germany are significantly higher than the other way around. The reason for this is the historically larger capacity located in Germany. This apparently led, to some extent, to differing preferences and a higher readiness of magazine publishers in the other countries to print abroad than is the case with German publishers. However, the exact definitions of the geographic market for these countries with the exception of Germany can be left open in this respect since even the narrowest possible delineation of the geographic markets as national markets does not raise any competition concerns in these countries' (para 70).

Hugin v Commission	**Market Definition**
Case 22/78	Narrow Markets
ECJ, [1979] ECR 1869, [1979] 3 CMLR 345	Aftermarket – Spare Parts

Facts

Hugin was fined by the European Commission for refusing to supply spare parts for its cash registers to Liptons, an independent company which operated outside the Hugin distribution system. The Commission found Hugin's refusal to supply to constitute an abuse of a dominant position (IV/29.132 Hugin/Liptons). Hugin appealed the decision and challenged, among other things, the Commission's definition of the market.

Held (on market definition)

'... it is necessary, first, to determine the relevant market. In this respect account must be taken of the fact that the conduct alleged against Hugin consists in the refusal to supply spare parts to Liptons and, generally, to any independent undertaking outside its distribution network. The question is, therefore, whether the supply of spare parts constitutes a specific market or whether it forms part of a wider market. To answer that question it is necessary to determine the category of clients who require such parts.' (para 5)

'In this respect it is established, on the one hand, that cash registers are of such a technical nature that the user cannot fit the spare parts into the machine but requires the services of a specialized technician and, on the other, that the value of the spare parts is of little significance in relation to the cost of maintenance and repairs. That being the case, users of cash registers do not operate on the market as purchasers of spare parts, however they have their machines maintained and repaired. Whether they avail themselves of Hugin's after-sales service or whether they rely on independent undertakings engaged in maintenance and repair work, their spare part requirements are not manifested directly and independently on the market. While there certainly exists amongst users a market for maintenance and repairs which is distinct from the market in new cash registers, it is essentially a market for the provision of services and not for the sale of a product such as spare parts, the refusal to supply in which forms the subject-matter of the Commission's Decision.' (para 6)

'On the other hand, there exists a separate market for Hugin spare parts at another level, namely that of independent undertakings which specialize in the maintenance and repair of cash registers, in the reconditioning of used machines and in the sale of used machines and the renting out of machines. The role of those undertakings on the market is that of businesses which require spare parts for their various activities. They need such parts in order to provide services for cash register users in the form of maintenance and repairs and for the reconditioning of used machines intended for re-sale or renting out. Finally, they require spare parts for the maintenance and repair of new or used machines belonging to them which are rented out to their clients. It is, moreover, established that there is a specific demand for Hugin spare parts, since those parts are not interchangeable with spare parts for cash registers of other makes.' (para 7)

'Consequently the market thus constituted by Hugin's spare parts required by independent undertakings must be regarded as the relevant market for the purposes of the application of [Article 82] to the facts of the case. It is in fact the market on which the alleged abuse was committed.' (para 8)

Comment

The court distinguished between the demand characteristics at the consumer level and that at the maintenance level. In the latter, where Liptons operated, the lack of interchangability between Hugin spare parts and spare parts of other makes led to a finding of a narrow market for 'Hugin spare parts'.

Where customers in the aftermarket, that is the market for replacement parts, accessories, or service for a product, are captive and unable to use other brands to service the product, that market may constitute a separate product market. Note the Commission *Nintendo* decision (COMP/35.587) page 31 below, which further highlights the considerations relevant to aftermarkets and 'locked in customers'.

Hilti AG v Commission	**Market Definition**
Case T–30/89	Narrow Markets
CFI, [1991] ECR II–1439, [1992] 4 CMLR 16	Aftermarket

Facts

The Commission fined Hilti AG for abusing its dominant position by tying the sale of nails to the sale of cartridge strips. The finding of dominance stemmed from the Commission's narrow market definition. In its decision the Commission identified three separate product markets which were (a) the market for nail guns, (b) the market for Hilti-compatible cartridge strips and (c) the market for Hilti-compatible nails. On appeal, Hilti contested, among other things, the Commission's definition of the product market and asserted that the three markets comprise one single product market.

Held

'The Court takes the view that nail guns, cartridge strips and nails constitute three specific markets. Since cartridge strips and nails are specifically manufactured, and purchased by users, for a single brand of gun, it must be concluded that there are separate markets for Hilti-compatible cartridge strips and nails, as the Commission found in its decision (paragraph 55).' (para 66)

'With particular regard to the nails whose use in Hilti tools is an essential element of the dispute, it is common ground that since the 1960s there have been independent producers, including the interveners, making nails intended for use in nail guns. Some of those producers are specialized and produce only nails, and indeed some make only nails specifically designed for Hilti tools. That fact in itself is sound evidence that there is a specific market for Hilti-compatible nails.' (para 67)

'Hilti's contention that guns, cartridge strips and nails should be regarded as forming an indivisible whole, 'a powder-actuated fastening system' is in practice tantamount to permitting producers of nail guns to exclude the use of consumables other than their own branded products in their tools. However, in the absence of general and binding standards or rules, any independent producer is quite free, as far as Community competition law is concerned, to manufacture consumables intended for use in equipment manufactured by others, unless in doing so it infringes a patent or some other industrial or intellectual property right. Even on the assumption that, as the applicant has argued, components of different makes cannot be interchanged without the system characteristics being influenced, the solution should lie in the adoption of appropriate laws and regulations, not in unilateral measures taken by nail gun producers which have the effect of preventing independent producers from pursuing the bulk of their business.' (para 68)

'The conclusion must be that the relevant product market in relation to which Hilti's market position must be appraised is the market for nails designed for Hilti nail guns.' (para 77)

As far as the definition of the geographic market is concerned, there appear to be large price differences for Hilti products between the Member States. In addition the transport costs for nails are low. Subsequently, parallel trading is highly likely between the national markets and the Commission was right in taking the view that the relevant geographic market in this case is the Community as a whole. (paras 79–81)

Comment

For another example of a finding of a distinct market for consumables, see Case C–333/94 *Tetra Pak International SA v Commission* [1996] ECR I–5951, [1997] 4 CMLR 662 (an appeal on the CFI decision in Case T–83/91, [1994] ECR II–755, [1997] 4 CMLR 726). In paragraph 83 of its judgment the CFI noted that 'any independent producer is …[free] to manufacture consumables intended for use in equipment manufactured by others …' (the ECJ confirmed this finding in paragraph 36 of its judgment). Tetra Pak was not alone in being able to manufacture cartons for use in its machines. That finding of a separate market for consumables led to finding of abusive tying of sales of cartons and filling machines. See detailed discussion on page 176 below.

PO Video Games, PO Nintendo Distribution, Omega-Nintendo
COMP/35.587, 35.706, 36.321
European Commission, [2003] OJ L 255/33

Market Definition
Switching Costs

Facts

The European Commission found that Nintendo, a Japanese video games maker, and seven of its official distributors in Europe, infringed Article 81 EC by colluding to maintain artificially high price differences for play consoles and games in the EU. According to the arrangements, distributors prevented parallel trade from their territories, thus hindering exports to high-priced from low-priced territories.

Held (on market definition)

Game consoles are not substitutable with personal computers. They may be divided into two distinct markets: static game consoles and portable, hand-held game consoles. Each of these comprises products intended to fulfil different user needs, and displaying different technical capabilities and price range. (paras 19–34)

Game cartridges are purchased by the users separately and are used with the game consoles. Due to different technical specifications, a cartridge with a game designed for a specific console cannot be used with any other console and, once a particular game console is chosen, only game cartridges compatible with the chosen console can be used. (paras 35, 36)

'As a result, in the event of a small, permanent increase in the price of a particular game cartridge, a user of a given game console is unlikely to switch to a game cartridge compatible with a different console. This is due to the fact that the user has to bear the cost not only of the new cartridge, but also that of buying a new console able to interoperate with that cartridge. It is uncontested that the number of game cartridges that need to be purchased to make switching worthwhile is far in excess of the average number of game cartridges owned by the average game console owner ...' (para 37)

'... current owners of a game console would face substantial switching costs if they switched to different game cartridges, and are generally "locked in" for a period of at least three to four years, usually until their current game console becomes obsolete. For them, competition took place at the time of deciding what console to buy. Their reaction to a small, permanent price increase in game cartridges compatible with their console would be limited because buying an incompatible game only makes sense if the console associated with that new game is bought at the same time.' (para 46)

'For consumers who do not yet own a console ... prices for game cartridges may be one of the competitive variables used by console manufacturers to compete in that market. However, there are no indications in the file to support that prices of games are more or less important than other elements such as the price of the console itself, its technical capabilities ... the availability and types of games ...' (para 48)

Subsequently, 'contrary to Nintendo's argument about system's competition, game cartridges compatible with a particular game console belong to a different market than those compatible with another.' (para 51)

Comment

The analysis shares similarities with the approach taken in Case 22/78 *Hugin v Commission* (page 29 above) where the finding of a group of locked-in customers led to a narrow market definition.

The market definition in this case raises interesting questions with respect to 'whole-life costing'. Do consumers take into account the prices of the secondary product (video games) when making a decision to purchase the main platform? If they do, then changes at the secondary market are likely to affect the competitiveness of the primary market (para 48). The consumers' ability to whole-life cost depends on the price difference between the secondary and primary products, the availability of information on the cost of spare parts and the frequency with which they are required. On this point see the UK OFT Guidelines 403.

Commercial Solvents v Commission	**Market Definition**
Case 6/73	Market for Raw Materials
ECJ, [1974] ECR 223, [1974] 1 CMLR 309	

Facts

Commercial Solvents Corporation (CSC) was the main supplier of the chemical amino-butanol, which can be used as raw material for the production of other chemicals. One of CSC's customers, Zoja, purchased large quantities of this raw material and used it for the manufacturing of another chemical, ethambutol. CSC informed Zoja that it would stop supplying it with the raw material necessary for the production of ethambutol. This decision coincided with CSC's decision to engage itself in the production of ethambutol. The Commission found this refusal to supply to constitute an infringement of Article 82 EC. CSC applied for the annulment of the Commission's Decision.

Held (on market definition)

CSC disputes the Commission's finding according to which it has a dominant position in the common market for the raw material necessary for the manufacture of ethambutol. For this purpose it argues, among other things, that ethambutol can be produced from other raw materials and not only from the chemicals produced by CSC. However, according to an expert opinion presented by the Commission, these processes would be possible only at considerable expense and at some risk. (paras 9–14)

'This dispute is of no great practical importance since it relates mainly to processes of an experimental nature, which have not been tested on an industrial scale and which have resulted in only a modest production. The question is not whether Zoja, by adapting its installations and its manufacturing processes, would have been able to continue its production of ethambutol based on other raw materials, but whether CSC had a dominant position in the market in raw material for the manufacture of ethambutol. It is only the presence on the market of a raw material which could be substituted without difficulty for nitropropane or aminobutanol for the manufacture of ethambutol which could invalidate the argument that CSC has a dominant position within the meaning of [Article 82]. On the other hand reference to possible alternative processes of an experimental nature or which are practiced on a small scale is not sufficient to refute the grounds of the Decision in dispute.' (para 15)

CSC further challenges the Commission's conclusion that the relevant market for determining the dominant position is the one of ethambutol. Such a market, it argues, does not exist since ethambutol is only a part of a larger market in anti-tuberculosis drugs, where it is in competition with other drugs which are to a large extent interchangeable. 'Contrary to the arguments of the applicants it is in fact possible to distinguish the market in raw material necessary for the manufacture of a product, from the market on which the product is sold. An abuse of a dominant position on the market in raw materials may thus have effects restricting competition in the market on which the derivatives of the raw material are sold and these effects must be taken into account in considering the effects of an infringement, even if the market for the derivative does not constitute a self-contained market.' (paras 22, 19–22)

Comment

The product market definition stemmed from the market in which CSC's alleged anticompetitive activity took place. The court therefore focused on Zoja's inability to use other raw materials to produce the final derivative.

The fact that the derivative did not constitute a self-contained market did not affect the ECJ finding of two distinct markets, an upstream market for raw materials and a downstream for the derivatives of the raw material. This finding facilitated the conclusion regarding refusal to supply (see below Chapter 5, page 165). An interesting extension to this analysis of a downstream market may be found in Case C–418/01 *IMS Health*, where the ECJ identified a hypothetical downstream market (see below Chapter 5, page 170).

3

Article 81 EC

Article 81 EC

1. The following shall be prohibited as incompatible with the common market: all agreements between undertakings, decisions by associations of undertakings and concerted practices which may affect trade between Member States and which have as their object or effect the prevention, restriction or distortion of competition within the common market, and in particular those which:

   (a) directly or indirectly fix purchase or selling prices or any other trading conditions;
   (b) limit or control production, markets, technical development, or investment;
   (c) share markets or sources of supply;
   (d) apply dissimilar conditions to equivalent transactions with other trading parties, thereby placing them at a competitive disadvantage;
   (e) make the conclusion of contracts subject to acceptance by the other parties of supplementary obligations which, by their nature or according to commercial usage, have no connection with the subject of such contracts.

2. Any agreements or decisions prohibited pursuant to this Article shall be automatically void.

3. The provisions of paragraph 1 may, however, be declared inapplicable in the case of:
   – any agreement or category of agreements between undertakings;
   – any decision or category of decisions by associations of undertakings;
   – any concerted practice or category of concerted practices,
   which contributes to improving the production or distribution of goods or to promoting technical or economic progress, while allowing consumers a fair share of the resulting benefit, and which does not:
   (a) impose on the undertakings concerned restrictions which are not indispensable to the attainment of these objectives;
   (b) afford such undertakings the possibility of eliminating competition in respect of a substantial part of the products in question.

The application of Article 81 EC depends on a series of distinct conditions being satisfied. For ease of analysis Article 81 EC may be divided into four main questions:

1. Is there an agreements between undertakings, decisions by associations of undertakings or concerted practices?
2. Is its Object or Effect the prevention, restriction or distortion of competition within the Common Market?

3. Does it affect trade between Member States?
4. Could it benefit from an exemption under Article 81(3) EC?

Agreement between Undertakings

The concept of 'undertaking' is discussed in Chapter 1 above. The following section is concerned with the criteria for establishing the existence of an agreement between undertakings.

Generally, in order for there to be an agreement caught under Article 81 EC, it is sufficient that at least two undertakings have expressed their joint intention to conduct themselves in a specific way on the market. The concept of an agreement centres on the existence of a concurrence of wills between the parties, the form in which it is manifested being insignificant. The following cases provide a good illustration of the notion of agreement and the distinction between agreements and unilateral actions:

107/82	*AEG–Telefunken v Commission*	40
25 & 26/84	*Ford v Commission*	41
T–41/96	*Bayer v Commission*	42
T–208/01	*Volkswagen v Commission*	44

See also summary references to:

277/87	*Sandoz Prodotti Farmaceutici SpA v Commission*	40, 43
41/69	*ACF Chemiefarma NV v Commission*	41
C–279/87	*Tipp-Ex v Commission*	43
C–338/00 P	*Volkswagen v Commission*	44

Concerted Practice

At times it is possible for some form of cooperation between undertakings to take place without giving rise to an agreement. To ensure the effectiveness of the competition provisions, Article 81 EC is also applicable to 'concerted practices'. The concept of 'concerted practice' refers to forms of coordination between companies, which, without reaching the level of an agreement, have nevertheless established practical cooperation between them. This cooperation substitutes the risk of competition to the detriment of consumers.

Concerted practice is commonly proven by showing parallel conduct between companies, which cannot be explained by any other reason but cooperation. It is therefore of major importance to distinguish between anticompetitive parallel conduct and similarity of conduct which results from the competitive process. Accordingly, concerted practice will not be established when market conditions provide an explanation to the parallel conduct or where companies adapt themselves intelligently and unilaterally to the existing and anticipated conduct of their competitors.

On the concept of concerted practice, see:

48/69	*ICI v Commission (Dyestuffs)*	45
40/73 etc	*Suiker Unie and others v Commission*	46
89/85 etc	*A Ahlström Osakeyhtiö and others v Commission* (Wood Pulp Cartel)	48
C–199/92	*Hüls AG v Commission*	49
C–204/00 etc	*Aalborg Portland A/S and others v Commission*	51

See also summary reference to:

Joint Classification and Single Overall Agreement

When dealing with complex cartel arrangements that involve different levels of cooperation, one can use a joint classification to establish coordination without distinguishing between agreements or concerted practice. In addition, in such circumstances the Commission is not required to establish the exact level of participation of each cartel member and may rely on the concept of a 'single overall agreement'.

See also summary reference to:

Decision by an Association

Article 81 EC also applies to decisions by associations of undertakings, thus preventing the use of associations as a vehicle to coordinate and promote anticompetitive activities.

See also summary reference to:

Object or Effect

Agreements, concerted practices or decisions of associations of undertakings are caught under Article 81 EC when they have the object or effect of preventing, restricting or distorting competition within the Common Market. The following cases illustrate the distinction between object and effect and the depth of analysis called for when assessing anticompetitive effect:

| T–328/03 | *O2 (Germany) GmbH & Co OHG v Commission* | 64 |

On the distinction between restrictions by object and restrictions by effect and their asessment, see also paragraphs 17–27, Commission Guidelines on the Application of Article 81(3) of the Treaty [2004] OJ C 101/94.

Scope of Analysis under Article 81(1) EC and the 'Rule of Reason'

Whilst the evaluation of the effect an agreement may generate under Article 81(1) EC takes account of its economic context, it does not encompass a balancing exercise of the competitive benefits and harms. Such balancing exercise is confined to the analysis under Article 81(3) EC.

Subsequently, Article 81(1) EC does not encompass a 'rule of reason' consideration and is limited in its scope in so much that it does not overlap with the Article 81(3) EC analysis.

T–328/03	*O2 (Germany) GmbH & Co OHG v Commission*	64
T–112/99	*Métropole Télévision (M6) v Commission*	66
C–519/04 P	*Meca-Medina and Majcen v Commission*	68

See also summary references to:

| T–17/93 | *Matra Hachette v Commission* | 65 |
| C–309/99 | *Wouters* | 65 |

Ancillary Restraints

The concept of ancillary restraints covers restrictions of competition which are directly related to and necessary for the implementation of a main non-restrictive transaction and proportionate to it. Accordingly, a restriction which is ancillary to an agreement that does not infringe Article 81(1) EC, or is exempted under Article 81(3) EC, will be allowed as long as it is objectively necessary for the operation of the agreement and is proportionate to it.

The application of the ancillary restraint concept differs from the balancing exercise under Article 81(3) EC and does not involve weighing of procompetitive and anticompetitive effects. It should also not be mistaken to constitute a 'Rule of Reason' analysis under Article 81(1) EC.

42/84	*Remia BV v Commission*	69
C–250/92	*Gottrup-Klim v Dansk Landbrugs Grovvareselskab AmbA*	70
T–112/99	*Métropole Télévision (M6) v Commission*	72
C–309/99	*Wouters*	74

On ancillary restraints also note paragraphs 28–31, Commission Guidelines on the Application of Article 81(3) of the Treaty, [2004] OJ C 101/94.

Appreciable Effect (de minimis)

The de minimis doctrine excludes from the application of Article 81 EC agreements that do not have an appreciable effect on competition or on trade between Member States.

The Commission published a notice which clarified the scope of the doctrine. See the Commission Notice on Agreements of Minor Importance which do not Appreciably Restrict Competition under Article 81(1) of the Treaty Establishing the European Community (de minimis), [2001] OJ C 368/13.

The thresholds in the notice are neither absolute nor binding. They reflect the Commission's view on which agreements are not likely to have an appreciable effect on competition or trade between Member States. It is therefore possible to find agreements which exceed the thresholds yet do not have an appreciable effect on competition, and vice versa. Also note that whereas the de minimis doctrine is applicable to agreements with both object or effect (see Case 5/69 *Volk*, below), the Commission's notice excludes from its scope agreements which include hard core restrictions.

5/69	*Franz Volk v SPRL Est J Vervaecke*	76
T–7 /93	*Langnese-Iglo GmbH v Commission*	76
T–374/94 etc	*European Night Services Ltd and others v Commission*	76

Effect on Trade Between Member States

Article 81(1) EC applies only to agreements between undertakings, decisions by associations of undertakings and concerted practices which may affect trade between Member States. In general, an agreement will be found to affect trade between Member States when it has an actual or potential, direct or indirect, positive or negative influence on patterns of trade between Member States. See the following cases which illustrate the European courts' broad interpretation of 'effect on trade':

56/65	*Société Technique Minière v Maschinenbau Ulm GmbH*	77
56/64 etc	*Consten & Grundig v Commission*	77
8/72	*Vereeniging van Cementhandelaren v Commission*	77
23/67	*SA Brasserie de Haecht v Consorts Wilkin-Janssen*	78
107/82	*AEG–Telefunken v Commission*	78

For additional discussion on 'effect on trade', see the Commission Guidelines on the Effect on Trade Concept Contained in Articles 81 and 82 of the Treaty, [2004] OJ C 101/81.

Article 81(2) EC

Article 81(2) EC provides that any agreements or decisions prohibited under Article 81(1) EC and not exempted under Article 81(3) EC are automatically void. The automatic nullity under Article 81(2) EC only applies to those parts of the agreement affected by the prohibition, or to the agreement as a whole when those parts are not severable from the agreement itself.

56/64 etc	*Consten and Grundig v Commission* (inc advocate general opinion)	79

See also summary references to:

56/65	*Société Technique Minière v Maschinenbau Ulm GmbH*	79
T–9/99	*HFB Holding and others v Commission*	79
English CA	*David John Passmore v Morland and others*	79

Not also the discussion in Chapter 7 below on Euro defence and the use of Article 81 EC in the National Court.

Article 81(3)

Article 81(3) provides a possible exemption route for agreements, concerted practices or decision by associations of undertakings which were found to restrict competition by their effect or object. Accordingly it stipulates that the provisions of Article 81(1) EC may be declared inapplicable in the case of agreement, decision or concerted practice 'which contributes to improving the production or distribution of goods or to promoting technical or economic progress, while allowing consumers a fair share of the resulting benefit, and which does not: (a) impose on the undertakings concerned restrictions which are not indispensable to the attainment of these objectives; (b) afford such undertakings the possibility of eliminating competition in respect of a substantial part of the products in question.'

Exemptions under Article 81(3) make take one of two forms:

(a)   Block Exemptions apply Article 81(3) to categories of agreements. Agreements covered by block exemptions are presumed to fulfil the conditions laid down in Article 81(3), thus relieving the parties to these agreements from the burden under Article 2 of Regulation 1/2003 of establishing that the agreement satisfies the conditions of Article 81(3) EC. A complete list of block exemption regulations may be found on the European Commission competition website (http://www.europa.eu.int/comm/dgs/competition). Agreements which are covered by one of the block exemption regulations are 'legally valid and enforceable even if they are restrictive of competition within the meaning of Article 81(1). Such agreements can only be prohibited for the future and only upon formal withdrawal of the block exemption by the Commission or a national competition authority. Block exempted agreements cannot be held invalid by national courts in the context of private litigation' (para 2, Guidelines on the Application of Article 81(3) of the Treaty, [2004] OJ C101/97).

(b)   Exemptions may also be granted in individual cases by the European Commission, national competition agencies or national courts, when an agreement, although found to infringe Article 81(1) EC, satisfies the cumulative conditions in Article 81(3) EC. In such cases, it is for the party seeking to defend the validity of the agreement to satisfy the cumulative conditions of Article 81(3) EC and to show that the agreement:

1.   contributes to improving the production or distribution of goods or to promoting technical or economic progress;
2.   allows consumers a fair share of the resulting benefit;
3.   does not impose restrictions which are not indispensable to the attainment of these objectives;
4.   does not eliminate competition in respect of a substantial part of the products in question.

Many of the cases concerning the realm of Article 81(3) EC date back to Regulation 17/62, which preceded Regulation 1/2003. Needless to say, the change in the enforcement regime and the abolition of the notification system did not affect the substantive analysis of Article 81(3) EC. As part of the modernisation package which accompanied the coming into force of Regulation 1/2003, the European Commission published a set of Guidelines on the Application of Article 81 (3) of the Treaty ([2004] OJ C101/97). These Guidelines, although not binding on national courts and national competition authorities, embody the European case law and establish an analytical framework for the application of Article 81(3) EC.

The following cases illustrate the scope and nature of analysis under Article 81(3) EC. On consideration of the first two (positive) conditions, namely the improvement of production or distribution of goods, the promotion of technical or economic progress and consumers' fair share of the resulting benefits, see:

56/64 etc	*Consten and Grundig v Commission*	80
26/76	*Metro v Commission*	81
C–360/92 P	*Publishers Association v Commission*	82
T–168/01	*GlaxoSmithKline Services Unlimited v Commission*	83

See also summary references to:

On consideration of the last two (negative) conditions, namely the requirement for indispensability and the need to avoid substantial elimination to competition, see:

See also summary references to:

On the scope of judicial review on decisions concerning exemption under Article 81(3) EC, see:

See also summary references to:

AEG–Telefunken v Commission	**Article 81 EC**
Case 107/82	Agreement
ECJ, [1983] ECR 3151, [1984] 3 CMLR 325	Selective Distribution System

Facts

AEG – Telefunken (AEG), a German company which manufactures and markets consumer electronic products, notified the Commission of a selective distribution system (SDS) for its branded products. The Commission did not object to the SDS, yet later found that the actual application of the SDS by AEG and its subsidiaries did not correspond to the scheme notified to it. Subsequently, the Commission found that AEG had infringed Article 81 EC and improperly applied its SDS by discriminating against certain distributors and by influencing dealers' resale prices. AEG appealed to the ECJ, arguing, among other things, that its actions were unilateral and did not constitute an agreement under Article 81 EC. The ECJ dismissed the appeal.

Held (on the existence of Agreement)

A selective distribution system (SDS) may include acceptable limitations leading to a reduction of price competition in favour of competition relating to factors other than price. This would be the case, for example, when an SDS is used to attain legitimate goals such as the maintenance of a specialist trade capable of providing specific services as regards high-quality and high-technology products. The criteria for permissible SDS were laid down by the Court in *Metro v Commission* and were not met in this case. (paras 33–7, 40–3)

A refusal by AEG to approve distributors who satisfy the qualitative criteria of the SDS, with a view to maintaining a high level of prices, is unlawful. Such refusal does not constitute unilateral conduct on the part of AEG and therefore does not exempt it from the prohibition contained in Article 81(1) EC. 'On the contrary, it forms part of the contractual relations between the undertaking and resellers. Indeed, in the case of the admission of a distributor, approval is based on the acceptance, tacit or express, by the contracting parties of the policy pursued by AEG which requires inter alia the exclusion from the network of all distributors who are qualified for admission but are not prepared to adhere to that policy.' (para 38)

'The view must therefore be taken that even refusals of approval are acts performed in the context of the contractual relations with authorised distributors inasmuch as their purpose is to guarantee observance of the agreements in restraint of competition which form the basis of contracts between manufacturers and approved distributors. Refusals to approve distributors who satisfy the qualitative criteria mentioned above therefore supply proof of an unlawful application of the system if their number is sufficient to preclude the possibility that they are isolated cases not forming part of systematic conduct.' (para 39)

Comment

The refusal by AEG to approve distributors that did not accept its price policy arose out of the agreement between AEG and its existing distributors. Those existing distributors accepted, tacitly or expressly, the policy pursued by AEG. The refusal formed an agreement, the provisions of which are subjected to Article 81(1) EC.

See Case C–227/87 *Sandoz Prodotti Farmaceutici SpA v Commission*, [1990] ECR I–45, in which Sandoz attempted to deter parallel import to countries where prices of its pharmaceutical products were not controlled. It did so by adding the words 'export prohibited' to invoices sent to its distributors. The ECJ rejected Sandoz's claim that this was a unilateral conduct and found this to form part of an agreement between Sandoz and its distributors. The distributors tacitly accepted Sandoz's wish by placing repeated orders without contesting the restrictive conditions. The tacit acceptance constituted an agreement subject to Article 81 EC, despite it not constituting a valid and binding contract under national law.

Ford Werke AG, Ford Europe Inc v Commission	**Article 81 EC**
Cases 25 & 26/84	Agreement
ECJ, [1985] ECR 2725, [1985] 3 CMLR 528	Selective Distribution System

Facts

In the early 1980s prices for Ford's right-hand-drive cars sold in Germany were considerably lower than those sold on the British market. Subsequently, a growing number of British customers were buying those vehicles from German dealers. Ford Werke AG (Ford AG) was concerned about the effects of such sales on the position of Ford Britain and its distribution network. Consequently, in April 1982 it notified the German Ford dealers who were part of its selective distribution system that it would no longer accept their orders for right-hand-drive cars. All such cars would have to be purchased either from a Ford dealer established in the United Kingdom or from a subsidiary of Ford Britain. The Commission found that Ford AG's conduct constituted an anticompetitive agreement between Ford AG and its distributors. Ford appealed to the ECJ, arguing that, among other things, its decision to stop supplies was unilateral, did not form part of an agreement and was therefore not subjected to Article 81 EC. Ford's appeal was dismissed.

Held

'It must be observed in this regard that agreements which constitute a selective distribution system and which, as in this case, seek to maintain a specialized trade capable of providing specific services for high-technology products are normally concluded in order to govern the distribution of those products for a certain number of years. Because technological developments are not always foreseeable over such a period of time, those agreements necessarily have to leave certain matters to be decided later by the manufacturer.' Such later decisions were provided for in 'schedule 1' of the Ford AG selective distribution agreement, as far as the models to be delivered under the terms of that agreement were concerned. (para 20)

'Such a decision on the part of the manufacturer does not constitute, on the part of the undertaking, a unilateral act which, as the applicants claim, would be exempt from the prohibition contained in [Article 81(1) EC]. On the contrary, it forms part of the contractual relations between the undertaking and its dealers. Indeed, admission to the Ford AG dealer network implies acceptance by the contracting parties of the policy pursued by ford with regard to the models to be delivered to the German market.' (para 21)

The applicants' argument based on the unilateral nature of the withdrawal of right-hand-drive cars from Ford AG' s model range must be rejected.

Comment

Similarly to AEG (page 40 above) the court found that the activity formed part of an ongoing relationship between the appellants and the distributors. The two cases are distinguished by the fact that AEG's policies benefited its own distributors, whereas Ford AG's change of policy did not benefit its German distributors.

Ford AG v Commission can be regarded as an extension of the AEG ruling, since despite the conduct not operating to the distributors' advantage it was found to form part of the agreement between the manufacturer and distributor.

Note generally that in order for there to be 'agreement' within the meaning of Article 81(1) EC it is sufficient that the undertakings in question have expressed their joint intention to conduct themselves on the market in a specific way. (Case 41/69 *ACF Chemiefarma NV v Commission*, [1970] ECR 661 (paras 106–13)).

Bayer v Commission	**Article 81 EC**
Case T–41/96	Agreement
CFI, [2000] ECR II–3383, [2001] 4 CMLR 4	Export Ban/Parallel Imports

Facts

Bayer AG (Bayer), the parent company of one of the main European chemical and pharmaceutical groups, manufactures and markets a range of medicinal products under the trade name 'Adalat'. The price of Adalat is fixed by the national health authorities in most Member States. Between 1989 and 1993, the prices for Adalat in Spain and France were, on average, 40 per cent lower than prices in the United Kingdom. These price differences provided a business opportunity to wholesalers in Spain and France that started exporting Adalat to the United Kingdom.

The parallel imports lead to a sharp drop in sales of Adalat and loss of revenue by Bayer's British subsidiary. In an attempt to stop the parallel imports the Bayer group began to cease fulfilling all of the increasingly large orders placed by wholesalers in Spain and France with its Spanish and French subsidiaries.

Some of the wholesalers concerned complained to the Commission. Following its investigation, the Commission found that Bayer France and Bayer Spain identified wholesalers who engaged in export to the United Kingdom and applied successive reductions in the volumes delivered to them. The two subsidiaries imposed an export ban as part of their continuous commercial relations with their customers and were therefore found to enter an agreement contrary to Article 81(1) EC.

Bayer appealed to the CFI, claiming, among other things, that its conduct was unilateral.

Held (on the concept of agreement)

'… in order for there to be an agreement within the meaning of [Article 81(1) EC] it is sufficient that the undertakings in question should have expressed their joint intention to conduct themselves on the market in a specific way (Case 41/69 *ACF Chemiefarma v Commission* [1970] ECR 661, paragraph 112).' (para 67)

'As regards the form in which that common intention is expressed, it is sufficient for a stipulation to be the expression of the parties' intention to behave on the market in accordance with its terms (see, in particular, *ACF Chemiefarma*, paragraph 112, and *Van Landewyck*, paragraph 86), without its having to constitute a valid and binding contract under national law (Sandoz, paragraph 13).' (para 68)

The concept of an agreement within the meaning of Article 81(1) EC 'as interpreted by the case-law, centres around the existence of a concurrence of wills between at least two parties, the form in which it is manifested being unimportant so long as it constitutes the faithful expression of the parties' intention.' (para 69)

'… a distinction should be drawn between cases in which an undertaking has adopted a genuinely unilateral measure, and thus without the express or implied participation of another undertaking, and those in which the unilateral character of the measure is merely apparent. Whilst the former do not fall within [Article 81(1) EC] the latter must be regarded as revealing an agreement between undertakings and may therefore fall within the scope of that article. That is the case, in particular, with practices and measures in restraint of competition which, though apparently adopted unilaterally by the manufacturer in the context of its contractual relations with its dealers, nevertheless receive at least the tacit acquiescence of those dealers.' (para 71)

The Commission cannot hold that apparently unilateral conduct on the part of a manufacturer, adopted in the context of the contractual relations which it maintains with his dealers, forms the basis of an agreement between the parties unless it establishes the existence of an acquiescence by the other partners, express or implied, in the attitude adopted by the manufacturer. (para 72)

In this case, in the absence of evidence of the conclusion of an agreement between the parties concerning the limitation of exports, the Commission has relied on the conduct of the applicant and the wholesalers to establish the concurrence of wills. It therefore found the unilateral decision as to the export ban, to form the subject-matter of an agreement between the applicant and the wholesalers as the latter adopted an implicit acquiescence in the export ban. (paras 73–6)

'In those circumstances, in order to determine whether the Commission has established to the requisite legal standard the existence of a concurrence of wills between the parties concerning the limitation of parallel exports, it is necessary to consider whether, as the applicant maintains, the Commission wrongly assessed the respective intentions of Bayer and the wholesalers.' (para 77)

The Commission has not proven to the requisite legal standard either that the subsidiaries imposed an export ban on their respective wholesalers, or that Bayer systematically monitored the export of Adalat, or that it applied a policy of threats and sanctions against exporting wholesalers, or that it made supplies of this product conditional on compliance with the alleged export ban. (paras 81–109)

The Commission did not prove the intention of the wholesalers to adhere to the export ban and cannot view the reduction in orders as a sign that the wholesalers had accepted Bayer's requirements. On the contrary, the wholesalers continued to try to obtain extra quantities of Adalat for export and demonstrated a firm intention to continue carrying on parallel exports of Adalat. The Commission was therefore wrong in holding that the actual conduct of the wholesalers constitutes sufficient proof in law of their acquiescence in the applicant's policy designed to prevent parallel imports. (paras 110–57)

Comment

The case was appealed to the ECJ (Joined Cases C–2/01 P, C–3/01 P *Bundesverband der Arzneimittel-Importeure v Bayer and Commission*). The ECJ dismissed the appeals.

Both the CFI and ECJ referred in their decisions to the case law relied on by the Commission in its decision and distinguished between those cases and the circumstances in the present case. Note in particular the Courts' references to the following two cases.

In Case C–277/87 *Sandoz v Commission* [1990] ECR I–45, the manufacturer had sent invoices to its suppliers carrying the express words 'export prohibited', which had been tacitly accepted by the suppliers. The ECJ found the repeated orders of the products and the successive payments without protest by the customer of the words 'export prohibited' to constitute a tacit acquiescence. It therefore held that the whole of the continuous commercial relations, of which the 'export prohibited' clause formed an integral part, established between Sandoz PF and its customers, were governed by a pre-established general agreement applicable to the innumerable individual orders for Sandoz products. The facts in Sandoz are distinguishable from the present case as in Bayer there was no formal clause prohibiting export and no conduct of non-contention or acquiescence, either in form or in reality.

Bayer v Commission is also distinguishable from Case C–279/87 *Tipp-Ex v Commission*, [1990] ECR I–261, which concerned an exclusive distribution agreement between Tipp-Ex and its French distributor, DMI. The latter had complied with the manufacturer's demand that the prices charged to a customer should be raised so far as was necessary to eliminate any economic interest on its part in parallel export. In *Tipp-Ex*, unlike the situation in the Bayer case, there was no doubt as to the fact that the policy of preventing parallel exports was established by the manufacturer with the cooperation of the distributors. That intention was manifested in the oral and written contracts between the two parties.

Volkswagen AG v Commission	**Article 81 EC**
Cases T–208/01	Agreement
CFI, [2003] ECR II–5141, [2004] 4 CMLR 14	Selective Distribution System

Facts

Volkswagen AG (VW) produces motor vehicles and sells them throughout the Community via a system of selective and exclusive distribution agreements signed with authorised dealers. The dealership agreements stipulate, among other things, that that the dealers will comply with all instructions issued by VW for the purposes of the agreement regarding the distribution of new cars and that VW will issue non-binding price recommendations concerning retail prices and discounts.

Between 1996 and 1998 VW issued several calls to its distributors in Germany requiring them to comply with a strict price discipline for the sale of its Passat model. The Commission found this to infringe Article 81 EC and imposed a fine on VW. VW appealed to the CFI, arguing its conduct was unilateral.

Held (on the existence of agreement within the meaning of Article 81 EC)

'… the concept of "agreement" within the meaning of Article 81(1) EC, as interpreted by the case-law, centres around the existence of a concurrence of wills between at least two parties, the form in which it is manifested being unimportant so long as it constitutes the faithful expression of the parties' intention (the *Bayer* judgment, paragraph 69).' (para 32)

A distinction should be drawn between cases in which an undertaking has adopted a genuinely unilateral measure, and those in which the unilateral character of the measure is merely apparent. (para 35)

The Commission's argument, according to which a dealer who has signed a dealership agreement which complies with competition law is deemed to have accepted in advance a later unlawful variation of that contract, even though, by virtue of its compliance with competition law, that contract could not enable the dealer to foresee such a variation, cannot succeed. (paras 43, 44)

'… a contractual variation could be regarded as having been accepted in advance, upon and by the signature of a lawful dealership agreement, where it is a lawful contractual variation which is foreseen by the contract, or is a variation which, having regard to commercial usage or legislation, the dealer could not refuse. By contrast, it cannot be accepted that an unlawful contractual variation could be regarded as having been accepted in advance, upon and by the signature of a lawful distribution agreement. In that case, acquiescence in the unlawful contractual variation can occur only after the dealer has become aware of the variation desired by the manufacturer.' (para 45)

Comment

The Commission did not establish in its decision that the dealers followed and implemented VW's pricing policy. The facts in this case are distinguishable from Case C–338/00 P *Volkswagen v Commission* [2003] ECR I–9189, [2004] 4 CMLR 7, where VW's anti-competitive initiatives were accepted by its dealers and put into effect. It was this implementation of initiatives in that case which led the CFI (Case T–62/98) and ECJ (Case C–338/00 P) to reject the plea for annulment of the Commission's decision based on Volkswagen's allegedly unilateral initiatives.

In its judgment, the CFI distinguished between the facts in this case and the *AEG* judgment (page 40 above). In *AEG* in order to establish agreement the ECJ relied on tacit or express acceptance by the distributors of the policy pursued by AEG. The ECJ did not suggest that the distributors' consent to AEG's anticompetitive policy was given in advance, upon signature of the contract, to an as of yet unknown policy of the manufacturer. (paras 47–50)

Imperial Chemical Industries (ICI) v Commission (Dyestuffs)   **Article 81 EC**
Case 48/69   Concerted Practice
ECJ, [1972] ECR 619, [1972] CMLR 557   Price Announcements

Facts

Following uniform increases in the prices of dyestuffs in the Community, the Commission found several producers of dyestuffs had infringed Article 81 EC by taking part in a concerted practice which led to the price increase. On appeal to the ECJ, Imperial Chemical Industries (ICI) challenged the Commission's finding of concerted practice.

Held

'By its very nature … a concerted practice does not have all the elements of a contract but may inter alia arise out of coordination which becomes apparent from the behaviour of the participants.' (para 65)

'Although parallel behaviour may not by itself be identified with a concerted practice, it may however amount to strong evidence of such a practice if it leads to conditions of competition which do not correspond to the normal conditions of the market, having regard to the nature of the products, the size and number of the undertakings, and the volume of the said market.' (para 66)

'This is especially the case if the parallel conduct is such as to enable those concerned to attempt to stabilize prices at a level different from that to which competition would have led, and to consolidate established positions to the detriment of effective freedom of movement of the products in the common market and of the freedom of consumers to choose their suppliers.' (para 67)

The finding of concerted practice can only be correctly determined when considering the evidence of price increase while taking account of the specific market features in this case, including the market concentration, the production patterns and cost structures of the manufacturers, the demand for dyestuffs and the geographical markets for dyestuffs. In this context the simultaneous increases in price and price announcements reveal progressive cooperation between the undertakings concerned with the common intention to adjust the level of prices and avoid the risks of competition. (paras 68–119)

Advance price announcements by some of the undertakings concerned allowed the undertakings to observe each other's reactions on the different markets, and to adapt accordingly. '

By means of these advance announcements the various undertakings eliminated all uncertainty between them as to their future conduct and, in doing so, also eliminated a large part of the risk usually inherent in any independent change of conduct on one or several markets.' They therefore temporarily eliminated with respect to prices some of the preconditions for competition on the market. (paras 101, 100–03)

'The function of price competition is to keep prices down to the lowest possible level and to encourage the movement of goods between the Member States, thereby permitting the most efficient possible distribution of activities in the matter of productivity and the capacity of undertakings to adapt themselves to change.' (para 115)

Comment

Note the weight attributed to price announcements in this case (paras 100–03). Contrast this approach with the ECJ judgment in *Ahlström Osakeyhtiö and others v Commission* (Wood Pulp Cartel). There, while considering the pulp market conditions, the ECJ held that a system of quarterly price announcements did not eliminate uncertainty as to the future conduct of the others and therefore was not to be regarded as constituting in itself an infringement of Article 81 EC. (See page 48 below.)

Suiker Unie and others v Commission	**Article 81 EC**
Joined Cases 40, 48, 50, 54–56, 111, 113,114/73	Concerted Practice
ECJ, [1975] ECR 1663, [1976] 1 CMLR 295	

Facts

A Commission investigation into the sugar market led to a decision (IV/26.918 – European sugar industry) finding a number of undertakings to have infringed Article 81 EC. A central part of the decision referred to the existence of concerted practices in the market for sugar which led to price alignment, control of deliveries of sugar and other limitations on sales. On appeal, nine undertakings argued, among other things, that the common organisation of the sugar market, the involvement of Member States in setting the prices for sugar, and fixing basic and maximum quotas for sugar eliminated any effective competition.

On appeal, the court considered separately each of the nine applications for the annulment. The following analysis focuses on the Italian and Netherlands markets as the court's analysis of these two is most illustrative.

Held

'The concept of a "concerted practice" refers to a form of coordination between undertakings, which, without having been taken to the stage where an agreement properly so-called has been concluded, knowingly substitutes for the risks of competition, practical cooperation between them which leads to conditions of competition which do not correspond to the normal conditions of the market, having regard to the nature of the products, the importance and number of the undertakings as well as the size and nature of the said market.' (para 26)

'Such practical cooperation amounts to a concerted practice, particularly if it enables the persons concerned to consolidate established positions to the detriment of effective freedom of movement of the products in the common market and of the freedom of consumers to choose their suppliers.' (para 27)

'In a case of this kind the question whether there has been a concerted practice can only be properly evaluated if the facts relied on by the Commission are considered not separately but as a whole, after taking into account the characteristics of the market in question.' (para 28)

The Italian market

With respect to the Commission's finding of a concerted practice having as its object and effect the control of deliveries of sugar on the Italian market, it is necessary to consider whether Community rules together with the measures taken by national authorities left opportunity for competition on the market. From examination of the market it emerges that Italian regulations and the way in which they have been implemented had a determinative effect on some of the most important aspects of the course of conduct of the undertakings concerned, so that it appears that, had it not been for these Regulations and their implementation, the cooperation, which is the subject-matter of these proceedings, either would not have taken place or would have assumed a form different from that found to have existed by the Commission. The Commission has not made sufficient allowance for the effect of those regulations and has consequently overlooked a crucial factor in the evaluation of the infringements which it alleges. (paras 29–73)

The Netherlands market

'The criteria of coordination and cooperation laid down by the case-law of the court, which in no way requires the working out of an actual plan, must be understood in the light of the concept inherent in the provisions of the Treaty relating to competition that each economic operator must determine independently the policy which he intends to adopt on the common market including the choice of the persons and undertakings to which he makes offers or sells.' (para 173)

'Although it is correct to say that this requirement of independence does not deprive economic operators of the right to adapt themselves intelligently to the existing and anticipated conduct of their competitors, it does however strictly preclude any direct or indirect contact between such operators, the object or effect whereof is either to influence the conduct on the market of an actual or potential competitor or to disclose to such a competitor the course of conduct which they themselves have decided to adopt or contemplate adopting on the market.' (para 174)

'The documents quoted show that the applicants contacted each other and that they in fact pursued the aim of removing in advance any uncertainty as to the future conduct of their competitors.' (para 175)

The evidence in this case supports the Commission finding of coordination and cooperation in the Netherlands to the detriment of the effective freedom of movement of the products in the Common Market and of the freedom enjoyed by consumers to choose their suppliers. The practices to which the Commission refers to in its decision were not the natural consequence of market conditions. These practices intended to ward off the risk of competition to which the undertakings could by no means be certain that they would not be exposed, if there was no concerted action. The concerted action in question and the practices whereby it was implemented were likely to remove any doubts the Netherlands producers had as to their chances of maintaining the position which they had established. (paras 74–180)

Comment

The concept of 'concerted practice' subjects to the competition rules forms of communication between undertakings which do not amount to an agreement. The Commission is not required to distinguish between concerted practice and agreement and may rely on 'joint classification' to catch any form of communication between undertakings, the result of which is the restriction of competition. On joint classification see page 52 below.

The concept of a concerted practice, 'as it results from the actual terms of Article 81(1) EC, implies, besides undertakings' concerting with each other, subsequent conduct on the market, and a relationship of cause and effect between the two.' Case C–199/92 P *Hüls AG v Commission* (para 161), page 50 below.

Parallel conduct cannot be regarded as furnishing proof of concerted practice unless it constitutes the only plausible explanation for such conduct. The undertakings may therefore be able to disprove the existence of concerted practice if they can provide an alternative explanation for their parallel behaviour in the market. Such an explanation might, for example, include evidence on changes in the market which affected all undertakings and led to alignment of price, or evidence concerning the market structure and the undertakings' rational and independent operation in the market. See decisions on page 45 above and pages 48–51 below.

Some oligopolistic markets may, under certain conditions, enable undertakings to sustain joint policies without entering into agreement or concerted practice. In such markets the rational and independent behaviour of the undertakings may lead to parallel behaviour without entering into cooperation. This phenomena is often referred to by economists as 'tacit collusion' and is discussed in Chapter 6 below. Note that tacit collusion falls outside the realm of Article 81 EC which is only applicable to agreements, concerted practices or decisions of associations of undertakings.

A Ahlström Osakeyhtiö and others v Commission (Wood Pulp Cartel)	**Article 81 EC**
Joined Cases 89, 104, 114, 116, 117, 125, 129/85	Concerted Practice
ECJ, [1993] ECR I–1307, [1993] 4 CMLR 407	Price Announcements

Facts

The Commission found forty wood pulp producers and three of their trade associations to have infringed Article 81 EC by forming a price-fixing cartel. The market for pulp was characterised by long-term supply contracts and by 'quarterly price announcements' by which producers communicated to their customers the prices of pulp. The Commission found the practice of price announcement to facilitate concentration between the undertakings on the transaction prices for pulp (IV/29.725 – Woodpulp). On appeal to the ECJ, the undertakings contested, among other things, the Commission's finding of concerted practice.

Held

A concerted practice refers to a form of coordination between undertakings which, without having been taken to the stage where an agreement properly so-called has been concluded, knowingly substitutes for the risks of competition. In this case, the communications arising from the price announcements did not lessen each undertaking's uncertainty as to the future attitude of its competitors. The system of quarterly price announcements did not eliminate uncertainty as to the future conduct of the others and therefore is not to be regarded as constituting in itself an infringement of Article 81 EC. (paras 59–65)

The system of price announcements could, however, constitute evidence of concentration at an earlier stage. In its decision, the Commission stated that, as proof of such concentration, it relied on the parallel conduct of the pulp producers, the simultaneous price announcements and similarity in price and on different kinds of direct or indirect exchange of information. (paras 66–9)

'Since the Commission has no documents which directly establish the existence of concentration between the producers concerned, it is necessary to ascertain whether the system of quarterly price announcements, the simultaneity or near-simultaneity of the price announcements and the parallelism of price announcements … constitute a firm, precise and consistent body of evidence of prior concentration.' (para 70)

'In determining the probative value of those different factors, it must be noted that parallel conduct cannot be regarded as furnishing proof of concentration unless concentration constitutes the only plausible explanation for such conduct … [Article 81 EC] does not deprive economic operators of the right to adapt themselves intelligently to the existing and anticipated conduct of their competitors'. (para 71)

'In this case, concentration is not the only plausible explanation for the parallel conduct. To begin with, the system of price announcements may be regarded as constituting a rational response to the fact that the pulp market constituted a long-term market and to the need felt by both buyers and sellers to limit commercial risks. Further, the similarity in the dates of price announcements may be regarded as a direct result of the high degree of market transparency, which does not have to be described as artificial. Finally, the parallelism of prices and the price trends may be satisfactorily explained by the oligopolistic tendencies of the market and by the specific circumstances prevailing in certain periods. Accordingly, the parallel conduct established by the Commission does not constitute evidence of concentration.' (paras 126, 72–126)

Comment

Contrast the treatment of price announcements in this case with the court's approach in Case 48/69 *Imperial Chemical Industries (ICI) v Commission* (Dyestuffs), page 45 above.

Hüls AG v Commission	**Article 81 EC**
Case C–199/92 P	Concerted Practice
ECJ, [1999] ECR I–4287, [1999] 5 CMLR 1016	Burden of Proof/Cartel Meetings

Facts

This case arose out of the Commission's Polypropylene decision (IV/31.149 – Polypropylene) in which it found Hüls AG (Hüls) to infringed Article 81(1) EC by participating with other undertakings in an agreement and concerted practice aimed at coordinating their commercial practices and fixing the prices of polypropylene. Hüls appealed unsuccessfully to the CFI (Case T–9/89 *Hüls v Commission*). On appeal to the ECJ, it argued, among other things, that the Commission and CFI decisions were based on insufficient evidence as to its regular participation in the producers' meetings and did not establish the evidential requirements in respect of concerted practices within the meaning of Article 81(1) EC.

Held

On the burden of proof and the presumption of innocence

The presumption of innocence resulting in particular from Article 6(2) of the ECHR is one of the fundamental rights which are protected in the Community legal order. In this case the Commission successfully established that Hüls had participated in meetings between undertakings of a manifestly anticompetitive nature. Subsequently the burden of proof reversed and it was for Hüls to put forward evidence to establish that its participation was without any anticompetitive intention by demonstrating that it had indicated to its competitors that it was participating in those meetings in a spirit that was different from theirs. (paras 141–55)

On concerted practice

'The Court of Justice has consistently held that a concerted practice refers to a form of coordination between undertakings which, without having been taken to a stage where an agreement properly so-called has been concluded, knowingly substitutes for the risks of competition practical cooperation between them (see Joined Cases 40/73 [...] *Suiker Unie and others v Commission* [1975] ECR 1663, paragraph 26, and Joined Cases C–89/85 [...] *Ahlstrom Osakeyhtio and others v Commission* [1993] ECR I–1307, paragraph 63).' (para 158)

Each economic operator must determine independently the policy it adopts on the market. 'Although that requirement of independence does not deprive economic operators of the right to adapt themselves intelligently to the existing and anticipated conduct of their competitors, it does however strictly preclude any direct or indirect contact between such operators, the object or effect whereof is either to influence the conduct on the market of an actual or potential competitor or to disclose to such a competitor the course of conduct which they themselves have decided to adopt or contemplate adopting on the market, where the object or effect of such contact is to create conditions of competition which do not correspond to the normal conditions of the market in question, regard being had to the nature of the products or services offered, the size and number of the undertakings and the volume of the said market. (See, to that effect, *Suiker Unie and others v Commission*, paragraph 174.)' (paras 159, 160)

'It follows, first, that the concept of a concerted practice, as it results from the actual terms of Article 81(1) EC, implies, besides undertakings' concerting with each other, subsequent conduct on the market, and a relationship of cause and effect between the two.' (para 161)

'However, subject to proof to the contrary, which the economic operators concerned must adduce, the presumption must be that the undertakings taking part in the concerted action and remaining active on the market take account of the information exchanged with their competitors for the purposes of determining their conduct on that market. That is all the more true where the undertakings concert together on a regular basis over a long period, as was the case here, according to the findings of the Court of First Instance.' (para 162)

Although the concept of a concerted practice presupposes conduct by the participating undertakings on the market, it does not necessarily mean that such conduct should produce the specific effect of restricting, preventing or distorting competition. A concerted practice is therefore caught by Article 81(1) EC, even in the absence of anticompetitive effects on the market and is prohibited, regardless of its effect, when it has an anticompetitive object. (paras 163–6)

'Consequently, contrary to Hüls's argument, the Court of First Instance was not in breach of the rules applying to the burden of proof when it considered that, since the Commission had established to the requisite legal standard that Hüls had taken part in polypropylene producers' concerting together for the purpose of restricting competition, it did not have to adduce evidence that their concerting together had manifested itself in conduct on the market or that it had had effects restrictive of competition; on the contrary, it was for Hüls to prove that that did not have any influence whatsoever on its own conduct on the market.' (para 167)

Since none of the pleas in law put forward by Hüls have been upheld, the appeal must be dismissed in its entirety.

Comment

The courts laid down the elements constituting concerted practice. These include (1) undertakings concerting with each other, (2) subsequent conduct on the market, and (3) a relationship of cause and effect between the two. (para 161)

Note that the above elements do not include a requirement for effect on the market. The court held in paragraph 163 of its decision that 'a concerted practice as defined above is caught by Article 81(1) EC, even in the absence of anti-competitive effects on the market.' Accordingly, 'as in the case of agreements between undertakings and decisions by associations of undertakings, concerted practices are prohibited, regardless of their effect, when they have an anti-competitive object. … Although the very concept of a concerted practice presupposes conduct by the participating undertakings on the market, it does not necessarily mean that that conduct should produce the specific effect of restricting, preventing or distorting competition.' (paras 164, 165)

See Commission decision in Case IV/37.614/F3 *PO/Interbrew and Alken-Maes*, [2003] OJ L200/1, where the Commission noted that 'behaviour can be regarded as a "concerted practice" where the parties have not reached agreement in advance on a common plan defining their action on the market but have adopted or adhered to collusive devices which facilitate the coordination of their commercial behaviour'. (para 221) 'Although it is clear from the actual terms of Article 81(1) of the EC Treaty that the concept of a concerted practice implies, besides undertakings consulting with each other, subsequent conduct on the market, and a relationship of cause and effect between the two, the presumption must be, subject to proof to the contrary which the economic operators concerned must adduce, that the undertakings taking part in the consultation and remaining active on the market take account of the information exchanged with their competitors for the purposes of determining their conduct on that market. That is all the more true where the undertakings consult together on a regular basis over a long period. A concerted practice is caught by Article 81(1) even in the absence of anti-competitive effects on the market'. (para 222)

With regard to the participation in meetings (paras 141–55), note Joined Cases T–25/95 etc *Cimenteries CBR SA v Commission*, where the CFI held that in the absence of positive evidence disassociating the undertakings from the anticompetitive objectives of the meetings, producers in attendance at the meetings were participants in concerted practice. Those who did not attend the meetings, but aligned their behaviour at a later stage to give effect to the objective of the meetings, were also liable. However, their liability ran only from the dates of the action of alignment and not from the date of the meeting. Also note Joined Cases C–204/00 *Aalborg Portland A/S and others v Commission*, page 51 below.

Aalborg Portland A/S and others v Commission		**Article 81 EC**
Joined Cases C–204, 205, 211, 213, 217, 219/00 P		Concerted Practice
ECJ, [2004] ECR I–123, [2005] 4 CMLR 4		Cartel Meetings – Single Agreement

Facts

Following an investigation into the European cement market, the Commission uncovered a series of anticompetitive agreements and concerted practices which facilitated, among other things, exchange of information on prices, supply and demand, and the regulation of cement transfers. The Commission adopted a decision that found producers and trade associations in this sector to have participated in a cartel contrary to Article 81 EC (Cases IV/33.126 and 33.322 Cement). On appeal to the CFI, the court confirmed most of the infringements found in the Commission Decision. On appeal to the ECJ, the undertakings disputed, among other things, the CFI's findings concerning their participation in the cartel.

Held

'According to settled case-law, it is sufficient for the Commission to show that the undertaking concerned participated in meetings at which anti-competitive agreements were concluded, without manifestly opposing them, to prove to the requisite standard that the undertaking participated in the cartel. Where participation in such meetings has been established, it is for that undertaking to put forward evidence to establish that its participation in those meetings was without any anti-competitive intention by demonstrating that it had indicated to its competitors that it was participating in those meetings in a spirit that was different from theirs (see Case C–199/92 P *Huls v Commission* [1999] ECR I–4287, paragraph 155, and Case C–49/92 P *Commission v Anic* [1999] ECR I–4125, paragraph 96).' (para 81)

'The reason underlying that principle of law is that, having participated in the meeting without publicly distancing itself from what was discussed, the undertaking has given the other participants to believe that it subscribed to what was decided there and would comply with it.' (para 82)

That principle of law also applies to participation in the implementation of a single agreement. 'In order to establish that an undertaking has participated in such an agreement, the Commission must show that the undertaking intended to contribute by its own conduct to the common objectives pursued by all the participants and that it was aware of the actual conduct planned or put into effect by other undertakings in pursuit of the same objectives or that it could reasonably have foreseen it and that it was prepared to take the risk' (*Commission v Anic*, paragraph 87). (para 83)

'In that regard, a party which tacitly approves of an unlawful initiative, without publicly distancing itself from its content or reporting it to the administrative authorities, effectively encourages the continuation of the infringement and compromises its discovery. That complicity constitutes a passive mode of participation in the infringement which is therefore capable of rendering the undertaking liable in the context of a single agreement.' (para 84)

The fact that an undertaking does not act on the outcome of a meeting with an anticompetitive purpose does not relieve it of responsibility for participation in a cartel, unless it has publicly distanced itself from what was agreed in the meeting. Similarly, it is immaterial for the establishment of infringement that an undertaking has not taken part in all aspects of an anticompetitive scheme or that it played only a minor role in it. Those factors are taken into consideration only when the gravity of the infringement is assessed and if and when it comes to determining the fine. (paras 85, 86)

Comment

On participation in cartel meetings see also Case C–199/92 P page 49 above, Cases T–25/95 page 50 above, and Joined Cases T–305/94, page 52 below.

Limburgse Vinyl Maatschappij NV and others v Commission	**Article 81 EC**
Joined Cases T–305–7, 313–318, 325, 328–9, 335/94	Joint Classification
CFI, [1999] ECR II–931, [1999] 5 CMLR 303	

Facts

A Commission investigation into the polypropylene sector led to a decision finding several polyvinyl chloride (PVC) producers to have infringed Article 81 EC by taking part in cartel activities (IV/31.865 PVC). The Commission decision stated that the undertakings infringed the Treaty provision by participating in an agreement and/or concerted practice by which the producers supplying PVC in the Community took part in regular meetings in order to fix target prices and quotas and plan concerted initiatives to raise price levels. On appeal to the CFI, some of the appellants argued, among other things, that the Commission was wrong to allege an alternative in relation to Article 81EC in the relevant part of the Decision in that the undertakings had participated in an agreement 'and/or' a concerted practice.

Held

'In the context of a complex infringement which involves many producers seeking over a number of years to regulate the market between them the Commission cannot be expected to classify the infringement precisely, for each undertaking and for any given moment, as in any event both those forms of infringement are covered by [Article 81 EC].' (para 696)

'The Commission is therefore entitled to classify that type of complex infringement as an agreement "and/or" concerted practice, inasmuch as the infringement includes elements which are to be classified as an "agreement" and elements which are to be classified as a "concerted practice".' (para 697)

'In such a situation, the dual classification must be understood not as requiring simultaneous and cumulative proof that every one of those factual elements reveals the factors constituting an agreement and a concerted practice, but rather as designating a complex whole that includes factual elements of which some have been classified as an agreement and others as a concerted practice within the meaning on [Article 81 EC], which does not provide for any specific classification in respect of that type of complex infringement.' (para 698)

Comment

In Case C–49/92 P, *Commission v Anic Partecipazioni SpA*, the ECJ held that 'whilst the concepts of an agreement and of a concerted practice have particularly different elements, they are not mutually incompatible … the Court of First Instance did not therefore have to require the Commission to categorise either as an agreement or as a concerted practice each form of conduct found but was right to hold that the Commission had been entitled to characterise some of those forms of conduct as principally "agreements" and others as "concerted practices" … it must be pointed out that this interpretation is not incompatible with the restrictive nature of the prohibition laid down in [Article 81 EC]. … Far from creating a new form of infringement, the arrival at that interpretation merely entails acceptance of the fact that, in the case of an infringement involving different forms of conduct, these may meet different definitions whilst being caught by the same provision and being all equally prohibited.' (paras 132, 133)

In Case IV/37.614/F3 *PO/Interbrew and Alken-Maes*, [2003] OJ L200/1, the Commission noted that 'The concepts of "agreement" and "concerted practice" are variable and may overlap. Realistically, it may even be impossible to make such a distinction, since an infringement may simultaneously have the characteristics of both forms of prohibited behaviour, whereas, taken separately, some of its elements may correctly be regarded as one rather than the other form. It would also be artificial from an analytical point of view to split what is clearly a continuous, collective enterprise with a single objective into several forms of infringement. A cartel may for instance constitute an agreement and a concerted practice at the same time …' (para 223)

Limburgse Vinyl Maatschappij NV and others v Commission   **Article 81 EC**
Joined Cases T–305–7, 313–318, 325, 328–9, 335/94   Single Overall Agreement
CFI, [1999] ECR II–931, [1999] 5 CMLR 303

Facts

A Commission investigation into the polypropylene sector led to a decision finding several polyvinyl chloride (PVC) producers to have infringed Article 81 EC by taking part in cartel activities (IV/31.865 – PVC). The Commission in its decision stated that it was not necessary for it to prove that each participant had taken part in every manifestation of the infringement, but only that it had participated in the cartel as a whole: 'In the present case it has not been possible, given the absence of pricing documentation, to prove the actual participation of every producer in concerted price initiatives. The Commission has therefore considered in relation to each suspected participant whether there is sufficient reliable evidence to prove its adherence to the cartel as a whole rather than proof of its participation in every manifestation thereof' (point 25 of the Decision). 'The essence of the present case is the combination of the producers over a long period toward a common unlawful end, and each participant must not only take responsibility for its own direct role as an individual, but also share responsibility for the operation of the cartel as a whole' (point 31 of the Decision). The appellants challenged the Commission approach and its alleged reliance on collective responsibility.

Held

In its decision the Commission was aware of the need to prove the participation of each undertaking in the cartel. 'For that purpose, it referred to the concept of the cartel considered "as a whole". That does not justify the conclusion, however, that the Commission applied the principle of collective responsibility, in the sense that it deemed certain undertakings to have participated in actions with which they were not concerned simply because the participation of other undertakings in those actions was established.' (paras 769–71)

'The concept of the cartel considered "as a whole" is indissociable from the nature of the infringement in question. That consisted, as the examination of the facts shows, in the regular organisation over the years of meetings of rival producers, the aim of which was to establish illicit practices intended to organise artificially the functioning of the PVC market.' (para 772)

'An undertaking may be held responsible for an overall cartel even though it is shown to have participated directly only in one or some of its constituent elements if it is shown that it knew, or must have known, that the collusion in which it participated, especially by means of regular meetings organised over several years, was part of an overall plan intended to distort competition and that the overall plan included all the constituent elements of the cartel.' (para 773)

'In this case, even if in the absence of documentation the Commission was not able to prove the participation of every undertaking in the implementation of the price initiatives, such implementation being one of the manifestations of the cartel, it nevertheless considered itself able to demonstrate that each undertaking had in any event participated in the producer meetings, the purpose of which was, *inter alia*, to fix prices in common.' (para 774)

'The Commission did not impute collective responsibility to each undertaking, or responsibility in respect of a manifestation of the cartel in which that undertaking did not become involved, but responsibility for the actions in which each had participated.' (para 778)

Comment

The CFI annulled part of the Commission's decision for failure to establish infringement of Article 81 EC with respect to one of the undertakings involved. The fines imposed on three of the appellants were reduced. The reminder of the action was dismissed.

Daimler Chrysler AG v Commission	**Article 81 EC**
Case T–325/01	Association of Undertakings
CFI, [2005] ECR II–3319, [2007] 4 CMLR 15	Cartel Meetings

Facts

An action for the annulment of a Commission Decision (Case COMP/36.264 – *Mercedes-Benz*) in which the Commission found Mercedes-Benz and two of its subsidiaries to have infringed Article 81(1) EC by engaging in various anticompetitive agreements in connection with the retailing of its passenger cars. Part of the Commission's decision referred to an agreement between Mercedes-Benz Belgium SA (MBBel) and the Belgian Mercedes-Benz dealers' association, which limited discounts on vehicles and had as its object the restriction of price competition in Belgium. The appellants challenged the Commission's finding and argued that the Belgian dealers' association had no power to take a decision which would bind its members and enter them into an anticompetitive agreement.

Held

'… where it has been established that an undertaking has participated in meetings between undertakings of a manifestly anticompetitive nature, it is for that undertaking to put forward evidence to establish that its participation in those meetings was without any anti-competitive intention, by demonstrating that it had indicated to its competitors that it was participating in those meetings in a spirit that was different from theirs. … In the absence of evidence of that distancing, the fact that an undertaking does not abide by the outcome of those meetings is not such as to relieve it of full responsibility for the fact that it participated in the concerted practice (Case T–347/94 *MayrMelnhof v Commission* [1998] ECR II–1751, paragraph 135, and Joined Cases T–25/95, [...] *Cimenteries CBR and others v Commission* [2000] ECR II–491, paragraph 1389).' (para 202)

It is not disputed that MBBel was present at the meeting of the dealers' association in which price slashing and the intention to take steps to detect and prevent various discounts were referred to. MBBel did not publicly distance itself from the discussions and led the other participants to believe that it accepted the decisions taken at the meeting and that it intended to contribute by its own conduct to the common objectives of the meeting. (paras 203–07)

'As regards the applicant's argument that the dealers' association did not have the authority to take decisions binding its members, but only to formulate recommendations, it is settled case-law that a measure may be categorised as a decision of an association of undertakings for the purposes of Article 81(1) EC even if it is not binding on the members concerned, at least to the extent that the members to whom the decision applies comply with its terms (see, by way of analogy, Joined Cases 96/82 [...] *IAZ and others v Commission* [1983] ECR 3369, paragraph 20; [Joined Cases 209/78 [...] *Van Landewyck and others v Commission* [1980] ECR 3125, at paragraphs 88 and 89]; and Case T–136/94 *Eurofer v Commission* [1999] ECR II–263, paragraph 15). That requirement is sufficiently established in this case by the fact that the members of the dealers' association in Belgium and MBBel decided at the meeting of 20 April 2005 to monitor, using ghost purchasing by members of an outside agency, the level of discounts given for the W 210 vehicle model and that ghost shoppers did indeed make visits to dealers. That information shows that the course of action decided upon at the meeting of 20 April 1995 was implemented.' (para 210)

Comment

In Joined Cases 209/78 etc *Van Landewyck and others v Commission* the ECJ held that Article 81(1) EC also applies to non-profit-making associations 'in so far as their own activities or those of the undertakings belonging to them are calculated to produce the results which it aims to suppress' (para 88). The court rejected an argument that the decisions of the association in question were not binding and pointed to the compliance with the recommendation by several of the undertakings involved. (para 89)

Also note Case C–309/99 *Wouters* (page 11 above, 74 below) and Case T–35/92 *John Deer* (page 103 below).

Société Technique Minière v Maschinenbau Ulm GmbH	**Article 81 EC**
Case 56/65	Object or Effect
ECJ, [1966] ECR 235, [1966] CMLR 357	Distribution Agreement

Facts

The French Cour d'appel de Paris made an application for a preliminary ruling concerning the interpretation of Article 81 EC and its application to exclusive distribution agreements. According to the agreement in question, a German manufacturer granted exclusive right of sale to a French distributor, yet did not prohibit it from selling to other territories, nor did it prohibit dealers in other territories from selling the products in the territory which was the primary responsibility of the distributor with whom the agreement was made. A dispute between the parties led to legal proceedings in which the French distributor argued that the agreement infringed Article 81(1) EC and was void under Article 81(2) EC.

Held

'For the agreement at issue to be caught by the prohibition contained in [Article 81(1)] it must have as its object or effect the prevention, restriction or distortion of competition within the common market.' (p. 249)

'The fact that these are not cumulative but alternative requirements, indicated by the conjunction "or", leads first to the need to consider the precise purpose of the agreement, in the economic context in which it is to be applied. This interference with competition referred to in [Article 81(1) EC] must result from all or some of the clauses of the agreement itself. Where, however, an analysis of the said clauses does not reveal the effect on competition to be sufficiently deleterious, the consequences of the agreement should then be considered and for it to be caught by the prohibition it is then necessary to find that those factors are present which show that competition has in fact been prevented or restricted or distorted to an appreciable extent.' (p. 249)

'The competition in question must be understood within the actual context in which it would occur in the absence of the agreement in dispute. In particular it may be doubted whether there is an interference with competition if the said agreement seems really necessary for the penetration of a new area by an undertaking. Therefore, in order to decide whether an agreement containing a clause "granting an exclusive right of sale" is to be considered as prohibited by reason of its object or of its effect, it is appropriate to take into account in particular the nature and quantity, limited or otherwise, of the products covered by the agreement, the position and importance of the grantor and the concessionaire on the market for the products concerned, the isolated nature of the disputed agreement or, alternatively, its position in a series of agreements, the severity of the clauses intended to protect the exclusive dealership or, alternatively, the opportunities allowed for other commercial competitors in the same products by way of parallel re-exportation and importation.' (p. 250)

Comment

The agreement was found not to infringe Article 81 EC. Contrast the nature of the agreement in this case with the distribution agreement in *Consten and Grundig* (page 56 below). There, the distribution agreement was found to infringe Article 81 EC as it resulted in absolute territorial protection.

Note the Commission Guidelines on Vertical Restraints, [2000] OJ C291/1, which outline the principles for the assessment of vertical agreements under Article 81 EC. Paragraphs 161–77 lay down the analytical framework for the analysis of exclusive distribution agreements. Also note the Vertical Block Exemption Regulation under which an exclusive distribution agreement is exempted when the supplier's market share does not exceed 30 per cent and the agreement does not contain hard-core vertical restraints (Regulation (EC) No 2790/1999 on the Application of Article 81(3) of the Treaty to Categories of Vertical Agreements and Concerted Practices, [1999] OJ L336/21).

Consten SaRL and Grundig-Verkaufs-GmbH v Commission	**Article 81 EC**
Joined Cases 56 and 58/64	Object or Effect
ECJ, [1966] ECR 299, [1966] CMLR 418	Distribution Agreement

Facts

The case concerned an exclusive distribution agreement between Consten and Grundig under which the former received exclusive rights to sell Grundig products in France in return for its promise not to handle competing brands. Under the agreement Grundig agreed to impose restrictions on its distributors in other Member States to prevent parallel import into Consten's exclusive territory. In addition, the Grundig trademark 'Gint' was registered in France under Consten's name, thus providing it with absolute territorial protection. The Commission found the agreement to infringe Article 81 EC. The companies appealed to the ECJ.

Held

Article 81 EC does not lay down any distinction between horizontal and vertical agreements and applies to all agreements which distort competition within the common market. (p. 339)

'... an agreement between producer and distributor which might tend to restore the national divisions in trade between Member States might be such as to frustrate the most fundamental objections of the Community. The Treaty, whose preamble and content aim at abolishing the barriers between states, and which in several provisions gives evidence of a stern attitude with regard to their reappearance, could not allow undertakings to reconstruct such barriers. [Article 81(1) EC] is designed to pursue this aim, even in the case of agreements between undertakings placed at different levels in the economic process.' (p. 340)

'... For the purpose of applying [Article 81(1)EC], there is no need to take account of the concrete effects of an agreement once it appears that it has as its object the prevention, restriction or distortion of competition.' (p. 342)

The court needs to consider whether in this case the agreement in question had the object of restricting competition. 'The infringement which was found to exist by the contested Decision results from the absolute territorial protection created the said contract in favour of Consten on the basis of French law. The applicants thus wished to eliminate any possibility of competition at the wholesale level in Grundig products in the territory specified in the contract essentially by two methods.' (p. 342)

'First, Grundig undertook not to deliver even indirectly to third parties products intended for the area covered by the contract. The restrictive nature of that undertaking is obvious if it is considered in the light of the prohibition on exporting which was imposed not only on Consten but also on all the other sole concessionaires of Grundig, as well as the German wholesalers. Secondly, the registration in France by Consten of the Gint trade mark, which Grundig affixes to all its products, is intended to increase the protection inherent in the disputed agreement, against the risk of parallel imports into France of Grundig products, by adding the protection deriving from the law on industrial property rights. Thus no third party could import Grundig products from other Member States of the Community for resale in France without running serious risks.' (p. 343)

'The defendant properly took into account the whole distribution system thus set up by Grundig. In order to arrive at a true representation of the contractual position the contract must be placed in the economic and legal context in the light of which it was concluded by the parties ...' (p. 343)

'The situation as ascertained above results in the isolation of the French market and makes it possible to charge for the products in question prices which are sheltered from all effective competition. In addition, the more producers succeed in their efforts to render their own makes of product individually distinct in the eyes of the consumer, the more the effectiveness of competition between producers tends to diminish. Because of the considerable impact of 'distribution costs on the aggregate cost price, it seems important that competition between dealers should also be stimulated. The efforts of the dealer are stimulated by competition between distributors of products of the same make. Since the agreement thus aims at isolating the French market for Grundig products and maintaining artificially, for products of a very well-known brand, separate national markets within the Community, it is therefore such as to distort competition in the common market.' (p. 343)

'It was therefore proper for the contested Decision to hold that the agreement constitutes an infringement of [Article 81(1) EC]. No further considerations, whether of economic data (price differences between France and Germany, representative character of the type of appliance considered, level of overheads borne by Consten) or of the correction of the criteria upon which the Commission relied in its comparisons between the situations of the French and German markets, and no possible favourable effects of the agreement in other respects, can in any way lead, in the face of the abovementioned restrictions, to a different solution under [Article 81(1) EC].' (p. 343)

'Consten's right under the contract to the exclusive use in France of the Gint trade mark, which may be used in a similar manner in other countries, is intended to make it possible to keep under surveillance and to place an obstacle in the way of parallel imports. Thus, the agreement by which Grundig, as the holder of the trade-mark by virtue of an inter-national registration, authorized Consten to register it in France in its own name tends to restrict competition.' (p. 345)

'That agreement therefore is one which may be caught by the prohibition in [Article 81(1) EC]. The prohibition would be ineffective if Consten could continue to use the trade-mark to achieve the same object as that pursued by the agreement which has been held to be unlawful.' (p. 345)

Comment

The Consten and Grundig distribution agreement led to absolute territorial protection by prohibiting parallel export and using trademark law to seal the market. Such an agreement is considered as having the object of restricting competition.

'The assessment of whether or not an agreement has as its object the restriction of competition is based on a number of factors. These factors include, in particular, the content of the agreement and the objective aims pursued by it. It may also be necessary to consider the context in which it is (to be) applied and the actual conduct and behaviour of the parties on the market. In other words, an examination of the facts underlying the agreement and the specific circumstances in which it operates may be required before it can be concluded whether a particular restriction constitutes a restriction of competition by object. The way in which an agreement is actually implemented may reveal a restriction by object even where the formal agreement does not contain an express provision to that effect. Evidence of subjective intent on the part of the parties to restrict competition is a relevant factor but not a necessary condition.' (para 22, Commission Guidelines on the Application of Article 81(3) of the Treaty [2004] OJ C 101/94)

Note Case T–168/01 *GlaxoSmithKline Services Unlimited v Commission*, in which the ECJ clarified that in *Consten and Grundig v Commission* the court 'did not hold that an agreement intended to limit parallel trade must be considered by its nature, that is to say, independently of any competitive analysis, to have as its object the restriction of competition. On the contrary, the Court of Justice merely held, first, that an agreement between a producer and a distributor which might tend to restore the national divisions in trade between Member States might be such as to frustrate the most fundamental objectives of the Community (p. 340). … The Court of Justice then carried out a competitive analysis, abridged but real, during the course of which it held, in particular, that the agreement in question sought to eliminate any possibility of competition at the wholesale level in order to charge prices which were sheltered from all effective competition, considerations which led it to reject a plea alleging that there was no restriction of competition (pp. 342 and 343).' '… while it is accepted that an agreement intended to limit parallel trade must in principle be considered to have as its object the restriction of competition, that applies in so far as the agreement may be presumed to deprive final consumers of those advantages.' (paras 120, 121). For detailed analysis of this case, see page 62 below.

SA Brasserie de Haecht v Consorts Wilkin-Janssen	**Article 81 EC**
Case 23/67	Object or Effect
ECJ, [1967] ECR 407, [1968] CMLR 26	Exclusive Distribution Agreement

Facts

A reference for a preliminary ruling from the Belgian Tribunal de Commerce de Liège. The Belgian court requested that the ECJ clarify whether when assessing the possible anticompetitive effects of an exclusive distribution agreement which forms part of a large number of similar agreements it should review the agreement in isolation or take account of the existence of a network of distribution agreements.

Held

'Agreements whereby an undertaking agrees to obtain its supplies from one undertaking to the exclusion of all others do not by their very nature necessarily include all the elements constituting incompatibility with the common market as referred to in [Article 81(1)EC]. Such agreements may, however, exhibit such elements where, taken either in isolation or together with others, and in the economic and legal context in which they are made on the basis of a set of objective factors of law or of fact, they may affect trade between Member States and where they have either as their object or effect the prevention, restriction or distortion of competition.' (p. 416)

Article 81(1) implies that regard must be had to the effects an agreement may have on competition in the economic and legal context in which they occur. 'In fact, it would be pointless to consider an agreement, decision or practice by reason of its effects if those effects were to be taken distinct from the market in which they are seen to operate and could only be examined apart from the body of effects, whether convergent or not, surrounding their implementation. Thus in order to examine whether it is caught by [Article 81(1) EC] an agreement cannot be examined in isolation from the above context, that is, from the factual or legal circumstances causing it to prevent, restrict or distort competition. The existence of similar contracts may be taken into consideration for this objective to the extent to which the general body of contracts of this type is capable of restricting the freedom of trade.' (p. 415)

Comment

'If an agreement is not restrictive of competition by object it must be examined whether it has restrictive effects on competition. Account must be taken of both actual and potential effects. In other words the agreement must have likely anti-competitive effects. In the case of restrictions of competition by effect there is no presumption of anti-competitive effects. For an agreement to be restrictive by effect it must affect actual or potential competition to such an extent that on the relevant market negative effects on prices, output, innovation or the variety or quality of goods and services can be expected with a reasonable degree of probability. Such negative effects must be appreciable. The prohibition rule of Article 81(1) does not apply when the identified anti-competitive effects are insignificant. This test reflects the economic approach which the Commission is applying. The prohibition of Article 81(1) only applies where on the basis of proper market analysis it can be concluded that the agreement has likely anti-competitive effects on the market. It is insufficient for such a finding that the market shares of the parties exceed the thresholds set out in the Commission's de minimis notice. Agreements falling within safe harbours of Block Exemption regulations may be caught by Article 81(1) but this is not necessarily so. Moreover, the fact that due to the market shares of the parties, an agreement falls outside the safe harbour of a Block Exemption is in itself an insufficient basis for finding that the agreement is caught by Article 81(1) or that it does not fulfil the conditions of Article 81(3). Individual assessment of the likely effects produced by the agreement is required.' (para 24, Commission Guidelines on the Application of Article 81(3) of the Treaty [2004] OJ C 101/94)

For a detailed evaluation of effect, see for example Case C–234/89 *Stergios Delimitis v Henninger Bräu AG* (page 60 below), Case T–168/01 *GlaxoSmithKline Services Unlimited v Commission* (page 62 below)

European Night Services Ltd v Commission	**Article 81 EC**
Joined Cases T–374, 375, 384 and 388/94	Object or Effect
CFI, [1998] ECR II–3141, [1998] 5 CMLR 718	

Facts

European Night Services Ltd (ENS), a cooperative joint venture, intended to operate in conjunction with several railway companies a night passenger services through the Channel Tunnel. Following notification of the agreement, the Commission concluded that the ENS agreements restricted competition among the ENS parent companies, and between the parent companies, ENS and third parties, and that it restricted competition as a result of the presence of networks of joint ventures on the market for rail transport. The Commission found, nonetheless, that the agreements qualified for an exemption under Article 81(3) EC, on condition that the railway companies who were party to the ENS agreements should supply the same necessary rail services as they have agreed to supply to ENS to third parties. (IV/34.600 – Night Services). On appeal ENS challenged, among other things, the Commission's analysis as regards restrictions of competition under Article 81(1) EC.

Held

When assessing an agreement under Article 81(1) EC, 'account should be taken of the actual conditions in which it functions, in particular the economic context in which the undertakings operate, the products or services covered by the agreement and the actual structure of the market concerned, … unless it is an agreement containing obvious restrictions of competition such as price-fixing, market-sharing or the control of outlets. … In the latter case, such restrictions may be weighed against their claimed pro-competitive effects only in the context of [Article 81(3) EC], with a view to granting an exemption from the prohibition in [Article 81(1) EC].' (para 136)

'It must also be stressed that the examination of conditions of competition is based not only on existing competition between undertakings already present on the relevant market but also on potential competition, in order to ascertain whether, in the light of the structure of the market and the economic and legal context within which it functions, there are real concrete possibilities for the undertakings concerned to compete among themselves or for a new competitor to penetrate the relevant market and compete with the undertakings already established.' (para 137)

In this case the Commission failed to make a correct and adequate assessment of the economic and legal context in which the ENS agreements were concluded. It therefore did not demonstrate that the agreements restrict competition within the meaning of Article 81(1) EC and therefore need to be exempted under Article 81(3) EC. (paras 138–60)

The Commission decision was therefore annulled.

Comment

The agreements in this case did not contain restrictions which by their nature are regarded as having the object of restricting competition; therefore the Commission was expected to conduct a more thorough evaluation and take into consideration the economic and legal context in which the ENS agreements were concluded.

In its judgment the CFI provided a few examples of agreements which by their nature can be regarded as having the object of restricting competition. These include 'price-fixing, market-sharing or the control of outlets' (para 136). Note, however, that the object 'tag' is not absolute and in some instances the courts and Commission may find a 'hard-core' restriction not to amount to 'object'. See for example Case T–168/01 *GlaxoSmithKline v Commission* (page 62 below), Case C–306/96 *Javico v Yves St Laurent* (page 106 below), and Case COMP/29.373 *Visa International – Multilateral Interchange Fee* (page 85 below).

Also note paragraphs 21–3, Commission Guidelines on the Application of Article 81(3) [2004] OJ C 101/97 which discuss restrictions of competition by object.

Stergios Delimitis v Henninger Bräu AG	**Article 81 EC**
Case C–234/89	Object or Effect
ECJ, [1991] ECR I–935, [1992] 5 CMLR 210	Beer Supply Agreements

Facts

A reference for a preliminary ruling to the ECJ by the Higher Regional Court in Frankfurt concerning the legality of a beer supply agreement. The case concerned a financial dispute between Delimitis, a former licensee of a public house, and the brewery, Henninger Bräu AG. The agreement between the parties required Delimitis to obtain a minimum quantity of beer and soft drinks from the brewery and its subsidiaries. Failure to reach the minimum quantity resulted in a penalty for non-performance. On termination of the agreement the brewery refused to return the full deposit to Delimitis and deducted sums of money it considered owed to it. Delimitis challenged the deduction made by the brewery and brought proceedings against it before the Regional Court. In support of its claim, it contended, among other things, that the contract was void by virtue of Article 81(2) EC. Following an appeal, the case reached the Higher Regional Court, which referred it to the ECJ for a preliminary ruling on the compatibility of the beer supply agreements with Community competition rules.

Held

The beer supply agreements in this case do not have as their object the restriction of competition within the meaning of Article 81(1). Subsequently it is for the Court to consider whether they have the effect of preventing, restricting or distorting competition. (paras 10–13)

The effects of the beer supply agreement have to be assessed in the context in which they occur. When the agreement is part of a larger web of similar contracts the cumulative effect on competition needs to be considered. Consequently, it is necessary to analyse the effects of the cumulative effect on the opportunities of national competitors or those from other Member States, to gain access to the market for beer consumption or to increase their market share and, accordingly, the effects on the range of products offered to consumers. (paras 14, 15)

In order to ascertain the effects of the agreement one first needs to define the relevant market on the basis of the nature of the economic activity in question, in this case the sale of beer. In this case the market is the one for the distribution of beer in premises for the sale and consumption of drinks in Germany. (paras 16–18)

Following the definition of the market, one needs to assess whether the existence of several beer supply agreements impedes access to the market. 'The effect of those networks of contracts on access to the market depends specifically on the number of outlets thus tied to national producers in relation to the number of public houses which are not so tied, the duration of the commitments entered into, the quantities of beer to which those commitments relate, and on the proportion between those quantities and the quantities sold by free distributors.' (para 19)

The existence of a web of similar contracts, even if it has a considerable effect on the access to the market, is only one of the factors that needs to be taken into account and cannot in itself support a finding that the relevant market is inaccessible. (para 20)

One factor to be taken into account is the opportunity for access. The court needs to consider whether a new competitor could enter the market by acquiring a brewery already established on the market or by opening new public houses. 'For that purpose it is necessary to have regard to the legal rules and agreements on the acquisition of companies and the establishment of outlets, and to the minimum number of outlets necessary for the economic operation of a distribution system. The presence of beer wholesalers not tied to producers who are active on the market is also a factor capable of facilitating a new producer's access to that market since he can make use of those wholesalers' sales networks to distribute his own beer.' (para 21)

Another factor to be taken into account is the conditions under which competitive forces operate on the relevant market. For this purpose it is necessary to consider the number and size of the competitors, the level of market concentration and customer fidelity to existing brands. (para 22)

'If an examination of all similar contracts entered into on the relevant market and the other factors relevant to the economic and legal context in which the contract must be examined shows that those agreements do not have the cumulative effect of denying access to that market to new national and foreign competitors, the individual agreements comprising the bundle of agreements cannot be held to restrict competition within the meaning of [Article 81 (1) EC]. They do not, therefore, fall under the prohibition laid down in that provision. (para 23)

'If, on the other hand, such examination reveals that it is difficult to gain access to the relevant market, it is necessary to assess the extent to which the agreements entered into by the brewery in question contribute to the cumulative effect produced in that respect by the totality of the similar contracts found on that market. Under the Community rules on competition, responsibility for such an effect of closing off the market must be attributed to the breweries which make an appreciable contribution thereto. Beer supply agreements entered into by breweries whose contribution to the cumulative effect is insignificant do not therefore fall under the prohibition under [Article 81(1)].' (para 24)

The contribution of the individual agreement in question to the cumulative sealing-off effect depends on several factors, including the market position of the contracting parties, the number of outlets tied to the brewery in relation to the total number of public houses in the relevant market and the duration of the agreement in relation to the average duration of other beer supply agreements. 'A brewery with a relatively small market share which ties its sales outlets for many years may make as significant a contribution to a sealing-off of the market as a brewery in a relatively strong market position which regularly releases sales outlets at shorter intervals.' (paras 25, 26)

Comment

The analysis in this case was influenced by the characteristics of the beer supply market. It was therefore divided into two stages; first, the court considered the sealing-off effect brought about by the totality of the beer distribution agreements. Following this, the contribution of the agreement to the foreclosure of the market was considered.

The ECJ was concerned with the sealing-off effect the agreement might generate. The Commission Guidelines on Vertical Restraints [2000] OJ C 291/1 elaborate on the potential negative effects of vertical restraints (paras 103–05). Of main concern is the risk that the vertical agreement would lead to market foreclosure by raising bariers to entry and reducing inter-brand competition. (See Guidelines on Vertical Restraints, paras 106–08 dealing with single branding.)

Note that 'for most vertical restraints, competition concerns can only arise if there is insufficient inter-brand competition, i.e. if there is some degree of market power at the level of the supplier or the buyer or at both levels. If there is insufficient inter-brand competition, the protection of inter- and intra-brand competition becomes important.' (para 6, Guidelines on Vertical Restraints)

Contrast the analysis in this case with the one in *Consten and Grundig* in terms of both the finding of object and the focus on inter- or intra-brand competition (page 56 above). Note that there, the distribution agreement lead to absolute territorial protection and was held to have the object of restricting competition.

GlaxoSmithKline Services Unlimited v Commission	**Article 81 EC**
Case T–168/01	Object or Effect
CFI, [2006] ECR II–2969 5 CMLR 29	Parallel Trade

Facts

GlaxoSmithKline (GSK) (formerly Glaxo Wellcome SA (GW)), a producer of pharmaceutical products, notified the Commission of a 'General Sales Conditions' document it issued to its Spanish wholesalers. The document included in Clause 4 a 'dual pricing mechanism' which resulted in a distinction between prices charged from wholesalers for medicines sold domestically and higher prices charged in the case of exports to other Member States. The Commission found the document to constitute an agreement. In addition it observed that the ECJ and CFI always have qualified agreements containing export bans, dual-pricing systems or other limitations of parallel trade as restricting competition 'by object'. It therefore found Clause 4 to have both the object and the effect of restricting competition by limiting parallel trade between Spain and other Member States.

GSK appealed to the CFI, challenging among other things the finding of an agreement between undertakings, the existence of anticompetitive object and effect, and the Commission's refusal to exempt the agreement under Article 81(3).

Held

'… the characterisation of a restriction of competition within the meaning of Article 81(1) EC must take account of the actual framework and, therefore, of the legal and economic context in which the agreement to which that restriction is imputed is deployed. Such an obligation is imposed for the purpose of ascertaining both the object and the effect of the agreement.' (para 110)

'… when examination of the clauses of an agreement, carried out in their legal and economic context, reveals in itself the existence of an alteration of competition, it may be presumed that that agreement has as its object the prevention, restriction or distortion of competition … so that there is no need to examine its effect.' (para 111)

It follows from the case-law that agreements which ultimately seek to prohibit parallel trade must in principle be regarded as having the restriction of competition as their object. Similarly, agreements that clearly intend to treat parallel trade unfavourably must in principle be regarded as having the restriction of competition as their object. (paras 115, 116)

Yet, in this case, having regard to the legal and economic context, 'the Commission could not rely on the mere fact that Clause 4 of the General Sales Conditions established a system of differentiated price intended to limit parallel trade as the basis for its conclusion that that provision had as its object the restriction of competition.' (para 117)

'… the objective assigned to Article 81(1) EC, which constitutes a fundamental provision indispensable for the achievement of the missions entrusted to the Community, in particular for the functioning of the internal market … is to prevent undertakings, by restricting competition between themselves or with third parties, from reducing the welfare of the final consumer of the products in question. … The application of Article 81(1) EC to the present case cannot depend solely on the fact that the agreement in question is intended to limit parallel trade in medicines … but also requires an analysis designed to determine whether it has as its object or effect the prevention, restriction or distortion of competition on the relevant market, to the detriment of the final consumer. (paras 118, 119)

'In particular, in *Consten and Grundig v Commission,* … the Court of Justice, contrary to the Commission's contention in its written submissions, did not hold that an agreement intended to limit parallel trade must be considered by its nature, that is to say, independently of any competitive analysis, to have as its object the restriction of competition. On the contrary, the Court of Justice merely held, first, that an agreement between a producer and a distributor which might tend to restore the national divisions in trade between Member States might be of such a kind as to frustrate the most fundamental objectives of the Community (p. 340), a consideration which led it to reject a plea alleging that Article 81(1) EC was not applicable to vertical agreements (pp. 339 and 340). The Court of Justice then carried out a competitive analysis, abridged but real, during the course of which it held, in particular, that the agreement in question sought to eliminate any possibility of competition at the wholesale level in order to charge prices which were sheltered from all effective competition, considerations which led it to reject a plea alleging that there was no restriction of competition (pp. 342 and 343).' (para 120)

'Consequently, while it is accepted that an agreement intended to limit parallel trade must in principle be considered to have as its object the restriction of competition, that applies in so far as the agreement may be presumed to deprive final consumers of those advantages.' (para 121)

In the present case, taking account of the legal and economic context in which GSK's General Sales Conditions are applied, since the prices of the medicines concerned are to a large extent shielded from the free play of supply and demand owing to the applicable regulations and are set or controlled by the public authorities, one cannot presume that parallel trade tends to reduce those prices and thus to increase the welfare of final consumers. (paras 122–147)

From a reading of the terms of the agreement, in its context, one cannot infer that it is restrictive of competition. It is therefore necessary to consider the effects of the agreement. (para 147)

Comment

The CFI went on to find that the Commission was correct in finding that Clause 4 of the General Sales Conditions had the effect of reducing the welfare of final consumers (paras 148–190). As for the Commission's decision not to grant exemption under Article 81(3) EC, the CFI found that the Commission failed to carry out a proper examination and upheld GSK's plea regarding Article 81(3) EC.

In this case, the exceptional characteristics of the pharmaceuticals sector meant that prices of medicines were to a large extent shielded from the free forces of supply and demand due to state regulations. In such circumstances the CFI considered it impossible to infer merely from a reading of the terms of the agreement that it has the object of restricting competition.

This unprecedented scenario and sector characteristics led the CFI to distinguish between this case and earlier decisions of the European Courts. It did so by focusing on the objectives assigned to Article 81(1) EC, and its role in protecting the welfare of the final consumer. Consequently, it held that an agreement intended to limit parallel trade would in principle be considered to have as its 'object' the restriction of competition, only in so far as the agreement may be presumed to deprive final consumers of those advantages.

This analysis by the CFI requires the Commission and Courts to go beyond the agreement and consider the legal and economic context before concluding that the agreement has as its object the restriction of competition. Note, however, that in the majority of sectors where restrictions on parallel trade harm the welfare of the end consumer, this effect-oriented analysis will still lead to a finding that the object of the agreement is to restrict competition.

Note that in both cases of object and effect the parties may seek exemption under Article 81(3) EC. In doing so, they will bare the burden of proving the existence of the conditions in Article 81(3).

The Commission appealed the CFI's judgment and argued, among other things, that the CFI's analysis confirming the existence of the restrictive 'effects' constituted in reality an analysis of the restrictive 'object' of the agreement having due regard to the legal and economic context (Case 513/06 P, judgment pending).

O2 (Germany) GmbH & Co OHG v Commission	**Article 81 EC**
Case T–328/03	Object or Effect
CFI, [2006] ECR II–1231, [2006] 5 CMLR 5	Rule of Reason

Facts

O2 (Germany) GmbH & Co OHG (O2) and T–Mobile Deutschland GmbH (T–Mobile), two operators of digital mobile telecommunications networks, entered into an infrastructure sharing agreement in Germany for third-generation GSM mobile telecommunications. Following the notification of the agreement, the Commission found no grounds for action with respect to the site sharing agreement between the parties but raised concerns as to the compatibility of the provisions relating to national roaming between network operators with Article 81(1) EC. In its decision the Commission granted exemption to the provisions for limited periods under Article 81(3) EC. O2 appealed the decision to the CFI contesting, among other things, the finding that the provisions relating to national roaming restricted competition between the operators.

Held

'In order to assess whether an agreement is compatible with the common market in the light of the prohibition laid down in Article 81(1) EC, it is necessary to examine the economic and legal context in which the agreement was concluded (Case 22/71 *Beguelin Import* [1971] ECR 949, paragraph 13), its object, its effects, and whether it affects intra-Community trade taking into account in particular the economic context in which the undertakings operate, the products or services covered by the agreement, and the structure of the market concerned and the actual conditions in which it functions (Case C–399/93 *Oude Luttikhuis and others* [1995] ECR I–4515, paragraph 10).' (para 66)

'That method of analysis is of general application and is not confined to a category of agreements (see, as regards different types of agreements, Case 56/65 *Société Technique Minière* [1966] ECR 235, at 249–250; Case C–250/92 DLG [1994] ECR I5641, paragraph 31; Case T35/92 *John Deere v Commission* [1994] ECR I–957, paragraphs 51 and 52; and Joined Cases T–374/94, T–375/94, T–384/94 and T–388/94 *European Night Services and others v Commission* [1998] ECR II–3141, paragraphs 136 and 137).' (para 67)

'Moreover, in a case such as this, where it is accepted that the agreement does not have as its object a restriction of competition, the effects of the agreement should be considered, and for it to be caught by the prohibition it is necessary to find that those factors are present which show that competition has in fact been prevented or restricted or distorted to an appreciable extent. The competition in question must be understood within the actual context in which it would occur in the absence of the agreement in dispute; the interference with competition may in particular be doubted if the agreement seems really necessary for the penetration of a new area by an undertaking (*Société Technique Minière* at 249–250).' (para 68)

'Such a method of analysis, as regards in particular the taking into account of the competition situation that would exist in the absence of the agreement, does not amount to carrying out an assessment of the pro- and anti-competitive effects of the agreement and thus to applying a rule of reason, which the Community judicature has not deemed to have its place under Article 81(1) EC (Case C–235/92 P *Montecatini v Commission* [1999] ECR I–4539, paragraph 133; *M6 and others v Commission*, paragraphs 72 to 77; and Case T–65/98 *Van den Bergh Foods v Commission* [2002] ECR II–4653, paragraphs 106 and 107).' (para 69)

'In this respect, to submit, as the applicant does, that the Commission failed to carry out a full analysis by not examining what the competitive situation would have been in the absence of the agreement does not mean that an assessment of the positive and negative effects of the agreement from the point of view of competition must be carried out at the stage of Article 81(1) EC. Contrary to the defendant's interpretation of the applicant's arguments, the applicant relies only on the method of analysis required by settled case-law.' (para 70)

'The examination required in the light of Article 81(1) EC consists essentially in taking account of the impact of the agreement on existing and potential competition (see, to that effect, Case C–234/89 *Delimitis* [1991] ECR I–935, paragraph 21) and the competition situation in the absence of the agreement (*Société Technique Minière* at 249–250), those two factors being intrinsically linked.' (para 71)

'The examination of competition in the absence of an agreement appears to be particularly necessary as regards markets undergoing liberalisation or emerging markets, as in the case of the 3G mobile communications market here at issue, where effective competition may be problematic owing, for example, to the presence of a dominant operator, the concentrated nature of the market structure or the existence of significant barriers to entry – factors referred to, in the present case, in the Decision.' (para 72)

'In order to take account of the two parts which this plea actually contains, it is therefore necessary to examine, first, whether the Commission did in fact consider what the competition situation would have been in the absence of the agreement and, second, whether the conclusions which it drew from its examination of the impact of the agreement on competition are sufficiently substantiated.' (para 73)

'It follows from the foregoing that the [Commission's Decision], in so far as it concerns the application of Article 81(1) EC and Article 53(1) of the EEA Agreement, suffers from insufficient analysis, first, in that it contains no objective discussion of what the competition situation would have been in the absence of the agreement, which distorts the assessment of the actual and potential effects of the agreement on competition and, second, in that it does not demonstrate, in concrete terms, in the context of the relevant emerging market, that the provisions of the agreement on roaming have restrictive effects on competition, but is confined, in this respect, to a "petitio principii" and to broad and general statements.' (para 116)

Comment

Note the CFI's clear comment in paragraph 69 regarding the scope of analysis under Article 81(1) EC. The court held that the examination of effect under Article 81(1) EC 'as regards in particular the taking into account of the competition situation that would exist in the absence of the agreement, does not amount to carrying out an assessment of the pro-and anti-competitive effects of the agreement and thus to applying a rule of reason, which the Community judicature has not deemed to have its place under Article 81(1) EC.'

Métropole Télévision (M6) and others v Commission	**Article 81 EC**
Case T–112/99	Scope of Analysis
CFI, [2001] ECR II–2459, [2001] 5 CMLR 33	Rule of Reason

Facts

'Télévision Par Satellite' (TPS) was set up as a partnership by six major companies active in the television sector. Its aim was to devise, develop and broadcast a range of television programmes, against payment, to French-speaking television viewers in Europe. The agreements forming the TPS partnership were notified to the Commission in order to obtain negative clearance and/or exemption. In its decision the Commission did not object to the creation of TPS. However, the Commission raised concerns with respects to the impact of non-competition, exclusivity and other clauses in the agreement and subsequently granted limited negative clearance and exemption.

With reference to the non-competition clause the Commission held that there were no grounds for action in respect of that clause for a period of three years. With regard to an exclusivity clause and the clause relating to special-interest channels, the Commission held that those provisions could benefit from an exemption under Article 81(3) EC for a period of three years. (Case No IV/36.237 – TPS)

The applicants challenged the Commission's decision and the limited period for which negative clearance and exemption were granted. Among other things, the applicants argued that the Commission failed to apply a rule of reason when considering the agreements under Article 81(1) EC.

Held

'[Article 81 EC] expressly provides, in its third paragraph, for the possibility of exempting agreements that restrict competition where they satisfy a number of conditions, in particular where they are indispensable to the attainment of certain objectives and do not afford undertakings the possibility of eliminating competition in respect of a substantial part of the products in question. It is only in the precise framework of that provision that the pro and anti-competitive aspects of a restriction may be weighed (see, to that effect, Case 161/84 *Pronuptia* [1986] ECR 353, paragraph 24, and Case T–17/93 *Matra Hachette v Commission* [1994] ECR II–595, paragraph 48, and *European Night Services and others v Commission*, [[1998] ECR II–3141], paragraph 136). [Article 81(3) EC] of the Treaty would lose much of its effectiveness if such an examination had to be carried out already under [Article 81(1) EC].' (para 74)

'It is true that in a number of judgments the Court of Justice and the Court of First Instance have favoured a more flexible interpretation of the prohibition laid down in [Article 81(1) EC] (see, in particular, *Société technique minière* and *Oude Luttikhuis* and others, [[1995] ECR I–4515, paragraph 10], *Nungesser and Eisele v Commission* and *Coditel* and others, [[1982] ECR 3381], *Pronuptia*, cited in paragraph 74 above, and *European Night Services and others v Commission*, cited in paragraph [74] above, as well as the judgment in Case C–250/92 DLG [1994] ECR I–5641, paragraphs 31 to 35).' (para 75)

'Those judgments cannot, however, be interpreted as establishing the existence of a rule of reason in Community competition law. They are, rather, part of a broader trend in the case-law according to which it is not necessary to hold, wholly abstractly and without drawing any distinction, that any agreement restricting the freedom of action of one or more of the parties is necessarily caught by the prohibition laid down in [Article 81(1) EC]. In assessing the applicability of [Article 81(1) EC] to an agreement, account should be taken of the actual conditions in which it functions, in particular the economic context in which the undertakings operate, the products or services covered by the agreement and the actual structure of the market concerned (see, in particular, *European Night Services and others v Commission*, paragraph 136, *Oude Luttikhuis*, paragraph 10, and *VGB and others v Commission*, paragraph 140, …). (para 76)

'That interpretation, while observing the substantive scheme of [Article 81 EC] and, in particular, preserving the effectiveness of [Article 81(3) EC], makes it possible to prevent the prohibition in [Article 81(1) EC] from extending wholly abstractly and without distinction to all agreements whose effect is to restrict the freedom of action of one or more of the parties. It must, however, be emphasised that such an approach does not mean that it is necessary to weigh the pro and anti-competitive effects of an agreement when determining whether the prohibition laid down in [Article 81(1) EC] applies.' (para 77)

In this case the Commission correctly applied Article 81(1) EC to the exclusivity clause and the clause relating to the special-interest channels inasmuch as it was not obliged to weigh the pro- and anticompetitive aspects of those agreements outside the specific framework of Article 81(3) EC. (paras 78, 79)

Comment

In paras 75 and 76 the CFI explained that the analysis under Article 81(1) may include some evaluation of the agreement so to avoid the conclusion that 'any agreement restricting the freedom of action of one or more of the parties is necessarily caught by the prohibition laid down in [Article 81(1) EC].' Such approach does not amount to a rule of reason, and is aimed at enabling the courts to apply a more flexible analysis grounded in facts rather than a wholly abstract analysis.

Note the CFI comment in Case T–17/93 *Matra Hachette SA v Commission*, [1994] ECR II–595, where it held that 'the assessment of the extent of the anti-competitive effect of an agreement for which an exemption is requested is entirely unconnected with the assessment of the substantive scope of [Article 81(1) EC] and must be carried out by the Commission not under [Article 81(1)EC] but under [Article 81(3) EC], in relation, in particular, to the indispensability of the restrictions of competition.' (para 48)

Note that following the coming into force of Regulation 1/2003, the national courts and national competition agencies may apply Article 81 EC in its entirety. Subsequently, the rule of reason debate lost much of its significance following the abolition of notifications. However, the debate is still relevant for two purposes. First, due to the shift in the burden of proof when considering Article 81(3) provisions. Secondly, as to the nature of the considerations used to counterbalance anticompetitive effects. In this respect, whereas Article 81(3) EC provides for a structured framework of analysis based on competitive variables, Article 81(1) EC does not. The latter thus allows for a more flexible framework in which a balancing exercise may take place. See for example the *Wouters* decision, page 74 below, where the ECJ balanced between public interest and anticompetitive effect within the framework of Article 81 EC.

Note Case T–328/03 *O2 (Germany) GmbH & Co OHG v Commission* (page 64 above) in which the CFI held that the analysis under Article 81(1) EC 'does not amount to carrying out an assessment of the pro-and anti-competitive effects of the agreement and thus to applying a rule of reason'. (para 69)

See also the discussion of ancillary restraints which includes additional references to the scope of analysis under Article 81 EC. Pages 68–75 below.

Meca-Medina and Majcen v Commission	**Article 81 EC**
Case C–519/04 P	Scope of Analysis
ECJ, [2006] ECR I–6991, [2006] 5 CMLR 18	Rule of Reason/ Ancillary Restraints

Facts

Mr Meca-Medina and Mr Majcen, two professional athletes, were suspended by the International Olympic Committee (IOC) for a period of four years following a positive anti-doping test for Nandrolone. The two athletes lodged a complaint with the Commission alleging that certain rules adopted by the IOC and certain practices relating to doping control were in breach of EC competition law and freedom of movement provisions. The Commission rejected their complaint. On appeal, the CFI dismissed their action for annulment of the Commission's decision (Case T–313/02) and held, with reference to competition law, that Articles 81 EC and 82 EC do not apply to purely sporting rules. An appeal to the ECJ raised important questions as to the application of EC Treaty provisions to sports bodies' rules and with respect to exemption on the grounds of legitimate objectives.

Held

The general objective of the anti-doping rules is to combat doping in order for competitive sport to be conducted fairly. The rules safeguard equal chances for athletes, athletes' health, the integrity and objectivity of competitive sport, and ethical values in sport. (paras 43, 44)

Subsequently, 'even if the anti-doping rules at issue are to be regarded as a decision of an association of undertakings limiting the appellants' freedom of action, they do not, for all that, necessarily constitute a restriction of competition incompatible with the common market, within the meaning of Article 81 EC, since they are justified by a legitimate objective. Such a limitation is inherent in the organisation and proper conduct of competitive sport and its very purpose is to ensure healthy rivalry between athletes.' (para 45)

'It must be acknowledged that the penal nature of the anti-doping rules at issue and the magnitude of the penalties applicable if they are breached are capable of producing adverse effects on competition because they could, if penalties were ultimately proven to be unjustified, result in an athlete's unwarranted exclusion from sporting events, and thus in impairment of the conditions under which the activity at issue is engaged in. It follows that, in order not to be covered by the prohibition laid down in Article 81(1) EC, the restrictions thus imposed by those rules must be limited to what is necessary to ensure the proper conduct of competitive sport.' (para 47) In this case the appellant failed to establish that the Commission made a manifest error of assessment in finding those rules to be justified.

The current restrictions imposed on professional sportsmen do not appear to go beyond what is necessary in order to ensure that sporting events take place and function properly. (paras 48–55)

Comment

Some commentators view this decision as one that introduces a rule of reason element to Article 81(1) EC, as the ECJ in paragraph 45 balances between the legitimate objectives of the provision and the restriction of competition. Accordingly, the decision shares similarities with Case C–309/99 *Wouters* (page 74 below), and on the other hand stands at odds with the CFI approach in Case T–112/99 *Métropole* (page 66 above) and Case T–328/03 O2 (page 64 above).

On the other hand, one can read paragraph 45 as one which merely distinguishes between a restriction on the freedom of action and a restriction of competition, holding that the former would not necessarily result in the latter. The possible restriction of competition may then be regarded as ancillary, objectively necessary and proportionate to the anti-doping rules. (See further discussion on ancillary restraints on pages 69–75 below and in particular Case C–309/99 *Wouters*, page 74 below.)

Remia BV and Nv Verenigde Bedrijven Nutricia v Commission	**Article 81 EC**
Case 42/84	Ancillary Restraints
ECJ, [1985] ECR 2545, [1987] 1 CMLR 1	Non-Compete Obligation

Facts

Nv Verenigde Bedrijven Nutricia (Nutricia), a manufacturer of health and baby foods, transferred two of its subsidiaries, Remia and Luycks, to third parties. The agreements contained non-competition clauses intended to protect the purchasers from competition from the vendor (Nutricia) in the same market immediately after the transfers. Following the notification of the transfer agreements to the Commission, it found that the duration and scope of the restrictions were excessive, that they constituted a restriction on competition and that they were not eligible for exemption under Article 81 (3) EC. On appeal to the ECJ the parties contested the decision.

Held

'It should be stated at the outset that the Commission has rightly submitted – and the applicants have not contradicted it on that point – that the fact that non-competition clauses are included in an agreement for the sale of an undertaking is not of itself sufficient to remove such clauses from the scope of [Article 81 (1) EC].' (para 17)

'In order to determine whether or not such clauses come within the prohibition in [Article 81(1) EC], it is necessary to examine what would be the state of competition if those clauses did not exist.' (para 18)

'If that were the case, and should the vendor and the purchaser remain competitors after the transfer, it is clear that the agreement for the transfer of the undertaking could not be given effect. The vendor, with his particularly detailed knowledge of the transferred undertaking, would still be in a position to win back his former customers immediately after the transfer and thereby drive the undertaking out of business. Against that background non-competition clauses incorporated in an agreement for the transfer of an undertaking in principle have the merit of ensuring that the transfer has the effect intended. By virtue of that very fact they contribute to the promotion of competition because they lead to an increase in the number of undertakings in the market in question.' (para 19)

'Nevertheless, in order to have that beneficial effect on competition, such clauses must be necessary to the transfer of the undertaking concerned and their duration and scope must be strictly limited to that purpose. The Commission was therefore right in holding that where those conditions are satisfied such clauses are free of the prohibition laid down in [Article 81 (1) EC].' (para 20)

The Commission correctly assessed the facts of the case before coming to the conclusion that the period of the prohibition agreed upon between the parties was excessive and that a shorter duration of four years was objectively justified. (paras 21–36)

The Commission did not err in its decision to refuse exemption under Article 81(3) EC. (paras 37–48)

Comment

The Court accepted that a non-compete clause is necessary in order to ensure the viability of the transaction and as such is procompetitive. It did, however, hold that the duration and scope of the non-compete clause need not go beyond what is necessary to facilitate the transaction.

Note also Case T–112/99 *Métropole Télévision* where the court assessed the Commission decision concerning the creation of the Joint venture 'Television Par Satellite' (Case No IV/36.237 – TPS) (page 72 below).

Gottrup-Klim v Dansk Landbrugs Grovvareselskab AmbA	**Article 81 EC**
Case C–250/92	Ancillary Restraints
ECJ, [1994] ECR I–5641, [1996] 4 CMLR 191	Non-Compete Obligation

Facts

Dansk Landbrugs Grovvareselskab AmbA (DLG), a Danish cooperative association distributing farm supplies, was established to provide its members with farm supplies, including fertilisers and plant protection products, at the lowest prices. In 1975 a group of DLG members formed a national union of cooperative associations (LAG) which specialised in the distribution of farm supplies. In 1988 DLG amended its statutes because of increasing competition from LAG and excluded from its membership members who were also part of LAG. The amendment was intended to induce LAG members to stop purchasing fertilisers and plant protection products from anyone other than DLG, so that within the cooperative sector in Denmark there would be just one large association purchasing supplies on behalf of Danish farmers. This, it was hoped, would enable DLG to obtain better prices for its members. By March 1989, 37 local associations who continued their participation in LAG were excluded from DLG. These associations brought an action against DLG before the Danish court for the annulment of the amendments to the statutes. They claimed that the object or effect of the amendments to the statutes was to restrict competition, as it aimed at putting an end to members' purchasing through LAG in competition with DLG.

The Danish court referred the matter to the ECJ asking, among other things, whether a provision in the statutes of a cooperative purchasing association, the effect of which is to forbid its members from participating in other forms of organised cooperation which are in direct competition with it, is caught by the prohibition in Article 81(1) EC.

Held

A cooperative purchasing association is a voluntary association established in order to pursue common commercial objectives. The compatibility of the statutes of such an association with the Community rules on competition cannot be assessed in the abstract. It depends on the particular clauses in the statutes and the economic conditions prevailing on the markets concerned. (paras 30, 31)

'In a market where product prices vary according to the volume of orders, the activities of cooperative purchasing associations may, depending on the size of their membership, constitute a significant counterweight to the contractual power of large producers and make way for more effective competition.' (para 32)

'Where some members of two competing cooperative purchasing associations belong to both at the same time, the result is to make each association less capable of pursuing its objectives for the benefit of the rest of its members, especially where the members concerned, as in the case in point, are themselves cooperative associations with a large number of individual members.' (para 33)

'It follows that such dual membership would jeopardize both the proper functioning of the cooperative and its contractual power in relation to producers. Prohibition of dual membership does not, therefore, necessarily constitute a restriction of competition within the meaning of [Article 81 EC] and may even have beneficial effects on competition.' (para 34)

'Nevertheless, a provision in the statutes of a cooperative purchasing association, restricting the opportunity for members to join other types of competing cooperatives and thus discouraging them from obtaining supplies elsewhere, may have adverse effects on competition. So, in order to escape the prohibition laid down in [Article 81 EC], the restrictions imposed on members by the statutes of cooperative purchasing associations must be limited to what is necessary to ensure that the cooperative functions properly and maintains its contractual power in relation to producers.' (para 35)

'The particular features of the case at issue in the main proceedings, which are referred to in the questions submitted by the national court, must be assessed in the light of the foregoing considerations. In addition, it is necessary to establish whether the penalties for non-compliance with the statutes are disproportionate to the objective they pursue and whether the minimum period of membership is unreasonable.' (para 36)

'First of all, the amendment of DLG's statutes is restricted so as to cover only fertilizers and plant protection products, the only farm supplies in respect of which a direct relationship exists between sales volume and price.' (para 37)

'Furthermore, even after DLG has amended its statutes and excluded the plaintiffs, it is open to "non-members" of the association, including the plaintiffs, to buy from it the whole range of products which it sells, including fertilizers and plant protection products, on the same commercial terms and at the same prices as members, except that "non-members" are obviously not entitled to receive a yearly discount on the amount of the transactions carried out.' (para 38)

'Finally, DLG's statutes authorize its members to buy fertilizers and plant protection products without using DLG as an intermediary, provided that such transactions are carried out otherwise than through an organized consortium. In that context, each member acts individually or in association with others but, in the latter case, only in making a one-off common purchase of a particular consignment or shipload.' (para 39)

'Taking all those factors into account, it would not seem that restrictions laid down in the statutes, of the kind imposed on DLG members, go beyond what is necessary to ensure that the cooperative functions properly and maintains its contractual power in relation to producers.' (para 40)

'As regards the penalties imposed on the plaintiffs as a result of their exclusion for infringing DLG's rules, these would not appear to be disproportionate, since DLG has treated the plaintiffs as if they were members exercising their right to withdraw.' (para 41)

'The answer to the second set of questions referred by the national court must therefore be that a provision in the statutes of a cooperative purchasing association, forbidding its members to participate in other forms of organized cooperation which are in direct competition with it, is not caught by the prohibition in Article [Article 81 EC], so long as the abovementioned provision is restricted to what is necessary to ensure that the cooperative functions properly and maintains its contractual power in relation to producers.' (para 45)

Comment

'… The application of the ancillary restraint concept does not involve any weighing of pro-competitive and anti-competitive effects. Such balancing is reserved for Article 81(3). The assessment of ancillary restraints is limited to determining whether, in the specific context of the main non-restrictive transaction or activity, a particular restriction is necessary for the implementation of that transaction or activity and proportionate to it. If on the basis of objective factors it can be concluded that without the restriction the main non-restrictive transaction would be difficult or impossible to implement, the restriction may be regarded as objectively necessary for its implementation and proportionate to it. If, for example, the main object of a franchise agreement does not restrict competition, then restrictions, which are necessary for the proper functioning of the agreement, such as obligations aimed at protecting the uniformity and reputation of the franchise system, also fall outside Article 81(1). Similarly, if a joint venture is not in itself restrictive of competition, then restrictions that are necessary for the functioning of the agreement are deemed to be ancillary to the main transaction and are therefore not caught by Article 81(1) …' (paras 30, 31, Commission Guidelines on the Application of Article 81(3) of the Treaty [2004] OJ C 101/94)

Métropole Télévision (M6) and others v Commission	**Article 81 EC**
Case T–112/99	Ancillary Restraints
CFI, [2001] ECR II–2459, [2001] 5 CMLR 33	

Facts

'Télévision Par Satellite' (TPS), was set up as a partnership by six major companies active in the television sector. Its aim was to devise, develop and broadcast a range of television programmes, against payment, to French-speaking television viewers in Europe. The agreements forming the TPS partnership were notified to the Commission in order to obtain negative clearance and/or exemption. In its decision the Commission did not object to the creation of TPS. The Commission raised concerns with respects to some of the provisions in the agreement and granted limited negative clearance and exemption. With reference to the non-competition clause which formed part of the agreement, the Commission held that there were no grounds for action in respect of that clause for a period of three years. With regard to an exclusivity clause which formed part of the agreement, and the clause relating to special-interest channels, the Commission held that those provisions could benefit from an exemption under Article 81(3) EC for a period of three years (Case No IV/36.237 – TPS). The applicants challenged the Commission's decision and argued, among other things, that the exclusivity clause and the clause relating to the special-interest channels are ancillary restrictions.

Held

The concept of an ancillary restriction covers any restriction which is directly related and necessary to the implementation of a main operation. To establish that a restriction is necessary a twofold examination is required, first, assessing whether the restriction is objectively necessary for the implementation of the main operation and, second, whether it is proportionate to it. (paras 104–06)

'As regards the objective necessity of a restriction … it would be wrong, when classifying ancillary restrictions, to interpret the requirement for objective necessity as implying a need to weigh the pro and anti-competitive effects of an agreement. Such an analysis can take place only in the specific framework of [Article 81(3)]. … That approach is justified not merely so as to preserve the effectiveness of [Article 81(3)] of the Treaty, but also on grounds of consistency. As [Article 81(1)] of the Treaty does not require an analysis of the positive and negative effects on competition of a principal restriction, the same finding is necessary with regard to the analysis of accompanying restrictions.' (paras 107, 108)

'Consequently, as the Commission has correctly asserted, examination of the objective necessity of a restriction in relation to the main operation cannot but be relatively abstract. It is not a question of analysing whether, in the light of the competitive situation on the relevant market, the restriction is indispensable to the commercial success of the main operation but of determining whether, in the specific context of the main operation, the restriction is necessary to implement that operation. If, without the restriction, the main operation is difficult or even impossible to implement, the restriction may be regarded as objectively necessary for its implementation.' (para 109)

'Where a restriction is objectively necessary to implement a main operation, it is still necessary to verify whether its duration and its material and geographic scope do not exceed what is necessary to implement that operation. If the duration or the scope of the restriction exceed what is necessary in order to implement the operation, it must be assessed separately under [Article 81(3) EC] (see, to that effect, Case T–61/89 *Dansk Pelsdyravlerforening v Commission* [1992] ECR II–1931, paragraph 78).' (para 113)

'Lastly, it must be observed that, inasmuch as the assessment of the ancillary nature of a particular agreement in relation to a main operation entails complex economic assessments by the Commission, judicial review of that assessment is limited to verifying whether the relevant procedural rules have been complied with, whether the statement of the reasons for the decision is adequate, whether the facts have been accurately stated and whether there has been a manifest error of appraisal or misuse of powers (see, to that effect, with regard to assessing the permissible duration of a non-competition clause, *Remia v Commission*, … paragraph 34).' (para 114)

As a consequence of classification as an ancillary restriction, the compatibility of that restriction with the competition rules must be examined with that of the main operation. If the main operation does not infringe Article 81(1) EC, the same holds for the restrictions directly related and necessary for that operation. Similarly, if the main operation benefits from an exemption under Article 81(3) EC, that exemption also covers those ancillary restrictions. (para 116)

Exclusivity clause

It is necessary to examine, whether in the present case the Commission committed a manifest error of assessment in not classifying the exclusivity clause as a restriction that was ancillary to the creation of TPS. The applicants submit that the exclusivity clause is ancillary to the creation of TPS as the clause is indispensable to allow TPS to penetrate the pay-TV market in France. Yet, it must, however, be observed that the fact that the exclusivity clause would be necessary to allow TPS to establish itself on a long-term basis on that market, it is not relevant to the classification of that clause as an ancillary restriction. 'Such considerations, relating to the indispensable nature of the restriction in light of the competitive situation on the relevant market, are not part of an analysis of the ancillary nature of the restrictions. They can be taken into account only in the framework of [Article 81(3)] of the Treaty.' (paras 108–21)

'Next, it must be observed that although, in the present case, the applicants have been able to establish to the requisite legal standard that the exclusivity clause was directly related to the establishment of TPS, they have not, on the other hand, shown that the exclusive broadcasting of the general-interest channels was objectively necessary for that operation. As the Commission has rightly stated, a company in the pay-TV sector can be launched in France without having exclusive rights to the general-interest channels. That is the situation for CanalSatellite and AB-Sat, the two other operators on that market.' (para 122)

'Even if the exclusivity clause was objectively necessary for the creation of TPS, the Commission did not commit a manifest error of assessment in taking the view that this restriction was not proportionate to that objective.' The exclusivity clause is for an initial period of ten years which is excessive as TPS has to establish itself on the market before the end of that period. Moreover, the exclusivity clause is disproportionate in so far as its effect is to deprive TPS's actual and potential competitors of any access to the programmes that are considered attractive by a large number of French television viewers. (paras 123–25)

Special-interest clause

Similarly, the Commission did not commit a manifest error of assessment in not classifying the clause relating to the special-interest channels as a restriction that was ancillary to the creation of TPS. The Commission rightly refused to classify the clause as an ancillary restriction as it limited the supply of special-interest channels and television services and had a negative impact on the situation of third parties over a long period of ten years which exceeded what was necessary for the creation of TPS. (paras 126–35)

Comment

The Court accepted the Commission's conclusion that the exclusivity clause and the clause relating to the special-interest channels were not ancillary to the creation of TPS. The court noted that even when the clause is directly related to the main operation it needs to be objectively necessary for that operation and proportionate to it.

Wouters v Algemene Raad van de Nederlandse Orde van Advocaten	**Article 81 EC**
Case C–309/99	Ancillary Restraints
ECJ, [2002] ECR I–1577, [2002] 4 CMLR 27	

Facts

The case arose out of a dispute between Mr Wouters and the Dutch Bar on the basis that the Bar's regulations prohibited its members from practising in full partnership with accountants. Mr Wouters argued that the prohibition was incompatible with Community rules on competition and freedom of establishment. The Dutch court referred the case to the ECJ asking, among other things, whether a regulation which, in order to guarantee the independence and loyalty to the client of members of the Bar who provide legal assistance in conjunction with members of other liberal professions, adopts universally binding rules governing the formation of multi-disciplinary partnerships, has the object or effect of restricting competition within the common market.

Held

'The prohibition at issue … prohibits all contractual arrangements between members of the Bar and accountants which provide in any way for shared decision-making, profit-sharing or for the use of a common name, and this makes any form of effective partnership difficult.' (para 84)

'It appears to the Court that the national legislation at issue in the main proceedings has an adverse effect on competition and may affect trade between Member States.' (para 85)

'As regards the adverse effect on competition, the areas of expertise of members of the Bar and of accountants may be complementary. Since legal services, especially in business law, more and more frequently require recourse to an accountant, a multi-disciplinary partnership of members of the Bar and accountants would make it possible to offer a wider range of services, and indeed to propose new ones. Clients would thus be able to turn to a single structure for a large part of the services necessary for the organisation, management and operation of their business (the one-stop shop advantage).' (para 87)

Furthermore, a multi-disciplinary partnership of members of the Bar and accountants would satisfy the needs created by the increasing interpenetration of national markets and might have positive effects on the cost of services. (paras 88, 89)

A prohibition of such multi-disciplinary partnerships 'is therefore liable to limit production and technical development within the meaning of [Article 81(1)(b)] of the Treaty.' (para 90)

On the other hand, it is true that the accountancy market is highly concentrated, to the extent that the firms dominating it are at present known as the Big Five. 'The prohibition of conflicts of interest with which members of the Bar in all Member States are required to comply with may constitute a structural limit to extensive concentration of law-firms and so reduce their opportunities of benefiting from economies of scale or of entering into structural associations with practitioners of highly concentrated professions.' (paras 91, 92)

'In those circumstances, unreserved and unlimited authorisation of multi-disciplinary partnerships between the legal profession, the generally decentralised nature of which is closely linked to some of its fundamental features, and a profession as concentrated as accountancy, could lead to an overall decrease in the degree of competition prevailing on the market in legal services, as a result of the substantial reduction in the number of undertakings present on that market.' (para 93)

'Nevertheless, in so far as the preservation of a sufficient degree of competition on the market in legal services could be guaranteed by less extreme measures than national rules such as the 1993 Regulation, which prohibits absolutely any form of multi-disciplinary partnership, whatever the respective sizes of the firms of lawyers and accountants concerned, those rules restrict competition.' (para 94)

'However, not every agreement between undertakings or every decision of an association of undertakings which restricts the freedom of action of the parties or of one of them necessarily falls within the prohibition laid down in [Article 81(1) EC]. For the purposes of application of that provision to a particular case, account must first of all be taken of the overall context in which the decision of the association of undertakings was taken or produces its effects. More particularly, account must be taken of its objectives, which are here connected with the need to make rules relating to organisation, qualifications, professional ethics, supervision and liability, in order to ensure that the ultimate consumers of legal services and the sound administration of justice are provided with the necessary guarantees in relation to integrity and experience (see, to that effect, Case C–3/95 *Reiseburo Broede* [1996] ECR I–6511, paragraph 38). It has then to be considered whether the consequential effects restrictive of competition are inherent in the pursuit of those objectives.' (para 97)

Account should be taken of the legal framework applicable in the Netherlands to members of the Bar, including the obligation of the Bar to ensure the proper practice of the profession, the duty to act for clients in complete independence and in their sole interest, and the duty to avoid all risk of conflict of interest and to observe strict professional secrecy. (paras 98–102)

No comparable requirements of professional conduct are imposed on accountants in the Netherlands. In addition, there may be a degree of incompatibility between the advisory activities carried out by a member of the Bar and the supervisory activities carried out by an accountant. The Bar was entitled to consider that its members might not be in a position to advise and represent their clients independently and in strict professional secrecy if they belonged to a multi-disciplinary partnership. (paras 103–05)

The Regulation in question could therefore reasonably be considered to be necessary in order to ensure the proper practice of the legal profession. To that extent even if multi-disciplinary partnerships of lawyers and accountants are allowed in other Member States, the Bar is entitled to consider that the objectives pursued by the Regulation cannot be attained by less restrictive means (paras 106–10)

Comment

Paragraphs 84–90 highlight the anticompetitive effect of the Regulation. From paragraph 91 onwards the ECJ treats the Regulation and the anticompetitive effects it generates as restraints necessary in order to fulfil the legal obligations of the Bar. In this respect the analysis resembles an ancillary restraint argument, although the restraint here does not facilitate a commercial agreement but rather a regulatory based obligation.

In its decision the ECJ balanced in paragraphs 91–110 between public interest and anticompetitive effect. This exercise raises two main difficulties. First, the anticompetitive effects of the Regulation were counterbalanced by reference to non-economic variables. Second, this exercise was conducted under Article 81(1) EC and resembles a rule of reason analysis. One would have expected the balancing exercise to take place under Article 81(3) EC. Yet, it is questionable whether non-economic variables such as public interest could have been integrated into the framework of Article 81(3) EC. It is possible that Article 81(1) EC provided the court with a more flexible framework to consider non-qualifying elements such as public interest.

Following *Wouters*, it may be possible to argue that a 'public interest arguments' can be heard as part of the Article 81(1) analysis. Such balancing exercise will not necessarily overlap with the Article 81(3) analysis as most public interest arguments are external to Article 81(3) EC. It is therefore best viewed as a widening of the variables considered under Article 81(1); a tool allowing the Court to balance anticompetitive effects against a range of non-qualifying policy variables. Although attractive in its ability to protect national public interests, the risk associated with such a flexible approach in a decentralised enforcement regime is clear.

Note the ECJ decision in Case C–519/04 P *Meca-Medina and Majcen v Commission*, page 68 above.

Franz Volk v SPRL Est J Vervaecke	**Article 81 EC**
Case 5/69	Appreciable Effect (de minimis)
ECJ, [1969] ECR 295, [1969] CMLR 273	

'... the prohibition in [Article 81(1) EC] is applicable only if the agreement in question also has as its object or effect the prevention, restriction or distortion of competition within the common market. Those conditions must be understood by reference to the actual circumstances of the agreement. Consequently an agreement falls outside the prohibition in [Article 81(1) EC] when it has only an insignificant effect on the markets, taking into account the weak position which the persons concerned have on the market of the product in question. Thus an exclusive dealing agreement, even with absolute territorial protection, may, having regard to the weak position of the persons concerned on the market in the products in question in the area covered by the absolute protection, escape the prohibition laid down in [Article 81(1) EC].' (para 7)

Langnese-Iglo GmbH v Commission	**Article 81 EC**
Case T–7 /93	Appreciable Effect (de minimis)
CFI, [1995] ECR II–1533, [1995] 5 CMLR 602	

'It must be borne in mind that [the Commission Notice on Agreements of Minor Importance] is intended only to define those agreements which, in the Commission's view, do not have an appreciable effect on competition or trade between Member States. The Court considers that it cannot however be inferred with certainty that a network of exclusive purchasing agreements is automatically liable to prevent, restrict or distort competition appreciably merely because the ceilings laid down in it are exceeded. Moreover, it is apparent from the actual wording of paragraph 3 of that notice that it is entirely possible, in the present case, that agreements concluded between undertakings which exceed the ceilings indicated, affect trade between Member States or competition only to an insignificant extent and consequently are not caught by [Article 81(1) EC].' (para 98)

European Night Services Ltd and others v	**Article 81 EC**
Commission	Appreciable Effect (de minimis)
Joined Cases T–374, 375, 384, 388/94	
ECJ, [1998] ECR II–3141, [1998] 5 CMLR 718	

'... it must be borne in mind that, according to the case-law, an agreement may fall outside the prohibition in [Article 81(1) EC] if it has only an insignificant effect on the market, taking into account the weak position which the parties concerned have on the product or service market in question. ... With regard to the quantitative effect on the market, the Commission has argued that, in accordance with its notice on agreements of minor importance, cited above, [Article 81(1)] applies to an agreement when the market share of the parties to the agreement amounts to. ... However, the mere fact that that threshold may be reached and even exceeded does not make it possible to conclude with certainty that an agreement is caught by [Article 81(1)]. Point 3 of that notice itself states that .the quantitative definition of "appreciable" given by the Commission is, however, no absolute yardstick' and that 'in individual cases ... agreements between undertakings which exceed these limits may ... have only a negligible effect on trade between Member States or on competition, and are therefore not caught by [Article 81(1)]. ... It is noteworthy, moreover, if only as an indication, that that analysis is corroborated by the Commission's 1997 notice on agreements of minor importance (OJ 1997 C 372, p 13) replacing the notice of 3 September 1986, cited above, according to which even agreements which are not of minor importance can escape the prohibition on agreements on account of their exclusively favourable impact on competition.' (para 102)

Société Technique Minière v Maschinenbau Ulm GmbH	**Article 81 EC**
Case 56/65	Effect on Trade
ECJ, [1966] ECR 235, [1966] CMLR 357	

'… It is in fact to the extent that the agreement may affect trade between Member States that the interference with competition caused by that agreement is caught by the prohibitions in Community law found in [Article 81 EC], whilst in the converse case it escapes those prohibitions. For this requirement to be fulfilled it must be possible to foresee with a sufficient degree of probability on the basis of a set of objective factors of law or of fact that the agreement in question may have an influence, direct or indirect, actual or potential, on the pattern of trade between Member States. Therefore, in order to determine whether an agreement which contains a clause "granting an exclusive right of sale" comes within the field of application of [Article 81 EC], it is necessary to consider in particular whether it is capable of bringing about a partitioning of the market in certain products between Member States and thus rendering more difficult the interpenetration of trade which the Treaty is intended to create.' (para 249)

Consten SaRL and Grundig-Verkaufs-GmbH v Commission	**Article 81 EC**
Joined Cases 56 and 58/64	Effect on Trade
ECJ, [1966] ECR 299, [1966] CMLR 418	

'The concept of an agreement "which may affect trade between Member States" is intended to define, in the law governing cartels, the boundary between the areas respectively covered by Community law and national law. It is only to the extent to which the agreement may affect trade between Member States that the deterioration in competition caused by the agreement falls under the prohibition of Community law contained in [Article 81 EC] otherwise it escapes the prohibition.' (para 341)

'In this connection, what is particularly important is whether the agreement is capable of constituting a threat, either direct or indirect, actual or potential, to freedom of trade between Member States in a manner which might harm the attainment of the objectives of a single market between states. Thus the fact that an agreement encourages an increase, even a large one, in the volume of trade between states is not sufficient to exclude the possibility that the agreement may "affect" such trade in the abovementioned manner. In the present case, the contract between Grundig and Consten, on the one hand by preventing undertakings other than Consten from importing Grundig products into France, and on the other hand by prohibiting Consten from re-exporting those products to other countries of the common market, indisputably affects trade between Member States. These limitations on the freedom of trade, as well as those which might ensue for third parties from the registration in France by Consten of the Gint trade mark, which Grundig places on all its products, are enough to satisfy the requirement in question.' (p 341)'

Vereeniging van Cementhandelaren v Commission	**Article 81 EC**
Case 8/72	Effect on Trade
ECJ, [1972] ECR 977, [1973] CMLR 7	

'An agreement extending over the whole of the territory of a Member State by its very nature has the effect of reinforcing the compartmentalization of markets on a national basis, thereby holding up the economic interpenetration which the Treaty is designed to bring about and protecting domestic production.' (para 29)

'In particular, the provisions of the agreement which are mutually binding on the members of the applicant association and the prohibition by the association on all sales to resellers who are not authorized by it make it more difficult for producers or sellers from other Member States to be active in or penetrate the Netherlands market.' (para 30)

SA Brasserie de Haecht v Consorts Wilkin-Janssen	**Article 81 EC**
Case 23/67	Effect on Trade
ECJ, [1967] ECR 407, [1968] CMLR 26	

'… it is only to the extent to which agreements, Decisions or practices are capable of affecting trade between Member States that the alteration of competition comes under Community prohibitions. In order to satisfy this condition, it must be possible for the agreement, Decision or practice, when viewed in the light of a combination of the objective, factual or legal circumstances, to appear to be capable of having some influence, direct or indirect, on trade between Member States, of being conducive to a partitioning of the market and of hampering the economic interpenetration sought by the Treaty. When this point is considered the agreement, Decision or practice cannot therefore be isolated from all the others of which it is one.'

'The existence of similar contracts is a circumstance which, together with others, is capable of being a factor in the economic and legal context within which the contract must be judged. Accordingly, whilst such a situation must be taken into account it should not be considered as decisive by itself, but merely as one among others in judging whether trade between Member States is capable of being affected through any alteration in competition.' (p 416)

AEG–Telefunken AG v Commission	**Article 81 EC**
Case 107/82	Effect on Trade
ECJ, [1983] ECR 3151, [1984] 3 CMLR 325	

'As regards the second argument put forward by AEG, it must be pointed out that the risk of obstacles to potential trade cannot be ruled out on the basis of a mere allegation that the traders did not or were not in a position to carry on trade between Member States. In that connection it is important to stress that several of the undertakings mentioned in the Decision (for example, Diederichs in Belgium and the Auchan, Darty, Fnac and Conforama shops in France) actually undertook or were prepared to undertake parallel imports. The Ratio chain of stores in the Federal Republic of Germany on several occasions effected re-imports of Telefunken products from Austria and would no doubt have done so from Member States of the EEC if the re-importation from those states had brought it the same advantages.' (para 59)

'In any case it must be recalled that, according to the Miller judgment [Case 19/77 *Miller International Schallplatten GmbH v Commission*, [1978] ECR 131, [1978] 2 CMLR 334,] …, the mere fact that at a certain time traders applying for admission to a distribution network or who have already been admitted are not engaged in intra-Community trade cannot suffice to exclude the possibility that restrictions on their freedom of action may impede intra-Community trade, since the situation may change from one year to another in terms of alterations in the conditions or composition of the market both in the common market as a whole and in the individual national markets.' (para 60)

Consten SaRL and Grundig-Verkaufs-GmbH v Commission	**Article 81(2) EC**
Joined Cases 56 and 58/64	Severability
ECJ, [1966] ECR 299, [1966] CMLR 418	Temporaneous Nullity

Facts

An exclusive distribution agreement between Consten and Grundig under which the former received exclusive rights to sell Grundig products in France in return for its promise not to handle competing brands. The agreement led to absolute territorial protection and was found by the Commission to infringe Article 81 EC. On appeal to the ECJ, the companies argued that, among other things, the Commission did not exclude from the prohibition those clauses of the contract in respect of which there was found no effect capable of restricting competition.

Held

'The provision in [Article 81(2) EC] that agreements prohibited pursuant to [Article 81 EC] shall be automatically void applies only to those parts of the agreement which are subject to the prohibition, or to the agreement as a whole if those parts do not appear to be severable from the agreement itself. The Commission should, therefore, either have confined itself in the operative part of the contested Decision to declaring that an infringement lay in those parts only of the agreement which came within the prohibition, or else it should have set out in the preamble to the Decision the reasons why those parts did not appear to it to be severable from the whole agreement.' (p. 344)

'It follows, however, from Article 1 of the Decision that the infringement was found to lie in the agreement as a whole, although the Commission did not adequately state the reasons why it was necessary to render the whole of the agreement void when it is not established that all the clauses infringed the provisions of [Article 81(1) EC]. The state of affairs found to be incompatible with [Article 81(1) EC] stems from certain specific clauses of the contract of 1 April 1957 concerning absolute territorial protection and from the additional agreement on the Gint trade mark rather than from the combined operation of all clauses of the agreement, that is to say, from the aggregate of its effects. Article 1 of the contested Decision must therefore be annulled in so far as it renders void, without any valid reason, all the clauses of the agreement by virtue of [Article 81(2) EC].' (p. 344)

Comment

In *Société Technique Minière v Maschinenbau Ulm* GmbH (page 55 above) the ECJ held similarly that the automatic nullity under Article 81(2) EC only applies to those parts of the agreement affected by the prohibition, or to the agreement as a whole if it appears that those parts are not severable from the agreement itself.

'The fact that only binding agreements can, by their nature, be rendered void [under Article 81(2) EC] does not mean that non-binding agreements must escape the prohibition laid down in [Article 81(1)] of the Treaty.' (Case T–9/99 *HFB Holding and others v Commission*, para 101, [2002] ECR II–1487)

In *David John Passmore v Morland and others*, [1999] 1 CMLR 1129, the English Court of Appeal held that an agreement which falls outside Article 81(1) EC at the time when it is entered, may nonetheless be prohibited under the Article when, for example, a change in market conditions influences the economic effects generated by it. The same is true for agreements which were prohibited under Article 81(1) EC, but do to changes in circumstances, no longer have anticompetitive effects. (paras 26, 27) Subsequently, Article 81(2) 'has to be construed in light of an appreciation that the prohibition in [Article 81(1)] is not an absolute prohibition. ... The prohibition is temporaneous (or transient) rather than absolute; in the sense that it endures for a finite period of time–the period of time for which it is needed–rather than for all time ...' (para 28) '... the nullity imposed by [Article 81(2)] is an exact reflection of the prohibition imposed by [Article 81(1)]. If the prohibition is temporaneous (or transient) then so is the nullity.' (para 34)

Consten SaRL and Grundig-Verkaufs-GmbH v Commission	**Article 81(3) EC**
Joined Cases 56 and 58/64	First and Third Conditions
ECJ, [1966] ECR 299, [1966] CMLR 418	

Facts

An exclusive distribution agreement between Consten and Grundig under which the former received exclusive rights to sell Grundig products in France in return for its promise not to handle competing brands. The agreement led to absolute territorial protection and was found by the Commission to infringe Article 81 EC. On appeal to the ECJ the possibility for exemption under Article 81(3) was considered.

Held

When assessing the conditions for exemption under Article 81(3) 'the Commission may not confine itself to requiring from undertakings proof of the fulfilment of the requirements for the grant of the exemption but must, as a matter of good administration, play its part, using the means available to it, in ascertaining the relevant facts and circumstances. Furthermore, the exercise of the Commission's powers necessarily implies complex evaluations on economic matters. A judicial review of these evaluations must take account of their nature by confining itself to an examination of the relevance of the facts and of the legal consequences which the Commission deduces therefrom. This review must in the first place be carried out in respect of the reasons given for the Decisions which must set out the facts and considerations on which the said evaluations are based.' (p 347)

'The question whether there is an improvement in the production or distribution of the goods in question, which is required for the grant of exemption, is to be answered in accordance with the spirit of [Article 81 EC]. First, this improvement cannot be identified with all the advantages which the parties to the agreement obtain from it in their production or distribution activities. These advantages are generally indisputable and show the agreement as in all respects indispensable to an improvement as understood in this sense. This subjective method, which makes the content of the concept of "improvement" depend upon the special features of the contractual relationships in question, is not consistent with the aims of [Article 81 EC]. Furthermore, the very fact that the Treaty provides that the restriction of competition must be "indispensable" to the improvement in question clearly indicates the importance which the latter must have. This improvement must in particular show appreciable objective advantages of such a character as to compensate for the disadvantages which [are caused] in the field of competition.' (p. 348)

'In its evaluation of the relative importance of the various factors submitted for its consideration, the Commission ... had to judge their effectiveness by reference to an objectively ascertainable improvement in the production and distribution of the goods, and to decide whether the resulting benefit would suffice to support the conclusion that the consequent restrictions upon competition were indispensable. The argument based on the necessity to maintain intact all arrangements of the parties in so far as they are capable of contributing to the improvement sought cannot be reconciled with the view propounded in the last sentence ...' (p 348)

Comment

The Court emphasised that when considering the benefits stemming from the agreement, under the first condition in Article 81(3) EC, account should only be taken of objective benefits which generate value to the Community as a whole and not to subjective benefit which the parties obtain from the agreement (see p 348).

For a detailed account of the different categories of efficiencies, see paras 48–72, the Commission Guidelines on the Application of Article 81(3) of the Treaty, [2004] OJ C101/97.

Metro SB-Großmarkte GmbH & Co KG v Commission	**Article 81(3) EC**
Case 26/76	First Condition
ECJ, [1977] ECR 1875, [1978] 2 CMLR 1	Policy Considerations

Facts

Following a complaint submitted by Metro, the Commission started an investigation into a selective distribution system for electric goods, operated by SABA. The Commission concluded that the distribution system did infringe Article 81 EC. It found that the conditions of sale for the domestic market as laid down in the distribution system did not fall within the prohibition in Article 81(1) EC and that the other provisions in the distribution agreement qualified for an exemption under Article 81(3) EC. Metro applied for annulment of the Commission decision. On appeal the ECJ considered, among other things, the Commission's evaluation of the distribution system under Article 81(3). Application was dismissed.

Held

The Court needs to consider whether the supply contracts which form part of the selective distribution system satisfy the conditions under Article 81(3) EC. With regard to the first condition in Article 81(3) EC, 'the conclusion of supply contracts for six months, taking account of the probable growth of the market, should make it possible to ensure both a certain stability in the supply of the relevant products, which should allow the requirements of persons obtaining supplies from the wholesaler to be more fully satisfied, and, since such supply contracts are of relatively short duration, a certain flexibility, enabling production to be adapted to the changing requirements of the market. Thus a more regular distribution is ensured, to the benefit both of the producer, who takes his share of the planned expansion of the market in the relevant product, of the wholesaler, whose supplies are secured, and, finally, of the undertakings which obtain supplies from the wholesaler, in that the variety of available products is increased. ... Furthermore, the establishment of supply forecasts for a reasonable period constitutes a stabilizing factor with regard to the provision of employment which, since it improves the general conditions of production, especially when market conditions are unfavourable, comes within the framework of the objectives to which reference may be had pursuant to [Article 81(3)].' (para 43)

Comment

The ECJ considered that employment was a relevant factor under the first condition of Article 81(3). Employment considerations constitute a non-efficiency variable which the court considered relevant in balancing the anticompetitive effects of the agreement under Article 81(3) EC.

This broad approach opens the door to variables that are not directly linked to efficiencies. In Case T–528/93 *Métropole Télévision SA v Commission*, [1996] ECR II–649, 1996] 5 CMLR 386, the CFI held that: 'Admittedly, in the context of an overall assessment, the Commission is entitled to base itself on considerations connected with the pursuit of the public interest in order to grant exemption under [Article 81(3)] of the Treaty ...' (para 118)

Contrast with the CFI comment in Case T–17/93 *Matra Hachette SA v Commission*, [1994] ECR II–595, where in paragraph 139 it seems to suggest that considerations as to public infrastructures, employment and European integration were external to the analysis of Article 81(3) EC.

Also note the restrictive attitude as indicated in the (post-modernisation) Guidelines on Article 81(3). The Guidelines, in line with the new decentralised enforcement regime, seem to foster a rather restrictive approach and focus primarily on cost and qualitative efficiencies. This restrictive approach is aimed at minimising divergence between national courts and competition authorities when considering individual exemptions. Note, however, that the Guidelines are not binding, and national courts and competition authorities are free to follow the more permissive case-law if they wish to do so.

Publishers Association v Commission	**Article 81(3) EC**
Case C–360/92 P	First Condition
ECJ, [1995] ECR I–23, [1995] 5 CMLR 33	Externalities of Effect

Facts

The Publishers Association (PA) brought an appeal against the CFI judgment in Case T–66/89 ([1992] ECR II–1995), in which the Court dismissed its application for annulment of the Commission Decision. The case concerned the lawfulness of two agreements which were concluded in the United Kingdom under the aegis of the PA and established a 'net price system' for books. The system included provisions for fixing prices and sale conditions for books. It was established, among other things, in order to avoid the decline in stock levels and to prevent an increase in book prices. The Commission found the agreements to constitute an infringement of Article 81(1) and rejected the PA's application for an exemption under Article 81(3) on the ground that the restrictions imposed by the agreements were not indispensable to the attainment of its stated objectives.

Held

In its review of the lawfulness of the Commission's refusal to grant an exemption under Article 81(3) for the 'net price system for books', the CFI failed to consider the existence of a single language area forming a single market for books in Ireland and the United Kingdom. 'Having regard to the single language area, the objectives pursued by the agreements and the restrictions of competition arising therefrom, and the relationship between the objectives and the restrictions were to be assessed in the same way or differently, depending on whether the assessment related to the national territory alone or to the Community market.' (paras 24–7)

'In paragraph 84 of the judgment under appeal, the Court then held that "the PA, which is an association consisting of publishers established in the United Kingdom, is not entitled to rely on any negative effects which might be felt on the Irish market, even though that market belongs to the same language area". That finding is vitiated by an error of law. Nothing in the wording or the spirit of [Article 81(3)] of the Treaty allows that provision to be interpreted as meaning that the possibility for which it provides, of declaring the provisions of paragraph 1 inapplicable in the case of certain agreements which contribute to improving the production or distribution of goods or to promoting technical or economical progress, is subject to the condition that those benefits should occur only on the territory of the Member State or States in which the undertakings who are parties to the agreement are established and not in the territory of other Member States. Such an interpretation is incompatible with the fundamental objectives of the Community and with the very concepts of common market and single market.' (paras 28, 29)

Comment

In Case T–131/99, *Michael Hamilton Shaw and others v Commission* [2002] ECR II–2023, the CFI reached a similar conclusion, holding that examination of the grant of an individual exemption had to be made within the same analytical framework as that used for assessing the restrictive effects. (para 163)

See also para 43, Guidelines on Article 81(3) according to which 'the conditions that consumers must receive a fair share of the benefits implies in general that efficiencies generated by the restrictive agreement within the relevant market must be sufficient to outweigh the anti-competitive effects produced by the agreement within the same relevant market. Negative effects on consumers in one geographic market or product market cannot normally be balanced against and compensated by positive effects for consumers in another unrelated geographic market or product market. However, where two markets are related, efficiencies achieved on separate markets can be taken into account provided that the group of consumers affected by the restriction and benefiting from the efficiency gains are substantially the same. Indeed, in some cases only consumers in a downstream market are affected by the agreement in which case the impact of the agreement on such consumers must be assessed. This is for instance so in the case of purchasing agreements.'

Facts

GlaxoSmithKline (GSK) (formerly Glaxo Wellcome, SA (GW)), a producer of pharmaceutical products, notified the Commission of a 'General Sales Conditions' document it issued to its Spanish wholesalers. The document included in Clause 4 a 'dual pricing mechanism' which resulted in a distinction between prices charged from wholesalers for medicines sold domestically and higher prices charged in the case of exports to other Member State. The Commission found Clause 4 to have both the object and the effect of restricting competition by limiting parallel trade between Spain and other Member States. The Commission rejected GW's request for exemption under Article 81(3) EC. GSK appealed the decision, and contested among other things the Commission refusal to grant an exemption under Article 81(3) EC.

Held (on Article 81(3) EC)

'Any agreement which restricts competition, whether by its effects or by its object, may in principle benefit from an exemption…' (para 233)

A person who relies on Article 81(3) EC must demonstrate that the four conditions in that Article are satisfied. The Commission, for its part, must adequately examine the arguments and evidence. 'In certain cases, those arguments and that evidence may be of such a kind as to require the Commission to provide an explanation or justification, failing which it is permissible to conclude that the burden of proof borne by the person who relies on Article 81(3) EC has been discharged. … As the Commission agrees in its written submissions, in such a case it must refute those arguments and that evidence.' (paras 236, 234–36)

'… the Court dealing with an application for annulment of a decision applying Article 81(3) EC carries out, in so far as it is faced with complex economic assessments, a review confined, as regards the merits, to verifying whether the facts have been accurately stated, whether there has been any manifest error of appraisal and whether the legal consequences deduced from those facts were accurate (*Consten and Grundig v Commission*, … p. 347; Case 26/76 *Metro v Commission*, paragraph 25; *Remia and others v Commission*, … paragraph 34; and *Aalborg Portland and others v Commission*, [Joined Cases C–204/00 etc, [2004] ECR I–123, paragraph 279).' (para 241)

Under the first condition in Article 81(3) EC, an agreement must be found to yield appreciable objective advantages. The Commission is required first to 'examine whether the factual arguments and the evidence submitted to it show, in a convincing manner, that the agreement in question must enable appreciable objective advantages to be obtained … it being understood that these advantages may arise not only on the relevant market but also on other markets (Case T–86/95 *Compagnie Générale Maritime and others v Commission* [2002] ECR II–1011, paragraph 343).' (paras 248, 247–8)

'In the affirmative, it is for the Commission, in the second place, to evaluate whether those appreciable objective advantages are of such a kind as to offset the disadvantages identified for competition in the context of the examination carried out under Article 81(1) EC (see, to that effect, [Case 209/78] *Van Landewyck and others v Commission*, [1980] ECR 3125, paragraphs 183 to 185).' (para 250)

In the present case, 'the Commission did not validly take into account all the factual arguments and the evidence pertinently submitted by GSK, did not refute certain of those arguments even though they were sufficiently relevant and substantiated to require a response, and did not substantiate to the requisite legal standard its conclusion that it was not proved, first, that parallel trade was apt to lead to a loss in efficiency by appreciably altering GSK's capacity for innovation and, second, that Clause 4 of the General Sales Conditions was apt to enable a gain in efficiency to be achieved by improving innovation.' (paras 303, 251–306)

'After concluding its examination of the factual arguments and the evidence submitted by GSK and finding that they did not demonstrate the existence of an appreciable objective advantage, the Commission did not carry out the complex assessment (see paragraph 241 above) which would have been involved by the exercise seeking to balance that advantage against the disadvantage for competition identified in the part of the Decision devoted to the application of Article 81(1) EC, as it stated on a number of occasions at the hearing.' (paras 304, 251–306)

The Commission's conclusions regarding the advantages being passed on to the consumer, the indispensability of Clause 4 of the General Sales Conditions and the absence of the elimination of competition were based on its conclusion relating to the lack of efficiency gain. Insofar as that conclusion is vitiated by illegality, those conclusions are themselves invalid. (paras 309, 310)

Comment

The Court upheld the plea alleging infringement of Article 81(3) EC. Note that this does not amount to clearance of the distribution system but only to rejection of the Commission's analysis.

In paragraph 248 the CFI noted that it is possible to balance between advantages in one market and detriment in another. Contrast this statement with para 43, Guidelines on Article 81(3) and with Case C–360/92 P *Publishers Association v Commission* (page 82 above).

GSK argued, among other things, that in the unique condition of the pharmaceutical market parallel trade leads to free riding, loss of efficiency and income. To address this, Clause 4 of the GSK General Sales Conditions optimised income and neutralised parallel trade. According to GSK, a rational producer is likely to reinvest those additional profits, made due to the restriction on parallel trade, in innovation. (paras 269–74) The Court noted that although parallel trade seems not to be the main factor underlying decisions on R&D it was for the Commission to conduct a more thorough examination of this point. (para 277)

In paragraph 273 the CFI refers to the final consumer, noting that 'The legitimacy of that transfer of wealth from producer to intermediary is not in itself of interest to competition law, which is concerned only with its impact on the welfare of the final consumer. In so far as the intermediary participates in intrabrand competition, parallel trade may have a pro-competitive effect …'. Contrast this with para 84, Guidelines on Article 81(3) which states that 'consumers within the meaning of Article 81(3) are the customers of the parties to the agreement and subsequent purchasers.'

In paragraph 313 the CFI noted that due to the special characteristics of the pharmaceutical market, in terms of innovation and competition, GSK's market position and market shares 'do not in itself make it possible to conclude, in a convincing manner, that competition would be eliminated for a substantial part of the relevant products.'

The Commission appealed the CFI's judgment (Case 513/06 P, judgment pending).

Visa International – Multilateral Interchange Fee	**Article 81(3) EC**
Case No COMP/29.373	The Four Conditions
European Commission, [2002] OJ L 318/17	Price Fixing

Facts

The Commission reviewed various rules and regulations governing the Visa association and its members. In particular the Commission focused on a proposed modified Visa EU intra-regional interchange reimbursement fee scheme which sets the inter-bank payments made for each transaction carried out with a Visa payment card. The Commission found the scheme to appreciably restrict competition within the meaning of Article 81(1) EC by creating an agreement between competitors which restrict the freedom of banks individually to decide their own pricing policies and distorts the conditions of competition on the Visa issuing and acquiring markets. Following its finding, the Commission considered whether the scheme may be exempted under Article 81(3) EC. It concluded, subject to certain obligations, that the scheme fulfils the conditions for an exemption under Article 81(3) EC.

Decision (on exemption criteria)

First condition

The Commission accepted Visa's view that the multilateral interchange fee scheme (MIF) generates positive network effects and promotes the wider distribution and acceptance of Visa cards and all the services they provide. In the absence of the scheme there would be fewer Visa cardholders and fewer merchants accepting Visa cards. The Commission concluded that the Visa International Rules meet the first condition in Article 81(3) as they contribute to the existence of a large-scale international payment system with positive network externalities. (paras 79–91)

Second condition

'… four-party payment card schemes like that of Visa are networks with two distinct and interdependent types of consumers, merchants and cardholders. Each type of consumer would prefer the costs of the system to be paid by the other user. … The Visa network, like any network characterized by network externalities, will provide greater utility to each type of user, the greater the number of users of the other type: the more merchants in the system, the greater the utility to cardholders and vice versa. The maximum number of users in the system will be achieved if the cost to each category of user is as closely as possible equivalent to the average marginal utility of the system to that category of user.' (paras 82, 83)

The proposed MIF is based on objective criteria and is transparent for users of the Visa scheme who end up paying the MIF in whole or in part. It can be said to provide a fair share of the benefits to each category of user of the Visa system. (paras 84–92)

Third condition

The Commission considered the indispensability of the proposed MIF scheme for the achievement of the benefits identified under the first and second conditions of Article 81(3), in particular, the positive network externalities. It found that 'without some kind of multilateral interchange fee arrangement, it would not be possible for issuers to recover from merchants the costs of services which are provided ultimately to the benefit of merchants, and this would lead to negative consequences, to the detriment of the entire system and all of its users.' (para 98)

The Commission was content that the proposed MIF, based as it was on objective criteria and being transparent is the least restrictive of competition out of all the possible types of MIF and satisfies the condition of indispensability. (paras 96–103)

Fourth condition

'The MIF does not eliminate competition between issuers, which remain free to set their respective client fees. Moreover, although it sets de facto a floor in the merchant fees it does not eliminate competition between acquirers either, since acquiring banks remain free to set the merchant fees and can still compete on the other components of the merchant fee apart from the MIF. Nor does it eliminate competition between Visa and its competitors …' (para 106)

Comment

Although exceptional, as a matter of law, any agreement, including a price fixing agreement, could benefit from exemption under Article 81(3). In Case T–17/93 *Matra Hachette v Commission*, [1994] ECR II–595, the CFI held that 'In principle, no anti-competitive practice can exist which, whatever the extent of its effects on a given market, cannot be exempted, provided that all the conditions laid down in [Article 81(3)] of the Treaty are satisfied …' See similarly *Consten and Grundig v Commission*, page 80 above, paragraph 110, *GlaxoSmithKline Services Unlimited v Commission*, page 83 above, paragraph 233.

In *Reims II* (Case IV/36.748) (OJ 1999 L275/17, 2000 4 CMLR 704) the Commission granted exemption under Article 81(3) EC to an agreement between sixteen European postal operators on the fixing of fees for the costs of delivering cross-border mail. Although the agreement was found to be a price-fixing agreement and led to price increases for some customers, these negative effects were offset by the elimination of cross-subsidies and the improvement in service. The agreement was exempted subject to conditions.

Note that the MIF scheme in the Visa International case is not a 'classic' price-fixing agreement. The scheme does not set a price which is charged from a customer but establishes a remuneration mechanism between banks. Therefore although it restricted the freedom of the banks involved it did not result in subsequent restriction on competition. The scheme may be viewed as an example of a price-fixing mechanism which does not have as its object the restriction of competition. Note in this respect the discussion on page 59 above on the possibility of finding 'hard core' restriction as not having the object of restricting competition.

With respect to the third condition under Article 81(3) EC (indispensability), note that 'the decisive factor is whether or not the restrictive agreement and individual restrictions make it possible to perform the activity in question more efficiently than would likely have been the case in the absence of the agreement or the restriction concerned. The question is not whether in the absence of the restriction the agreement would not have been concluded, but whether more efficiencies are produced with the agreement or restriction than in the absence of the agreement or restriction. (para 74, Guidelines on Article 81(3))

With respect to the fourth condition under Article 81(3) EC (no elimination of competition), note that 'Whether competition is being eliminated within the meaning of the last condition of Article 81(3) depends on the degree of competition existing prior to the agreement and on the impact of the restrictive agreement on competition, i.e. the reduction in competition that the agreement brings about. The more competition is already weakened in the market concerned, the slighter the further reduction required for competition to be eliminated within the meaning of Article 81(3). Moreover, the greater the reduction of competition caused by the agreement, the greater the likelihood that competition in respect of a substantial part of the products concerned risks being eliminated. (para 107, Guidelines on Article 81(3))

GlaxoSmithKline Services Unlimited v Commission	**Article 81(3) EC**
Case T–168/01	Judicial Review
CFI, [2006] ECR II–2969 5 CMLR 29	Third Party Rights

Facts

GlaxoSmithKline (GSK) (formerly Glaxo Wellcome, SA (GW)), a producer of pharmaceutical products, notified the Commission of a selective distribution agreement. The Commission found Clause 4 of the agreement to have both the object and the effect of restricting competition by limiting parallel trade between Member States and rejected GW request for exemption under Article 81(3) EC. GSK appealed the decision, and contested the Commission's refusal to grant an exemption under Article 81(3) EC.

Held (on the scope of judicial review)

'In that regard, the Court dealing with an application for annulment of a decision applying Article 81(3) EC carries out, in so far as it is faced with complex economic assessments, a review confined, as regards the merits, to verifying whether the facts have been accurately stated, whether there has been any manifest error of appraisal and whether the legal consequences deduced from those facts were accurate (*Consten and Grundig v Commission*, [Joined Cases 56/64 etc, [1966] ECR 299], p 347; *Metro I*, [Case 26/76 ,[1977] ECR 1875], paragraph 25; *Remia and others v Commission*, [Case 42/84, [1985] ECR 2545], paragraph 34; and *Aalborg Portland and others v Commission*, [Joined Cases C–204/00 P etc, [2004] ECR I–123] paragraph 279).' (para 241)

'It is for the Court to establish not only whether the evidence relied on is factually accurate, reliable and consistent, but also whether it contains all the information which must be taken into account for the purpose of assessing a complex situation and whether it is capable of substantiating the conclusions drawn from it (Case C–12/03 P *Commission v Tetra Laval* [2005] ECR I–987, paragraph 39, and Case T–210/01 *General Electric v Commission* [2005] ECR II–5575, paragraphs 62 and 63).' (para 242)

'On the other hand, it is not for the Court to substitute its own economic assessment for that of the institution which adopted the decision the legality of which it is requested to review.' (para 243)

'The Commission has, in particular, a margin of discretion which is subject to a restricted judicial review, in the operation consisting, once it has been ascertained that one of the criteria on which Article 81(3) EC makes provision for an exemption was satisfied, in weighing up the advantages expected from the implementation of the agreement and the disadvantages which the agreement entails for the final consumer owing to its impact on competition, which takes the form of a balancing exercise carried out in the light of the general interest appraised at Community level.' (para 244)

'Furthermore, review of the Commission's decision is carried out solely by reference to the elements of fact and of law existing on the date of adoption of the contested decision, without prejudice to the possibility afforded to the parties, in the exercise of their rights of defence, to supplement them by evidence established after that date but for the specific purpose of contesting or defending that decision …' (para 245)

Comment

The Court adopted a non-interventionist approach and did not substitute its own economic assessment for that of the Commission. The Court noted especially the Commission's margin of discretion in weighing up the advantages and disadvantages which the agreement entails.

Note that, according to Regulation 1/2003, national competition authorities and national courts may exempt under Article 81(3) EC agreements, decisions and concerted practices caught by Article 81(1) EC. These decisions at the national level, when appealed, will be heard by the relevant appeal court within the national jurisdiction. One would expect to see a similar non-interventionist approach at the national level when judicial authorities review decisions of the national competition agency or lower courts concerning exemptions under Article 81(3) EC.

Under Article 230 of the Treaty, a natural or legal person may institute proceedings against a decision addressed to another person if the decision in question is of direct and individual concern to the former. In the context of Article 81(3) EC this provision opens the door to third parties who can contest the Commission's decision to clear an agreement under Article 81(3) EC. In Case 26/76 *Metro SB-Großmarkte GmbH & Co KG v Commission*, page 81 above, the court accepted an application for annulment of the Commission's decision granting exemption under Article 81(3) EC, from a third party (Metro) which was held to be directly and individually concerned by the contested Decision.

Similarly, in Case T–528/93 etc *Métropole Télévision SA and others v Commission*, [1996] ECR II–649, [1996] 5 CMLR 386, the court noted in para 60 that '… provisions of the Treaty concerning the right of interested persons to bring an action must not be interpreted restrictively, and hence, where the Treaty makes no provision, a limitation in that respect cannot be presumed to exist. Persons other than those to whom a decision is addressed may only claim to be individually concerned if that decision affects them by reason of certain attributes which are peculiar to them or by reason of circumstances in which they are differentiated from all other persons and by virtue of these factors distinguishes them individually just as in the case of the person addressed …' The court then concluded that 'Antena 3' and 'RTI' were individually concerned by the Decision within the meaning of Article 230 of the Treaty. (paras 61–5, 78)

4

Horizontal and Vertical Agreements

This chapter supplements Chapter 3 by providing a (non-exhaustive) review of different categories of agreements which may raise competitive concerns.

Horizontal Agreements

Horizontal agreements are those concluded between undertakings operating at the same level of production or distribution. These agreements may reduce competition when they involve price fixing, sharing of markets or other restrictions on business operations. They may also reduce competition when they involve softer forms of cooperation which increase the transparency in the market and reduce uncertainty concerning the competitors' conduct. On the other hand, they may at times yield substantial efficiencies and economic benefits, allowing companies to cope better with changing market realities, when they deal, for example, with research and development, production, purchasing, commercialisation, standardisation and environmental matters.

Cartel Agreements

The term 'cartel' usually refers to practices such as market sharing (Case IV/30.907), price fixing (Case C–199/92, 40/73, 2005/1071) and bid rigging (Case T–9/99) which have as their object the restriction of competition. When putting their case forward, competition authorities are not required to distinguish between agreements or concerted practice to establish the infringement (Case T–305/94) and may rely on the concept of single overall agreement to prove membership in the cartel (Case T–305/94, C–204/00, T–325/01). Undertakings that take part in cartel meetings may be responsible for the conduct of other cartel members (Case T 8/99). See:

With summary references to:

On the enforcement powers of the European Commission, the European leniency programme, administrative fines and the Commission's inspection powers, see Chapter 8 below.

Price Fixing

Price fixing shields cartel members from price competition and transfers wealth from consumers to the conspiring undertakings. Article 81(1) EC provides that agreements, decisions or concerted practices which have as their object or effect the direct or indirect fixing of price would be prohibited. The European courts and Commission have generally treated price-fixing arrangements as having the object of restricting competition (above, Case C–199/92, 40/73). Such arrangements may be caught in cases of indirect communication between undertakings (Case 2005/1071 etc) and would rarely benefit from exemption under Article 81(3) (Case COMP/29.373).

| 2005/1071 etc | *Argos, Littlewoods and others v Office of Fair Trading* | 98 |

With summary references to:

| 12/1981 | *Camera Care v Victor Hasselblad AB* | 99 |
| COMP/29.373 | *Visa International – Multilateral Interchange Fee* | 99 |

Market Sharing

Article 81(1) EC, subsections (b) and (c) specifically refer to the limitation or control of markets and the sharing of markets. Market sharing allows competitors to shield themselves from the pressures of competition by dividing the market between them, thereby allowing them to exercise a large degree of market power within their exclusive territory.

| IV/30.907 | *Peroxygen products* | 100 |

See also summary references to:

| COMP/37.978 | *Methylglucamine* | 100 |

Collusive Tendering

A system of tendering relies on the absence of coordination or communication between the bidders to achieve a competitive result in areas where it might otherwise be absent. When tenders submitted by bidders are not the result of individual economic calculation, but of knowledge of the submissions of the other participants, competition is prevented, or at least restricted. See:

| 1061/1/1/06 | *Makers UK Ltd v Office of Fair Trading* | 101 |

With summary reference to:

2005/1071 etc	*Argos, Littlewoods and others v Office of Fair Trading*	101
IV/26 918	*European Sugar Industry*	101
IV/35.691.E-4	*Pre-Insulated Pipe Cartel*	101

Horizontal Cooperation Agreements

By contrast to the anticompetitive horizontal agreements discussed above, it is important to note that horizontal agreements can lead to efficiency gains, allowing medium and small sized companies to achieve greater efficiencies and cope with dynamic markets. The European Commission published Guidelines on the Applicability of Article 81 of the EC Treaty to Horizontal Cooperation Agreements (Text with EEA relevance) [2001] OJ C 3/2. The Guidelines provide an analytical framework for the most common types of horizontal cooperation, ie agreements on research and development, production, purchasing, commercialisation, standardisation, and environmental matters.

Also note the two Block Exemption Regulations which cover specialization and research and development agreements:

- Commission Regulation (EC) No 2658/2000 on the Application of Article 81(3) of the Treaty to Categories of Specialisation Agreements, [2000] OJ L 304/3
- Commission Regulation (EC) No 2659/2000 on the Application of Article 81(3) of the Treaty to Categories of Research and Development Agreements, [2000] OJ L 304/7

Information Exchange Arrangements

Information exchange, even between competitors, may serve legitimate goals when it concerns, for example, general information, standardisation or developments of new technologies. 'The exchange of information may however have an adverse effect on competition where it serves to reduce or remove uncertainties inherent in the process of competition. … Whether or not exchange of information has an appreciable effect on competition will depend on the circumstances of each individual case: the market characteristics, the type of information and the way in which it is exchanged…' (see UK OFT Guidelines on Agreements and Concerted Practices, OFT 401, 3.17–3.23)

The following cases illustrate the Courts' and Commission's approach toward information exchange:

T–34/92	*Fiatagri UK Ltd and New Holland Ford Ltd v Commission*	102
T–35/92	*John Deere v Commission*	103
C–89/85	*A Ahlström Osakeyhtiö and others v Commission*	104

With summary reference to:

T–141/94	*Thyssen Stahl AG v Commission*	103
T–25/95	*Cimenteries CBR and others v Commission*	103
48/69	*Imperial Chemical Industries v Commission*	104

Vertical Agreements

Vertical agreements are agreements entered into between companies operating at different levels of the production or distribution chain. These agreements differ in their potential anticompetitive effect from horizontal agreements. Whereas the latter may eliminate competition between competing undertakings, the former concerns the relationship between upstream operator and downstream distributor or retailer. As a result, vertical agreements often generate positive effects and would raise concerns predominantly when there is some degree of market power at the upstream and/or down stream levels.

The Commission published detailed guidelines on the application of Article 81(1) and 81(3) to vertical agreements. See Commission Guidelines on Vertical Restraints [2000] OJ C 291/1 (the Vertical Guidelines).

Also note Commission Regulation (EC) No 2790/1999 on the Application of Article 81(3) of the Treaty to Categories of Vertical Agreements and Concerted Practices, [1999] OJ L 336/21 (the Vertical Block Exemption). The Vertical Block Exemption creates a presumption of legality for vertical agreements depending on the market share of the supplier or the buyer and the nature of the vertical restriction.

Export Bans

Distribution agreements which include restriction of export from one territory to another are generally regarded as having the object of restricting competition. The Vertical Block Exemption makes a direct reference to these restrictions in Article 4, treating them as hard-core restrictions which do not benefit from exemption. In line with this, export bans are unlikely to benefit from an individual exemption under Article 81(3) EC.

Note, however, that export bans have been held as having the object of restricting competition only when they deprive the final consumers of the advantages of competition (T–168/01). On export bans, see:

19/77	*Miller International Schallplatten GmbH v Commission*	105
31/85	*ETA Fabriques d'Ebauches v SA DK Investment and others*	107

With summary reference to:

56/64 etc	*Consten and Grundig v Commission*	105
C–279/87	*Tipp-Ex v Commission*	105
COMP/35.587	*PO Video Games (Nintendo)*	106
T–168/01	*GlaxoSmithKline Services Unlimited v Commission*	106
C–306/96	*Javico v Yves St Laurent*	106

Exclusive Distribution Agreements

Exclusive distribution agreements generally involve a supplier's commitment to sell his products to a single distributor in a designated territory, in return for a commitment from the distributor not to engage in active sales in other exclusively allocated territories. Such agreements are exempted by the Vertical Block Exemption when the supplier's market share does not exceed 30 per cent and the agreement does not include hard-core restrictions (Article 4, Vertical Block Exemption). When combined with selective distribution, these agreements are exempted if active selling in other territories is not restricted. On exclusive distribution agreements, see for example:

03/2005	*Sarl Kitch Moto v SA Suzuki France*	108

With summary reference to:

56/64 etc	*Consten and Grundig v Commission*	108
56/65	*Société Technique Minière v Maschinenbau Ulm GmbH*	108

On the analysis of exclusive distribution agreements see also paragraphs 161–83, Vertical Guidelines.

Selective Distribution Agreements

Selective distribution agreements restrict the number of distributors by applying selection criteria for admission as an authorised distributor. These systems are commonly used to maintain a specialist distribution chain capable of providing specific services to branded high-quality or high-technology products. Purely qualitative selective distribution systems are in general considered to fall outside Article 81(1) for lack of anticompetitive effects (Case 26/76). Both qualitative and quantitative selective distribution systems are exempted by the Vertical Block Exemption when the supplier's market share does not exceed 30 percent, provided that active selling by the authorised distributors to each other and to end users is not restricted. On selective distribution systems, see:

With summary reference to:

On the analysis of selective distribution agreements see also paras 184–98, Vertical Guidelines.

Single Branding Agreements

A non-compete arrangement is based on an obligation of a buyer to purchase all or most of his requirements of particular group of products from one supplier. These agreements are exempted under the Vertical Block Exemption when the supplier's market share does not exceed 30 per cent and subject to a limitation in time of five years for the non-compete obligation.

With summary references to:

On the analysis of single barnding agreements see also paras 138–60, Vertical Guidelines.

Franchise Agreements

A franchise agreement allows the franchisor to expand his brand without investing its own capital and allows the franchisee to benefit from the reputation and experience of the franchisor. Under a franchise agreement, the franchisor which has established itself on a given market licenses trade marks, business systems and know-how to independent traders (franchisee) in exchange for a fee. On the analysis of these agreements under Article 81 EC, see:

With summary reference to:

On the analysis of franchise agreements see also paragraphs 199–201, Vertical Guidelines.

Resale Price Maintenance

Restriction of the buyer's ability to determine its sale price is generally regarded as having the object of restricting competition. Such restriction on pricing policies should be distinguished from recommended and maximum resale prices which may have the effect of restricting competition but are not considered as having the object of restricting competition.

The Vertical Block Exemption includes within its black list restrictions of the buyer's ability to determine the sale price (Article 4(a)). Note, however, the different approach to resale price maintainance in the United States (06–480).

243/85	*SA Binon & Cie v SA Agence et Messageries de la Presse*	115

See also summary references to:

161/84	*Pronuptia de Paris GmbH v Pronuptia de Paris Irmgard Schillgallis*	116
26/76	*Metro SB-Großmarkte GmbH & Co KG v Commission*	116
IV/30.658	*Polistil/Arbois*	116
06–480	*Leegin Creative Leather Products, Inc v PSKS, Inc*	116

On resale price maintenance note also paragraphs 225–8, Vertical Guidelines.

Agency Agreements

An agent is vested with the power to negotiate and conclude an agreement on behalf of the principal. Agreements entered into between an agent and its principal will not be subjected to the prohibitions laid down under Article 81(1) EC where an agent, although having separate legal personality, does not independently determine his own conduct on the market, but carries out the instructions given to him by his principal. In such circumstances the agreement between the two parties will not amount to an agreement between undertakings. See:

T–325/01	*DaimlerChrysler AG v Commission*	117

See also summary references to:

40/73 etc	*Suiker Unie and others v Commission*	118
C–266/93	*Bundeskartellamt v Volkswagen AG and VAG Leasing GmbH*	118

On agency agreements note also paragraphs 12–20, Vertical Guidelines.

Tate & Lyle plc and others v Commission	**Horizontal Agreements**
Joined Cases T 02, 204, 207/98	Cartel Agreement
CFI, [2001] ECR II–2035, [2001] 5 CMLR 22	

Facts

Application for annulment of Commission decision in which it found a number of undertakings which took part in various meetings with other sugar producers to infringe of Article 81(1) EC by engaging in anti-competitive agreements or concerted practice on the industrial and retail sugar markets. (Case IV/F-3/33.708 *British Sugar plc*, Case IV/F-3/33.709 *Tate & Lyle plc*, Case IV/F-3/33.710 *Napier Brown & Company Ltd*, Case IV/F-3/33.711 *James Budgett Sugars Ltd*) ([1999] OJ L 76/1).

Held

The undertakings involved do not deny their participation in meetings but challenge the Commission finding that such meetings had an anticompetitive purpose. In particular they argue that the nature of the Community sugar market and the Community sugar scheme do not allow producers the freedom to determine themselves the price of products. This argument cannot be accepted. Price competition is still possible between the minimum price offered by the Community sugar scheme and the prices decided upon by the undertakings. The Commission was therefore right to take the view that the purpose of those meetings was to restrict competition by the coordination of pricing policies. (paras 42–3)

'… the fact that only one of the participants at the meetings in question reveals its intentions is not sufficient to exclude the possibility of an agreement or concerted practice. The criteria of coordination and cooperation laid down by the case-law on restrictive practices, far from requiring the working out of an actual plan, must be understood in the light of the concept inherent in the provisions of the Treaty relating to competition that each economic operator must determine independently the policy which he intends to adopt on the common market (40/73 etc *Suiker Unie* [1975] ECR 1663, paragraph 173).' (paras 54, 55)

'Although it is correct to say that that requirement of independence does not deprive economic operators of the right to adapt intelligently to the existing and anticipated conduct of their competitors, it does however strictly preclude any direct or indirect contact between such operators, the object or effect whereof is either to influence the conduct on the market of an actual or potential competitor or to disclose to such a competitor the course of conduct which they themselves have decided to adopt or contemplate adopting on the market (*Suiker Unie*, paragraph 174).' (paras 56)

'In the present case, it is undisputed that there were direct contacts between the three applicants, whereby British Sugar informed its competitors, Tate & Lyle and Napier Brown, of the conduct which it intended to adopt on the sugar market in Great Britain. In Case T–1 /89 *Rhône-Poulenc v Commission* [1991] ECR II–867, in which the applicant had been accused of taking part in meetings at which information was exchanged amongst competitors concerning, inter alia, the prices which they intended to adopt on the market, the Court of First Instance held that an undertaking, by its participation in a meeting with an anti-competitive purpose, not only pursued the aim of eliminating in advance uncertainty about the future conduct of its competitors but could not fail to take into account, directly or indirectly, the information obtained in the course of those meetings in order to determine the policy which it intended to pursue on the market (*Rhône-Poulenc*, paragraphs 122 and 123). This Court considers that that conclusion also applies where, as in this case, the participation of one or more undertakings in meetings with an anti-competitive purpose is limited to the mere receipt of information concerning the future conduct of their market competitors.' (paras 57, 58)

Comment

Note para 58 in which the CFI condemned not only the exchange of information but also the receipt of information in a meeting, as both have the same impact of eliminating in advance uncertainty about the competitors future conduct. See also Case T–8/99 and commentary on pages 96 and 97 below.

Sigma Tecnologie di Rivestimento Srl v Commission	**Horizontal Agreements**
Case T–28/99	Cartel Agreement
CFI, [2002] ECR II–1845	

Facts

An application for annulment of Commission decision in Case No IV/35.691/E-4 *Pre-Insulated Pipe* Cartel ([1999] OJ L 24/1) in which the Commission found that various undertakings and, in particular, Sigma Tecnologie di Rivestimento Srl (STR), had participated in a European-wide cartel agreement, fixed quotes and shared with others the market for heating pipes. In addition the Commission found that STR had participated in an Italian cartel in which members fixed quotes between them. STR contested the findings and argued, among other things, that it did not take part in all the cartel meetings and did not know of or take part in the European cartel agreements.

Held

'It is settled case-law that an undertaking which has participated in a multiform infringement of the competition rules by its own conduct, which met the definition of an agreement or concerted practice having an anti-competitive object within the meaning of [Article 81(1) EC] and was intended to help bring about the infringement as a whole, may also be responsible for the conduct of other undertakings followed in the context of the same infringement throughout the period of its participation in the infringement, where it is proved that the undertaking in question was aware of the unlawful conduct of the other participants, or could reasonably foresee such conduct, and was prepared to accept the risk (Case C–49/92 P *Commission v Anic Partecipazioni* [1999] ECR I–4125, paragraph 203).' (para 40)

The Commission established that STR participated in cartel meetings concerning the Italian market. Since STR accepts that it participated, at least in some of the cartels meetings, it must be concluded that the Commission properly established its participation in an agreement on the Italian market. (paras 41 3)

'However, the Commission did not show that [STR], when participating in the agreement on the Italian market, was aware of the anti-competitive conduct at the European level of the other undertakings, or that it could reasonably have foreseen such conduct.' (para 44)

'The mere fact that there is identity of object between an agreement in which an undertaking participated and a global cartel does not suffice to render that undertaking responsible for the global cartel. It is only if the undertaking knew or should have known when it participated in the cartel that in doing so it was joining in the global cartel that its participation in the agreement concerned can constitute the expression of its accession to that global cartel.' (para 45)

'It follows from all the foregoing that the Commission has failed to adduce evidence sufficiently precise and consistent to found the firm conviction that [STR] knew or should have known that by participating in the agreement on the Italian market it was joining the European cartel. Accordingly, the decision must be annulled in so far as the applicant is alleged, in addition to participating in an agreement on the Italian market, to have participated in the cartel covering the whole of the common market.' (paras 51, 52)

Comment

In C–204/00 etc *Aalborg Portland A/S and others v Commission* the ECJ held that to prove membership in a cartel, 'it is sufficient for the Commission to show that the undertaking concerned participated in meetings at which anti-competitive agreements were concluded, without manifestly opposing them, to prove to the requisite standard that the undertaking participated in the cartel. Where participation in such meetings has been established, it is for that undertaking to put forward evidence to establish that its participation in those meetings was without any anti-competitive intention by demonstrating that it had indicated to its competitors that it was participating in those meetings in a spirit that was different from theirs (see Case C–199/92 P

Huls v Commission [1999] ECR I–4287, paragraph 155, and Case C–49/92 P *Commission v Anic* [1999] ECR I–4125, paragraph 96).' (para 81) For detailed analysis of this case see page 51 above, Chapter 3.

In Joined Cases T–305/94 etc, *LVM and others v Commission*, the CFI held that in the context of a complex cartel infringement which involves many producers seeking over a number of years to regulate the market between them the Commission is not expected to classify the infringement precisely, as an agreement or concerted practice and is entitled to classify that type of complex infringement as an agreement 'and/or' concerted practice. The CFI also held that 'An undertaking may be held responsible for an overall cartel even though it is shown to have participated directly only in one or some of its constituent elements if it is shown that it knew, or must have known, that the collusion in which it participated, especially by means of regular meetings organised over several years, was part of an overall plan intended to distort competition and that the overall plan included all the constituent elements of the cartel.' For detailed analysis of this case see pages 52, 53 above, Chapter 3.

In T–325/01 *Daimler Chrysler AG v Commission* the CFI held that where it has been established that an undertaking has participated in cartel meetings 'it is for that undertaking to put forward evidence to establish that its participation in those meetings was without any anti-competitive intention, by demonstrating that it had indicated to its competitors that it was participating in those meetings in a spirit that was different from theirs. … In the absence of evidence of that distancing, the fact that an undertaking does not abide by the outcome of those meetings is not such as to relieve it of full responsibility for the fact that it participated in the concerted practice (Case T–347/94 *MayrMelnhof v Commission* [1998] ECR II–1751, paragraph 135, and Joined Cases T–25/95, […] *Cimenteries CBR and others v Commission* [2000] ECR II–491, paragraph 1389).' (para 202). For detailed analysis of this case see page 54 above, Chapter 3.

In Case C–199/92 *Hüls AG v Commission* the ECJ considered the Commission's Polypropylene decision (IV/31.149 – *Polypropylene*) in which it found Hüls AG to have infringed Article 81(1) EC by participating with other undertakings in an agreement and concerted practice aimed at coordinating their commercial practices and fixing the prices of polypropylene. For detailed analysis of this case, see page 49 above, Chapter 3.

In Case 40/73 etc *Suiker Unie and others v Commission*, the ECJ considered a Commission decision (IV/26.918 – *European sugar industry*) finding a number of undertakings to collude in the market for sugar by aligning prices, control deliveries of sugar and applying other limitations on sales. For detailed analysis of this case, see page 46 above, Chapter 3.

Argos, Littlewoods and others v Office of Fair Trading	**Horizontal Agreements**
Case No 2005/1071, 1074 and 1623	Price Fixing
Court of Appeal, [2006] EWCA Civ 1318	Indirect Price Fixing

Facts

The appeals arose of two distinct investigations by the UK Office of Fair Trading (OFT) under the UK Competition Act 1998. In the first decision the OFT found a price-fixing agreement in the toys and games market between Hasbro UK Ltd, Argos Ltd and Littlewoods Ltd. In the second decision the OFT found that a number of companies fixed the prices of replica football kits. Both decisions were appealed (separately) to the UK Competition Appeal Tribunal (the Tribunal) (Football Shirts decision, Toys and Games decision). The Tribunal's decisions were appealed to the Court of Appeal (CA). In both cases the appellants challenged the OFT and Tribunal holding that there was a horizontal agreement between competitors (the appellants accepted the OFT's finding of an anticompetitive vertical agreement).

The CA judgment is long and detailed, not least as it concerns two different sets of facts. The analysis includes very interesting comments on indirect price fixing. Extracts of the analysis concerning the football shirt cartel are given below.

Held

'Although the concept of a concerted practice implies the existence of reciprocal contacts, that requirement may be met where one competitor discloses its future intentions or conduct on the market to another when the latter requests it or, at the very least, accepts it …' (para 21(V))

'It is not in dispute that there could be a trilateral or multilateral agreement or concerted practice between two or more customers and their common supplier, nor that this might come about by virtue of indirect contact between the customers via that supplier. Equally it is clear that there could be a series of bilateral vertical agreements between one supplier and several of its customers, none of the customers being aware of the fact or nature of the agreements between the supplier and other customers, such that there would be no horizontal element to the customers' agreements. If, on the other hand, each customer did know of the other agreements, it could be equivalent to a multilateral agreement between the supplier and each of the customers.' (para 31)

'… Mr Lasok QC, for JJB, criticised as too general paragraph 664 of the [Tribunal] judgment, as follows: "The cases about complaints cited above, notably *Suiker Unie* … and the Commission's decision in *Hasselblad* …, show that if a competitor (A) complains to a supplier (B) about the market activities of another competitor (C), and the supplier B acts on A's complaint in a way which limits the competitive activity of C, then A, B and C are all parties to a concerted practice to prevent, restrict or distort competition. We can see the sense of that case law. Were it otherwise, established customers would always be able to exert pressure on suppliers not to supply new and more competitive outlets, free of any risk of infringing the Chapter I prohibition. A competitor who complains to a supplier about the activities of another competitor should not in our view be absolved of responsibility under the Act if the supplier chooses to act on the complaint."' (para 33)

'Mr Lasok submitted that the law as to complaints does not permit a conclusion that, merely by complaining, the complainer is party to an agreement or concerted practice with the undertaking to which the complaint is made, let alone with the party complained about. Of course there is and could be no general rule on the point. There can be complaints of all sorts, by no means all of which are made in the expectation that anything will be done about the matter complained about, still less something that might amount to a breach of the Chapter I prohibition. In the present case, however, as the Tribunal pointed out at paragraph 667, the complaints were vigorous and repeated, they were made at the highest levels, and they were backed up by an implicit threat arising from the strength of JJB's commercial position in relation to Umbro.' (para 72)

'Mr Lasok submitted that, for an undertaking to be involved in an anti-competitive arrangement reached between others, it must know of the arrangement, not merely of the possibility that there might be such an arrangement. He cited passages from the judgment of the CFI in *Cimenteries v Commission*, Cases T–25/95 etc [2000] ECR II–491 for this proposition, where the CFI considered whether one undertaking … was aware that the others with whom it was dealing were themselves part of a much wider and more serious agreement or concerted practice, and concluded that it was not, and was therefore not to be penalised on the basis that it was a participant in the more serious breach of Article 81.' (para 87) 'In general that is no doubt the case, but it seems to us that, where the first undertaking, in effect, asks the second to do something in relation to a third which would be an anti-competitive agreement or concerted practice, and the second does do so, the first cannot rely on the fact that it may not have known whether the second and third did enter into such an agreement or concerted practice in order to assert that it was not involved as a participant in what they did. No doubt Umbro's staff did not perceive JJB's conduct as "asking" Umbro to act in relation to Sports Soccer, but it did amount to a particularly forceful form of request or demand.' (para 88)

'… we do not need to decide, in the context of the Football Shirts appeal, whether Mr Lasok's criticism of paragraph 659 of the Tribunal's judgment … is justified. But it does seem to us that the Tribunal may have gone too far, in that paragraph, insofar as it suggests that if one retailer (A) privately discloses to a supplier (B) its future pricing intentions "in circumstances where it is reasonably foreseeable that B might make use of that information to influence market conditions" and B then passes that pricing information on to a competing retailer (C) then A, B and C are all to be regarded as parties to a concerted practice having as its object or effect the prevention, restriction or distortion of competition. The Tribunal may have gone too far if it intended that suggestion to extend to cases in which A did not, in fact, foresee that B would make use of the pricing information to influence market conditions or in which C did not, in fact, appreciate that the information was being passed to him with A's concurrence . This is not such a case on the facts.' (para 91)

'… the Tribunal was entitled to find that (1) JJB provided confidential price information to Umbro in circumstances in which it was obvious that it would or might be passed on to Sports Soccer in support of Umbro' s attempt to persuade Sports Soccer to raise its prices … (2) Umbro did use the information in relation to Sports Soccer in that way, (3) Sports Soccer did agree to raise its prices in reliance on this information … and (4) Umbro did tell JJB of this, thereby making it clear to JJB that it would be able to maintain its prices at their current level, as it did. It also seems to us that the Tribunal was right to hold that this sequence of events amounted to a concerted practice … whereby the two retailers coordinated their conduct on the market in such a way as, knowingly, to substitute practical cooperation between them for the risks of competition …' (paras 102, 103)

Comment

Indirect communication in which a retailer discloses commercial information to its supplier with the intention that this information will be communicated to its competitor would amount to concerted practice when the competitor acted on that information. On the other hand, communication between retailer and supplier on commercial information which is not intended to be passed to the competitor, does not amount to concerted practice. The same would apply to a complaint to a supplier concerning business terms.

In paragraph 91 of the judgment the CA held that in order to prove concerted practice one must show that the retailer foresaw that the supplier would make use of the information to influence market conditions and that the competitor appreciated that the information was being passed to him with the retailer's concurrence.

In paragraphs 72–80 the CA referred to the facts in *Camera Care v Victor Hasselblad AB* [1982] CMLR 233, [1984] ECR 883, there, the Commission found undertakings to rely on a complaint mechanism to affect their actions on the market. This enabled the undertakings involved to indirectly raise concerns regarding the sales by other undertakings in some territories and obtain their commitment to withdraw from those markets.

Note generally Case No COMP/29.373 *Visa International – Multilateral Interchange Fee*, where a banking system which restricted the freedom of banks to decide their own pricing policies was exempted under Article 81(3) EC (page 85 above). More generally, note the example of price fixing on page 96 above.

Peroxygen products	**Horizontal Agreements**
IV/30.907	Market Sharing
European Commission, [1985] OJ L 35/1	

Facts

A Commission investigation into the 'hydrogen peroxide and sodium perborate' market led to a finding of several anticompetitive agreements or concerted practices between several undertakings under which they agreed that each national market was to be reserved for those producers which manufacture inside the territory in question (the 'home market rule').

Decision

'The EEC markets for both hydrogen peroxide and sodium perborate are strictly divided on national lines. Each producer limits its sales to end-users in those Member States where it possesses production facilities. … The strict separation of the national markets and the absence of intra-Community exchanges is all the more remarkable given the very considerable price differences, particularly as between France and the neighbouring Member States.' (para 10) 'A similar market division is apparent in sodium perborate …' (para 11)

'The Commission does not accept that the strict market separation on national lines, which is a characteristic of both the hydrogen peroxide and sodium perborate sectors in the EEC, results from natural market forces or the independent commercial judgment of the producers. It considers that the market separation is the result of an arrangement or understanding of long duration (from at least 1961) between the producers, originally based on an acceptance of the "home market principle", i.e. that the national markets would be reserved for domestic producers …' (para 23)

'It is not necessary, for the establishment of a concerted practice, for the parties to have agreed a precise or detailed plan in advance. … The criteria of coordination and cooperation laid down in the case law of the Court must be understood in the light of the concept inherent in the provisions of the Treaty relating to competition that each economic operator must determine independently the policy which he intends to adopt on the common market. … The documents show that the decision by each producer of its markets and customers was not the subject of independent commercial judgment. The "home market rule" is expressly and consistently mentioned as the basis on which they conducted their activities …' (para 45)

'The overall market division and sharing arrangement, and the individual agreements covering particular geographical areas and products, together regulate almost all trade in the products concerned in a major part of the common market, and involved all the principal producers in the European market for a major industrial sector. The "home market" arrangement … delineated the territories in which each producer was to supply and consolidated the established positions of those producers to the detriment of effective freedom of movement in the common market …' (para 50)

'The complex of arrangements made on a European (and world) level between the major producers of peroxygen products had the effect of excluding virtually all trade between Member States except through channels subject to control by restrictive agreement …' (para 51)

Comment

In the EU, market sharing raises concerns not only due to its anticompetitive effects but also as it undermines the goal of achieving market integration.

Note the Commission decision in Case COMP/E-2/37.978/*Methylglucamine*, [2004] OJ L 38/18, where the Commission exposed a cartel between producers of methylglucamine, which lasted nine years and eliminated competition through market sharing and price fixing.

Makers UK Ltd v Office of Fair Trading	**Horizontal Agreements**
Case No 1061/1/1/06	Collusive Tendering
The Competition Appeal Tribunal, [2007] CAT 11	Price Fixing

Facts

Makers UK Limited (Makers) appealed to the Tribunal against the Office of Fair Trading (OFT) Decision in which various roofing contractors, including Makers, were found to collude in the making of bids tendered for flat-roof and car-park surfacing contracts. The collusion at issue was that of 'cover bidding' which occurs when a contractor that is not intending to win the contract submits a price for it after communicating and agreeing the price with the designated winner. The OFT's case against Makers, rested on the fact that the figures submitted in Makers' tender bid were identical to figures submitted by another undertaking (Asphaltic). Makers argued that it had made speculative contacts with Asphaltic and requested a subcontractor quotation. Accordingly, it asserted that the figures used in its bid did not amount to collusive tendering but rather constituted a quotation from Asphaltic for carrying out the work as a subcontractor.

Held

'… Cover pricing gives the impression of competitive bidding but, in reality, contractors agree to submit token bids that are higher than the bid of the contractor that is seeking the cover. The issue in this case is whether Makers had been involved in cover pricing with either or both of Asphaltic and Rock.' (para 14)

'… In *Apex Asphalt and Paving Co Limited v Office of Fair Trading* [2005] CAT 4 ("Apex"), the Tribunal noted that when an undertaking (which for whatever reason does not wish to win the tender) opts to put in a cover bid rather than declining to bid, it deprives a bidder with the genuine intention to win the tender of the opportunity to take its place and put in a competitive bid. The CAT said: "the tendering process provides for the tenderee to receive independent bids following the acceptance of an invitation to tender, alternatively for the invited tenderer to decline the invitation to bid so that the tenderee has the opportunity to replace that undertaking with another competitor. … The effect of the conduct … was to deprive the tenderee of a similar opportunity. In this respect also the concerted practice has as its object or effect the prevention, restriction or distortion of competition."' (para 15)

The burden of proof in this case lies on the OFT and the standard of proof is the balance of probabilities, taking into account the gravity of what is alleged. The Tribunal has to consider whether the evidence before it provides a "plausible" explanation for the events other than collusion. (paras 45–50)

Maker failed to provide a plausible explanation for the identical bid. Its explanation regarding the sub contractor quote lacks commercial sense. 'We agree with the inference drawn by the OFT that Maker knew when they incorporated the figures into their own bid to AKS, that the figures represented a cover price for another bidder …' Even if Makers' explanation was true, Makers submitted a bid which was influenced by the figures provided by Asphaltic and thus infringed the Chapter I prohibition. (paras 93, 54–110)

Comment

In paragraphs 99–100, the Tribunal distinguished between this case and *Argos & Littlewoods* (page 98 above) where an undertaking operating at the retail level of the market disclosed information to an undertaking operating at the supplier level of the market, followed by the subsequent disclosure of that information by that supplier to a different retailer.

Note the Commission's decision in IV/26 918 – *European Sugar Industry*, [1973] OJ L 140/17, where the Commission noted that in a system of tendering, competition is of the essence and that it would be restricted if tenders were not the result of individual economic calculation. Also note Commission decision Case No IV/35.691.E-4 *Pre-Insulated Pipe Cartel* in which several producers of heating pipes were found to have participated in a cartel involved price fixing, market sharing and bid-rigging arrangements, [1999] OJ L 24/1.

Fiatagri UK Ltd and New Holland Ford Ltd v Commission	**Horizontal Agreements**
Case T–34/92	Information Exchange
CFI, [1994] ECR II–905	

Facts

The UK Agricultural Engineers Trade Association (AEA) notified to the Commission an information exchange agreement concerning data on the registrations of agricultural tractors. In its decision the Commission held that the agreement, which was open to all and not confined to members of the AEA, infringed Article 81 EC as it facilitated exchange of information identifying sales of individual competitors, as well as information on dealer sales and imports of own products. The decision in this case was the first one in which the Commission prohibited an information exchange system which did not directly concern prices or underpin any other anti-competitive arrangement (IV/31.370 and 31.446 – *UK Agricultural Tractor Registration Exchange*, [1992] OJ L 68/19). An appeal to the CFI.

Held

'As the applicants correctly argue, in a truly competitive market transparency between traders is in principle likely to lead to the intensification of competition between suppliers, since in such a situation the fact that a trader takes into account information made available to him in order to adjust his conduct on the market is not likely, having regard to the atomized nature of the supply, to reduce or remove for the other traders any uncertainty about the foreseeable nature of its competitors' conduct. On the other hand, the Court considers that, as the Commission argues this time, general use, as between main suppliers, of exchanges of precise information at short intervals, identifying registered vehicles and the place of their registration is, on a highly concentrated oligopolistic market such as the market in question … and on which competition is as a result already greatly reduced and exchange of information facilitated, likely to impair considerably the competition which exists between traders. In such circumstances, the sharing, on a regular and frequent basis, of information concerning the operation of the market has the effect of periodically revealing to all the competitors the market positions and strategies of the various individual competitors.' (para 91)

The exchange of information presupposes an agreement or tacit agreement, between the traders to define the boundaries of dealer sales territories by reference to the United Kingdom postcode system, as well as a framework for information exchange between traders through the trade association to which they belong. The information agreement is also disadvantageous for a trader wishing to penetrate the United Kingdom agricultural tractor market. If the trader does not join the information exchange agreement it will not benefit from the information and market knowledge which is available to its competitors under the information exchange. On the other hand, if it decides to become a member of the agreement, its business strategy is then immediately revealed to all its competitors by means of the information which they receive. (para 92)

'It follows that the applicants are wrong in arguing that the information exchange agreement at issue is likely to intensify competition on the market and that the Commission has not established to the requisite legal standard the anti-competitive nature of the agreement at issue. The fact that the Commission is not able to demonstrate the existence of an actual effect on the market … has no bearing on the outcome of this case since [Article 81(1) EC] prohibits both actual anti-competitive effects and purely potential effects, provided that these are sufficiently appreciable, as they are in this case, having regard to the characteristics of the market as described above.' (para 93)

Comment

See the comments below in Case T–35/92 *John Deere Ltd v Commission* which dealt with the same information exchange arrangement (page 103).

John Deere Ltd v Commission	**Horizontal Agreements**
Case T–35/92	Information Exchange
CFI, [1994] ECR II–957	

Facts

The UK Agricultural Engineers Trade Association (AEA) notified to the Commission an agreement relating to an information system based on data held by the United Kingdom Department of Transport relating to registrations of agricultural tractors, called the 'UK Agricultural Tractor Registration Exchange'. Membership of the notified agreement was open to all manufacturers or importers of agricultural tractors in the United Kingdom, whether or not they are members of the AEA. The AEA provides the secretariat for the agreement. In its decision the Commission held that the agreement infringed Article 81 EC as it facilitated exchange of information identifying sales of individual competitors, as well as information on dealer sales. The Commission refused to grant exemption under Article 81(3).

This is the same information agreement considered by the CFI in Case T–34/92 *Fiatagri UK Ltd and New Holland Ford Ltd v Commission* (*Fiatagri*) (above, page 102). The CFI analysis in paragraphs 51 and 52 of this decision is identical to its analysis in paragraphs 91 and 92 in *Fiatagri* and is therefore not repeated below.

Held

'… with regard to the type of information exchanged, the Court considers that, contrary to the applicant's contention, the information concerned, which relates in particular to sales made in the territory of each of the dealerships in the distribution network, is in the nature of business secrets. Indeed, this is admitted by the members of the agreement themselves, who strictly defined the conditions under which the information received could be disseminated to third parties, especially to members of their distribution network. The Court also observes that, as stated above (in paragraph 51), having regard to its frequency and systematic nature, the exchange of information in question makes the conduct of a given trader's competitors all the more foreseeable for it in view of the characteristics of the relevant market as analyzed above, since it reduces, or even removes, the degree of uncertainty regarding the operation of the market, which would have existed in the absence of such an exchange of information, and in this regard the applicant cannot profitably rely on the fact that the information exchanged does not concern prices or relate to past sales. Accordingly, the first part of the plea, to the effect that there is no restriction of competition as a result of alleged "prevention of hidden competition", must be dismissed.' (para 81)

Comment

Note case T–141/94 *Thyssen Stahl AG v Commission*, [1999] ECR II–347, where the CFI held that it is not necessary, to demonstrate that exchanges of information led to a specific result or were put into effect on the market in order to establish the existence of concerted practice. (CFI judgment upheld on appeal in Case C–194/99 P)

Note Case T–25/95 *Cimenteries CBR and others v Commission*, [2000] ECR II–491, [2000] 5 CMLR 204, where the CFI considered that exchange of price information has as its object the restriction of competition. (para 1531)

'Whether or not exchange of information has an appreciable effect on competition will depend on the circumstances of each individual case: the market characteristics, the type of information and the way in which it is exchanged.' See the OFT Guidelines (401) on Agreements and Concerted Practices which consider the pro and anticompetitive effects of information exchange. (paras 3.17–3.23)

Ahlström Osakeyhtiö and others v Commission	**Horizontal Agreements**
Joined Cases C–89, 104, 114, 116, 117, 125, 129/85	Information Exchange
ECJ, [1993] ECR I–1307, [1993] 4 CMLR 407	Price Announcements

Facts

The Commission found forty wood pulp producers and three of their trade associations to have infringed Article 81 EC by forming a price-fixing cartel. The market for pulp was characterised by long-term supply contracts and by 'quarterly price announcements' by which producers communicated to their customers the prices of pulp.

According to the Commission's hypothesis, the system of quarterly price announcements constitutes in itself the infringement of Article 81 EC and was deliberately introduced by the pulp producers in order to enable them to ascertain the prices charged by their competitors in the following quarters. The disclosure of prices to third parties well before their application at the beginning of a new quarter had the effect of making the market artificially transparent and gave the producers sufficient time to adjust their own prices before that quarter and to apply them from the commencement of that quarter. In addition the Commission put forward a second hypothesis according to which the system of price announcements constitutes evidence of concentration.

Held

'According to the Court's judgment in *Suiker Unie* … a concerted practice refers to a form of coordination between undertakings which, without having been taken to the stage where an agreement properly so-called has been concluded, knowingly substitutes for the risks of competition practical cooperation between them. … the Court added that the criteria of coordination and cooperation must be understood in the light of the concept inherent in the provisions of the Treaty relating to competition that each economic operator must determine independently the policy which he intends to adopt on the Common Market.' (para 63)

'In this case, the communications arise from the price announcements made to users. They constitute in themselves market behaviour which does not lessen each undertaking's uncertainty as to the future attitude of its competitors. At the time when each undertaking engages in such behaviour, it cannot be sure of the future conduct of the others.' (para 64)

'Accordingly, the system of quarterly price announcements on the pulp market is not to be regarded as constituting in itself an infringement of [Article 81(1) EC].' (para 65)

As for the Commission's second hypothesis; in this case, the system of price announcements does not provide sufficient evidence of concentration as such concentration is not the only plausible explanation for the parallel conduct of the undertakings. (paras 66–126)

Comment

On price announcements note Case 48/69 *Imperial Chemical Industries v Commission* where the Court held that advance price announcements eliminated all uncertainty between the undertakings as to their future conduct and, in doing so, also eliminated a large part of the risk usually inherent in any independent change of conduct on one or several markets. For detailed analysis of this case see page 45 above.

'The exchange of information on prices may lead to price co-ordination and therefore diminish competition which would otherwise be present between the undertakings. This will be the case whether the information exchanged relates directly to the prices charged or to the elements of a pricing policy, for example discounts, costs, terms of trade and rates and dates of change. The more recent or current the information exchanged, the more likely it is that exchange will have an appreciable effect on competition …' (OFT Guidelines (401) on Agreements and Concerted Practices, paras 3.20–3.21)

Miller International Schallplatten GmbH v Commission	**Vertical Agreements**
Case 19/77	Export Ban
ECJ, [1978] ECR 131, [1978] 2 CMLR 334	

Facts

Miller International Schallplatten GmbH (Miller) produced sound recordings (records, cassettes and tapes) which were sold chiefly on the German market. As part of its distribution strategy, Miller required its distributors to refrain from exporting its products outside their allocated territory. These restrictions allowed Miller to charge its German customers prices differing sharply from the export prices, the latter being lower than the prices charged to wholesalers and department stores.

Held

'... by its very nature, a clause prohibiting exports constitutes a restriction on competition, whether it is adopted at the instigation of the supplier or of the customer since the agreed purpose of the contracting parties is the endeavour to isolate a part of the market. Thus the fact that the supplier is not strict in enforcing such prohibitions cannot establish that they had no effect since their very existence may create a "visual and psychological" background which satisfies customers and contributes to a more or less rigorous division of the markets. The market strategy adopted by a producer is frequently adapted to the more or less general preferences of his customers ...' (para 7)

'... Miller continues to maintain that neither its German customers nor its exporters or foreign customers were interested in intra-Community trade, so that the prohibitions on exports did not interfere with their freedom of competition. Furthermore, the higher prices charged to resellers resident in the Federal Republic of Germany in themselves rendered exports to the other Member States unprofitable.' (para 13)

'Arguments based on the current situation cannot sufficiently establish that clauses prohibiting exports are not such as to affect trade between Member States. Furthermore, as has already been observed above, the fact that resellers, as customers of the applicant, prefer to limit their commercial operations to more restricted markets, whether regional or national, cannot justify the formal adoption of clauses prohibiting exports, either in particular contracts or in conditions of sale, any more than the desire of the producer to wall off sections of the common market. Finally, the existence of the clauses in dispute has at least assisted Miller in maintaining its policy of lowering export prices.' (para 14)

Comment

The export ban was regarded as an activity which by its very nature constituted a restriction on competition. Subsequently, the analysis did not include an examination of the market and the effects the provisions have on competition.

In Case 56/64 etc *Consten & Grundig v Commission* the ECJ held that 'an agreement between producer and distributor which might tend to restore the national divisions in trade between Member States might be such as to frustrate the most fundamental objections of the Community' (p. 340). The agreement in this case lead to absolute territorial protection and was found to have the object of restricting competition. For a full analysis of this case see page 56 above, Chapter 3.

Note also Case C–279/87 *Tipp-Ex v Commission* [1990] ECR I–261, where the court held that 'the absolute territorial protection granted to a distributor under an exclusive distribution agreement, designed to enable parallel imports to be controlled and hindered, leads to separate national markets being maintained artificially, contrary to the Treaty, and is therefore such as to infringe Article 81 EC.' This case, together with Case 19/77 *Miller v Commission*, were referred to in Case C–306/96 *Javico v Yves St Laurent* [1998] ECR I–1983 to support a conclusion that an 'agreement which requires a reseller not to resell contractual products outside the contractual territory has as its object the exclusion of parallel imports within the Community and consequently restriction of competition in the common market'. (para 14)

In case COMP/35.587 PO *Video Games (Nintendo)* [2003] OJ L 255/33 the Commission found Nintendo and seven of its distributors to have infringed Article 81 EC by colluding to maintain artificially high price differences for game consoles and games in the EU. According to the arrangements, distributors prevented parallel trade from their territories thus hindering exports to high-priced territories from low-priced territories. Nintendo and its distributors combated parallel trade by, among other things, establishing a system of information exchange and practical collaboration that enabled it to locate deviations from the restriction. The system facilitated tracing sources of parallel trade and restricting them. Although export bans only need to be enforced in low-price territories and not in high-price territories, the Commission held that all distributors who took part in this scheme were jointly responsible for the infringement. It noted that 'even if certain distributors did not have to take steps to prevent exports from their territories they were fundamental to the infringement's efficient operation, as they regularly warned [Nintendo] that parallel imports were taking place into their respective territories' (para 282) On the liability of an undertaking which takes part in a multiform infringement to the conduct of others see *Sigma v Commission*, page 96 above and *LVM and others v Commission*, page 97 above.

Note, however, the CFI decision in Case T–168/01 *GlaxoSmithKline Services Unlimited v Commission*. Here the court held that 'while it is accepted that an agreement intended to limit parallel trade must in principle be considered to have as its object the restriction of competition, that applies in so far as the agreement may be presumed to deprive final consumers of those advantages.' (para 121) The exceptional characteristics of the pharmaceuticals sector meant that prices of medicines were to a large extent shielded from the free play of supply and demand due to state regulations. In such circumstances the CFI considered it impossible to infer merely from a reading of the terms of the agreement that it has the object of restricting competition. The CFI went on to find that the agreement had the effect of reducing the welfare of final consumers. For a full analysis of this case, see page 62, Chapter 3 above.

Also note Case C–306/96 *Javico v Yves St Laurent* [1998] ECR I–1983 where the ECJ considered whether an export ban which prohibits a European supplier entrusted with the distribution of products in a territory outside the Community from making any sales in a territory other than the contractual territory, including the territory of the Community, would infringe Article 81 EC. In a preliminary ruling the ECJ held that such agreement 'must be construed not as being intended to exclude parallel imports and marketing of the contractual product within the Community but as being designed to enable the producer to penetrate a market outside the Community by supplying a sufficient quantity of contractual products to that market. That interpretation is supported by the fact that, in the agreements at issue, the prohibition of selling outside the contractual territory also covers all other non-member countries. It follows that an agreement in which the reseller gives to the producer an undertaking that he will sell the contractual products on a market outside the Community cannot be regarded as having the object of appreciably restricting competition within the common market or as being capable of affecting, as such, trade between Member States.' (paras 19, 20)

Note the hardcore restriction set out in Article 4(b) of the Vertical Block Exemption concerning market partitioning by territory or by customer. Also note paragraphs 49–56, 113–14, Vertical Guidelines.

ETA Fabriques d'Ebauches v SA DK Investment and others	**Vertical Agreements**
Case 31/85	Exclusive Distribution
ECJ, [1985] ECR 3933, [1986] 2 CMLR 674	Restrictions on Parallel Trade

Facts

Eta Fabriques d'Ebauches SA (Eta), a mass-producer of inexpensive 'Swatch' quartz watches, used a network of exclusive distributors to market its watches. In Belgium it assigned the exclusive distribution of 'Swatch' watches to an authorised dealer and undertook not to offer or sell its products in that territory to anyone but the dealer and to pass on to him any order relating to that territory. For his part, the authorised dealer undertook not to buy the products otherwise than from Eta, not to sell them, either directly or indirectly, outside the territory allotted and to pass on to Eta any order relating to the distribution of the products outside that territory. The watches sold by Eta were covered by a guarantee against technical defects for a period of 12 months after sale to the consumer, subject to a maximum of 18 months following delivery to the dealer. The defendants in the main proceedings sold 'Swatch' watches which they obtained by way of parallel imports, together with the guarantee certificate which referred to the 'Swatch' repair service in Switzerland. Eta applied to the Tribunal de Commerce, Brussels, for an injunction restraining the defendants from selling 'Swatch' watches with the guarantee granted by Eta to its authorised dealers by virtue of its contractual relationship with them. It argued that the guarantee provided is contractual in nature and is binding upon it only as against the recognised distributors. In a preliminary reference the ECJ considered the legality of the practice of not extending the guarantee to parallel imports.

Held

'The crucial element to be taken into consideration … is the actual or potential effect of withholding the guarantee on the competitive position of parallel distributors. In that connection it is necessary to consider whether parallel imports may be hindered, or whether opportunities for marketing such products may be restricted, regard being had in particular to the reaction of consumers and to the importance of the guarantee as an incentive to buy the products.' (para 12)

'A guarantee scheme under which a supplier of goods restricts the guarantee to customers of his exclusive distributor places the latter and the retailers to whom he sells in a privileged position as against parallel importers and distributors and must therefore be regarded as having the object or effect of restricting competition within the meaning of [Article 81(1) EC].' (para 14)

'The refusal to grant the guarantee cannot be justified by the need to ensure observance of the maximum storage period. The watches in question do not belong to a category of products in respect of which it is necessary to accept certain restrictions which are an inherent feature of a selective distribution system and are motivated by the desire to maintain a network of specialized dealers able to provide specific services for technically sophisticated, high-quality products. The battery is expressly excluded from the guarantee, its replacement does not pose any particular technical difficulties and, by its own admission, Eta honours the guarantee within the official distribution network beyond the six-month storage period, should the battery need to be replaced. The fact that, according to the parties, a defective watch cannot be repaired but can only be replaced is not without relevance in this regard.' (para 16)

Comment

The practice of not extending the guarantee to parallel imports indirectly hindered the imports of 'swatch' watches and distorted competition and trade between Member States.

See comments on export bans, page 105 above.

Sarl Kitch Moto v SA Suzuki France	**Vertical Agreements**
Court of Appeal, Paris, [2006] ECC 2 C d'A (Paris)	Exclusive Distribution

Facts

An appeal on a decision from the Tribunal de Commerce (Paris). Sarl Kitch Moto (the distributor) was an authorised distributor of SA Suzuki France (the manufacture). A new distribution contract between the two parties was agreed in 2001 with the aim of bringing the parties' relations into line with EC Regulation 2790/99. Article 2 of the contract stipulated that 'The distributor is prohibited from selling actively or passively from any establishment not approved by Suzuki France. It is prohibited from selling to any unauthorised resellers. Any sales to resellers not authorised by Suzuki in the European Union shall be regarded as unlawful. Where a sale is made to another reseller, the distributor shall be obliged to establish that the purchaser is a distributor approved by Suzuki in the European Union.' Following a few incidents in which the distributor sold motorcycles outside its own territory, the manufacturer terminated the distribution agreement. The distributor brought an action in the Paris Commercial Court, complaining of the excessive and unjustified nature of the termination. On appeal to the Paris court of Appeal the court commented on the Vertical Block Exemption and the legality of Article 2 of the distribution agreement.

Held

Kitch Moto, in invoking EC Regulation 2790/1999 on the application of Art 81(3) of the Treaty to categories of vertical agreements and concerted practices in order to argue that the prohibition of passive sales referred to in Art 2 of the distribution contract was unlawful, and in relying on Art 4(b) of that Regulation prohibiting restriction of: 'the territory into which, or of the customers to whom, the [distributor] may sell the contract goods … except the restriction of active sales into the exclusive territory, or to an exclusive customer group reserved to the supplier or allocated by the supplier to another [distributor], where such a restriction does not limit sales by the customers of the [distributor]' to argue that 'only active sales outside the network may be prohibited' and to ask the court to declare Art 2 of the distribution contract void, fails to observe, first, that the appellant does not show how the clauses criticised might restrict sales by its customers, and secondly, that the territorial clause set out in this article is not contrary to the provisions of Art 4(c) of the above-mentioned Regulation, which permit the supplier to prohibit 'a member of the system from operating out of an unauthorised place of establishment'. (para 8)

Comment

Note that a provision in a vertical agreement which does not satisfy the conditions of the Block Exemption is not necessarily void. The Block Exemption lists restrictions which do not benefit from an outright exemption (see Article 4 (hard core), Article 5 (no compete)). Such provisions, although not benefiting from the Block Exemption may still benefit from an individual exemption, or be found not to infringe Article 81 EC.

In order to succeed in its claim, it was for the distributor (Sarl Kitch Moto) to show that Article 2 of the distribution agreement infringed Article 81(1) EC by its object or effect. This would have shifted the burden of proof to the manufacturer (SA Suzuki France) which would then have to prove that despite infringing Article 81 (1) EC the agreement benefits from an exemption under Article 81(3) EC.

In this case, the Court of Appeal seemed to suggest that the agreement benefited from the safe heaven of the Vertical Block Exemption since the article in question did not infringe the provisions of Article 4(c) of the Block Exemption.

Note Case 56/65 *Société Technique Minière v Maschinenbau Ulm* (page 55 above) and Case 23/67 *SA Brasserie de Haecht v Consorts Wilkin-Janssen* (page 58 above), where the court considered the legality of exclusive distribution agreements. Also note Case 56/64 etc *Consten & Grundig v Commission* (page 56 above), where absolute territorial protection was found to have the object of restricting competition.

Metro SB-Großmarkte GmbH & Co KG v Commission	**Vertical Agreements**
Case 26/76	Selective Distribution
ECJ, [1977] ECR 1875, [1978] 2 CMLR 1	

Facts

Following a complaint submitted by Metro the Commission started an investigation into a selective distribution system for electric goods, operated by SABA. The Commission found that the conditions of sale for the domestic market as laid down in the distribution system did not fall within the prohibition in Article 81(1) EC and that the other provisions in the distribution agreement qualify for an exemption under Article 81(3) EC. Metro applied for an annulment of the Commission decision. On appeal the ECJ considered, among other things, the characteristics of selective distribution systems. The Application was dismissed.

Held

'The requirement contained in [Articles 3(1) and 81 EC] that competition shall not be distorted implies the existence on the market of workable competition, that is to say the degree of competition necessary to ensure the observance of the basic requirements and the attainment of the objectives of the Treaty, in particular the creation of a single market achieving conditions similar to those of a domestic market. In accordance with this requirement the nature and intensiveness of competition may vary to an extent dictated by the products or services in question and the economic structure of the relevant market sectors. In the sector covering the production of high quality and technically advanced consumer durables, where a relatively small number of large- and medium-scale producers offer a varied range of items which, or so consumers may consider, are readily interchangeable, the structure of the market does not preclude the existence of a variety of channels of distribution adapted to the peculiar characteristics of the various producers and to the requirements of the various categories of consumers. On this view the Commission was justified in recognizing that selective distribution systems constituted, together with others, an aspect of competition which accords with [Article 81(1) EC], provided that resellers are chosen on the basis of objective criteria of a qualitative nature relating to the technical qualifications of the reseller and his staff and the suitability of his trading premises and that such conditions are laid down uniformly for all potential resellers and are not applied in a discriminatory fashion.' (para 20)

'It is true that in such systems of distribution price competition is not generally emphasized either as an exclusive or indeed as a principal factor. This is particularly so when, as in the present case, access to the distribution network is subject to conditions exceeding the requirements of an appropriate distribution of the products. However, although price competition is so important that it can never be eliminated it does not constitute the only effective form of competition or that to which absolute priority must in all circumstances be accorded. The powers conferred upon the Commission under [Article 81(3) EC] show that the requirements for the maintenance of workable competition may be reconciled with the safeguarding of objectives of a different nature and that to this end certain restrictions on competition are permissible, provided that they are essential to the attainment of those objectives and that they do not result in the elimination of competition for a substantial part of the common market. For specialist wholesalers and retailers the desire to maintain a certain price level, which corresponds to the desire to preserve, in the interests of consumers, the possibility of the continued existence of this channel of distribution in conjunction with new methods of distribution based on a different type of competition policy, forms one of the objectives which may be pursued without necessarily falling under the prohibition contained in [Article 81(1) EC], and, if it does fall thereunder, either wholly or in part, coming within the framework of [Article 81(3) EC]. This argument is strengthened if, in addition, such conditions promote improved competition inasmuch as it relates to factors other than prices.' (para 21)

Comment

'To assess the possible anti-competitive effects of selective distribution under Article 81(1), a distinction needs to be made between purely qualitative selective distribution and quantitative selective distribution. Purely qualitative selective distribution selects dealers only on the basis of objective criteria required by the nature of the product such as training of sales personnel, the service provided at the point of sale, a certain range of the products being sold etc. The application of such criteria does not put a direct limit on the number of dealers. Purely qualitative selective distribution is in general considered to fall outside Article 81(1) for lack of anti-competitive effects, provided that three conditions are satisfied. First, the nature of the product in question must necessitate a selective distribution system, in the sense that such a system must constitute a legitimate requirement, having regard to the nature of the product concerned, to preserve its quality and ensure its proper use. Secondly, resellers must be chosen on the basis of objective criteria of a qualitative nature which are laid down uniformly for all potential resellers and are not applied in a discriminatory manner. Thirdly, the criteria laid down must not go beyond what is necessary. Quantitative selective distribution adds further criteria for selection that more directly limits the potential number of dealers by, for instance, requiring minimum or maximum sales, by fixing the number of dealers, etc.' (Vertical Guidelines, para 185)

The product in question must necessitate a selective distribution system. For example:

(a)   In case T–88/92 *Groupement d'achat Edouard Leclerc v Commission,* [1996] ECR II–1961, (appeal by a third party on the Commission's decision to grant exemption to the Givenchy distribution system (Case IV/33.542 *Parfums Givenchy* system of selective distribution)) the CFI held that luxury cosmetics are sophisticated and high-quality products with a distinctive luxury image which is important in the eyes of consumers. 'In the luxury cosmetics sector, qualitative criteria for the selection of retailers which do not go beyond what is necessary to ensure that those products are suitably presented for sale are in principle not covered by [Article 81(1) EC], in so far as they are objective, laid down uniformly for all potential retailers and not applied in a discriminatory fashion.' (para 117)

(b)   In Case 31/85 *ETA Fabriques d'Ebauches v SA DK Investment and others* (page 107 above), mass produced 'swatch' watches were considered not to belong to a category of products which require a selective distribution system. On the other hand, in Case IV/5715 *Junghans* [1977] OJ L 30/10, quality, sophisticated watches were found to justify conditions in a selective distribution system relating to the technical qualification of dealers and specialist knowledge of their staff.

(c)   In Case 243/83 *SA Binon & Cie v SA Agence et Messageries de la Presse* (page 115 below) the special characteristics of newspapers and periodicals distribution were held to justify a system of selective distribution.

When the selective distribution agreement is part of a wider network of selective distribution, a 'simple' selective distribution system may give rise to competitive concerns. In Metro II, Case 75/84 *Metro SB-Großmarkte GmbH & Co KG v Commission,* [1986] ECR 3021, [1987] 1 CMLR 118, the court held that 'although the court has held in previous Decisions that "simple" selective distribution systems are capable of constituting an aspect of competition compatible with [Article 81(1) EC], there may nevertheless be a restriction or elimination of competition where the existence of a certain number of such systems does not leave any room for other forms of distribution based on a different type of competition policy or results in a rigidity in price structure which is not counterbalanced by other aspects of competition between products of the same brand and by the existence of effective competition between different brands.' (para 40)

In Case 107/82 *AEG v Commission* the ECJ held that selective distribution systems may include acceptable limitations to attain legitimate goals such as the maintenance of a specialist trade capable of providing specific services as regards high-quality and high-technology products. Such limitations lead to a reduction of price competition in favour of competition relating to factors other than price. For detailed analysis see page 40, Chapter 3 above.

Van den Bergh Foods Ltd v Commission	**Vertical Agreements**
Case T–65/98 R	Single Branding
CFI, [2003] ECR II–4653, [2004] 4 CMLR 1	Cabinet Exclusivity

Facts

Van den Bergh Foods (formerly HB Ice Cream), supplied ice-cream retailers with freezer cabinets free of charge or at a nominal rent, provided that they were used exclusively for HB ice creams. The Commission found HB's exclusive cabinet distribution agreements incompatible with Articles 81 and 82 EC. HB applied for the annulment of the Commission Decision arguing that freezer-cabinet exclusivity was not to be regarded as outlet exclusivity since retailers were entitled to terminate the contract with HB or to install other freezers not belonging to HB. According to HB, the retailers' freedom of choice contradicted any conclusion that the agreements foreclosed the market. Additionally HB challenged the Commission's finding that 40 per cent of sales outlets in Ireland were *de facto* tied to HB by the exclusivity clause. The Application was dismissed.

Held

The cabinet exclusivity clause was not, in formal terms, an exclusive purchasing obligation whose object was to restrict competition. The Commission was therefore required to prove that the effect of such a clause would be to lead to a sufficiently high degree of foreclosure as to constitute an infringement of Article 81(1) of the Treaty. (para 80) Such an inquiry would rely on the specific economic context in which the agreements operated. (para 84)

The nature of the product market, the limited space in outlets and the popularity of HB's product range would have lead retailers bound by the agreement to stock HB ice-cream and to refrain from stocking a second range of impulse ice-cream. The cabinet exclusivity clause would have motivated rational retailers in small outlets to favour HB's products over products of other ice-cream manufacturers, regardless of their popularity on the market. (para 97)

Despite the fact that it was theoretically possible for retailers who only had an HB freezer cabinet to sell the ice-creams of other manufacturers, the practical effect of HB's network of distribution agreements and exclusivity clause was to restrict the commercial freedom of retailers to choose the products they wished to sell. (paras 99, 101)

The retailers' right to terminate their distribution agreements with HB at any time was not often exercised and did not operate *de facto* to reduce the degree of foreclosure of the relevant market. (para 105)

Although freezer-cabinet exclusivity may be a standard practice in the market and is part of an agreement concluded in the interests of both the retailers and HB, it constituted in the present market conditions an abuse when engaged by a dominant undertaking. (paras 159, 160)

Comment

The market in this case displays unique characteristics. The cost of freezer cabinets, cost of maintenance and cost of space in outlets, would lead a rational retailer to favour the dominant undertaking over competitors. Optimal allocation of space in small outlets would make it unprofitable to stock additional brands in a second freezer unless the profit generated is greater than the potential profit generated from using this space for displaying other goods. These unique characteristics created a strong disincentive for retailers to allow a new competitor into the outlet either instead of HB freezers or in addition to them. In other words, the retailers' legal right to terminate an agreement was of no consequence as they lacked the incentive to do so. Subsequently, freezer exclusivity transformed into outlet exclusivity in the circumstances of this case.

Note Case T–7/93 *Langnese-Iglo v EC Commission*, [1995] ECR II–1533, [1995] 5 CMLR 602 (upheld on appeal to the ECJ: Case C–279/95, [1998] ECR I–5609, [1998] 5 CMLR 933). There the court considered the legality of a distribution agreement in the German market for impulse ice-cream. The agreement included an exclusive purchase obligation which required distributors of 'Scholler Lebensmittel GmbH & Co KG' (Scholler) to obtain their ice-cream supply solely from Scholler. These provisions included freezer exclusivity but were wider as they also referred to the outlet as a whole. The Court noted that in order to determine whether the 'exclusive purchasing agreements fall within the prohibition contained in [Article 81(1) EC], it is appropriate, according to the case-law, to consider whether, taken together, all the similar agreements entered into in the relevant market and the other features of the economic and legal context of the agreements at issue show that those agreements cumulatively have the effect of denying access to that market for new domestic and foreign competitors. If, on examination, that is found not to be the case, the individual agreements making up the bundle of agreements as a whole cannot undermine competition within the meaning of [Article 81(1) EC]. If, on the other hand, such examination reveals that it is difficult to gain access to the market, it is necessary to assess the extent to which the contested agreements contribute to the cumulative effect produced, on the basis that only agreements which make a significant contribution to any partitioning of the market are prohibited (*Delimitis*, paragraphs 23 and 24).' (para 99) The court agreed with the Commission concussions that access to the market for new competitors was made difficult by the existence of a system under which a large number of freezer cabinets were lent by Scholler to retailers and retailers were obliged to use them exclusively for the applicant's products. 'The necessary consequence of that situation is that any new competitor entering the market must either persuade the retailer to exchange the freezer cabinet installed by [Scholler] for another, which involves giving up the turnover in the products from the previous supplier, or to persuade the retailer to install an additional freezer cabinet, which may prove impossible, particularly because of lack of space in small sales outlets. Moreover, if the new competitor is able to offer only a limited range of products, as in the case of the intervener, it may prove difficult for it to persuade the retailer to terminate its agreement with the previous supplier.' (para 108) The court upheld the Commission decision finding the agreements to give rise to an appreciable restriction of competition on the relevant market.

In Case C–234/89 *Stergios Delimitis v Henninger Bräu AG*, [1991] ECR I–935, the ECJ, in a preliminary reference, held that in order to assess the effects of a single branding agreement (beer supply agreement) the national court should analyse its effects, 'taken together with other contracts of the same type, on the opportunities of national competitors or those from other Member States, to gain access to the market for beer consumption or to increase their market share and, accordingly, the effects on the range of products offered to consumers.' (para 15) In order to do so the relevant market needs to be defined and the agreements on this market examined in their totality, to conclude whether the network of agreements forecloses the market. For a detailed analysis of this case see page 60, Chapter 3 above.

The Vertical Guidelines (paras 138–60) outline the possible anticompetitive effects of non-compete obligations and the variables relevant in the assessment of such agreements under Article 81 EC.

Non-compete obligations (single branding agreements) are exempted under the Vertical Block Exemption when the supplier's market share does not exceed 30 per cent and subject to a limitation in time of five years for the non-compete obligation.

Pronuptia de Paris GmbH v Pronuptia de Paris Irmgard Schillgallis	**Vertical Agreements**
Case 161/84	Franchise Agreements
ECJ, [1986] ECR 353, [1986] 1 CMLR 414	

Facts

A reference for a preliminary ruling from the German Federal Court of Justice concerning the application of Article 81 EC to franchise agreements. The questions arose in proceedings between Pronuptia de Paris GmbH (the franchisor), a distributor of wedding dresses which was a subsidiary of the French company of the same name, and Mrs Schillgalis, an independent retailer who acted as the franchisee in Hamburg, Oldenburg and Hanover.

Held

'... a distinction must be drawn between different varieties of franchise agreements. In particular, it is necessary to distinguish between (i) service franchises, under which the franchisee offers a service under the business name or symbol and sometimes the trade-mark of the franchisor, in accordance with the franchisor's instructions, (ii) production franchises, under which the franchisee manufactures products according to the instructions of the franchisor and sells them under the franchisor's trade-mark, and (iii) distribution franchises, under which the franchisee simply sells certain products in a shop which bears the franchisor's business name or symbol. In this judgment the court is concerned only with this third type of contract, to which the questions asked by the national court expressly refer.' (para 13)

In a system of distribution franchises the franchisor which has established itself in a given market grants independent traders, for a fee, the right to establish themselves in other markets using its business name and the business methods that have made it successful. The system allows the franchisor to expand without investing its own capital and the franchisee to benefit from the reputation and experience of the franchisor. 'In order for the system to work two conditions must be met. First, the franchisor must be able to communicate his know-how to the franchisees and provide them with the necessary assistance in order to enable them to apply his methods, without running the risk that that know-how and assistance might benefit competitors, even indirectly. It follows that provisions which are essential in order to avoid that risk do not constitute restrictions on competition for the purposes of [Article 81(1)]. That is also true of a clause prohibiting the franchisee, during the period of validity of the contract and for a reasonable period after its expiry, from opening a shop of the same or a similar nature in an area where he may compete with a member of the network. The same may be said of the franchisee's obligation not to transfer his shop to another party without the prior approval of the franchisor; that provision is intended to prevent competitors from indirectly benefiting from the know-how and assistance provided. Secondly, the franchisor must be able to take the measures necessary for maintaining the identity and reputation of the network bearing his business name or symbol. It follows that provisions which establish the means of control necessary for that purpose do not constitute restrictions on competition for the purposes of [Article 81(1)].' (paras 15–17)

'The same is true of the franchisee's obligation to apply the business methods developed by the franchisor and to use the know-how provided. That is also the case with regard to the franchisee's obligation to sell the goods covered by the contract only in premises laid out and decorated according to the franchisor's instructions, which is intended to ensure uniform presentation in conformity with certain requirements. The same requirements apply to the location of the shop, the choice of which is also likely to affect the network's reputation. It is thus understandable that the franchisee cannot transfer his shop to another location without the franchisor's approval. The prohibition of the assignment by the franchisee of his rights and obligations under the contract without the franchisor's approval protects the latter's right freely to choose the franchisees, on whose business qualifications the establishment and maintenance of the network's reputation depend.' (paras 18–20)

The control exerted by the franchisor on the selection of goods offered by the franchisee enables the public to obtain goods of the same quality from each franchisee and is necessary for the protection of the network's reputation. Such control should not prevent the franchisee from obtaining those goods from other franchisees. (para 21)

A provision requiring the franchisee to obtain the franchisor's approval for all advertising is essential for the maintenance of the network's identity, so long as it concerns only the nature of the advertising. (para 22)

Certain provision may restrict competition between the members of the network and may lead to the sharing of the market. 'In that regard the attention of the national court should be drawn to the provision which obliges the franchisee to sell goods covered by the contract only in the premises specified therein. That provision prohibits the franchisee from opening a second shop. Its real effect becomes clear if it is examined in conjunction with the franchisor's undertaking to ensure that the franchisee has the exclusive use of his business name or symbol in a given territory. In order to comply with that undertaking the franchisor must not only refrain from establishing himself within that territory but also require other franchisees to give an undertaking not to open a second shop outside their own territory. A combination of provisions of that kind results in a sharing of markets between the franchisor and the franchisees or between franchisees and thus restricts competition within the network. As is clear from [Joined cases 56, 58/64 *Consten and Grundig v Commission* (1966) ECR 299)], a restriction of that kind constitutes a limitation of competition for the purposes of [Article 81 (1)] if it concerns a business name or symbol which is already well-known. It is of course possible that a prospective franchisee would not take the risk of becoming part of the chain, investing his own money, paying a relatively high entry fee and undertaking to pay a substantial annual royalty, unless he could hope, thanks to a degree of protection against competition on the part of the franchisor and other franchisees, that his business would be profitable. That consideration, however, is relevant only to an examination of the agreement in the light of the conditions laid down in [Article 81 (3)].' (paras 24, 26)

The franchisor may provide the franchisee with price guidelines as long as these do not impair the franchisee's freedom to determine its own prices, and so long as there is no concerted practice between the franchisor and franchisees or between the franchisees themselves for the actual application of such prices. (para 25)

Comment

The provisions of the franchise agreement were analysed as ancillary restraints. The Court considered whether they are necessary for achieving the objectives of the franchise system. It considered provisions protecting know-how, branding advertising and product choice to be necessary in this respect. On the other hand a franchising agreement which leads to market sharing was held as restricting competition. (para 24)

A combination of exclusivity and territorial allocation (para 24) led to absolute territorial protection and, in line with *Consten and Grundig v Commission*, was found to restrict competition.

The Commission noted in several cases that clauses which are essential to prevent the know-how supplied and assistance provided by the franchisor from benefiting competitors and clauses which provide for the control that is essential for preserving the common identity and reputation of the network do not constitute restrictions of competition within the meaning of Article 81 (1) EC. See, for example, Commission decision granting exemption under Article 81(3) in Case IV/31.697, *Charles Jourdan*, [1989] OJ L 35/31, and Commission decision in Cases IV/31.428 to 31.432, *Yves Rocher* [1987] OJ L 8/49.

The Commission Guidelines on Vertical Restraints [2000] OJ C 291 consider the analysis of franchise agreements (paras 199–201) as well as the transfer of know-how and licensing of intellectual property rights (paras 23–45).

SA Binon & Cie v SA Agence et Messageries de la Presse Case 243/83 ECJ, [1985] ECR 2015,[1985] 3 CMLR 800	**Vertical Agreements** Resale Price Maintenance

Facts

SA Agence et Messageries de la Presse (AMP) operated a selective distribution system for newspapers and periodicals in Belgium and was responsible for close to 70 per cent of the distribution of Belgian newspapers and periodicals. AMP refused to supply newspapers to SA Binon & Cie (Binon). The dispute between the two companies reached the Brussels Commercial Court. The court, in a preliminary reference referred to the ECJ several questions, one of which concerned the legality of a clause in AMP's selective distribution system according to which the distributor reserved the right to fix prices and compel retailers to respect those prices.

Held (on the fixing of prices)

'Finally, the third question is concerned with the problem whether the fact that, within the framework of a selective distribution system of newspapers and periodicals, fixed prices must be observed renders the system incompatible with the prohibition laid down in [Article 81 EC].' (para 39)

'AMP contends in that regard that the prices of newspapers and periodicals are fixed by the publishers and not, as the national court seems to think, by the distribution agency. Observance by retailers of the prices fixed by publishers arises from the aforementioned special characteristics of the distribution of newspapers and periodicals.' (para 40)

'The government of the Federal Republic of Germany, which took part in the proceedings solely in order to submit observations with regard to the third question, considers that the freedom of the press, as a fundamental right protected by the constitutional law of the Member States and by the court's case-law, entails the freedom to contribute to the formation of public opinion. For that reason newspapers and periodicals as well as their distribution have special characteristics. The nature of newspapers and periodicals requires an extremely rapid system for their distribution in view of the very limited period during which they can be sold before they are out of date; at the end of that period, the length of which varies according to the specific publication in question, newspapers and periodicals have practically no value. To those factors must be added the heterogeneity of newspapers and periodicals and the lack of elasticity in demand since each newspaper or periodical has more or less its own body of customers.' (para 41)

'The German government concludes that, from the point of view of competition, the position of the market in newspapers and periodicals is so special that it is not possible to apply to it without modification principles which have been developed in completely different contexts. If the possibility of fixing prices for newspapers and periodicals is not accepted any effective distribution system for such products would be incompatible with the rules on competition and the effect on the diversity and freedom of the press would be disastrous. From that point of view it is not unimportant to note that systems of fixed prices in relation to the distribution of newspapers and periodicals are accepted under the legislation of most Member States or are operated without encountering any difficulties.' (para 42)

'In the Commission's opinion any price-fixing agreement constitutes, of itself, a restriction on competition and is, as such, prohibited by [Article 81(3) EC]. The Commission does not deny that newspapers and periodicals and the way they are distributed have special characteristics but considers that these cannot lead to an exclusion of such products and their distribution from the scope of [Article 81(3) EC]. On the contrary, those characteristics should be put forward by the undertakings relying upon them in the context of an application for exemption under [Article 81(3) EC].' (para 43)

'It should be observed in the first place that provisions which fix the prices to be observed in contracts with third parties constitute, of themselves, a restriction on competition within the meaning of [Article 81(1) EC] which refers to agreements which fix selling prices as an example of an agreement prohibited by the Treaty.' (para 44)

Such agreement may benefit from an exemption under Article 81(3) EC. In considering the availability of exemption account should be taken of the possibility that the fixing of the retail price by publishers constitutes the sole means of supporting the financial burden resulting from the taking back of unsold copies and the possibility that the latter practice constitutes the sole method by which a wide selection of newspapers and periodicals can be made available to readers. (para 46)

Comment

In Case 161/84 *Pronuptia de Paris GmbH v Pronuptia de Paris Irmgard Schillgallis* (page 113 above) the ECJ held that 'provisions which impair the franchisee's freedom to determine his own prices are restrictive of competition'. On the other hand it noted that would not be the case 'where the franchisor simply provides franchisees with price guidelines, so long as there is no concerted practice between the franchisor and the franchisees or between the franchisees themselves for the actual application of such prices.' (para 25)

Note also Case 26/76 *Metro SB-Großmarkte GmbH & Co KG v Commission* (page 109 above), where the ECJ commented in the context of selective distribution systems that 'it is true that in such systems of distribution price competition is not generally emphasized either as an exclusive or indeed as a principal factor. ... However, although price competition is so important that it can never be eliminated it does not constitute the only effective form of competition or that to which absolute priority must in all circumstances be accorded ...' (para 21)

Also note the Commission decision in case IV/30.658 *Polistil/Arbois*, [1984] OJ L 136/9, where a clause in a distribution agreement was held to restrict 'Polistil's freedom to set its prices to Arbois according to conditions on the relevant market, the quantities supplied and its own commercial policy.' (para 45)

Contrast the above restrictive approach with the United States Supreme Court decision in *Leegin Creative Leather Products, Inc v PSKS, Inc*, 127 SCt 2705 US (2007). In that decision the US Supreme Court overruled the court's longstanding decision in *Dr Miles Medical Co v John D Park & Sons Co*, 220 US 373 (1911) and held that the 'application of per se rule, under which category of restraint of trade is deemed necessarily illegal under Sherman Act, is unwarranted as to vertical agreements to fix minimum resale prices ... [since] it cannot be stated with confidence that such agreements always or almost always tend to restrict competition and decrease output.' 'Economics literature is replete with procompetitive justifications for a manufacturer's use of resale price maintenance, and the few recent studies on the subject also cast doubt on the conclusion that the practice meets the criteria for a per se rule. The justifications for vertical price restraints are similar to those for other vertical restraints. Minimum resale price maintenance can stimulate interbrand competition among manufacturers selling different brands of the same type of product by reducing intrabrand competition among retailers selling the same brand. This is important because the antitrust laws' "primary purpose ... is to protect interbrand competition" ... A single manufacturer's use of vertical price restraints tends to eliminate intrabrand price competition; this in turn encourages retailers to invest in services or promotional efforts that aid the manufacturer's position as against rival manufacturers. Resale price maintenance may also give consumers more options to choose among low-price, low-service brands; high-price, high-service brands; and brands falling in between. Absent vertical price restraints, retail services that enhance interbrand competition might be underprovided because discounting retailers can free ride on retailers who furnish services and then capture some of the demand those services generate. Retail price maintenance can also increase interbrand competition by facilitating market entry for new firms and brands and by encouraging retailer services that would not be provided even absent free riding.' (pages 2714–16) 'Setting minimum resale prices may also have anticompetitive effects; and unlawful price fixing, designed solely to obtain monopoly profits, is an ever present temptation. Resale price maintenance may, for example, facilitate a manufacturer cartel or be used to organize retail cartels. It can also be abused by a powerful manufacturer or retailer. Thus, the potential anticompetitive consequences of vertical price restraints must not be ignored or underestimated.' (pages 2716–18)

DaimlerChrysler AG v Commission	**Agency Agreements**
Case T–325/01	
CFI, [2005] ECR II–3319, [2007] 4 CMLR 15	

Facts

An appeal on Commission decision (Case COMP/36.264 – *MercedesBenz*) ([2002], OJ L 257/1), in which the Commission found that Mercedes-Benz (MB) had itself or through its subsidiaries infringed Article 81(1)EC by restricting the export of MB passenger cars. The Commission rejected MB's argument that the agreements at issue were concluded with its German agents and were thus not subject to Article 81 EC. It found that the agents took on a considerable share of the commercial risk associated with the sale and transport of vehicles and used their own financial resources for sale promotions. Since those risks were not typical of those borne by a true commercial agents, the agreements between MB and its German agents were subject to Article 81 EC and were found to infringe Article 81 EC. MB appealed the decision, contesting, among other things, the finding concerning the commercial agent.

Held

'… in competition law the term "undertaking" must be understood as designating an economic unit for the purpose of the subject-matter of the agreement in question, even if in law that unit consists of several persons, natural or legal (Case 170/83 *Hydrotherm* [1984] ECR 2999, paragraph 11, and Case T–234/95 *DSG v Commission* [2000] ECR II–2603, paragraph 124). The Court of Justice has emphasised that, for the purposes of applying the competition rules, formal separation of two companies resulting from their having distinct legal identity, is not decisive. The test is whether or not there is unity in their conduct on the market. Thus, it may be necessary to establish whether two companies that have distinct legal identities form, or fall within, one and the same undertaking or economic entity adopting the same course of conduct on the market (see, to that effect, Case 48/69 *ICI v Commission* [1972] ECR 619, paragraph 140).' (para 85)

'The case-law shows that this sort of situation arises not only in cases where the relationship between the companies in question is that of parent and subsidiary. It may also occur, in certain circumstances, in relationships between a company and its commercial representative or between a principal and its agent. In so far as application of Article 81 EC is concerned, the question whether a principal and its agent or commercial representative form a single economic unit, the agent being an auxiliary body forming part of the principal's undertaking, is an important one for the purposes of establishing whether given conduct falls within the scope of that article. Thus, it has been held that if … an agent works for the benefit of his principal he may in principle be treated as an auxiliary organ forming an integral part of the latter's undertaking, who must carry out his principal's instructions and thus, like a commercial employee, forms an economic unit with this undertaking [Case 40/73 etc *Suiker Unie and others v Commission*, [1975] ECR 1663, para 480].' (para 86)

'The position is otherwise if the agreements entered into between the principal and its agents confer upon the agent or allow him to perform duties which from an economic point of view are approximately the same as those carried out by an independent dealer, because they provide for the agent accepting the financial risks of selling or of the performance of the contracts entered into with third parties (see, to that effect, *Suiker Unie and others v Commission* … at paragraph 541). It has therefore been held that an agent can lose his character as independent economic operator only if he does not bear any of the risks resulting from the contracts negotiated on behalf of the principal and he operates as an auxiliary organ forming an integral part of the principal's undertaking (see, to that effect, Case C–266/93 *Volkswagen and VAG Leasing*, [1995] ECR I–3477, at paragraph 19).' (para 87)

'Accordingly, where an agent, although having separate legal personality, does not independently determine his own conduct on the market, but carries out the instructions given to him by his principal, the prohibitions laid down under Article 81(1) EC do not apply to the relationship between the agent and the principal with which he forms an economic unit.' (para 88)

In this case it is not the agent but MB which determines the conditions applying to car sales and sale price, and which bears the principal risks associated with that activity. The German agent is prevented by the terms of the agency agreement from purchasing and holding stocks of vehicles for sale. In those circumstances, the agents should be treated in the same way as employees and considered as integrated in that undertaking and thus forming an economic unit with it. It follows that, in carrying on business on the market in question, the German MB agent does not himself constitute an 'undertaking' for the purposes of Article 81 EC. It follows that the Commission did not establish the existence of an agreement between undertakings for the purposes of Article 81(1) EC. (paras 89–119)

Comment

In Joined Cases 40/73 etc *Suiker Unie and others v Commission*, [1975] ECR 1663, the ECJ held that an agent may be regarded as an auxiliary organ forming an integral part of the principal when it works for the benefit of his principal and is required to carry out his principal's instructions without accepting the financial risks of the sales or of the performance of contracts entered into with third parties. (paras 480–485, 537–544)

In Case C–266/93 *Bundeskartellamt v Volkswagen AG and VAG Leasing GmbH*, [1995] ECR I–3477, Volkswagen AG (VAG) and VAG Leasing GmbH (VAG Leasing) argued that the relationship between VAG and its dealers, which was governed by a distribution agreement, was not subjected to Article 81 EC as the distributors were commercial agents which formed one economic unit with VAG and VAG Leasing. In a preliminary reference, the ECJ held that 'That argument must be rejected. Representatives can lose their character as independent traders only if they do not bear any of the risks resulting from the contracts negotiated on behalf of the principal and they operate as auxiliary organs forming an integral part of the principal's undertaking (see Joined Cases 40/73 … *Suiker Unie and others v Commission* [1975] ECR 1663, paragraph 539). However, the German VAG dealers assume, at least in part, the financial risks linked to the transactions concluded on behalf of VAG Leasing, in so far as they repurchase the vehicles from it upon the expiry of the leasing contracts. Furthermore, their principal business of sales and after-sales services is carried on, largely independently, in their own name and for their own account.' (para 19)

The Commission Vertical Guidelines (paras 12–20) outline the distinction between genuine and non-genuine agency agreements. Note in particular the impact risk allocation has on the classification of an agency agreement; 'The determining factor in assessing whether Article 81(1) is applicable is the financial or commercial risk borne by the agent in relation to the activities for which he has been appointed as an agent by the principal. … There are two types of financial or commercial risks that are material to the assessment of the genuine nature of an agency agreement under Article 81(1). First there are the risks which are directly related to the contracts concluded and/or negotiated by the agent on behalf of the principal, such as financing of stocks. Secondly, there are the risks related to market-specific investments. These are investments specifically required for the type of activity for which the agent has been appointed by the principal, i.e. which are required to enable the agent to conclude and/or negotiate this type of contract. Such investments are usually sunk, if upon leaving that particular field of activity the investment cannot be used for other activities or sold other than at a significant loss.' (paras 13, 14, Vertical Guidelines)

5

Article 82 EC

Article 82 EC

Any abuse by one or more undertakings of a dominant position within the common market or in a substantial part of it shall be prohibited as incompatible with the common market insofar as it may affect trade between Member States. Such abuse may, in particular, consist in:

(a) directly or indirectly imposing unfair purchase or selling prices or other unfair trading conditions;

(b) limiting production, markets or technical development to the prejudice of consumers;

(c) applying dissimilar conditions to equivalent transactions with other trading parties, thereby placing them at a competitive disadvantage;

(d) making the conclusion of contracts subject to acceptance by the other parties of supplementary obligations which, by their nature or according to commercial usage, have no connection with the subject of such contracts.'

For ease of analysis Article 82 EC may be divided into four main questions:

1.   Is there a dominant undertaking or a group of undertakings?

2.   Is this dominant position within the Common Market or in a substantial part of it?

3.   Is this dominant position being abused?

4.   Could this abuse of dominant position affect trade between Member States?

Although Article 82 EC does not include an exempting provision similar to Article 81(3) EC, conduct which is regarded as abusive may escape the prohibition in Article 82 EC if the dominant undertaking can objectively justify it. One can therefore qualify the third question by asking whether the undertaking's conduct can be objectively justified.

The analysis of Article 82 through these questions is illustrated below.

Dominance

Dominance is a position of economic strength enjoyed by an undertaking which enables it to prevent effective competition being maintained in the relevant market by affording it the power to behave to an appreciable extent independently of its competitors, customers and its consumers. The concept of dominance reflects the notion of market power and requires a preliminary consideration of the relevant market and its characteristics.

The process involves two distinct steps. First the boundaries of competition need be identified by defining the relevant product and geographical markets (see discussion in Chapter 2 above). Once the market has been defined, it is possible to proceed to the next step and assess whether the undertaking enjoys a position of dominance in that market. The analysis is based on, among other things, the market shares of the undertaking and its competitors, barriers to expansion and entry, and the market position of buyers. The following cases illustrate the process of establishing dominance and the weight attributed to market shares and to other market characteristics:

27/76	*United Brands v Commission*	127
85/76	*Hoffmann-La Roche v Commission*	129
C–62/86	*AKZO Chemie BV v Commission*	130
22/78	*Hugin v Commission*	131
322/81	*Nederlandsche Banden Industrie Michelin v Commission*	132
T–125/97	*The Coca-Cola Company v Commission*	133

See also summary references to:

COMP/34.780	*Virgin/British Airways*	130
27/76	*United Brands v Commission*	130
C–68/94	*France v Commission*	130

In 2005 the Commission published a Discussion Paper on the Application of Article 82 of the Treaty to Exclusionary Abuses. The paper provides a useful overview of the relevant case-law and the process of establishing dominance. Note in particular paragraphs 20–42 which outline the methodology of establishing dominance. The paper may be accessed through the European Commission website: http://ec.europa.eu/comm/competition/index_en.html.

Dominant Position within the Common Market or in a Substantial Part of It

After establishing the existence of a dominant or collective dominant position and before moving to consider the question of abuse, it is necessary to consider whether this position of power is within the Common Market or in a substantial part of it. This requirement acts as a threshold which ensures that Article 82 EC will only be applicable to dominant positions which occupies at least a substantial part of the Common Market. See:

40/73	*Suiker Unie and others v Commission*	134

Abuse

Dominance in itself is not prohibited under Article 82 EC. The Article targets the abuse of a dominant (or collectively dominant) position. 'The concept of abuse is an objective concept relating to the behaviour of an undertaking in a dominant position, which is such as to influence the structure of a market, where, as a result of the very presence of the undertaking in question, the degree of competition is weakened and which, through recourse to methods different from those which condition normal competition in products or services on the basis of the transactions of commercial operators, has the effect of hindering the maintenance of the degree of competition still existing in the market or the growth of that competition.' (Case 85/76 *Hoffmann-La Roche v Commission*)

The following sections outline different categories of abusive behaviour.

Predatory Pricing

Aggressive price rivalry is central to a healthy competitive market as it ensures that firms sell their products at the lowest profitable price. Yet, under certain circumstances price competition may harm customers rather than benefit them. Such is the case when a dominant firm abuses its dominant position by engaging in predatory pricing. The practice involves the deliberate lowering of prices by the dominant undertaking in the short term to a loss-making level, in an attempt to drive competitors out of the market or to prevent competitors from entering the market. Then, having eliminated the competition through predation, the dominant undertaking is capable of raising prices above competitive levels, ultimately harming customers by charging higher prices.

The following cases illustrate the analysis of predation:

C–62/86	*AKZO Chemie BV v Commission*	135
C–333/94 P	*Tetra Pak International SA v Commission*	137
T–340/03	*France Télécom SA v Commission*	138

See also summary references to:

07-D-09	*GlaxoSmithKline France*	137
COMP/38.233	*Wanadoo Interactive*	138
No 92–466	*Brooke Group Ltd v Brown & Williamson Tobacco Corp*	140
No 05–381	*Weyerhaeuser Co v Ross-Simmons Hardwood Lumber Co Inc*	140

Selective Price Cuts

Whereas healthy price competition may drive less-efficient undertakings out of the market, selective price cuts enable the dominant undertaking to eliminate an equally efficient competitor from the market by cutting its prices to above cost level. Selective price cuts may be abusive when the dominant undertaking selectively cuts its prices with the aims of driving out a competitor from the market. Contrary to predation cases, the analysis does not focus on the cost structure or profitability, but rather on the selectiveness aimed at excluding a competitor.

C–395/96 etc	*Compagnie Maritime Belge Transports v Commission*	141

See also summary references to:

IV/30.787 etc	*Eurofix-Bauco v Hilti*	141
T–228/97	*Irish Sugar v Commission*	141

Price Alignment

Dominant companies have a right to align their prices in good faith with prices charged by a competitor. In doing so they can 'meet' the competition but are prohibited from strengthening their dominant position and abusing it (for example, by engaging in predatory pricing).

IP/97/868	*Digital Equipment Corporation*	142
T–228/97	*Irish Sugar v Commission*	180

See also summary references to:

Price Discrimination

Article 82(c) EC stipulates that an abuse may consist in 'applying dissimilar conditions to equivalent transactions with other trading parties, thereby placing them at a competitive disadvantage'. The provision, which covers price discrimination, should be applied with caution, as it is generally accepted that price discrimination may at times increase welfare. This will be the case when by engaging in 'price differentiation' the undertaking is able to increase output. For example, by charging higher prices for peak-time rail travellers or lower prices for last-minute air travellers.

Article 82(c) EC has often been used in cases concerning abusive discount strategies. These are detailed blow under 'Rebates'. On its use to target geographical price discrimination, see:

See also summary references to:

Rebates

The European law concerning rebates generally distinguishes between quantity discounts, which are linked solely to the volume of purchases from the manufacturer concerned, and loyalty-inducing rebates. Whereas the former are considered valuable and acceptable components of price competition, the latter are held to be abusive. The European courts' approach, as evident from the cases below, has been criticised as too formalistic, failing to take into account the effects different discount schemes have on competition. The case-law is unsatisfactory in this respect, leaving uncertainties as to the dividing line between justifiable and anticompetitive discounts.

See also summary references to:

Note paragraphs 151–76 in the Commission Discussion Paper on the Application of Article 82 of the Treaty to Exclusionary Abuses (December 2005). There, the Commission outlines its proposed approach to assessing the effects of discounts on competition

Margin Squeeze

Margin squeeze (also known as price squeeze) refers to a situation where a vertically integrated dominant undertaking engages in a discriminatory strategy which aims to favour its own downstream operations. The strategy may, for example, take place when the dominant undertaking supplies input both to his own downstream operation and to other competitors in the downstream market and increases the price charged to competitors, to squeeze their profit and improve the position of its own downstream operation.

| COMP/C–1/37.451 | *Deutsche Telekom AG* | 156 |
| 1016/1/1/03 | *Genzyme Limited v Office of Fair Trading* | 157 |

See also summary references to:

| IV/30.178 | *Napier Brown/British Sugar* | 156 |
| CA98/20/2002 | *BSkyB* | 157 |

Excessive Pricing

A dominant undertaking may choose to take advantage of its market power and increase the price of its products above competitive levels. Such practice may amount to an abuse of a dominant position when it involves the imposition of unfair purchase or selling prices or the application of dissimilar conditions to equivalent transactions.

Excessive prices may be analysed using two of the subsections in Article 82 EC. Under Article 82(a) EC they may be challenged when they consist of: 'directly or indirectly imposing unfair purchase or selling prices or other unfair trading conditions'. Under Article 82(c) EC they may be objected to when they result in a discriminatory practice. The following cases provide an illustration of the Commission's and European courts' approach to excessive prices:

26/75	*General Motors v Commission*	158
27/76	*United Brands v Commission*	159
COMP/C–1/36.915	*Deutsche Post AG*	160
HC05C00510	*British Horseracing Board v Victor Chandler International*	161
A3/2006/0126	*At the Races v The British Horse Racing Limits and others*	163

See also summary references to:

395/87	*Ministère Public v Jean-Louis Tournier*	159
30/87	*Corinne Bodson v SA Pompes Funébres des Régions Libérées*	159
110/88	*Lucazeau v SACEM*	160
COMP/A.36.568D3	*Scandlines Sverige AB v Port of Helsingborg Case*	164

Refusal to Supply

The finding of dominance imposes responsibility on the dominant undertaking not to allow its behaviour to impair effective competition. In some cases, this responsibility may lead to restrictions on the dominant undertaking's freedom to choose its trading partners and to refuse to supply others with services or goods. Such will be the case when a dominant undertaking operates at both the upstream and downstream levels and refuses to supply a competitor which operates at the downstream level. Such refusal to supply is contrary to Article 82 EC when it eliminates competition in the downstream market (Case 6/73 below). Another form of refusal to supply that is objectionable occurs when a dominant undertaking controls the provision of an essential infrastructure, uses that essencial facility, but refuses other companies access to that facility without objective justification (Case IV/34.689 below). In other cases a refusal to supply may involve a refusal to licence intellectual property rights (Cases C–241/91P, T–504/93, C–418/01 below).

The analysis of refusal to supply is traditionally based on the finding of two markets: an upstream market dominated by the undertaking and a downstream market in which supply is refused. However, the requirement for two markets has been relaxed in some instances (Case C–418/01 below).

See also summary references to:

See also the Notice on the Application of the Competition Rules to Access Agreements in the Telecommunications Sector, [1998] 5 CMLR 821, where excessive pricing of essential facilities is considered.

Tying and Bundling

Tying and bundling commonly refer to a situation where a dominant undertaking links the sale of separate products requiring customers who wish to purchase one product to purchase the other as well. Such practice enables the dominant firm to leverage its market power from the market where it enjoys a dominant position to the tied product's market where it faces competition. This may be done by contractual arrangements, through discounts or other incentives. The practice may involve pure bundling, where the products are only offered together and cannot be purchased separately. Alternatively it may involve mixed bundling, where products are available separately outside the bundled package, but are offered at a discounted price when purchased as a bundle. Article 82(d) EC makes direct reference to these practices and treats as abusive 'making the conclusion of contracts subject to acceptance by the other parties of supplementary obligations which, by their nature or according to commercial usage, have no connection with the subject of such contracts.'

See also summary reference to:

Two lines of defence are noteworthy when considering claims of tying. The first stems from the need to identify the existence of two products or two markets in order to establish tying. Consequently, the dominant undertaking will often attempt to establish that the two products actually comprise one and therefore by their nature and characteristics should be sold together. Another common, yet rather more general, line of defence addresses the objective justifications, such as economies of scale, efficiencies and safety considerations which may justify tying the products. See below the discussion on objective justification.

Other Forms of Exclusivity

Exclusive dealing through contracts, tying or rebates enables the dominant undertaking to establish its position while excluding competitors from the market. Such practices, even when done at the request of the customer, risk foreclosing the market and may constitute an abuse under Article 82 EC. The economic implications of practices such as single branding and the application of Article 81 EC to these practices were discussed in Chapter 4 herein. See generally:

Objective Justification and Efficiency Defence

Article 82 EC does not include an exempting provision similar to Article 81(3) EC. Nonetheless, seemingly abusive conduct may escape prohibition under Article 82 EC if the dominant undertaking can provide an objective justification for its actions or show that the actions generate efficiencies which outweigh the anticompetitive effects. These defence claims are difficult to prove and have commonly been rejected by the Commission and courts. The Commission's proposed effects based approach to Article 82 EC may open the way for greater consideration of these claims.

See also summary references to:

On objective justification and efficiency defence, see further, the Commission discussion paper on the application of Article 82 of the Treaty to exclusionary abuses (paras 77–92).

Effect on Trade between Member States

Article 82 EC applies only to abuse which may affect trade between Member States. To be capable of affecting trade between Member States, it is sufficient to establish that the conduct is capable of having that effect. On the effect of trade between Member States, see Commission Guidelines on the Effect on Trade Concept Contained in Articles 81 and 82 of the Treaty, [2004] OJ C 101/81. For illustration, also note the following cases:

Nullity and Severance

Although Article 82 does not include a declaration of nullity equivalent to Article 81(2) EC it arguably generates a similar effect when an undertaking is found to abuse its dominant position. See the following judgment from the English court:

An Economic Approach to Article 82

The traditional approach to Article 82 EC as described above encompasses two distinct steps: first dominance needs to be established, following which the abuse of dominance is assessed. In July 2005 the Commission published a consultation paper titled 'An Economic Approach to Article 82' in which the Economic Advisory Group for Competition Policy (EAGCP) questioned the merit in this traditional approach. The paper advocates an effects-based approach which focuses on competitive harm and refrains from treating different categories of behaviour as abusive. It stems from the understanding that the same types of actions may result in different effects on the market, some abusive and others not. Similarly, different types of actions may lead to the same anticompetitive effect.

The paper has no binding power, nor does the Commission discussion paper on the application of Article 82 of the Treaty to exclusionary abuses, which was published in December 2005. Nevertheless, these publications provide an insight to the Commission's current thinking on Article 82 EC.

The economic approach to Article 82 EC remains at present the preserve of the Commission and does not seem to significantly affect the European Courts' analysis. Note, for example, the CFI decision in Case T–340/03 *France Télécom SA v Commission* (March 2007) (page 138 below), T–201/04 *Microsoft Corp v Commission* (17 September 2007) (page 173, 177 herein), and the ECJ decision in Case C–95/04 *British Airways v Commission* (April 2007) (page 152 below).

United Brands v Commission	**Article 82 EC**
Case 27/76	Dominant Position
ECJ, [1978] ECR 207, [1978] 1 CMLR 429	

Facts

In a Commission decision United Brands (UBC) was found to have infringed Article 82 EC by abusing its dominant position in the market for bananas. UBC appealed to the ECJ and challenged the Commission's conclusions with respect to the market definition, the dominant position and the abuse of the dominant position.

Held (on the question of dominance)

In order to determine whether UBC has a dominant position in the market for bananas it is necessary to define the relevant product and geographical markets. The market in this case, as defined by the Commission, is the market for bananas in a substantial part of the common market. (paras 10–57)

Dominant position in Article 82 EC is 'a position of economic strength enjoyed by an undertaking which enables it to prevent effective competition being maintained on the market by giving it the power to behave to an appreciable extent independently of its competitors, customers and ultimately its consumers.' (para 65)

'In order to find out whether UBC is an undertaking in a dominant position on the relevant market it is necessary first of all to examine its structure and then the situation on the said market as far as competition is concerned. In doing so it may be advisable to take account if need be of the facts put forward as acts amounting to abuses without necessarily having to acknowledge that they are abuses.' (paras 67, 68)

UBC resources for and methods of producing, packaging, transporting, selling and displaying its product should be examined.

UBC is vertically integrated to a high degree. This integration is evident at each of the stages from the plantation to the loading in the ports and after those stages, as far as ripening and sale prices are concerned. At the production stage UBC can supplement its own production when needed by obtaining supplies from independent planters. Additionally some independent planters grow the varieties of bananas which UBC has advised them to adopt. UBC plantations are spread over a wide geographic area, a fact which enables it to cope with regional natural disasters and comply with all the requests which it receives. At the packaging and distribution stages, UBC has at its disposal factories, manpower, plant and material which enable it to handle the goods independently. It uses its own transport means to deliver products from plantation to port and is the only undertaking of its kind which is capable of carrying two-thirds of its exports by means of its own banana fleet. UBC is able to transport regularly to Europe and to ensure, using its own ships, that three regular consignments reach Europe each week. This capacity guarantees its commercial stability and well-being. In the field of technical knowledge UBC keeps on improving the productivity and yield of its plantations and perfecting new ripening methods. Competing companies are unable to develop research at a comparable level and are in this respect at a disadvantage compared with UBC. (paras 70–84)

UBC has made its product distinctive by large-scale repeated advertising and promotion campaigns which have induced the consumer to show a preference for it in spite of price differences between the price of labelled and unlabelled bananas. It has revolutionized the commercial exploitation of the banana and made its brand name 'Chiquita' the premier brand name with the result that distributors cannot afford not to offer it to the consumer. (paras 91–3)

UBC is the largest banana group having accounted in 1974 for 35 per cent of all banana exports on the world market. Without going into a discussion about percentages, which when fixed are bound to be to some extent approximations, it can be considered to be an established fact that UBC's share of the relevant market is more than 40 per cent and nearly 45 per cent. (paras 97–108)

UBC's market share does not, however, permit the conclusion that UBC automatically controls the market. Dominance must be determined having regard to the strength and number of the competitors operating in the market. UBC's market share is several times greater than that of its competitor, Castle and Cooke, which is the best placed of all the competitors, the others lagging far behind. This fact, together with the others to which attention has already been drawn, may be regarded as a factor which affords evidence of UBC's preponderant strength. (paras 109–12)

An undertaking does not have to have eliminated all opportunity for competition in order to be in a dominant position. The market for bananas displayed lively competition struggles which on several occasions included large-scale promotion campaigns and price reduction. These periods of competition were, however, limited in time and did not cover the whole of the relevant geographical market. In spite of these efforts made by competitors, they have not succeeded in appreciably increasing their market share in the national markets where they launched their attacks. (paras 113–20)

Barriers to entry to the market include 'the exceptionally large capital investments required for the creation and running of banana plantations, the need to increase sources of supply in order to avoid the effects of fruit diseases and bad weather (hurricanes, floods), the introduction of an essential system of logistics which the distribution of a very perishable product makes necessary, economies of scale from which newcomers to the market cannot derive any immediate benefit and the actual cost of entry made up, inter alia, of all the general expenses incurred in penetrating the market such as the setting up of an adequate commercial network, the mounting of very large-scale advertising campaigns, all those financial risks, the costs of which are irrecoverable if the attempt fails.' (para 122)

Although competitors are able to use the same methods of production and distribution as UBC, they come up against almost insuperable practical and financial obstacles. That is another factor peculiar to a dominant position. (paras 123, 124)

'An undertaking's economic strength is not measured by its profitability; a reduced profit margin or even losses for a time are not incompatible with a dominant position, just as large profits may be compatible with a situation where there is effective competition. The fact that UBC's profitability is for a time moderate or non-existent must be considered in the light of the whole of its operations.' (paras 126, 127)

'The finding that, whatever losses UBC may make, the customers continue to buy more goods from UBC which is the dearest vendor, is more significant and this fact is a particular feature of the dominant position and its verification is determinative in this case.' (para 128)

The cumulative effect of all the advantages enjoyed by UBC thus ensures that is has a dominant position on the relevant market.

Comment

The finding of dominance stemmed from the Commission's finding that the relevant product market was the market for bananas. See detailed analysis of the market definition on page 21 above.

Dominance was referred to as the ability to behave to an appreciable extent independently of competitors, customers and ultimately consumers. (para 62) The ECJ later elaborated that an undertaking does not have to have eliminated all opportunity for competition in order to be in a dominant position. (para 113) In Case 85/76 *Hoffmann-La Roche* (page 129 below) the ECJ appeared to further relax this benchmark by holding that 'Such a position does not preclude some competition, which it does where there is a monopoly or quasi-monopoly, but enables the undertaking … if not to determine, at least to have an appreciable influence on the conditions under which that competition will develop, and in any case to act largely in disregard of it, so long that such conduct does not operate to its detriment.' (para 39)

Hoffmann-La Roche & Co v Commission	**Article 82 EC**
Case 85/76	Dominant Position
ECJ, [1979] ECR 461, [1979] 3 CMLR 211	

Facts

Hoffmann-La Roche (Roche) applied for the annulment of a Commission Decision IV/29.020 – Vitamins, which found Roche to have abused its dominant position in the market for vitamins A, B2, B3, B6, C, E and H. Roche challenged the decision on several points, including the finding of dominance and abuse.

Held (on the question of dominance)

A dominant position enables an undertaking 'to prevent effective competition being maintained on the relevant market by affording it the power to behave to an appreciable extent independently of its competitors, its customers and ultimately of the consumers.' (para 38)

'Such a position does not preclude some competition, which it does where there is a monopoly or a quasi-monopoly, but enables the undertaking which profits by it, if not to determine, at least to have an appreciable influence on the conditions under which that competition will develop, and in any case to act largely in disregard of it so long as such conduct does not operate to its detriment.' (para 39)

Very large market shares are in themselves, and save in exceptional circumstances, evidence of dominance. 'An undertaking which has a very large market share and holds it for some time, by means of the volume of production and the scale of the supply which it stands for – without holders of much smaller market shares being able to meet rapidly the demand from those who would like to break away from the undertaking which has the largest market share – is by virtue of that share in a position of strength which makes it an unavoidable trading partner and which, because of this alone, secures for it, at the very least during relatively long periods, that freedom of action which is the special feature of a dominant position.' (para 41)

Retention of market share may result from effective competition and is not – by itself – an indicator of dominance. However, when dominance is established, retention of market share supports a conclusion that the position of dominance has been maintained. (para 44) The facts that Roche produced a far wider range of vitamins than its competitors and that its turnover exceeded that of all the other competitors, were held to be immaterial to the finding of dominance. (paras 45–7)

Other factors indicating dominance include the disparity between the market share of the leading undertaking and the next largest competitor, the technological lead of an undertaking over its competitors, the existence of a highly developed sales network, barriers to entry and the absence of potential competition. (para 48)

The existence of lively competition on a particular market does not exclude the possibility that a dominant position exists on that market. In this case, price variation in the market did not lead to competitive pressure which was likely to jeopardise the marked degree of independence enjoyed by Roche. (paras 49–78)

The Commission was right to find dominance in the market for vitamins A, B2, B6, C, E and H.

The Commission was wrong in its finding of dominance in the vitamin B3 market.

Comment

Note that the two-stage analysis relies heavily on market definition, and subsequently market characteristics. Market share is only one of the indicators of dominance and should be analysed accordingly, bearing in mind the other market characteristics. Note especially that large market shares must exist 'for some time' and that in 'exceptional circumstances' they may not establish dominance. On market definition in this case see page 23 above. On the finding of abuse see page 145 below.

AKZO Chemie BV v Commission	**Article 82 EC**
Case C–62/86	Dominant Position
ECJ, [1991] ECR I–3359, 1993 5 CMLR 215	

Facts

AKZO Chemie (Akzo) applied for the annulment of a Commission decision (IV/30698 ECS/AKZO Chemie) in which the Commission found that Akzo had abused its dominant position in the organic peroxides market, by pursuing against one of its competitors a course of conduct intended to damage its business and secure its withdrawal from the market. Akzo challenged the decision on several grounds, one of them being the finding of dominance.

Held (on the question of dominance)

'With regard to market shares the Court has held that very large shares are in themselves, and save in exceptional circumstances, evidence of the existence of a dominant position. … That is the situation where there is a market share of 50% such as that found to exist in this case.' (para 60)

'Moreover, the Commission rightly pointed out that other factors confirmed AKZO's predominance in the market. In addition to the fact that AKZO regards itself as the world leader in the peroxides market, it should be observed that, as AKZO itself admits, it has the most highly developed marketing organization, both commercially and technically, and wider knowledge than that of their competitors with regard to safety and toxicology.' (para 61)

Comment

The court referred to Case 85/76 Roche (page 129 above) and held that a market share of 50 per cent is indicative of dominance. It thus established a rebuttable presumption of dominance in market shares of 50 per cent and above.

This rebuttable presumption shifts the burden of proof to the alleged dominant undertaking which has to establish that it is not dominant despite holding a market share of 50 per cent or more. The likelihood of successfully invalidating this presumption is eroded the larger the market share is. Yet, note that the market share serves only as one of several factors indicating the existence or lack of dominance.

Note that dominance can be found below the threshold of 50 per cent market share. See, for example, *Virgin/British Airways* (COMP/34.780, para 88), where the Commission found British Airways to dominate the market with a market share of 39.7 per cent. Also note *United Brands* (page 127 above) where a market share of 40–45 per cent supported a conclusion of dominance.

The Akzo presumption applies only to single firm dominance and not to collective dominance. See Chapter 6 herein and in particular *France v Commission (Kali und Salz)* (para 226) (C–68/94, [1998] ECR I–1375).

On single dominance, see also paragraphs 28–42, DG Competition Discussion Paper on the Application of Article 82 of the Treaty to Exclusionary Abuses (December 2005).

Hugin v Commission	**Article 82 EC**
Case 22/78	Dominant Position
ECJ, [1979] ECR 1869, [1979] 3 CMLR 345	

Facts

Hugin was fined by the European Commission for refusing to supply spare parts for its cash registers to Liptons, a company which was not part of the Hugin distribution system. The Commission found Hugin's refusal to supply to constitute an abuse of a dominant position (Case IV/29.132 *Hugin/Liptons*). On appeal to the ECJ, Hugin contested, among other things, the finding of dominance.

Held (on the question of dominance)

The definition of the market in question should take account of the fact that the conduct alleged against Hugin consists in the refusal to supply spare parts to independent undertakings outside its distribution network. 'The question is, therefore, whether the supply of spare parts constitutes a specific market or whether it forms part of a wider market. To answer that question it is necessary to determine the category of clients who require such parts.' (para 5)

Cash registers are of such a technical nature that the user cannot fit the spare parts into the machine but requires the services of a specialised technician. That being the case, users of cash registers do not operate on the market as purchasers of spare parts but require the service of undertakings engaged in maintenance and repair work. While there certainly exists amongst users a market for maintenance and repairs which is distinct from the market in new cash registers, it is essentially a market for the provision of services and not for the sale of a product such as spare parts, the refusal to supply which forms the subject-matter of the Commission's Decision. (para 6)

However, a separate market for Hugin spare parts does exists at the level of independent undertakings which specialise in the maintenance and repair of cash registers. Hugin spare parts are not interchangeable with spare parts for cash registers of other makes. Consequently, there is a specific demand for Hugin's spare parts from independent undertakings engaged in the activities of maintenance service and repairs of Hugin cash registers. It flows from this that the market constituted by Hugin spare parts required by independent undertakings must be regarded as the relevant market for the purposes of the application of Article 82 EC. This is also the market on which the alleged abuse was committed. (paras 7, 8)

It is necessary to examine next whether Hugin occupies a dominant position on that market. Hugin controls most, if not all, of the production and supply of spare parts which could be used in Hugin cash registers. Therefore, Hugin occupies a dominant position on the market for its own spare parts and enjoys a position which enables it to determine its conduct without taking account of competing sources of supply. (paras 9, 10)

Comment

This decision highlights the impact market definition has on the conclusion of dominance. Although Hugin was a relatively small undertaking which occupied a small share of the general market for cash registers, the definition of the market as the market for its own spare parts led to finding of dominance. In other words, despite its lack of market power on the primary product (cash registers) it was found to dominate the narrow market for the complementary product (spare parts).

After finding dominance the ECJ considered whether the Commission was successful in establishing all the other conditions of Article 82 EC. The ECJ found that Hugin's conduct was not capable of affecting trade between Member States and consequently annulled the Commission's decision. (paras 15–26)

Nederlandsche Banden Industrie Michelin v Commission	**Article 82 EC**
Case 322/81	Dominant Position
ECJ, [1983] ECR 3461, [1985] 1 CMLR 282	

Facts

Michelin NV was responsible for the production and sale of Michelin tyres in the Netherlands. The Commission found that Michelin abused its dominant position on the market for new replacement tyres for lorries, buses and similar vehicles by operating anticompetitive target-based discount schemes (Case iv/29.491). On appeal to the ECJ Michelin contested, among other things, the Commission's finding of a dominant position. To establish the existence of a dominant position the Court considered Michelin's share of the relevant product market as well as its position in relation to its competitors, customers and consumers. It subsequently accepted the Commission's definition of the relevant market and the finding concerning Michelin's market shares.

Held (on the question of dominance)

Michelin NV's share of the market in new replacement tyres for lorries, buses and similar vehicles in the Netherlands was between 57 and 65 per cent, whereas the market share of its main competitors was only 4–8 per cent (from 1975 to 1980). This market share constitutes a valid indication of Michelin's preponderant strength in relation to its competitors. (paras 22–52)

'In order to assess the relative economic strength of Michelin NV and its competitors on the Netherlands market the advantages which those undertakings may derive from belonging to groups of undertakings operating throughout Europe or even the world must be taken into consideration. Amongst those advantages, the lead which the Michelin group has over its competitors in the matters of investment and research and the special extent of its range of products, to which the Commission referred in its Decision, have not been denied. In fact in the case of certain types of tyre the Michelin group is the only supplier on the market to offer them in its range.' (para 55)

'That situation ensures that on the Netherlands market a large number of users of heavy-vehicle tyres have a strong preference for Michelin tyres. As the purchase of tyres represents a considerable investment for a transport undertaking and since much time is required in order to ascertain in practice the cost-effectiveness of a type or brand of tyre, Michelin NV therefore enjoys a position which renders it largely immune to competition. As a result, a dealer established in the Netherlands normally cannot afford not to sell Michelin tyres.' (para 56)

Michelin NV's large network of commercial representatives is not matched by its competitors, and gives Michelin NV direct access to tyre users at all times. This, and the standard of service which the network can give them, enables Michelin NV to maintain and strengthen its position on the market and to protect itself more effectively against competition. (para 58)

The existence of a dominant position in this case is not disproved by temporary unprofitability or losses. By the same token, the fact that the prices charged by Michelin NV do not constitute an abuse and are not particularly high is not inconsistent with the existence of a dominant position. (para 59) The finding of dominance simply means that the undertaking concerned has a special responsibility not to allow its conduct to impair genuine undistorted competition on the Common Market. (para 57)

Comment

In its decision the Commission relied on Michelin's price discrimination policy as evidence of dominance. The court did not comment on this part of the Commission decision. On the relationship between abuse and dominance, note the EAGCP paper on 'An Economic Approach to Article 82' (July 2005).

The Coca-Cola Company v Commission	**Article 82 EC**
Case T–125/97	Dominant Position
CFI, [2000] ECR II–1733, [2000] 5 CMLR 467	The Requirement for 'Fresh Analysis'

Facts

The Coca-Cola Company and Cadbury Schweppes plc operated in the UK partly through their subsidiary, Coca-Cola & Schweppes Beverages Ltd (CCSB). CCSB handled the bottling, distribution, promotion and marketing of beverages of the two companies. The Commission, in proceedings under the European Merger Regulation (Case IV/M.794 – *Coca-Cola/Amalgamated Beverages GB*) found, inter alia, that CCSB held a dominant position on the British cola market. However the Commission declared the notified operation compatible with the common market. On appeal, the companies challenged the Commission's finding of dominance.

Held

'It is settled case-law that any measure which produces binding legal effects such as to affect the interests of an applicant by bringing about a distinct change in his legal position is an act or decision which may be the subject of an action under [Article 230 EC] for a declaration that it is void (*IBM v Commission*, cited above, paragraph 9, Joined Cases C–68/94 and C–30/95 *France and others v Commission* [1998] ECR I–1375, paragraph 62, and Case T–87/96 *Assicurazioni Generali and Unicredito v Commission* [1999] ECR II–203, paragraph 37).' (para 77)

'… [A] finding of a dominant position by the Commission, even if likely in practice to influence the policy and future commercial strategy of the undertaking concerned, does not have binding legal effects as referred to in the IBM judgment. Such a finding is the outcome of an analysis of the structure of the market and of competition prevailing at the time the Commission adopts each decision. The conduct which the undertaking held to be in a dominant position subsequently comes to adopt in order to prevent a possible infringement of [Article 82 EC] is thus shaped by the parameters which reflect the conditions of competition on the market at a given time.' (para 81)

'Moreover, in the course of any decision applying [Article 82 EC], the Commission must define the relevant market again and make a fresh analysis of the conditions of competition which will not necessarily be based on the same considerations as those underlying the previous finding of a dominant position.' (para 82)

'… A national court which has to assess action taken by CCSB after the contested decision in the context of a dispute between CCSB and a third party is not bound by previous findings of the Commission. There is nothing to prevent it from concluding that CCSB is no longer in a dominant position, contrary to the Commission's finding at the time when the contested decision was adopted.' (para 85)

'It is clear from the foregoing considerations that the mere finding in the contested decision that CCSB holds a dominant position has no binding legal effects so that the applicants' challenge to its merits is not admissible.' (para 92)

Comment

Market definition and the finding of dominance provide an indication of the boundaries of competition and the market power of the undertakings involved, in a given time and with respect to a given product. As such, the empirical analysis cannot bind a future analysis of another product or alleged abuse at a later stage.

Suiker Unie and others v Commission	**Article 82 EC**
Joined Cases 40–48, 50, 54–56, 111, 113, 114/73	Substantial Part of the Common Market
ECJ, [1975] ECR 1663, [1976] 1 CMLR 295	

Facts

Joint appeal on the Commission decision in Case IV/26.918 – European Sugar Industry, in which the Commission found a number of undertakings to engage in concerted actions contrary to Article 81 EC with the aim of protecting national markets and eliminating interstate trade. In addition, the Commission accused some of the undertakings of abusing their dominant position by bringing economic pressure to bear on importers with the object of compelling them to restrict their imports. As part of its decision the ECJ considered whether the markets in question constituted a substantial part of the Common Market.

Held (on the Belgo-Luxembourg market)

'For the purpose of determining whether a specific territory is large enough to amount to "a substantial part of the common market" within the meaning of [Article 82 EC] the pattern and volume of the production and consumption of the said product as well as the habits and economic opportunities of vendors and purchasers must be considered.' (para 371)

'So far as sugar in particular is concerned it is advisable to take into consideration in addition to the high freight rates in relation to the price of the product and the habits of the processing industries and consumers, the fact that Community rules have consolidated most of the special features of the former national markets.' (para 372)

'From 1968/69 to 1971/72 Belgian production and total Community production increased respectively from 530 000 to 770 000 metric tons and from 6 800 000 to 8 100 000 metric tons. … During these marketing years Belgian consumption was approximately 350 000 metric tons whereas Community consumption increased from 5 900 000 to 6 500 000 metric tons…' (paras 373, 374)

'If the other criteria mentioned above are taken into account these market shares are sufficiently large for the area covered by Belgium and Luxembourg to be considered, so far as sugar is concerned, as a substantial part of the common market in this product.' (para 375)

Comment

The relative size of Belgian sugar production in comparison to the wider community production levels led to a finding that the area covered by Belgium and Luxembourg constituted a substantial part of the common market. Note that when assessing whether the market was 'substantial' the Court did not limit itself to the size of the geography but considered the pattern and volume of the production and consumption.

The requirement for 'substantial part of the common market' acts as a de minimis threshold. The finding of 'substantial part' should not be confused with the additional requirement of finding an effect on trade between Member States.

AKZO Chemie BV v Commission	**Article 82 EC**
Case C–62/86	Abuse
ECJ, [1991] ECR I–3359, [1993] 5 CMLR 215	Predatory Pricing

Facts

AKZO Chemie (Akzo) applied for the annulment of a Commission decision (IV/30.698 – ECS/AKZO Chemie) which found that Akzo had abused its dominant position in the organic peroxides market by endeavouring to eliminate one of its competitors (ECS) from the market mainly by massive and prolonged price-cutting in the flour additives sector. Akzo contested the Commission finding of pricing below average variable cost (AVC) and argued that it priced above AVC and therefore did not engage in predatory pricing.

Held (on the question of predation)

Article 82 EC prohibits a dominant undertaking from eliminating a competitor and thereby strengthening its position by using methods other than those which come within the scope of competition on the basis of quality. 'Prices below average variable costs (that is to say, those which vary depending on the quantities produced) by means of which a dominant undertaking seeks to eliminate a competitor must be regarded as abusive. A dominant undertaking has no interest in applying such prices except that of eliminating competitors so as to enable it subsequently to raise its prices by taking advantage of its monopolistic position, since each sale generates a loss, namely the total amount of the fixed costs (that is to say, those which remain constant regardless of the quantities produced) and, at least, part of the variable costs relating to the unit produced.' (paras 70, 71)

'Moreover, prices below average total costs, that is to say, fixed costs plus variable costs, but above average variable costs, must be regarded as abusive if they are determined as part of a plan for eliminating a competitor. Such prices can drive from the market undertakings which are perhaps as efficient as the dominant undertaking but which, because of their smaller financial resources, are incapable of withstanding the competition waged against them.' (para 72)

In this case AKZO directly threatened ECS that it would drop its prices in the flour additives sector if ECS continued to sell benzoyl peroxide in the plastics sector. The threats were aimed at convincing ECS to withdraw from the market. (paras 75–80)

AKZO's pricing strategy led to unreasonably low prices with the aim of damaging ECS's viability. AKZO maintained, as part of this strategy, the prices of some of its products at an artificially low level over a prolonged period without any objective justification. Akzo survived this pricing strategy because of its superior financial resources compared to those of ECS. (paras 83–109, 131–40)

Comment

In order to distinguish between permissible price competition and abusive predation, consideration needs to be given to the economics at the base of the pricing policies. In principle, competition law is not concerned with price competition which drives less-efficient undertakings out of the market; however, predation strategy enables the dominant undertaking to eliminate equally efficient competitors from the market and is therefore held abusive.

The evaluation of predation is predominantly based on cost. Two cost benchmarks were referred to in Akzo: (1) Average total costs (ATC), which reflects the total cost of production of one unit of output. This cost is calculated by taking both fixed and variable costs and dividing them by the number of units produced. (2) Average variable costs (AVC), which is the variable cost of production of one unit of output. This cost is calculated by dividing the variable costs (but not the fixed costs) by the number of units produced. This parameter ignores the fixed costs which were already incurred by the undertaking and measures the real cost of producing one unit of output. A third cost benchmark, which was not referred to in this case but is often mentioned in the literature, is average avoidable costs (AAC). AAC reflects the cost which would be avoided by not producing a unit of product. It reflects avoidable losses and may differ from AVC when the undertaking had to make a specific investment in order to be able to predate.

Following the Akzo judgment, predation is presumed where undertakings price products below AVC (or AAC). This is the case as the undertaking is losing money by producing the product and therefore the practice has no commercial justification. When prices are above AVC (and AAC) but below ATC the conduct may be held abusive when the undertaking intended to eliminate a competitor. At this level although the undertaking fails to cover its fixed costs it is able to sell above its variable costs and therefore can still benefit from the production of additional units. Above ATC, the undertaking is making profits and there is no indication of predation.

It is important to note that the presumption of predation below AVC is a rebuttable one. Such price policy can in some instances be objectively justifiable, for example when an undertaking engages in short-term promotion or has entered a market based on false assumptions of profitability.

Note that although abuse is an objective concept, when considering predation the party's intention to eliminate a competitor plays a role. Accordingly, predation may be established when pricing above AVC but below ATC with the intention of eliminating competition. See para 71 above.

In the US in order to establish predation it is necessary to show that the monopolist is able to recoup its short-run losses in the long run. The rational behind this condition is that in the absence of recoupment, a rational undertaking will not engage in predation. The ECJ did not consider recoupment as a necessary condition in its Akzo decision. On recoupment, note Case C–333/94 P *Tetra Pak v Commission*, page 137 below, and Case T–340/03 *France Télécom SA v Commission*, page 138 below.

On the feasibility of recouping losses, also note the UK Guidelines on Assessment of Individual Agreements and Conduct (OFT 414) 2.19–4.21. Also note OFT 657 'Assessing Profitability in Competition Policy Analysis (2003).

Tetra Pak International SA v Commission	**Article 82 EC**
Case C–333/94 P	Abuse
ECJ, [1996] ECR I–5951, [1997] 4 CMLR 662	Predatory Pricing – Recoupment

Facts

Tetra Pak International SA (Tetra Pak) specialises in equipment for the packaging of liquid or semi-liquid food products in cartons. The Commission found Tetra Pak to have abused its dominant position by, among other things, tying the sales of machinery for packaging with the sales of cartons, and by engaging in predatory pricing (IV/31.043 – *Tetra Pak II*). The CFI dismissed Tetra Pak's application for annulment of the Commission's decision. Tetra Pak appealed to the ECJ, asking it to quash the CFI judgment. On the issue of predatory pricing Tetra Pak argued that the CFI erred in its judgment when it failed to consider the prospect of recouping losses as part of the analysis of predation.

Held

In the judgment under appeal, the CFI carried out the examination of predation in line with the criteria set by the ECJ in the Akzo judgment. Accordingly, the CFI considered the prices of non-aseptic cartons in Italy between 1976 and 1981 and found that these were considerably lower than average variable costs. As indicated in Akzo, prices below average variable costs result in a loss for each item produced and sold. Such a pricing strategy must always be considered abusive as there is no conceivable economic purpose for it other than the elimination of a competitor. Proof of intention to eliminate competitors is not necessary when pricing below AVC. (paras 41, 42)

'It would not be appropriate, in the circumstances of the present case, to require in addition proof that Tetra Pak had a realistic chance of recouping its losses. It must be possible to penalize predatory pricing whenever there is a risk that competitors will be eliminated. The Court of First Instance found, at paragraphs 151 and 191 of its judgment, that there was such a risk in this case. The aim pursued, which is to maintain undistorted competition, rules out waiting until such a strategy leads to the actual elimination of competitors.' (para 44)

Comment

Note that the predatory practice took place in a market other than the one in which Tetra Pak held a dominant position. In paragraph 30 of its decision the ECJ held that the associative links between the non-aseptic and aseptic markets meant that the Commission was not required to show that Tetra Pak was dominant on the non-aseptic markets where it engaged in predatory pricing. For an example of weaker associated links between markets which led to a conclusion on predation, see the French Competition Council decision concerning GlaxoSmithKline (GSK). There, associative links between the 'Zinnat' and 'Zovirax' markets were established, leading to a finding that GSK abused its dominant position in the Zovirax market by engaging in predatory pricing in the Zinnat market. (Décision No 07-D-09 du 14 mars 2007 relative à des pratiques mises en oeuvre par le laboratoire GlaxoSmithKline France)

The Commission's Discussion Paper on the Application of Article 82 of the Treaty to Exclusionary Abuses suggests that recoupment may be presumed in most cases. 'It will in general be sufficient to show the likelihood of recoupment by investigating the entry barriers to the market, the (strengthened) position of the company and foreseeable changes to the future structure of the market. As dominance is already established this normally means that entry barriers are sufficiently high to presume the possibility to recoup.' (para 122)

In Case T–340/03 *France Télécom SA v Commission* (page 138 below) the CFI, referring to the Akzo and Tetra Pak judgments, held that when proving predation it is not necessary to establish that the undertaking had a realistic chance of recouping its losses. (para 227) On recoupment, see also comments on page 140 below.

France Télécom SA v Commission	**Article 82 EC**
Case T–340/03	Abuse
CFI, [2007] 4 CMLR 21	Predatory Pricing and Price Alignment

Facts

Wanadoo Interactive (Wanadoo), a subsidiary of France Télécom, was fined by the Commission for abusing its dominant position in the market for ADSL-based Internet access services for the general public by charging predatory prices for its Pack eXtense and Wanadoo ADSL services. The Commission found that this deliberate strategy restricted market entry and development potential for competitors in the market and was part of a plan aimed at pre-empting the market for high-output Internet access services. (Case COMP/38.233 *Wanadoo Interactive*)

In its analysis the Commission made adjustments to the application of the Akzo predation test, in the sense of greater flexibility. This was done in order to reflect the industry characteristics and the features peculiar to the launching of a new product. Accordingly, instead of simply examining costs and revenue as suggested in the Akzo judgment, the Commission has spread customer acquisition costs over 48 months, treating as it were these costs as a commercial investment to be written off over a customer's realistic lifetime. Moreover, in its assessment of the revenue generated by subscriptions, the Commission has taken into account a theoretical, nominal subscription revenue, and not the average revenue actually observed. The combined effect of these two corrections was to improve the cost recovery rates used in this decision compared with what they would have been had they simply been based on the unadjusted accounting data (Akzo). The Commission has also ignored the cost of capital in its analysis. These adjustments enabled the Commission to asses whether Wanadoo will be able to secure a return on its investment within a reasonable time, rather than to recover all its costs at once. (Commission Decision, paras 39–109, 257–70)

'The Commission considers that the legal precedents do not cover every possible predation scenario. Predation can take forms other than the radical elimination and wholesale ousting of competitors from the market. More generally, predation may simply consist in dictating or inhibiting the competitive behaviour of an existing or potential rival. Here, a predatory price is simply one which leads to a maximization of profits through its exclusionary or other anticompetitive effects.' (Commission Decision, para 266)

The Commission considers that proof of recoupment of losses is not a precondition for a finding of abuse through predatory pricing. 'While the recoupment of losses initially incurred may constitute a rational objective associated with predation, other scenarios are perfectly conceivable. In certain specific cases, the undertaking may embark upon a strategy of predation with aims other than the achievement of operating margins higher than those which would prevail in a competitive context. For example, in certain highly specific share ownership scenarios, the undertaking may attach only secondary importance to recoupment of its losses. It may also abandon the idea of recouping all its initial losses and concentrate instead on balancing its future costs and revenues. Lastly, it may aim at recoupment in the long term by means other than its operating results.' (Commission Decision, paras 333–9)

Wanadoo appealed to the CFI for the annulment of the Commission's decision, arguing that, among other things, the Commission committed serious errors of law and assessment, in formulating and implementing the test for predatory pricing that it used, and by failing to take account of the highly competitive market context.

Held

'It is clear from the case-law on predatory pricing that, first, prices below average variable costs give grounds for assuming that a pricing practice is eliminatory and that, if the prices are below average total costs but above average variable costs, those prices must be regarded as abusive if they are determined as part of a plan for eliminating a competitor (*AKZO v Commission … Tetra Pak v Commission …*).' (para 130)

It is clear from the Commission's decision that the application of the accounting method used in AKZO and Tetra Pak, which takes into account the costs simply as they appear in the undertaking's accounts, leads in the present case to very low rates of recovery. The Commission therefore corrected the data recorded on Wanadoo's accounts, in favour of Wanadoo, to take account of the particular context of the market. In doing so the Commission did not apply an unlawful test of recovery of costs. (paras 131–54)

Price Alignment

'It must be pointed out, first of all, that the Commission is in no way disputing the right of an operator to align its prices on those previously charged by a competitor. It states in recital 315 of the decision that "[w]hilst it is true that the dominant operator is not strictly speaking prohibited from aligning its prices on those of competitors, this option is not open to it where it would result in its not recovering the costs of the service in question". (para 176)

In *Akzo v Commission* the conferral on a dominant undertaking of a right to align its conduct was limited. That observation applies both to the Commission Decision 83/462 making an order for interim measures and the subsequent judgment of the Court of Justice (*AKZO v Commission* … paragraph 134). (para 178)

'Indeed, in Decision 83/462, the Commission did not permit AKZO to align its prices generally on those of its competitors but only, in respect of a particular customer, to align its prices on those of another supplier ready and able to supply to that customer. In addition, that authorisation to align prices in very precise circumstances was not contained in the final decision adopted in that case (Commission Decision 85/609/EEC of 14 December 1985 relating to a proceeding under Article [82 EC] (IV/30.698 – ECS/AKZO Chemie); [1985] OJ L 374, p 1).' (para 179)

'It should be recalled that, according to established case-law, although the fact that an undertaking is in a dominant position cannot deprive it of the right to protect its own commercial interests if they are attacked and such an undertaking must be allowed the right to take such reasonable steps as it deems appropriate to protect those interests, such behaviour cannot be countenanced if its actual purpose is to strengthen this dominant position and abuse it (*United Brands v Commission* … paragraph 189; Case T–65/89 *BPB Industries and British Gypsum v Commission* [1993] ECR II–389, paragraph 117; and *Compagnie Maritime Belge Transports and others v Commission* … paragraph 146).' (para 185)

'[Wanadoo] cannot therefore rely on an absolute right to align its prices on those of its competitors in order to justify its conduct. Even if alignment of prices by a dominant undertaking on those of its competitors is not in itself abusive or objectionable, it might become so where it is aimed not only at protecting its interests but also at strengthening and abusing its dominant position.' (para 187)

No Need to Prove Effect of Eliminating Competition

'As regards the conditions for the application of Article 82 EC and the distinction between the object and effect of the abuse, it should be pointed out that, for the purposes of applying that article, showing an anti-competitive object and an anti-competitive effect may, in some cases, be one and the same thing. If it is shown that the object pursued by the conduct of an undertaking in a dominant position is to restrict competition, that conduct will also be liable to have such an effect. Thus, with regard to the practices concerning prices, the Court of Justice held in *AKZO v Commission*, paragraph 100 above, that prices below average variable costs applied by an undertaking in a dominant position are regarded as abusive in themselves because the only interest which the undertaking may have in applying such prices is that of eliminating competitors, and that prices below average total costs but above average variable costs are abusive if they are determined as part of a plan for eliminating a competitor. In that case, the Court did not require any demonstration of the actual effects of the practices in question (see, to that effect, Case T–203/01 *Michelin v Commission* [2003] ECR II–4071, paragraphs 241 and 242).' (para 195)

'Furthermore, it should be added that, where an undertaking in a dominant position actually implements a practice whose object is to oust a competitor, the fact that the result hoped for is not achieved is not sufficient to prevent that being an abuse of a dominant position within the meaning of Article 82 EC (*Compagnie Maritime Belge Transports and others v Commission,* paragraph 104 above, paragraph 149, and Case T–228/97 *Irish Sugar v Commission* [1999] ECR II–2969, paragraph 191).' (para 196)

'It is clear therefore that, in the case of predatory pricing, the first element of the abuse applied by the dominant undertaking comprises non-recovery of costs. In the case of non-recovery of variable costs, the second element, that is, predatory intent, is presumed, whereas, in relation to prices below average full costs, the existence of a plan to eliminate competition must be proved. According to Case T83/91 *Tetra Pak v Commission,* paragraph 130 above, paragraph 151, that intention to eliminate competition must be established on the basis of sound and consistent evidence.' (para 197)

Recoupment of Losses

'In line with Community case-law, the Commission was … able to regard, as abusive, prices below average variable costs. In that case, the eliminatory nature of such pricing is presumed (see, to that effect, Case T–83/91 *Tetra Pak v Commission* … paragraph 148). In relation to full costs, the Commission had also to provide evidence that [Wanadoo's] predatory pricing formed part of a plan to pre-empt the market. In the two situations, it was not necessary to establish in addition proof that [Wanadoo] had a realistic chance of recouping its losses.' (paras 227, 224–8)

Action dismissed.

Comment

The CFI favoured a form-based approach to establishing predation. It rejected arguments concerning the need to demonstrate the actual effects of the practice (paras 195–7) and held that recoupment is not necessary when establishing predation.

This form-based approach is especially interesting in light of the Commission's attempt to foster an effects-based approach which focuses on consumer harm. See EAGCP report 'An Economic Approach to Article 82' (July 2005). Note in particular pages 50–53 on predation.

Contrast the CFI's approach with the requirement to show likelihood of recoupment under US law. See in particular the US Supreme Court decision in *Brooke Group Ltd v Brown & Williamson Tobacco Corp* 509 US 940 (1993). Also note the Supreme Court decision in *Weyerhaeuser Co v Ross-Simmons Hardwood Lumber Co Inc* 127 SCt 1069 (2007), dealing with predatory bidding.

Also note the UK Competition Commission's approach according to which 'in order to prove that an instance of below-cost selling is a predatory strategy, it is necessary to show that there is a strong likelihood that the predator will recoup the profit it has initially sacrificed. If the predator is unlikely to recoup its lost profit, then setting low prices is unlikely to be part of a predatory strategy. Recoupment is more likely the less profit is sacrificed and the greater the added market power the predator gains from excluding the target. Added market power from excluding the target is greater, the closer the target is as a competitor (i.e. the greater the constraint it exerts over the behaviour of the predator, while no other rivals maintain the same degree of competitive pressure) and the greater the barriers to entry and re-entry.' The AKZO test, which presumes predation if costs are below average variable cost, 'may be too rigid a test because of its apparent failure to acknowledge that prices below average variable cost may be set pro-competitively.' (UK Competition Commission 2007 'Pricing Practices Working Paper' (Groceries market inquiry) pages 6, 7)

On meeting the competition, note the CFI comments (paras 176–87) in which it held that predatory pricing cannot be justified by an alignment (meeting the competition) argument. The court held that a dominant company can protect its commercial interests but cannot, in doing so, strengthen its dominant position and abuse it.

Compagnie Maritime Belge Transports and others v Commission	**Article 82 EC**
Joined Cases C–395, 366/96 P	Abuse
ECJ, [2000] ECR I–1365, [2000] 4 CMLR 1076	Selective Price Cuts

Facts

Compagnie Maritime Belge Transports SA (CMB) was found by the Commission to have abused a collective dominant position that it held with other undertakings. Together, the companies formed the membership of a liner conference and implemented a cooperation agreement which aimed, through selective price cuts, to drive an independent competitor out of the market (a practice known as 'fighting ships'). The companies were also found to infringe Article 81 EC by entering into a non-competition agreement. The CFI dismissed an application by CMB to annul the Commission's decision. CMB appealed to the ECJ.

Held (on selective price cuts)

'In certain circumstances, abuse may occur if an undertaking in a dominant position strengthens that position in such a way that the degree of dominance reached substantially fetters competition'. (paras 112–13)

The conduct at issue here is that of a liner conference having a share of over 90 per cent of the market in question and only one competitor. The conference engaged in a practice known as fighting ships in an attempt to eliminate its only competitor from the market. (para 119)

'Where a liner conference in a dominant position selectively cuts its prices in order deliberately to match those of a competitor, it derives a dual benefit. First, it eliminates the principal, and possibly the only, means of competition open to the competing undertaking. Second, it can continue to require its users to pay higher prices for the services which are not threatened by that competition.' (para 117)

Comment

Distinction should be made between a permissible attempt by the dominant firm to meet the competition by lowering prices in a reasonable and proportional manner (above ATC) and an anticompetitive practice of selective price cuts aimed at beating the competition. In this respect note the special circumstances in CMB which included the undertakings' large market share, their intention to eliminate all competition in the market, the unique cost structure and characteristics of the maritime transport market, and the ability of the undertakings to share the losses of revenue among themselves. See also AG Fennelly opinion paras 131–7.

See the Commission's decision in Case IV/30.787 *Eurofix-Bauco v Hilti*, [1998] OJ L65/19, where it fined Hilti for abusing its dominant position by, among other things, targeting customers of its competitors and offering them especially favourable conditions. These conditions were selective and discriminatory and were not offered to existing customers. The Commission found that 'only a dominant undertaking such as Hilti could carry out such a strategy because it is able, through its market power, to maintain prices to all its other customers unaffected by its selective discriminatory discounts.' (para 80) Hilti also hindered competition by removing discounts from its own customers who purchased from its competitors. The decision did not involve assessment of cost structure and was argued on the basis that 'selective discriminatory pricing policy by a dominant firm designed purely to damage the business of, or deter market entry by, its competitors, whilst maintaining higher prices for the bulk of its customers, is both exploitive of these other customers and destructive of competition.' (para 81)

See also the CFI decision in Case T–228/97 *Irish Sugar v Commission*, [1999] ECR II–2969, where the CFI upheld the Commission's decision regarding the abusive nature of selective rebates to customers. Similarly to the other decisions, the significant variables in this case were the high market share of the dominant under-taking, the intention to exclude competitors, the lack of efficiency rational at the base of the practice and the harm to consumers.

Digital Equipment Corporation	**Article 82 EC**
Commission Press Release IP/97/868	Abuse
European Commission (10 October 1997)	Price Alignment

Facts

Following an investigation into the commercial practices of Digital Equipment Corporation (Digital), the Commission issued a formal statement of objections in which it found Digital to have abused its dominant position by developing a commercial policy typified by discriminatory practices and tying.

To resolve the Commission's concerns, Digital offered to modify its service portfolio and pricing practices. The formal undertakings provided by Digital included commitments according to which Digital undertook to pursue a transparent and non-discriminatory discount policy. Although Digital reserved the right to grant non-standard price reductions to meet competition, it undertook to verify that all discounted prices would remain above average total costs, would be proportionate and would not prevent or distort competition. Digital acknowledged that the Commission may initiate proceedings if service prices fall below their average total costs.

Comment

The nature of the commitment regarding meeting the competition highlights the relativity of the dominant company's right to align price. Accordingly, there is no absolute right to align prices.

In Case 27/76 *United Brands v Commission* the Court held that 'although it is true … that the fact that an undertaking is in a dominant position cannot disentitle it from protecting its own commercial interests if they are attacked, and that such an undertaking must be conceded the right to take such reasonable steps as it deems appropriate to protect its said interests, such behaviour cannot be countenanced if its actual purpose is to strengthen this dominant position and abuse it.' (para 189)

In Case T–228/97 *Irish Sugar v Commission* the CFI held that the grant by Irish Sugar of selective rebates to certain retailers established in the border area between Ireland and Northern Ireland was abusive. The CFI rejected Irish Sugar's argument that its practice was aimed at meeting the competition and was defensive in nature. The defensive nature of the practice did not alter the fact that the practice constituted an abuse for the purposes of Article 82(c). (paras 186–7). See page 180 below.

In Case T–340/03 *France Télécom SA v Commission* the CFI held that there is no absolute right to align prices and that predatory pricing cannot be justified by alignment (meeting the competition) argument. The Court held that a dominant company can protect it commercial interests but cannot, in doing so, strengthen its dominant position and abuse it. (paras 176–87) See page 138 above.

Note 'DG Competition Discussion Paper on the Application of Article 82 of the Treaty to Exclusionary Abuses where the Commission considers that a meeting-of-competition defence can only apply to individual and not to collective behaviour to meet competition. The action taken by the undertaking needs to be suitable, proportional and indispensable. In this respect, pricing below average avoidable cost (AAC) is in general neither suitable nor indispensable to minimise the dominant company losses. (paras 81–3)

United Brands v Commission	**Article 82 EC**
Case 27/76	Price Discrimination
ECJ, [1978] ECR 207, [1978] 1 CMLR 429	

Facts

In a Commission Decision, United Brands (UBC) was found to have infringed Article 82 EC by abusing its dominant position in the market for bananas. Among the different forms of abuse, UBC was accused of price discrimination. UBC appealed to the ECJ and challenged the Commission's conclusions with respect to the market definition, the dominant position and the abuse of the dominant position.

Held (on discriminatory prices)

The bananas marketed by UBC under the brand name 'Chiquita' have the same geographic origin, belong to the same variety and are of almost the same quality. They are unloaded in two ports, Rotterdam and Bremerhaven, where unloading costs are similar and are resold (except to Scipio and in Ireland) subject to the same terms of payment and conditions of sale. (paras 204–05)

This being so, UBC customers going to Rotterdam and Bremerhaven to obtain their supplies might be expected to be offered the same selling price for 'Chiquita' bananas. However, this is not the case. UBC's selling price differs appreciably according to the Member State where its customers are established. 'The greatest difference in price is 138% between the delivered Rotterdam price charged by UBC to its customers in Ireland and the f.o.r. Bremerhaven price charged by UBC to its customers in Denmark, that is to say the price paid by Danish customers is 2.38 times the price paid by Irish customers.' The Commission blames UBC for abusing its dominant position by applying dissimilar conditions to equivalent transactions with the other trading parties, thereby placing them at a competitive disadvantage. (paras 213, 207–14)

'The applicant states that its prices are determined by market forces and cannot therefore be discriminatory. Further … the price in any given week is calculated so as to reflect as much as possible the anticipated yellow market price in the following week for each national market. This price is fixed by the Rotterdam management after discussions and negotiations between the applicant's local representatives, and the ripener/distributors must take into account the different competitive contexts in which ripener/distributors in the different countries are operating. It finds its objective justification in the average anticipated market price. These price differences are in fact due to fluctuating market factors such as the weather, different availability of seasonal competing fruit, holidays, strikes, government measures [and] currency denominations.' (paras 215–20)

'In short the applicant has been asked by the Commission to take appropriate steps to establish a single banana market at a time when it has in fact been unable to do so.' (para 221)

'According to the applicant as long as the Community institutions have not set up the machinery for a single banana market and the various markets remain national and respond to their individual supply/demand situations, differences in prices between them cannot be prevented.' (para 222)

The price differences in question can reach 30 to 50% in some weeks, even though products supplied under the transactions are equivalent and despite them being freighted in the same ships, and unloaded at the same cost. (paras 223–6)

'[A]lthough the responsibility for establishing the single banana market does not lie with the applicant, it can only endeavour to take 'what the market can bear' provided that it complies with the rules for the Regulation and coordination of the market laid down by the Treaty.' (para 227)

'[O]nce it can be grasped that differences in transport costs, taxation, customs duties, the wages of the labour force, the conditions of marketing, the differences in the parity of currencies, the density of competition may eventually culminate in different retail selling price levels according to the Member States, then it follows those differences are factors which UBC only has to take into account to a limited extent since it sells a product which is always the same and at the same place to ripener/distributors who – alone – bear the risks of the consumers' market.' (para 228)

'[T]he interplay of supply and demand should, owing to its nature, only be applied to each stage where it is really manifest.' (para 229)

'[T]he mechanisms of the market are adversely affected if the price is calculated by leaving out one stage of the market and taking into account the law of supply and demand as between the vendor and the ultimate consumer and not as between the vendor (UBC) and the purchaser (the ripener/distributors).' (para 230)

'[T]hus, by reason of its dominant position UBC, fed with information by its local representatives, was in fact able to impose its selling price on the intermediate purchaser. This price and also the "weekly quota allocated" is only fixed and notified to the customer four days before the vessel carrying the bananas berths.' (para 231)

'[T]hese discriminatory prices, which varied according to the circumstances of the Member States, were ... obstacles to the free movement of goods and their effect was intensified by the clause forbidding the resale of bananas while still green and by reducing the deliveries of the quantities ordered.' (para 232)

'[A] rigid partitioning of national markets was thus created at price levels, which were artificially different, placing certain distributor/ripeners at a competitive disadvantage, since compared with what it should have been, competition had thereby been distorted.' (para 233) '[C]onsequently the policy of differing prices enabling UBC to apply dissimilar conditions to equivalent transactions with other trading parties, thereby placing them at a competitive disadvantage, was an abuse of a dominant position.' (para 234)

Comment

The Court accepted that different market conditions may require a supplier to charge different prices in different territories. However, in this case UBC did not operate at the downstream level and could only take these differences into account to a limited extent.

The ECJ decision was criticised as being too formalistic. It ignored the fact that the demand patterns at the downstream level are not confined to that level and are manifested through the distribution channels. In addition it encouraged UBC to charge a flat rate across the Community which would have resulted in customers in 'cheaper' territories paying more for bananas. Arguably, the judgment was primarily motivated by the ECJ's desire to avoid partitioning of the Common Market (paras 232–3) and is not necessarily indicative of the approach to price differentiation between markets with different demand patterns.

Note that Article 82(c) EC targets discrimination which places other trading parties at a competitive disadvantage. This type of competitive harm is often referred to as second-line injury as it concerns competition between undertakings at the downstream level. Despite this, in *United Brands* it was applied although the distributors did not compete with each other and did not suffer a competitive disadvantage. Similarly, in Case C–18/93 *Corsica Ferries Italia Srl v Corpo dei Piloti del Porto di Genova*, [1994] ECR I–1783, the ECJ appeared to apply Article 82(c) EC without establishing a 'competitive disadvantage'. Interesting in this respect is the comment made by AG Van Gerven in this case: 'It appears implicitly from the Community case-law, in particular the judgments in *United Brands* and in *Merci*, that the Court does not interpret [Article 82(c) EC] restrictively, with the result that it is not necessary, in order to apply it, that the trading partners of the undertaking responsible for the abuse should suffer a competitive disadvantage against each other or against the undertaking in the dominant position.' (para 34) Contrast this statement with the ECJ's clear holding in Case C–95/04 *British Airways v Commission* (page 154 below) where it clarified the need to verify the existence of 'competitive disadvantage' under Article 82(c) EC. Note however that the list of abusive conducts in Article 82 EC is not exhaustive and one can target discriminatory pricing outside the realm of Article 82(c) EC.

Hoffmann-La Roche & Co v Commission	**Article 82 EC**
Case 85/76	Abuse
ECJ, [1979] ECR 461, [1979] 3 CMLR 211	Rebates

Facts

Hoffmann-La Roche (Roche) applied for the annulment of a Commission decision (IV/29.020 – Vitamins) which found Roche to have abused its dominant position in the market for vitamins A, B2, B3, B6, C, E and H. In its decision, the Commission argued that exclusivity terms and fidelity rebates, which were part of Roche's network of agreements with large purchasers of vitamins, amounted to an abuse of a dominant position. Roche challenged the decision on several grounds, including the finding of abuse.

Held (on the question of abuse)

'An undertaking which is in a dominant position on a market and ties purchasers – even if it does so on their request – by an obligation or promise on their part to obtain all or most of their requirements exclusively from the said undertaking abuses its dominant position … whether the obligation in question is stipulated without further qualification or whether it is undertaken in consideration of a grant or rebate. The same applies if the said undertaking, without tying the purchaser by a formal obligation, applies, either under the terms of agreement concluded with these purchasers or unilaterally, a system of fidelity rebates, that is to say, discounts conditional on the customer's obtaining all or most of its requirements – whether the quantity of its purchases being large or small – from the undertaking in a dominant position.' (para 89)

'Obligations of this kind to obtain supplies exclusively from a particular undertaking, whether or not they are in consideration of rebates or of the granting of fidelity rebates intended to give the purchaser an incentive to obtain his supplies exclusively from the undertaking in a dominant position, are incompatible with the objective of undistorted competition within the common market, because – unless there are exceptional circumstances which may make an agreement between undertakings in the context of [Article 81 EC] and in particular of paragraph (3) of that Article, permissible – they are not based on an economic transaction which justifies this burden or benefit but are designed to deprive the purchaser of or restrict his possible choices of sources of supply and to deny other producers access to the market. The fidelity rebate, unlike quantity rebates exclusively linked with the volume of purchases from the producer concerned, is designed through the grant of a financial advantage to prevent customers from obtaining their supplies from competing producers. Furthermore the effect of fidelity rebates is to apply dissimilar conditions to equivalent transactions with other trading parties in that two purchasers pay a different price for the same quantity of the same product depending on whether they obtain their supplies exclusively from the undertaking in a dominant position or have several sources of supply. Finally these practices by an undertaking in a dominant position and especially on an expanding market tend to consolidate this position by means of a form of competition which is not based on the transactions effected and is therefore distorted.' (para 90)

'… The concept of abuse is an objective concept relating to the behaviour of an undertaking in a dominant position which is such as to influence the structure of a market where, as a result of the very presence of the undertaking in question, the degree of competition is weakened and which, through recourse to methods different from those which condition normal competition in products or services on the basis of the transactions of commercial operators, has the effect of hindering the maintenance of the degree of competition still existing in the market or the growth of that competition.' (para 91)

Fidelity rebates could be in the form of both fixed and progressive rates. The fidelity rebates are characterised by a case-by-case customer assessment, setting individual targets aimed at satisfying a maximum portion of the undertaking's demand for a product. On the other hand, quantitative rebates are set to increase the quantity purchased, are solely linked to the volume of purchase and apply to all purchasers. (paras 94–100)

The Commission was right to regard the contracts containing fidelity rebates as an abuse of a dominant position. An 'English clause' in a contract does not remove the discrimination resulting from the fidelity rebates. On the contrary, such a clause had provided Roche with information about market conditions and the pricing strategies of its competitors and aggravated the exploitation of its dominant position in an abusive way. (paras 102–08)

Comment

Fidelity rebates are objectionable when they stimulate customers to tie themselves to the dominant under-taking and create de facto exclusivity. Such rebates weaken the structure of competition in the market, strengthen the market power of the already dominant undertaking and act as a barrier to entry. It is therefore irrelevant that the tied undertaking willingly entered into the agreement and is benefiting in the short term from the rebates.

The ECJ distinguished between quantity (volume) rebates and a fidelity rebate which is designed to prevent customers from obtaining their supplies from competing producers. The latter was held abusive when it lead purchasers to obtain all or most of their requirements exclusively from the said undertaking. (para 89) Note the form-based language used by the court when dealing with fidelity rebates. Contrast this with the CFI approach in *British Airways v Commission* (page 152 below) where the court noted that fidelity rebates may be economically justified. (para 271)

The Commission, in its Discussion Paper on the Application of Article 82 of the Treaty to Exclusionary Abuses, addresses the distinction between volume and loyalty-inducing rebates and introduces an effect-based test to the analysis of rebates. (paras 151–76) The Commission notes in its paper that volume rebates (unconditional rebates) may also be found abusive when they are applied in a discriminatory manner to certain customers and not to others. (para 171)

In Case C–163/99 *Portuguese Republic v Commission*, [2001] ECR I–2613, [2002] 4 CMLR 31, the ECJ held that a volume discount on landing fees which was based on landing frequency of planes was abusive because of its 'de facto' discriminatory application. In that case the volume discount scheme, based on landing frequency, gave the Portuguese companies TAP and Portugalia average discounts of 30 and 22 per cent, respectively, on all their flights, whilst companies from other Member States with fewer planes received discounts of between 1 and 8 per cent. The court held that 'an undertaking occupying a dominant position is entitled to offer its customers quantity discounts linked solely to the volume of purchases made from it. ... However, the rules for calculating such discounts must not result in the application of dissimilar conditions to equivalent transactions with other trading parties within the meaning of subparagraph (c) of the second paragraph of [Article 82 EC].' (para 50) 'In that connection, it should be noted that it is of the very essence of a system of quantity discounts that larger purchasers of a product or users of a service enjoy lower average unit prices or – which amounts to the same – higher average reductions than those offered to smaller purchasers of that product or users of that service. It should also be noted that even where there is a linear progression in quantity discounts up to a maximum discount, initially the average discount rises (or the average price falls) mathematically in a proportion greater than the increase in purchases and subsequently in a proportion smaller than the increase in purchases, before tending to stabilise at or near the maximum discount rate. The mere fact that the result of quantity discounts is that some customers enjoy in respect of specific quantities a proportionally higher average reduction than others in relation to the difference in their respective volumes of purchase is inherent in this type of system, but it cannot be inferred from that alone that the system is discriminatory.' (para 51) 'None the less, where as a result of the thresholds of the various discount bands, and the levels of discount offered, discounts (or additional discounts) are enjoyed by only some trading parties, giving them an economic advantage which is not justified by the volume of business they bring or by any economies of scale they allow the supplier to make compared with their competitors, a system of quantity discounts leads to the application of dissimilar conditions to equivalent transactions.' (para 52) 'In the absence of any objective justification, having a high threshold in the system which can only be met by a few particularly large partners of the undertaking occupying a dominant position, or the absence of linear progression in the increase of the quantity discounts, may constitute evidence of such discriminatory treatment.' (para 53)

Nederlandsche Banden Industrie Michelin v Commission	**Article 82 EC**
Case 322/81 (Michelin I)	Abuse
ECJ, [1983] ECR 3461, [1985] 1 CMLR 282	Rebates

Facts

The Commission found Michelin NV (Michelin) to dominate the market for replacement tyres for buses and lorries. Michelin was further found to have abused this dominant position by operating a series of selective, target-based discounts, and target bonus schemes. The discount system applied by Michelin was based on the fixing of individual and selective sales targets which surpassed the target in the preceding period. The targets were discussed at the beginning of each year between the dealer and Michelin's commercial representative. The discount system and the scale of discounts were not published by Michelin and were not clearly defined in writing after the discussions. Michelin appealed to the CFI and argued, among other things, that the discounts were quantitative in nature and were legitimately aimed at inducing dealers to buy more tyres. Accordingly it submitted that the prohibition of these discounts would amount to condemning the dominant undertaking to lose ground and penalising it merely for having a dominant position.

Held

'In contrast to a quantity discount, which is linked solely to the volume of purchases from the manufacturer concerned, a loyalty rebate, which by offering customers financial advantages tends to prevent them from obtaining their supplies from competing manufacturers, amounts to an abuse.' (para 71)

'As regards the system at issue in this case, which is characterized by the use of sales targets, it must be observed that this system does not amount to a mere quantity discount linked solely to the volume of goods purchased since the progressive scale of the previous year's turnover indicates only the limits within which the system applies. Michelin NV has moreover itself pointed out that the majority of dealers who bought more than 3000 tyres a year were in any case in the group receiving the highest rebates. On the other hand, the system in question did not require dealers to enter into any exclusive dealing agreements or to obtain a specific proportion of their supplies from Michelin NV, and that this point distinguishes it from loyalty rebates of the type which the court had to consider in its judgment in *Hoffmann-La Roche*.' (para 72)

'In deciding whether Michelin NV abused its dominant position in applying its discount system it is therefore necessary to consider all the circumstances, particularly the criteria and rules for the grant of the discount, and to investigate whether, in providing an advantage not based on any economic service justifying it, the discount tends to remove or restrict the buyer's freedom to choose his sources of supply, to bar competitors from access to the market, to apply dissimilar conditions to equivalent transactions with other trading parties or to strengthen the dominant position by distorting competition.' (para 73)

The discount system in question was based on an annual reference period. This relatively long reference period has the inherent effect, at the end of that period, of increasing pressure on the buyer to reach the purchase figure needed to obtain the discount or to avoid suffering the expected loss for the entire period. In such circumstances, when the last order may affect the rate of discount over the whole year, it puts dealers under appreciable pressure since it has a significant impact on its profit. (para 81)

Michelin's large market share increased the impact of this practice. 'If a competitor wished to offer a dealer a competitive inducement for placing an order, especially at the end of the year, it had to take into account the absolute value of Michelin NV's annual target discount and fix its own discount at a percentage which, when related to the dealer's lesser quantity of purchases from that competitor, was very high. Despite the apparently low percentage of Michelin NV's discount, it was therefore very difficult for its competitors to offset the benefits or losses resulting for dealers from attaining or failing to attain Michelin NV's targets, as the case might be.' (para 82)

The lack of transparency of Michelin's discount system and the absence of written documentation of the target and discount sales created additional uncertainty and pressure. This was especially noticeable toward the end of a year, when dealers needed to attain Michelin's sales targets. (paras 83, 84)

The impact of this discount scheme was to prevent dealers from freely selecting the best available offers from the different competitors and to change suppliers accordingly. Subsequently, as it limited the dealers' choice of supplier it made access to the market more difficult for competitors. Such a discount system amounts to an abuse of Article 82 EC. (paras 85, 86)

Comment

The discount scheme was condemned due to the use of individual progressing sales targets, the long reference period and the lack of transparency.

On the long reference period, note the Commission Discussion Paper on the Application of Article 82 of the Treaty to Exclusionary Abuses. There the Commission considers the conditions under which a long reference period will result in foreclosure. 'Conditional rebates that are granted on all purchases in the reference period once a certain threshold is exceeded can have a strong foreclosure effect. To induce such an effect, it is necessary that the dominant supplier sets the threshold above the level that the buyer would purchase from the dominant company in the absence of any loyalty enhancing obligation or rebate … the dominant position will in general ensure that most buyers will anyhow purchase most of their requirements from the dominant supplier, for instance because its brand is a "must stock item" preferred by many final consumers or because the capacity constraints on the other suppliers are such that a good part of demand can only be provided by the dominant supplier. If the threshold is only set at the level that would anyhow be purchased by the buyer from the dominant company, the rebate will not have a loyalty enhancing effect. If the threshold is set above the amount that would otherwise be purchased, the rebate may induce the buyer to purchase more than it would otherwise do, in particular by diverting purchases from other suppliers to the dominant company, in order to be able to benefit from the rebate on all its purchases and thus effectively lower the price for all its purchases.' (para 152) The loyalty-enhancing effect depends on the level of the rebate percentage and on the level of the threshold. 'The higher the rebate percentage and the higher the amount that needs to be purchased before the rebate kicks in, the stronger the inducement just below the threshold. The fact that exceeding the threshold will not only reduce the price for all purchases above the threshold, but also for all previous purchases during the reference period, will create a so-called "suction" effect. The price of the units of the last transaction before the threshold is exceeded, will effectively be seriously lower, and is possibly even negative because this transaction triggers the rebate for all the purchases below the threshold in the reference period. The higher the amount that constitutes the threshold and the higher the rebate percentage, the stronger the suction effect will be near the threshold. The rebate enables the dominant supplier to use the inelastic or "non contestable" portion of demand of each buyer, i.e. the amount that would anyhow be purchased by the buyer, as leverage to decrease the price for the elastic or "contestable" portion of demand, i.e. the amount for which the buyer may prefer and be able to find substitutes.' (para 153)

On the use of individual progressing sales targets, note the CFI Decision in Case T–228/97 *Irish Sugar plc v Commission*, [1999] ECR II–2969, where the Court confirmed the Commission's objection to a sale target which was based on an increase in sales in comparison to the preceding period. (para 203) Also note Case T–219/99 *British Airways v Commission* (page 152 below).

In its discussion paper the Commission noted that 'Individualised volume targets allow the dominant supplier to create the same loyalty enhancing effect. Such requirement percentage targets and individualised volume targets are normally set in view of the purchases made by the same buyer in the previous period and may also take the form of growth targets. The loyalty enhancing effect may increase in case the threshold is adjusted to the individual demand of the customer in successive periods.' (para 158)

Manufacture Française des Pneumatiques Michelin v Commission
Case T–203/01 (Michelin II)
CFI, [2003] ECR II–4071, [2004] 4 CMLR 18

Article 82 EC
Abuse
Rebates

Facts

This case concerned the commercial policy pursued by Michelin in the French markets for new replacement tyres for trucks and for retreaded tyres for trucks. The Commission found Michelin to have abused its dominant position on this market via, among other things, its loyalty-inducing rebate system. An appeal to the CFI.

Held

A quantity rebate system linked solely to the volume of purchases made from a dominant undertaking is generally considered not to have the foreclosure effect prohibited by Article 82 EC. On the other hand a loyalty rebate, which is granted by a dominant undertaking in return for an undertaking by the customer to obtain his stock exclusively or almost exclusively from an undertaking in a dominant position, is contrary to Article 82 EC. Such a rebate is designed through the grant of financial advantage, to prevent customers from obtaining their supplies from competing producers. It thus has a foreclosure effect on the market and therefore is regarded as contrary to Article 82 EC. (paras 56–8)

'It follows that a rebate system in which the rate of the discount increases according to the volume purchased will not infringe Article 82 EC unless the criteria and rules for granting the rebate reveal that the system is not based on an economically justified countervailing advantage but tends, following the example of a loyalty and target rebate, to prevent customers from obtaining their supplies from competitors …' (para 59)

In assessing rebate systems it is necessary to consider in particular 'the criteria and rules governing the grant of the rebate, and to investigate whether, in providing an advantage not based on any economic service justifying it, the rebates tend to remove or restrict the buyer's freedom to choose his sources of supply, to bar competitors from access to the market, to apply dissimilar conditions to equivalent transactions with other trading parties or to strengthen the dominant position by distorting competition'. (para 60)

The mere fact that an undertaking characterises a discount system as 'quantity rebates' does not mean that the grant of such discounts is compatible with Article 82 EC. (para 62)

A loyalty-inducing rebate system applied by a dominant undertaking has foreclosure effects prohibited by Article 82 EC, irrespective of whether or not the rebate system is discriminatory. In the present case, the Commission concluded that the rebate system constitutes an infringement of Article 82 EC because it is unfair, it is loyalty-inducing and it has a partitioning effect. (paras 64–5)

'This Court considers that it is necessary, first, to consider whether the Commission had good reason to conclude, in the contested decision, that the quantity rebate system was loyalty-inducing or, in other words, that it sought to tie dealers to the applicant and to prevent them from obtaining supplies from the applicant's competitors. As the Commission acknowledges in its defence, moreover, the alleged unfairness of the system was closely linked to its loyalty-inducing effect. Furthermore, it must be held that a loyalty- inducing rebate system is, by its very nature, also partitioning, since it is designed to prevent the customer from obtaining supplies from other manufacturers.' (para 66)

The Quantity Rebates (these provided for an annual refund expressed as a percentage of the turnover achieved by the dealer)

Although a dominant undertaking can take reasonable steps to protect its commercial interests, not all competition on price can be regarded as legitimate. A loyalty-inducing discount system which seeks to tie dealers to a dominant undertaking by granting advantages which are not based on a countervailing economic advantage and seeks to prevent those dealers from obtaining their supplies from the undertaking's competitors infringes Article 82 EC. A quantity rebate system is compatible with Article 82 EC if the advantage conferred on dealers is economically justified by the volume of business they bring or by any economies of scale they allow the supplier to make. (paras 74–101)

'A quantity rebate system in which there is a significant variation in the discount rates between the lower and higher steps, which has a reference period of one year and in which the discount is fixed on the basis of total turnover achieved during the reference period, has the characteristics of a loyalty-inducing discount system.' (para 95)

Michelin failed to establish that the quantity rebate system, which presents the characteristics of a loyalty-inducing rebate system, was based on objective economic reasons. The fact that the rebate system was transparent does not affect this conclusion. A loyalty-inducing rebate system is contrary to Article 82 EC, whether it is transparent or not. (paras 107–111)

The Commission was therefore entitled to conclude, that 'the quantity rebate system at issue was designed to tie truck tyre dealers in France to the applicant by granting advantages which were not based on any economic justification. Because it was loyalty-inducing, the quantity rebate system tended to prevent dealers from being able to select freely at any time, in the light of the market situation, the most advantageous of the offers made by various competitors and to change supplier without suffering any appreciable economic disadvantage. The rebate system thus limited the dealers' choice of supplier and made access to the market more difficult for competitors, while the position of dependence in which the dealers found themselves, and which was created by the discount system in question, was not therefore based on any countervailing advantage which might be economically justified.' (para 110)

The Service Bonus (this was paid to specialist dealers, who achieved a minimum annual turnover, to improve their facilities and after-sales service)

Michelin argued that the aim of the service bonus was to encourage dealers to improve the quality of their services and the brand image of Michelin products through remuneration. This reward system was fixed annually by mutual agreement with the dealer according to the commitments entered into by him.

The Court pointed out that the fact that the service bonus remunerates services rendered by the dealer and is not formed as a discount has no relevance for the purpose of Article 82 EC. The question under Article 82 EC is whether the service bonus system was unfair and loyalty-inducing and had a tied sales effect.

'The granting of a discount by an undertaking in a dominant position to a dealer must be based on an objective economic justification. … It cannot depend on a subjective assessment by the undertaking in a dominant position of the extent to which the dealer has met his commitments and is thus entitled to a discount. As the Commission points out in the contested decision … [that] such an assessment of the extent to which the dealer has met his commitments enables the undertaking in a dominant position 'to put strong pressure on the dealer … and allow[s] it, if necessary, to use the arrangement in a discriminatory manner'. (para 140)

'It follows that a discount system which is applied by an undertaking in a dominant position and which leaves that undertaking a considerable margin of discretion as to whether the dealer may obtain the discount must be considered unfair and constitutes an abuse by an undertaking of its dominant position on the market within the meaning of Article 82 EC. …Because of the subjective assessment of the criteria giving entitlement to the service bonus, dealers were left in uncertainty and on the whole could not predict with any confidence the rate of discount which they would receive by way of service bonus.' (para 141)

Analysing 'Effect'

Michelin argued that the Commission did not examine the actual economic effect of the criticised practices and that such examination would have revealed that the conduct in question did not have the effect of either reinforcing its position or limiting the degree of competition on the market. In support of its argument,

Michelin referred to the consistent line of decisions which show that 'an "abuse" is an objective concept referring to the behaviour of an undertaking in a dominant position which is such as to influence the structure of a market and which has the effect of hindering the maintenance of the degree of competition still existing in the market or the growth of that competition.' (paras 236, 238)

'The Court points out that Article 82 EC prohibits, in so far as it may affect trade between Member States, any abuse of a dominant position within the common market or in a substantial part thereof. Unlike Article 81(1) EC, Article 82 EC contains no reference to the anti-competitive aim or anti-competitive effect of the practice referred to. However, in the light of the context of Article 82 EC, conduct will be regarded as abusive only if it restricts competition.' (para 237)

The 'effect' referred to in the case-law cited by Michelin does not necessarily relate to the actual effect of the abusive conduct complained of. 'For the purposes of establishing an infringement of Article 82 EC, it is sufficient to show that the abusive conduct of the undertaking in a dominant position tends to restrict competition or, in other words, that the conduct is capable of having that effect.' (para 239)

'For the purposes of applying Article 82 EC, establishing the anti-competitive object and the anti-competitive effect are one and the same thing. … If it is shown that the object pursued by the conduct of an undertaking in a dominant position is to limit competition, that conduct will also be liable to have such an effect.' (para 241)

'In the contested decision, the Commission demonstrated that the purpose of the discount systems applied by the applicant was to tie the dealers to the applicant. Those practices tended to restrict competition because they sought, in particular, to make it more difficult for the applicant's competitors to enter the relevant market.' (para 244)

Comment

The Court accepted in paragraph 59 that a rebate system based on an economically justified advantages will not infringe Article 82 EC. However, it later favored a simplified distinction between discounts which are economically justifiable and loyalty discounts which are regarded as abusive. The rhetoric of the court considers all loyalty-inducing discounts as abusive notwithstanding the actual effect on competition. Note especially paragraphs 237 and 239, where the Court established what may be regarded as a low threshold for proving abuse, finding that abuse could be a behaviour 'capable of limiting competition'. In the context of rebates, this low benchmark may result in a chilling effect on competition. Compare this statement with paragraph 293, *British Airways v Commission* (page 152 below).

The use of a low threshold to establish the abusive nature of rebates results in a formalistic per se restriction which does not involve an analysis of anticompetitive effects. At the practical level, this raises difficulties when dealing with borderline cases in which the company may or may not be dominant. In addition it categorically forbids discount schemes which may have efficiency justifications. At the policy level, this stands at odds to the Commission's attempt to advance an effect based approach to Article 82 EC.

According to the judgement, it was for Michelin to prove that the discount system was economically justifiable. The burden of proof was therefore on Michelin to show that the discounts reflect cost savings. Michelin failed to establish that the quantity rebate system, which presents the characteristics of a loyalty-inducing rebate system, was based on objective economic reasons. (paras 107–10).

With respect to the reference period, in its decision the Commission stated that the Court of Justice has ruled against the granting of quantity rebates by a dominant undertaking where the rebates exceed a reasonable period of three months on the grounds that such a practice is not in line with normal competition based on prices. The CFI rejected this proposition and noted that the ECJ did not expressly hold that the reference period could not exceed three months.

British Airways v Commission	**Article 82 EC**
Case T–219/99	Abuse
CFI, [2003] ECR II–5917, [2004] 4 CMLR 19	Rebates

Facts

British Airways (BA) operated a range of target incentives which were offered to travel agents. These commission schemes had one notable feature in common; in each case, meeting the targets for sales growth led to an increase in the commission paid on all tickets sold by the travel agent, not just on the tickets sold after the target was reached. The Commission found that this practice amounted to an abuse of BA's dominant position. More specifically, it asserted that BA's reward schemes caused discrimination between travel agents and produced an exclusionary effect in relation to competing airlines. BA appealed to the CFI for the annulment of the decision on the ground, among other things, of lack of abuse.

Held

On the Finding of Discrimination

The target schemes lead to an increase in the commission paid on all tickets sold during the reference period. Subsequently, two travel agents who sell different numbers of BA tickets may receive the same payments and two agents who sell the same number of BA tickets may receive different incentive payments. 'By remunerating at different levels, services that were nevertheless identical and supplied during the same reference period, those performance reward schemes distorted the level of remuneration which the parties concerned received in the form of commissions paid by BA.' The Commission was right to hold that this practice produced discriminatory effects within the network of travel agents, thereby inflicting on some of them a competitive disadvantage within the meaning of Article 82 (c). (paras 233–40)

On the Finding of Exclusionary Effect

Although an undertaking in a dominant position cannot be deprived of its entitlement to take reasonable steps to protect its commercial interests when they are attacked, such behaviour cannot be allowed if its purpose is to strengthen that dominant position and thereby abuse it. (para 243)

A fidelity rebate, granted by a dominant undertaking which has the effect of preventing customers from obtaining supplies from market competitors will be regarded as contrary to Article 82 EC, irrespective of whether the rebate system is discriminatory. The same applies to a fidelity-building' performance reward scheme practised by a purchaser in a dominant position in relation to its suppliers of services. (paras 244–9)

'In order to determine whether BA abused its dominant position by applying its performance reward schemes ... it is necessary to consider the criteria and rules governing the granting of those rewards, and to investigate whether, in providing an advantage not based on any economic service justifying it, they tended to remove or restrict the agents' freedom to sell their services to the airlines of their choice and thereby hinder the access of BA's competitor airlines to the United Kingdom market for air travel agency services'. (para 270)

'It needs to be determined in this case whether the marketing agreements and the new performance reward scheme had a fidelity-building effect in relation to travel agents established in the United Kingdom and, if they did, whether those schemes were based on an economically justified consideration.' (para 271)

(i) The Fidelity-Building Character

'Concerning, first, the fidelity-building character of the schemes in question, the Court finds that, by reason of their progressive nature with a very noticeable effect at the margin, the increased commission rates were capable of rising exponentially from one reference period to another, as the number of BA tickets sold by agents during successive reference periods progressed.' (para 272)

'Conversely, the higher revenues from BA ticket sales were, the stronger was the penalty suffered by the persons concerned in the form of a disproportionate reduction in the rates of performance rewards, even in the case of a slight decrease in sales of BA tickets compared with the previous reference period. BA cannot therefore deny the fidelity-building character of the schemes in question.' (para 273)

(ii) Economically Justified Consideration

'Concerning, secondly, the question whether the performance reward schemes applied by BA were based on an economically justified consideration, it is true that the fact that an undertaking is in a dominant position cannot deprive it of its entitlement, within reason, to perform the actions which it considers appropriate in order to protect its own commercial interests when they are threatened'. (para 279)

In order for such protection to be lawful, BA's scheme must, at the very least, be based on criteria of economic efficiency. In this case, the higher rates of commission were applied on all BA tickets handled during the reference period and not only on the tickets sold once those sales targets had been met. The additional remuneration of the agents cannot be regarded as constituting the consideration for efficiency gains or cost savings. 'On the contrary, that retrospective application of increased commission rates to all BA tickets sold by a travel agent during the reference period in question must even be regarded as likely to entail the sale of certain BA tickets at a price disproportionate to the productivity gain obtained by BA from the sale of those extra tickets.' (paras 280–85)

'Contrary to what BA maintains, its performance reward schemes could not therefore constitute a mode of exercise of the normal operation of competition or allow it to reduce its costs. The opposite arguments by BA in that regard are not capable of demonstrating that its performance reward schemes had an objective economic justification.' (para 291)

'BA cannot accuse the Commission of failing to demonstrate that its practices produced an exclusionary effect. In the first place, for the purposes of establishing an infringement of Article 82 EC, it is not necessary to demonstrate that the abuse in question had a concrete effect on the markets concerned. It is sufficient in that respect to demonstrate that the abusive conduct of the undertaking in a dominant position tends to restrict competition, or, in other words, that the conduct is capable of having, or likely to have, such an effect.' (para 293)

'[W]here an undertaking in a dominant position actually puts into operation a practice generating the effect of ousting its competitors, the fact that the hoped-for result is not achieved is not sufficient to prevent a finding of abuse of a dominant position within the meaning of Article 82 EC.' (para 297)

Moreover, the growth in the market shares of some of BA's airline competitors, which was modest in absolute value having regard to the small size of their original market shares, does not mean that BA's practices had no effect. In the absence of those practices, it may legitimately be considered that the market shares of those competitors would have been able to grow more significantly (see, to that effect, *Compagnie Maritime Belge Transports*, paragraph 149). (para 298)

Comment

The rebates were condemned both for their discriminatory (Article 82(c) EC) and exclusionary effect. On the long reference period and 'suction effect', see comments on page 148 above.

Interestingly, despite the fact that BA competitors gained market share during that period, the Court did not consider this to affect its conclusion. (para 298) The growth in market share could have been used as an indication of lack of anticompetitive effect, yet the CFI considered it possible that absent BA discount practice the competitors' market share would have grown even faster. This might have been the case, yet it is questionable whether the fact that a competitor is not better off should be used as a proxy to consumer harm.

British Airways v Commission	**Article 82 EC**
Case C–95/04	Abuse
ECJ, [2007] CEC 607, [2007] 4 CMLR 22	Rebates

Facts

British Airways (BA) brought an appeal on the CFI decision in Case T–219/99 (see page 152 above) in which the CFI dismissed its action for the annulment of Commission Decision (IV/D 2/34.780 – *Virgin/British Airways*). On appeal, BA argued, among other things, that the CFI erred in its analysis of the exclusionary effects and fidelity-building effects of its bonus scheme and in the application of Article 82(c) EC. Appeal dismissed.

Held

'In order to determine whether the undertaking in a dominant position has abused such a position by applying a system of [fidelity discounts] … the Court has held that it is necessary to consider all the circumstances, particularly the criteria and rules governing the grant of the discount, and to investigate whether, in providing an advantage not based on any economic service justifying it, the discount tends to remove or restrict the buyer's freedom to choose his sources of supply, to bar competitors from access to the market, to apply dissimilar conditions to equivalent transactions with other trading parties or to strengthen the dominant position by distorting competition (*Michelin*, paragraph 73).' (para 67)

'It then needs to be examined whether there is an objective economic justification for the discounts and bonuses granted. In accordance with the analysis carried out by the Court of First Instance in paragraphs 279 to 291 of the judgment under appeal, an undertaking is at liberty to demonstrate that its bonus system producing an exclusionary effect is economically justified.' (para 69)

Exclusionary Effect

Goal-related discounts or bonuses, that is to say those the granting of which is linked to the attainment of sales objectives defined individually, may give rise to an exclusionary effect. It is clear from the CFI judgment that the bonus schemes at issue were drawn up by reference to individual sales objectives, since the rate of the bonuses depended on the evolution of the turnover arising from BA ticket sales by each travel agent during a given period. (paras 70–72)

Long Reference Period

'It is also apparent from the case-law that the commitment of co-contractors toward the undertaking in a dominant position and the pressure exerted upon them, may be particularly strong where a discount or bonus does not relate solely to the growth in turnover in relation to purchases or sales of products of that undertaking made by those co-contractors during the period under consideration, but extends also to the whole of the turnover relating to those purchases or sales. In that way, relatively modest variations – whether upward or downward – in the turnover figures relating to the products of the dominant undertaking have disproportionate effects on co-contractors (see, to that effect, *Michelin*, paragraph 81).' (para 73)

The CFI found that the bonus schemes at issue gave rise to a similar situation. 'Attainment of the sales progression objectives gave rise to an increase in the commission paid on all BA tickets sold by the travel agent concerned, and not just on those sold after those objectives had been attained …' (para 74)

Objective Economic Justification

'Discounts or bonuses granted to its co-contractors by an undertaking in a dominant position are not necessarily an abuse and therefore prohibited by Article 82 EC. According to consistent case-law, only discounts or bonuses which are not based on any economic counterpart to justify them must be regarded as an abuse (see, to that effect, *Hoffmann-La Roche*, paragraph 90, and *Michelin*, paragraph 73).' (para 84)

'Assessment of the economic justification for a system of discounts or bonuses established by an undertaking in a dominant position is to be made on the basis of the whole of the circumstances of the case (see, to that effect, Michelin, paragraph 73) …' The CFI did not err in its finding that BA's bonus scheme was not based on any objective economic justification (paras 86, 86–91)

Probable Effects

'Concerning BA's argument that the Court of First Instance did not examine the probable effects of the bonus schemes at issue, it is sufficient to note that, in paragraphs 272 and 273 of the judgment under appeal, the Court of First Instance explained the mechanism of those schemes. Having emphasised the very noticeable effect at the margin, linked to the progressive nature of the increased commission rates, it described the exponential effect on those rates of an increase in the number of BA tickets sold during successive periods, and, conversely, the disproportionate reduction in those rates in the event of even a slight decrease in sales of BA tickets in comparison with the previous period. On that basis, the Court of First Instance was able to conclude, without committing any error of law, that the bonus schemes at issue had a fidelity-building effect. It follows that BA's plea accusing the Court of not examining the probable effects of those schemes is unfounded.' (paras 96–8)

Article 82(c) EC – The Findings of a Competitive Disadvantage

'The specific prohibition of discrimination in subparagraph (c) of the second paragraph of Article 82 EC forms part of the system for ensuring, in accordance with Article 3(1)(g) EC, that competition is not distorted in the internal market. The commercial behaviour of the undertaking in a dominant position may not distort competition on an upstream or a downstream market, in other words between suppliers or customers of that undertaking. Co-contractors of that undertaking must not be favoured or disfavoured in the area of the competition which they practise amongst themselves.' (para 143)

'Therefore, in order for the conditions for applying subparagraph (c) of the second paragraph of Article 82 EC to be met, there must be a finding not only that the behaviour of an undertaking in a dominant market position is discriminatory, but also that it tends to distort that competitive relationship, in other words to hinder the competitive position of some of the business partners of that undertaking in relation to the others (see, to that effect, Suiker Unie, paragraphs 523 and 524). (para 144)

'In that respect, there is nothing to prevent discrimination between business partners who are in a relationship of competition from being regarded as being abusive as soon as the behaviour of the undertaking in a dominant position tends, having regard to the whole of the circumstances of the case, to lead to a distortion of competition between those business partners. In such a situation, it cannot be required in addition that proof be adduced of an actual quantifiable deterioration in the competitive position of the business partners taken individually.' (para 145)

Comment

The ECJ upheld the CFI judgment in a relatively short and formalistic decision. It confirmed that the list of abusive behaviour in Article 82 EC is not exhaustive and upheld the CFI finding concerning fidelity-building effects. The ECJ did not accept BA's arguments concerning the examination of actual effects and consumer harm. The decision adds little to existing case law on rebates and as such stand at odds with the effect-based approach to Article 82 EC as manifested in recent years by the Commission.

Note the clear statement concerning Article 82(c) EC and the requirement for competitive disadvantage. Contrast this with *United Brands* (page 143 above) and *Corsica Ferries* (page 144 above). Note, however, that the list of abusive conducts in Article 82 EC is not exhaustive and abusive discrimination may be established outside the realm of Article 82(c) EC.

Deutsche Telekom AG	**Article 82 EC**
Case COMP/C–1/37.451, 37.578, 37.579	Abuse
European Commission, [2003] OJ L 263/9	Margin Squeeze

Facts

The Commission received complaints from various network operators in Germany, alleging that Deutsche Telekom AG (DT) engaged in unfair pricing strategy contrary to Article 82 EC. The complaints focused on prices charged to competitors and end-users by DT for access to its local networks, and accused DT of not allowing for sufficient margin to enable its competitors to compete with it to provide end-user access.

Held (on margin squeeze)

DT enjoys a dominant position on the German market for broadband access to local fixed networks, both at wholesale and at retail level. At wholesale level, DT is the only German network operator that possesses a network with nationwide coverage. In order to provide a variety of services to end-users, new entrants need access to this infrastructure on a wholesale basis. At retail level, DT holds around 90 per cent market share.

The Commission's assessment revealed that DT charged competitors more for unbundled access at wholesale level than it charged its subscribers for access at the retail level. This constitutes a margin squeeze as the charges to be paid to DT for wholesale access were so expensive that competitors were forced to charge their end-users prices higher than the prices DT charges its own end-users for similar services. Consequently new entrants were unable to compete with the DT and did not attain significant market share. (para 102)

The Commission's practice when dealing with margin squeeze has been to hold that 'there is an abuse of a dominant position where the wholesale prices that an integrated dominant undertaking charges for services provided to its competitors on an upstream market and the prices it itself charges end-users on a downstream market are in a proportion such that competition on the wholesale or retail market is restricted.' (para 106)

Comment

DT argued that since the wholesale charges in Germany were fixed by the regulatory authority it cannot be accused of margin squeeze. The Commission rejected this view and stated that although DT is subjected to price regulation, it has the commercial discretion to avoid or end the margin squeeze on its own initiative, for example by increasing the existing retail charges for its connections. (paras 163–75)

In order to establish the existence of a margin squeeze in this case it was essential that the wholesale and retail access services be comparable. In order to achieve a coherent comparison, the Commission used a weighted approach taking into account the numbers of DT's retail customers for the different access types on the retail level. (paras 107–62)

DT appealed to the CFI. See T–271/03 *Deutsche Telekom AG v Commission*. Appeal pending

In its Notice on the Application of Competition Rules to Access Agreements in the Telecommunication Sector (1998 OJ C265/2) the Commission refers to margin squeeze and states that it 'could be demonstrated by showing that the dominant company's own downstream operations could not trade profitably on the basis of the upstream price charged to its competitors by the upstream operating arm of the dominant company. A loss making downstream arm could be hidden if the dominant operator has allocated costs to its access operations which should properly be allocated to the downstream operations, or has otherwise improperly determined the transfer prices within the organisation …' (para 117)

Note the Commission's decision in Case IV/30.178 *Napier Brown/British Sugar* (OJ 1988 L284/41) where British Sugar (BS) was found to have engaged in margin squeeze. There, the margin allowed by BS between prices charged for bulk and packaged sugar did not allow its own downstream operation to trade profitably.

Genzyme Limited v Office of Fair Trading	**Article 82 EC**
1016/1/1/03	Abuse
Competition Appeal Tribunal, [2004] CAT 4, [2004] Comp AR 358	Margin Squeeze

Facts

Genzyme Limited appealed against a decision of the Office of Fair Trading (OFT) in which it was found to have abused its dominant position in the supply of Cerezyme, a treatment for Gaucher's disease, by bundling it with its homecare services and by engaging in margin squeeze against other providers of homecare services. The Competition Appeal Tribunal (CAT) allowed the appeal in part, accepted Genzyme's claims concerning the finding of bundling but upheld the OFT finding on margin squeeze.

Held (on margin squeeze)

A 'margin squeeze' may occur where a dominant undertaking in an upstream market 'supplies an essential input to its competitors in a downstream market, on which the dominant company is also active, at a price which does not enable its competitors on the downstream market to remain competitive. ... See Case T–5/97 *Industrie des Poudres Sphériques v Commission* [2000] ECR II–3755, at paragraph 178. ... In *National Carbonising Company*, OJ 1976 L36/6 the National Coal Board supplied coking coal for the manufacture of coke both to its own subsidiary, National Smokeless Fuels, and to an independent company National Carbonising. National Smokeless Fuels and National Carbonising were competitors in the downstream market for coke, which was derived from the coal supplied by the National Coal Board. National Carbonising complained that the price it had to pay the National Coal Board for coal was too high to enable it to sell coke competitively at the price charged by National Smokeless Fuels. The Commission held, at paragraph 14 of its decision, that: "an undertaking which is in a dominant position as regards the production of a raw material ... and therefore able to control its price to independent manufacturers of derivatives ... and which is itself producing the same derivatives in competition with these manufacturers, may abuse its dominant position if it acts in such a way as to eliminate the competition from these manufacturers in the market for derivatives. From this general principle the services of the Commission deduced that the enterprise in a dominant position may have an obligation to arrange its prices so as to allow a reasonably efficient manufacturer of the derivatives a margin sufficient to enable it to survive in the long term."' (para 491)

'The OFT argues that since May 2001 Genzyme has supplied Cerezyme to the NHS at the NHS list price, while supplying other homecare services providers at the same list price, £2.975 per unit. The effect of that is that other homecare service providers have no margin with which to compete with Genzyme Homecare, and are effectively eliminated from the supply of Homecare Services to Gaucher patients.' (para 478)

'In those circumstances it is likely to be wholly uneconomic for other homecare service providers to provide homecare services at no effective margin between its buying and selling price of Cerezyme. We therefore accept that Genzyme's pricing policy constitutes a margin squeeze, the effect of which is to force other providers to sustain a loss in the provision of Homecare Services to Gaucher patients. We also accept that no undertaking, regardless of how efficient it may be, could trade profitably in these circumstances in the downstream supply of homecare services. ... We share the OFT's conclusion that the effect of Genzyme's margin squeeze is to monopolise the supply of Homecare Services to Gaucher patients in favour of Genzyme, and to eliminate any competition in the supply of such services to Gaucher patients' (paras 552, 554, 549–55) Contrary to Genzyme's claim, the margin squeeze is not objectively justified. (paras 576–623)

Comment

In *BSkyB* (BSB) the UK OFT considered whether BSB had impeded competition from other pay-TV distributors by engaging in margin squeeze. The OFT tested whether BSB had set its wholesale prices at a level that would prevent an equally efficient distributor from earning a normal return on the distribution of BSB's premium channels. The investigation did not reveal conclusive evidence that BSB's downstream distribution operated at a loss. BSB was found not to engage in margin squeeze. (CA98/20/2002, OFT 623)

General Motors Continental v Commission	**Article 82 EC**
Case 26/75	Abuse
ECJ, [1975] ECR 1367, [1976] 1 CMLR 95	Excessive pricing

Facts

General Motors Continental (GMC) was found by the Commission to have abused its dominant position by charging excessive prices for producing certain documentation which was required by drivers of GM cars in Belgium. GMC appealed to the ECJ contesting the Commission's finding of excessive pricing.

Held

An undertaking in a dominant position may abuse it by imposing a price which is excessive in relation to the economic value of the service it provides, and which has the effects of curbing parallel imports or unfairly exploiting customers. (paras 11, 12)

It is not disputed that on several cases GMC imposed a charge which was excessive in relation to the economic value of the service it provided. However, the question whether GMC abused its dominant position must be considered in the light of the actual circumstances in which the charge in question was imposed. In this case the charge was confined to a limited number of cases, was imposed for a limited period and once identified was reduced by GMC. Additionally, GMC reimbursed those persons who had made complaints to it, and did so before any intervention on the part of the Commission. GMC therefore did not abuse its dominant position. (paras 16–22)

Comment

Because of the simple facts in this case the finding that the charge imposed by GM was excessive in comparison to its economic value was simple to make. In this respect the case does not reflect the practical difficulty in assessing cost and economic value of products and services. The challenge of assessing cost and establishing unfairness is better illustrated in *United Brands v Commission* (page 159 below), *Deutsche Post AG* (page 160 below) and *At the Races* (page 163 below).

Although excessive pricing is an abuse that directly affects customers and impacts on their welfare, it has seldom been the subject of formal decisions. This is largely the result of practical difficulties in assessment. Practical difficulties include the complexity of assessing the cost structure of the undertaking which is then used to establish a competitive price. This also includes the difficulty in identifying the competitive price, either by reference to cost or by comparison to other markets, and the difficulty in establishing what constitutes an unfair price.

In addition to the practical difficulties, some may object to price regulation from a policy perspective, arguing that in the absence of market failures, excessive prices motivate potential competitors to enter into the market and are therefore self-correcting. Accordingly, the regulation of excessive pricing is only called for where new entry would not occur due to high barriers to entry or other market failures. Supporting this non-interventionist approach is the risk that the prohibition of excessive pricing may, in some instances, have a detrimental effect, ex ante, on the incentives to innovate and invest, especially in dynamic markets.

United Brands v Commission	Article 82 EC
Case 27/76	Abuse
ECJ, [1978] ECR 207, [1978] 1 CMLR 429	Excessive Pricing

Facts

In a Commission Decision, United Brands (UBC) was found to have infringed Article 82 EC by abusing its dominant position in the market for bananas. Among the different abuses, the Commission investigated claims that UBC charged excessive and discriminatory prices for its 'Chiquita' brand bananas to its customers in Belgium, Luxembourg, Denmark and Germany. UBC appealed to the ECJ and argued that it had not charged discriminatory or unfair prices. On appeal, the ECJ accepted the Commission's finding on discriminatory pricing but rejected its economic analysis of excessive pricing.

Held (on unfair prices)

Article 82 EC applies to excessive pricing and may result in the finding of abuse when the dominant undertaking charges a price which is excessive, having no reasonable relation to the economic value of the product supplied. (paras 248–50) 'This excess could, inter alia, be determined objectively if it were possible for it to be calculated by making a comparison between the selling price of the product in question and its cost of production, which would disclose the amount of the profit margin; however the Commission has not done this since it has not analysed UBC's costs structure. The questions therefore to be determined are whether the difference between the costs actually incurred and the price actually charged is excessive, and, if the answer to this question is in the affirmative, whether a price has been imposed which is either unfair in itself or when compared to competing products.' (paras 251–2)

Working out the production costs may raise great difficulties, yet in this particular case 'the production costs of the banana do not seem to present any insuperable problems'. The Commission was therefore expected at the very least to require UBC to produce particulars of all the constituent elements of its production costs. (paras 254–5)

The Commission's comparison between prices charged by UBC in different Member States can in principle provide the basis for a finding of excessive pricing. In this case, however, the Commission failed to conduct a proper comparison of prices while taking all circumstances into account. (paras 258–67)

Comment

The ECJ establishes a two-tiered test. First the Commission should engage in cost analysis. Then, after establishing an unacceptable gap between costs and price, the actual price needs to be held unfair. The ECJ acknowledged that economic theorists may provide additional ways to determine whether the price of a product is unfair.

The Court accepted in principle that comparing prices between different Member States may be used to establish excessive pricing. Note also Case 395/87 *Ministère Public v Jean-Louis Tournier*, [1989] ECR 2521, where the ECJ indicated that when a dominant undertaking charges higher fees for its services in one Member State than in others, then 'where a comparison of the fee levels has been made on a consistent basis, that difference must be regarded as indicative of an abuse of a dominant position. In such a case it is for the undertaking in question to justify the difference by reference to objective dissimilarities between the situation in the Member State concerned and the situation prevailing in all the other Member States.' (para 38)

Also note Case 30/87 *Corinne Bodson v SA Pompes Funèbres des Régions Libérées*, [1988] ECR 2479, where the ECJ assessed the fairness of the price charged by an undertaking which held an exclusive concession for funeral services in a particular area, by comparing these charges with other areas in which the undertaking did not hold a dominant position.

Deutsche Post AG	**Article 82 EC**
Case COMP/C–1/36.915	Abuse
European Commission, [2001] OJ L331/40	Excessive Pricing

Facts

The Commission considered a complaint made by the British Post Office against Deutche Post AG (DPAG) which had a statutory monopoly that included, among other things, the delivery of cross-border mail in Germany. Following its investigation the Commission found that DPAG had abused its dominant position by discriminating between different customers and by refusing to supply its delivery service unless an unjustified surcharge was paid. It also found that the price charged by DPAG for the service was excessive and that its behaviour limited the development of the German market for the delivery of international mail and of the UK market for international mail bound for Germany.

In analysing the imposition of unfair selling prices, the Commission first sought to satisfy the 'economic value benchmark' as established in *General Motors v Commission*. According to this benchmark, excessive pricing may be established if the price charged by an undertaking was excessive in comparison to the economic value of the service.

The Commission noted that a 'price which is set at a level which bears no reasonable relation to the economic value of the service provided must be regarded as excessive in itself, since it has the effect of unfairly exploiting customers. In a market which is open to competition the normal test to be applied would be to compare the price of the dominant operator with the prices charged by competitors.' (para 159)

However, a price comparison analysis in this case proved impractical due to the existence of DPAG's wide-ranging monopoly. Furthermore, cost data provided by DPAG was not detailed enough to allow detailed analysis of DPAG's average costs.

The Commission resorted to the alternative benchmark to assess the fairness of the sale price. It compared DPAG's price for incoming cross-border mail with its domestic tariff. It then concluded that the price charged by DPAG for incoming cross-border mail exceeded the average economic value of that service by at least 25 per cent.

Comment

The Commission's analysis followed the comparative approach as accepted by the ECJ in *United Brands*. The comparative benchmark is used where cost is too difficult to ascertain. Accordingly, the price charged by the dominant undertaking is compared to prices charged in neighbouring markets for the same product. This benchmark is by no means problem-free. One notable difficulty is in attempting to import information from other markets in order to determine what the competitive market price might have been. Another clear difficulty is the possibility that this benchmark may lead to a conclusion of excessive pricing even when the dominant undertaking's profits are minimal.

The comparative benchmark has been used in a range of cases. In Case 30/87 *Corinne Bodson v SA Pompes Funèbres des Régions Libérées*, [1988] ECR 2479, [1989] 4 CMLR 984, the excessiveness was assessed by making comparisons with pricing in other regions where the market was competitive. In Case 110/88 *Lucazeau v SACEM*, [1989] ECR 2811, a comparison of prices charged by different undertakings for the same service in different Member States was held to form a reasonable basis for establishing excessiveness of price. Note also Case 395/87 *Ministère Public v Jean-Louis Tournier* (page 159 above).

British Horseracing Board v Victor Chandler International	**Article 82 EC**
HC05C00510	Abuse
High Court of Justice Chancery Division, [2005] EWHC 1074 (Ch)	Excessive Pricing

Facts

The British Horseracing Board (BHB) is a company which administrates British horseracing. As part of its activities, BHB compiles data related to horseracing and charges a fee for accessing this database. The claim arose out of the refusal of a bookmaking company, Victor Chandler International (VCI) to pay the charges for using data as agreed between BHB and VCI. BHB claimed damages for breach of contract against VCI. In its defence VCI alleged, among other things, that BHB infringed Article 82 EC by charging high prices and abusing its dominant position. BHB applied for summary judgment against that claim.

Held (The Hon Mr Justice Laddie)

On Excessive Pricing

VCI's claim that, in effect, high prices charged by a dominant undertaking are per se abusive, is unacceptable. 'This approach is based on a number of doubtful propositions. It assumes that in a competitive market prices end up covering only the cost of production plus the cost of capital. I am not convinced that that is so. Sometimes the price may be pushed much lower than this so that all traders are making a very small, if any, margin. Sometimes the desire of the customer for the product or service is so pressing that all suppliers, even if competing with one another, can charge prices which give them a much more handsome margin. In other words, even when there is competition, some markets are buyers' markets, some are sellers'. I do not see that there is any necessary correlation between the cost of production and the cost of capital and the price which can be achieved in the market place. Furthermore the question is not whether the prices are large or small compared to some stable reference point, but whether they are fair.' (paras 47, 48)

'In addition, this [approach] breaks down as soon as one applies it in the real world. What happens if there are only a few customers? Must the cost of production, including all research and development, be recovered from them? If so, does that mean that the price varies depending on the number of customers one has? Does it also mean that the price must go down once all the research and development costs have been recovered? Does it mean that traders cannot increase the price if they engage in successful advertising campaigns which whet the consumer's appetite? If Mr Turner's proposition were correct, it would mean that for most fashion products (clothes, cars, perfumes, cosmetics, electronics and so on) the prices charged would be deemed to be unfair. Indeed it must follow that if the price of a product differed significantly in a single market or between markets in different locations, one must assume that, at best, one set of customers is getting the fair price and all the ones being charged more are being charged an unfair price. This would be so, even though no trader occupies a dominant position.' (para 49)

In *United Brands v Commission* paragraph 252 the ECJ held that 'The questions therefore to be determined are whether the difference between the costs actually incurred and the price actually charged is excessive, and, if the answer to this question is in the affirmative, whether a price has been imposed which is either unfair in itself or when compared to competing products.' Contrary to VCI claim it appears from this paragraph that all the ECJ was saying was that comparing prices with costs determines the profit margin. 'Once that has been achieved it is necessary to go on to the next stage to determine whether the price is unfair. What it did not do was suggest that high prices or high margins are the same as unfair prices. Indeed, were [VCI] right, it seems to me that the law reports would be full of cases where undertakings in dominant positions would have been found guilty of abuse by simply charging high prices. As Mr Vaughan says, the reality is that there are no such cases.' (para 51)

'… [W]e still live in a free market economy where traders are allowed to run their businesses without undue interference. What Article 82 and Section 18 of the Act are concerned with is unfair prices, not high prices. In determining whether a price is unfair it is necessary to consider the impact on the end consumer and all of the market conditions. In a case where unfair pricing is alleged, assessment of the value of the asset both to the vendor and the purchaser must be a crucial part of the assessment. VCI's approach does not take into account value at all. It simply relates prices to the cost of acquisition or creation.' (para 56)

'Here, were one to consider value, there are numerous factors which would suggest that the allegation of unfair pricing is unjustified. This is not a case of a trader making bumper profits. On the contrary, this is concerned with undertakings, and particularly the Board, whose prime function is to nurture British horse-racing. It is non-profit making. Save for administration costs it feeds back all its income into the promotion and improvement of British horseracing not only for the benefit of the general public but also for the benefit of those who have a commercial interest in the sport including bookmakers like VCI.' (para 57)

On Euro Defence Summary Judgment

'… [P]articular care is to be expected of a party who pleads … an Article 82 offence. These are notoriously burdensome allegations, frequently leading to extensive evidence, including expert reports from economists and accountants. The recent history of cases in which such allegations have been raised illustrate that they can lead to lengthy and expensive trials. Mere assertion in a pleading will not do. Before a party has to respond to an allegation like this, it is incumbent on the party making the allegation to set out clearly and succinctly the major facts upon which it will rely.' (para 43)

'In the material before me, there is nothing to suggest that VCI have formulated a viable argument that BHB has breached either Section 18 or Article 82.' (para 60)

Comment

Note that the dispute arose between contracting parties and that the excessive price claim was part of a 'Euro defence'. The Court's approach to the excessive price argument is likely to have been influenced, to some extent, by this being an attempt by VCI to avoid its contractual obligations by contesting the legality of the agreement under Article 82 EC. On Euro defence, see Chapter 7 below.

In his comments Justice Laddie highlighted the practical difficulty of establishing what a fair price is. Even if one succeeds in accurately establishing the cost structure, it is still difficult to assess what might be a reasonable and fair profit margin.

The unease with which the national court approached the task of establishing the unfairness of the price was echoed in *At the Races Limited v The British Horse Racing Limits and others*. There, the Court commented that excessive price claims present the Court with a range of factual and legal problems of a kind which even specialist lawyers and economists regard as very difficult (see page 163 below).

At the Races Limited v The British Horse Racing Limits and others	**Article 82 EC**
A3/2006/0126	Abuse
England and Wales Court of Appeal (Civil Division), 2007 EWCA Civ 38	Excessive Pricing

Facts

An appeal on a judgment handed down by Etherton J in which he held that the British Horseracing Board Limited (BHB) had abused its dominant position, by unreasonably refusing to supply to At the Races Limited (ATR) pre-race data which was in its sole possession, and by excessively and unfairly pricing the data.

Held (on excessive pricing)

The claim of abuse in this case presents the Court with a range of factual and legal problems of a kind which even specialist lawyers and economists regard as very difficult. Difficulties in assessing when the price charged by the person controlling access to the information is excessive or unfair suggest that these problems may be solved 'more satisfactorily by arbitration or by a specialist body equipped with appropriate expertise and flexible powers. The adversarial procedures of an ordinary private law action, the limited scope of expertise in the ordinary courts and the restricted scope of legal remedies available are not best suited to helping the parties out of a deadlocked negotiating position or to achieving a business-like result reflecting both their respective interests and the public interest.' (paras 3–7)

In *United Brands* fair price was held to be one which represents or reflects the economic value of the product supplied. A price which significantly exceeds that will be prima facie excessive and unfair. In the following case it is for the Court to consider what constitutes economic value. (para 204)

'There is nothing in [Article 82 EC] or its jurisprudence to suggest that the index of abuse is the extent of departure from a cost + criterion. It seems to us that, in general, cost + has two other roles: one is as a baseline, below which no price can ordinarily be regarded as abusive: the other is as a default calculation, where market abuse makes the existing price untenable.' (para 207)

'Exceeding cost + is a necessary, but in no way a sufficient, test of abuse of a dominant position. … As already noted, the Commission's decision in Scandlines supports the view that the exercise under Article 82, while it starts from a comparison of the cost of production with the price charged, is not determined by the comparison. This in itself is sufficient to exclude a cost + test as definitive of abuse.' (paras 209–13)

In this case ATR's handsome revenues from overseas bookmakers enable it to pay the high prices demanded by BHB. The charges made by BHB eats into ATR's profit and may be unfair, but this alone does not make them abusive. The principal object of Article 82 EC is the protection of consumers, not of business competitors. Since BHB's practice did not lead to the distortion of competition it cannot be regarded as abusive. (paras 214–18)

'We appreciate that this [analysis] leaves the realistic possibility of a monopoly supplier not quite killing the goose that lays the golden eggs, but coming close to throttling her. We do not exclude the possibility that this could be held to be abusive, not least because of its potential impact on the consumer. But Article 82, as we said earlier, is not a general provision for the regulation of prices. It seeks to prevent the abuse of dominant market positions with the object of protecting and promoting competition. The evidence and findings here do not show ATR's competitiveness to have been, or to be at risk of being, materially compromised by the terms of the arrangements with or specified by BHB.' (para 217)

The Court of First Instance erred in holding that the economic value of the pre-race data was its competitive price based on cost +. 'This method of ascertaining the economic value of this product is too narrow in that it does not take account, or sufficient account, of the value of the pre-race data to ATR and in that it ties the costs allowable in cost+ too closely to the costs of producing the pre-race data.' (para 282)

Comment

The Court of Appeal held that 'economic value' should be assessed while taking into account the value to the purchaser. The court rejected the 'cost +' benchmark for assessing the economic value of the compiled data and noted that it should serve as a baseline, below which no price can ordinarily be regarded as abusive or as a default calculation where market abuse makes the existing price untenable.

The judgment is particularly important for cases involving intellectual property rights. In such cases the direct cost of acquiring intellectual property rights is often considerably lower than their economic value and price on the market.

Note that the pricing strategies in this case affected ATR's profit but not the final consumers. Although possibly unfair, the pricing policy was not considered as abusive since the end consumer was not harmed and competition was not distorted.

By focusing on the value of the product to the consumer, the judgment set the bar for proving excessive pricing at a high level. The Court accepted that this approach 'leaves the realistic possibility of a monopoly supplier not quite killing the goose that lays the golden eggs, but coming close to throttling her.' (para 217) Yet it concluded that this would not amount to an abuse under Article 82 EC. The difficulty with the court's approach is that it opened the door for the monopolist to increase the price as long as the customer can bare it. This in many ways is exactly what a rational monopolist would do when maximising its profits.

Note the Commission's decision in Case COMP/A.36.568.D3 *Scandlines Sverige AB v Port of Helsingborg*. There, the Commission dismissed a complaint by a ferry company of excessive and discriminatory port charges by the port operator. In the decision, while assessing the pricing strategy, the Commission considered it necessary to take account not only of the costs incurred by the port in providing its services, but also additional costs and other factors, such as the benefits to customers conferred by the particular location of the port and the frequent and short distance service. These benefits were held to represent 'an intangible value in itself, which must be taken into account as part of the assessment of the economic value of the services provided.' (paras 234–5) Accordingly, the economic value of the product/service should also reflect the demand-side features of this product/service. After considering all the relevant economic factors, the Commission concluded that there was insufficient evidence to conclude that the port charges would have 'no reasonable relation to the economic value' of the services and facilities provided to the ferry-operators. (paras 234–48)

Commercial Solvents v Commission	**Article 82 EC**
Case 6/73	Abuse
ECJ, [1974] ECR 223, [1974] 1 CMLR 309	Refusal to Supply

Facts

Commercial Solvents Corporation (CSC) was the main supplier of the chemical amino-butanol, which is a raw material for the production of other chemicals. One of CSC's customers, Zoja, purchased large quantities of this raw material and used it for the manufacture of another chemical, ethambutol. CSC informed Zoja that it would stop supplying it with the raw material necessary for the production of Ethambutol. This decision coincided with CSC's decision to engage in the production of ethambutol itself. The Commission found this refusal to supply to constitute an infringement of Article 82 EC. CSC applied for the annulment of the Commission's decision.

Held

It is possible to distinguish the market in a raw material necessary for the manufacture of a product from the market on which the product is sold. An abuse of a dominant position on the market in the raw material may restrict competition in the market on which the derivatives of the raw material are sold. (para 22)

'An undertaking being in a dominant position as regards the production of raw material and therefore able to control the supply to manufacturers of derivatives, cannot, just because it decides to start manufacturing these derivatives (in competition with its former customers) act in such a way as to eliminate their competition which in the case in question, would amount to eliminating one of the principal manufacturers of Ethambutol in the common market. Since such conduct is contrary to the objectives expressed in [Article 3(g) EC] and set out in greater detail in [Articles 81 and 82 EC], it follows that an undertaking which has a dominant position in the market in raw materials and which, with the object of reserving such raw materials for manufacturing its own derivatives, refuses to supply a customer, which is itself a manufacturer of these derivatives, and therefore risks eliminating all competition on the part of this customer, is abusing its dominant position within the meaning of [Article 82 EC]. In this context it does not matter that the undertaking ceased to supply in the spring of 1970 because of the cancellation of the purchases by Zoja, because it appears from the applicants' own statement that, when the supplies provided for in the contract had been completed, the sale of Amino-butanol would have stopped in any case.' (para 25)

Comment

Note that in this case the Court identified an upstream and downstream market. The undertaking dominated the upstream market and also operated at the downstream market. The refusal to supply a competitor at the downstream market would have eliminated the main competitor in this market and allowed the dominant undertaking to increase its holding in this market.

In subsequent cases the requirement for two distinct markets was relaxed. See in particular *IMS Health* (page 170 below) in which the ECJ satisfied itself with the existence of a hypothetical upstream market.

Sea Containers Ltd/Stena Sealink	**Article 82 EC**
Case IV/34.689, (Interim measures)	Abuse
European Commission, [1994] OJ L15/8	Refusal to Supply

Facts

Sealink was the owner and operator of the port of Holyhead in Anglesey, Wales, and operated ferry services between the United Kingdom, Ireland and France. Sea Containers Ltd (SC) operated passenger, car and freight ferry services and was looking to expand its ferry services. It entered into negotiations with Sealink in order to expand its access rights to the port of Holyhead. When Sealink refused to allow adequate access, SC complained to the Commission and argued that Sealink was abusing its dominant position by failing to allow SC access on a reasonable basis to an essential facility. After the complaint was made, but before the Commission's decision, the parties reached an agreement on schedule and access rights. Despite this, the Commission considered that there remains sufficient public interest in this case and issued a formal decision.

Decision

After establishing Sealink's dominant position in the market for the provision of port facilities for car and passenger ferry operations on the central corridor route between the United Kingdom and Ireland, the Commission considered the question of abuse.

'An undertaking which occupies a dominant position in the provision of an essential facility and itself uses that facility (i.e. a facility or infrastructure, without access to which competitors cannot provide services to their customers), and which refuses other companies access to that facility without objective justification or grants access to competitors only on terms less favourable than those which it gives its own services, infringes [Article 82 EC] if the other conditions of that Article are met. An undertaking in a dominant position may not discriminate in favour of its own activities in a related market. The owner of an essential facility which uses its power in one market in order to protect or strengthen its position in another related market, in particular, by refusing to grant access to a competitor, or by granting access on less favourable terms than those of its own services, and thus imposing a competitive disadvantage on its competitor, infringes [Article 82 EC].' (para 66)

Where the operator of an essential facility is required to provide access on non-discriminatory terms, interim measures to enable a new competitor to enter a market require stronger justification than measures maintaining the situation of an already established competitor. (paras 57, 67) In this case Sealink treated the request by SC in a discriminatory manner. It consistently delayed and raised difficulties concerning SC's possible use of existing facilities while rapidly approving its own fast ferry service. (paras 70–4)

'It is the Commission's view that in the circumstances of the present case an independent harbour authority, which would of course have had an interest in increasing revenue at the port, would at least have considered whether the interests of existing and proposed users of the port could best be reconciled by a solution involving modest changes in the allocated slot times or in any plans for the development of the harbour. In situations such as the present one, unless a solution is considered fully and discussed with all the interests involved, it is likely that a port authority which is not independent will prefer an arrangement which minimizes inconvenience to itself (especially in relation to its own operations as a user) but which does not necessarily provide non-discriminatory access to the new entrant. If Sealink, in drawing up the various versions of its redevelopment plan for the east side, had always duly consulted SC … it might have been possible to avoid the difficulty of reconciling the plan with SC's wish for temporary facilities there.' (para 75)

Comment

Note an earlier Commission decision in *Sealink/B&I Holyhead* (Interim measures), [1992] 5 CMLR 255, which dealt with similar facts. In cases involving ferry services, a central question is wherther the Commission was right in finding the port to be an essential facility. Much depends on the market definition which may result in a narow market served by one port or a wider market served by several facilities.

RTE & ITP v Commission **(The Magill Case)**	**Article 82 EC**
Joined Cases C–241, 242/91P	Abuse
ECJ, [1995] ECR I–743, [1995] 4 CMLR 718	Refusal to Supply

Facts

Magill TV Guide Ltd (Magill) wanted to introduce a new television publication which would provide a comprehensive weekly television guide in Ireland. To do so, it required the consent of the television stations, among them RTE and ITE, who owned the copyrights for the relevant information. Although at the time, the companies provided third parties with information on a daily basis, they refused to provide Magill with a weekly listing of programmes. The Commission found the refusal to constitute an abuse of Article 82 EC. RTE and ITP applied for the annulment of the Commission's decision. Following the CFI dismissal of the appeal, the companies appealed to the ECJ.

Held

'So far as a dominant position is concerned, it is to be remembered at the outset that mere ownership of an intellectual property right cannot confer such a position.' (para 46)

However, in this case, the television stations are the only source of information relating to the listings of their programmes and therefore hold a dominant position by reason of their de facto monopoly over the information. As such they are in a position to prevent effective competition on the market in weekly television magazines in the areas concerned. (para 47)

A refusal to grant a licence, even if it is the act of an undertaking holding a dominant position, cannot in itself constitute abuse of a dominant position. Nonetheless, the exercise of an exclusive right by the proprietor may, in exceptional circumstances, involve abusive conduct. (paras 49, 50)

In the present case, the refusal to provide information by relying on national copyright provisions prevented the appearance of a new product, a comprehensive weekly guide to television programmes, which the television companies did not offer and for which there was a potential consumer demand. There was no justification for such refusal which constitutes an abuse under Article 82(2)(b). (paras 51–5)

By their conduct, the television companies reserved to themselves the secondary market of weekly television guides by excluding all competition on that market. (para 56) The Court of First Instance did not err in law in holding that the appellants' conduct was an abuse of a dominant position.

Comment

The case demonstrates the possible tension between the protection granted to intellectual property rights and competition law. Note that mere ownership of an intellectual property right does not necessarily establish the existence of a dominant position.

The special circumstances in Magill which swung the balance in favour of an obligation to license were highlighted in Case C–7/97 *Oscar Bronner* (page 168 below): (1) the refusal in question concerned a product the supply of which was indispensable for carrying on the business in question; (2) such refusal prevented the appearance of a new product for which there was a potential consumer demand; (3) the refusal was likely to exclude all competition in the secondary market of television guides; and (4) it was not justified by objective considerations. (*Oscar Bronner*, paras 39–41)

Note that the case involved a 'weak copyright' concerning lists of television and radio programmes. The doubts raised as to the justification of the copyright protection in this case to 'compilation of banal information' may have played a role in the court's decision.

Oscar Bronner GmbH Co KG v Mediaprint	**Article 82 EC**
Case C–7/97	Abuse
ECJ, [1998] ECR I–7791, [1999] 4 CMLR 112	Refusal to Supply

Facts

Oscar Bronner GmbH & Co KG (Bronner) was the publisher of the Austrian daily newspaper *Der Standard*. Bronner wanted to use the nationwide home-delivery service for daily newspapers which was owned by the Mediaprint group and operated for the distribution of its own newspapers. Although there were a number of regional or local networks, Mediaprint's network was the only nationwide network in Austria. Mediaprint refused to provide Bronner with access to its delivery system. Bronner applied to the national Austrian court for an order requiring Mediaprint to refrain from abusing its alleged dominant position on the market and to allow Bronner access to its nationwide home-delivery service for daily newspapers. A preliminary reference from the Austrian court.

Held (on refusal to supply)

In order to assess whether the refusal by Mediaprint to allow access to the single nationwide home-delivery scheme in Austria constitutes an abuse of a dominant position, one needs to consider the indispensability of this scheme for the distribution of newspapers. It is undisputed that other methods of distributing daily newspapers, although maybe less advantageous for the distribution of certain newspapers, exist. These include distribution by post and through sale in shops and at kiosks. (paras 42–4)

Moreover, it does not appear that there are any technical, legal or even economic obstacles which prevent other publishers of daily newspapers from establishing a second nationwide home-delivery scheme. The fact that the small circulation prevents a publisher from setting up, alone or with others, a second nationwide home-delivery scheme does not make the access to existing nationwide home-delivery scheme indispensable. For this to be considered indispensable it is necessary to establish at the very least that that the creation of a second nationwide home-delivery scheme with a circulation comparable to that of the daily newspapers distributed by the existing scheme is not economically viable. (paras 45, 46)

Comment

The Court distinguished the facts in this case from the circumstances in *Commercial Solvents v Commission* where the refusal to supply would have eliminated all competition from the rival's business. (para 38)

The Court referred to the exceptional circumstances in Magill (page 167 above) which were not found in this case. There, (1) the refusal to supply concerned a product which was indispensable for carrying on the business in question, (2) the refusal prevented the appearance of a new product for which there was a potential consumer demand, (3) the refusal was likely to exclude all competition in the secondary market, and (4) it was not justified by objective considerations. (paras 39–41)

In his opinion, AG Jacobs commented on the careful balancing of conflicting considerations which is required before interfering with a dominant undertaking's freedom to contract: 'In the long term it is generally pro-competitive and in the interest of consumers to allow a company to retain for its own use facilities which it has developed for the purpose of its business. ... the incentive for a dominant undertaking to invest in efficient facilities would be reduced if its competitors were, upon request, able to share the benefits. Thus the mere fact that by retaining a facility for its own use a dominant undertaking retains an advantage over a competitor cannot justify requiring access to it. ... It is on the other hand clear that refusal of access may in some cases entail elimination or substantial reduction of competition to the detriment of consumers in both the short and the long term. ... In assessing such conflicting interests, particular care is required where the goods or services or facilities to which access is demanded represent the fruit of substantial investment. That may be true in particular in relation to refusal to license intellectual property rights...' (paras 57, 61, 62)

Tiercé Ladbroke SA v Commission	**Article 82 EC**
Case T–504/93	Abuse
CFI, [1995] ECR II–923, [1997] 5 CMLR 309	Refusal to Supply, Discrimination

Facts

Tiercé Ladbroke SA (Ladbroke) operated betting shops in Belgium. It approached the French Horse-Racing Associations and their affiliated companies (the Associations), and asked them to grant it the right to retransmit televised pictures and sound commentaries of French races in its betting outlets in Belgium. Following the Associations' refusal to grant the rights, Ladbroke lodged a complaint with the Commission alleging, among other things, that this refusal to supply constituted an abuse of a dominant position. The Commission rejected the complaint and Ladbroke appealed to the CFI.

Held

The relevant geographical market in this case is national and comprises Belgium. Consequently, the arbitrariness of the refusal of the Associations to supply French sound and pictures to Ladbroke cannot be assessed in light of the policy followed by the Associations on other, geographically distinct, markets. In other words the practice involves no discrimination as between operators on the same market. The fact that Ladbroke is prepared to pay an appropriate fee for the licence to transmit French races does not constitute sufficient evidence of an abuse in the absence of discrimination against it by the Associations in the relevant geographical market. (paras 126–9)

'The applicant cannot rely on the Magill judgment to demonstrate the existence of the alleged abuse, since that decision is not in point. In contrast to the position in Magill, where the refusal to grant a licence to the applicant prevented it from entering the market in comprehensive television guides, in this case the applicant is not only present in, but has the largest share of, the main betting market on which the product in question, namely sound and pictures, is offered to consumers whilst the [Associations], the owners of the intellectual property rights, are not present on that market. Accordingly, in the absence of direct or indirect exploitation by the [Associations] of their intellectual property rights on the Belgian market, their refusal to supply cannot be regarded as involving any restriction of competition on the Belgian market.' (para 130)

Moreover, the refusal to supply Ladbroke could not fall within the prohibition Article 82 EC unless it concerned a product or service which was either essential for the exercise of the activity in question, in that there was no real or potential substitute, or was a new product whose introduction might be prevented, despite specific, constant and regular potential demand from consumers. In the present case the televised broadcasting of horse races, although constituting an additional service for bettors, is not in itself indispensable for the exercise of Ladbroke's main activity on the Belgian betting market. (paras 131, 132)

For the same reasons, Ladbroke cannot rely on the *London European v Sabena* decision in which the action taken to exclude a competitor related to a market in which both Sabena and that competitor, London European, were operating, whereas in this case the Associations are not present on the Belgian market. The same applies to *ICI* and *Commercial Solvents v Commission*, where Commercial Solvents, like its customers, was present on the downstream market, namely the market in derivatives. (para 133)

Comment

The Court distinguished between the circumstances in Magill and those in this case. (para 130) In para 131 the Court noted that the refusal to supply 'could not fall within the prohibition laid down by [Article 82 EC] unless it concerned a product or service which was either essential for the exercise of the activity in question … or was a new product whose introduction might be prevented …' In doing so, the court widened the scope of the doctrine by treating conditions (1) and (2) in Magill as alternatives rather than cumulative conditions. For another example of a wide reading of the Magill conditions, see *Intel v Via* (page 172 below).

IMS Health GmbH & Co OHG v NDC Health GmbH & Co KG	**Article 82 EC**
Case C–418/01	Abuse
CFI, [2000] ECR I–5039, [2004] 4 CMLR 28	Refusal to Supply

Facts

A reference from the German court concerning a dispute between IMS and NDC regarding the use of IMS's '1,860 brick structure' by NDC. The system, owned by IMS, provided data on regional sales of pharmaceutical products in Germany according to a brick structure consisting of 1,860 bricks and a derived structure consisting of 2,847 bricks. IMS marketed its brick structures and also distributed them free of charge to pharmacies and doctors' surgeries. That practice helped those structures to become the normal industry standard to which its clients adapted their information and distribution systems. NDC (formerly PII), whose activity also consisted in marketing regional data on pharmaceutical products in Germany, designed a brick structure which was very similar to the IMS product. IMS applied to the German court for an interlocutory order prohibiting PII (NDC) from using any brick structure derived from the IMS 1,860 brick structure. The German court granted the order and based its decision on the finding that the brick structure used by IMS is a database which may be protected by copyright. As part of the main proceedings concerning this case, the German court stayed the proceedings and referred three questions to the ECJ, the central one being whether the refusal by a dominant undertaking to grant a licence to use a brick structure for which it has an intellectual property right, to another undertaking which wishes to provide such data in the same market and due to market characteristics has to use the same brick structure, constitutes an abuse of a dominant position.

Held

The question submitted by the German court is based on the premise, whose validity it is for the national court to ascertain, that the use of the 1,860 brick structure protected by an intellectual property right is indispensable in order to allow a potential competitor to have access to the market in which the undertaking which owns the right occupies a dominant position. In order to determine this indispensability the national court needs to consider whether there are products or services which constitute alternative solutions, even if they are less advantageous, and whether there are technical, legal or economic obstacles capable of making it impossible or at least unreasonably difficult to create the alternative products or services. As highlighted in paragraph 46 of the ECJ judgment in *Bronner*, in order to accept the existence of economic obstacles, it must be established, at the very least, that the creation of those products or services is not economically viable for production on a scale comparable to that of the undertaking which controls the existing product or service. (paras 22, 28)

A refusal to grant a licence, even if it is the act of an undertaking holding a dominant position, cannot in itself constitute abuse of a dominant position. However, the exercise of an exclusive right by the owner may, in exceptional circumstances, involve abusive conduct. (paras 34, 35)

Such exceptional circumstances were present in the case giving rise to the judgment in Magill which was later referred to in *Bronner*. There, the Court indicated that the exceptional circumstances in Magill were constituted by the fact that the refusal in question concerned a product the supply of which was indispensable for carrying on the business in question, the refusal prevented the emergence of a new product for which there was a potential consumer demand, the fact that it was not justified by objective considerations, and was likely to exclude all competition in the secondary market. (paras 36–8)

It is clear from that case-law that in order for the refusal by an undertaking which owns a copyright to give access to a product or service indispensable for carrying on a particular businesss to be treated as abusive, three cumulative conditions need to be satisfied: (1) the refusal is preventing the emergence of a new product for which there is a potential consumer demand; (2) the refusal is not justified by objective considerations; and (3) the refusal will exclude any competition on a secondary market. (paras 38, 52)

As for the first condition concerning the emergence of a new product, in the balancing of the interest in protection of the intellectual property right and the economic freedom of its owner, against the interest in protection of free competition, the latter can prevail only where refusal by the dominant undertaking to grant a licence to an indispensable product prevents the development of the secondary market to the detriment of consumers. Therefore, such refusal may be regarded as abusive only where the undertaking requesting the licence does not intend to limit itself to duplicating the goods or services already offered on the secondary market by the owner of the intellectual property right, but intends to produce new goods or services not offered by the owner of the right and for which there is a potential consumer demand. (paras 48, 49)

With respect to the second condition, relating to whether the refusal was unjustified, it is for the national court to examine whether the refusal is justified by objective considerations. (para 51)

With respect to the third condition, concerning the likelihood of excluding all competition on a secondary market, one needs to identify an upstream market, constituted by the product or service, and a secondary downstream market, on which the product or service in question is used for the production of another product or the supply of another service. The fact that the upstream product is not marketed separately does not preclude, from the outset, the possibility of identifying two separate markets. Such was the situation in Case C–7/97 *Bronner* where the home-delivery service was not marketed separately. (paras 40–43)

'For the purposes of the application of the earlier case-law, it is sufficient that a potential market or even a hypothetical market can be identified. Such is the case where the products or services are indispensable in order to carry on a particular business and where there is an actual demand for them on the part of undertakings which seek to carry on the business for which they are indispensable.' (para 44)

'Accordingly, it is determinative that two different stages of production may be identified and that they are interconnected, inasmuch as the upstream product is indispensable for the supply of the downstream product. Transposed to the facts of the case in the main proceedings, that approach prompts consideration as to whether the 1,860 brick structure constitutes, upstream, an indispensable factor in the downstream supply of German regional sales data for pharmaceutical products.' (paras 45, 46)

Comment

In paragraphs 44–6 the Court held that the finding of 'a potential market or even hypothetical market' would suffice. This proposition undermines the distinction between upstream and downstream markets. Note that the finding of a fictional upstream market may result in compulsory licensing from a dominant undertaking to its competitor. Contrast this approach with the US approach as evident in *Verizon Communications Inc v Trinko LLP*, 540 US 398. There the US Supreme Court considered the absence of two distinct markets as a relevant factor in its decision not to condemn a refusal to supply (para 5).

Arguably, by widening the breadth of the doctrine, the ruling risked undermining companies' incentive to innovate. However, similar to the Magill case, it is possible to question the justification of the copyright protection afforded in this case. Since IMS developed the brick structure in collaboration with pharmaceutical companies and it became the de facto industry standard, one might argue that competition law was used here to remedy unjustified over protection by the intellectual property laws.

Note that prior to the reference from the national court, the Commission also addressed the issue following a complaint made by NDC. In an interim decision the Commission, noting the *Ladbroke* decision, held that refusal to supply will be objectionable even without it preventing the emergence of a new product. On appeal the president of the CFI suspended the operation of the decision.

Note the Commission Discussion Paper on the Application of Article 82 of the Treaty to Exclusionary Abuses, in which the Commission makes reference to the requirement for a new product or service not offered by the owner of the right and for which there is a potential consumer demand.

Intel Corporation v Via Technologies Inc	**Article 82 EC**
Case No A3/2002/1380, A3/2002/1381	Abuse
English Court of Appeal, [2002] EWCA Civ 1905	Refusal to Supply

Facts

Two patent infringement actions brought by Intel Corporation (Intel) in the patent court against Via Technologies (Via), alleging that Via infringed five of Intel's patents. Via's defence in the patent court was based on, among other things, the claim that Intel's actions infringed Articles 81 and 82 EC. The Court awarded Intel summary judgment. Via appealed the summary judgment. On appeal the Court considered, among other things, whether Intel's refusal to licence a patent on reasonable terms may amount to an abuse of a dominant position. The Court made reference to the 'exceptional circumstances' benchmark in Magill (*RTE and others v European Commission*) and its interpretation in *IMS Health Inc v European Commission* and considered whether Via has pleaded facts which are capable of constituting such exceptional circumstances.

Held (on refusal to licence)

The Court does not accept Intel's argument that *IMS* and Magill show that there can only be exceptional circumstances within the Magill test if all the conditions in either Magill or *IMS* are satisfied. Thus, the result of the refusal must be to exclude an entirely new product from the market (Magill) or all competition to the patentee (*IMS*).

'Magill and *IMS* indicate the circumstances which the Court of Justice and the President of the Court of First Instance respectively regarded as exceptional in the cases before them. It does not follow that other circumstances in other cases will not be regarded as exceptional. In particular it is at least arguable, as the President recognised in *IMS*, that the Court of Justice will assimilate its jurisprudence under Article 82 more closely with that of the essential facilities doctrine applied in the United States. In that event there could be a breach of Article 82 without the exclusion of a wholly new product or all competition. This approach seems to me to be warranted by the width of the descriptions of abuse contained in Article 82 itself.' (paras 47, 48)

Accordingly the Court finds it arguable that the range of 'exceptional circumstances' which may give rise to an abuse by the owner of an intellectual property right of his dominant position can extend to the facts pleaded by Via.

Comment

In these proceedings the Appeal Court considered whether Via's defences under Articles 81 and 82 have real prospects of success. The Court therefore did not have to reach a final decision on the issues at stake but rather to consider whether these provide a sufficient basis which merits a permission to appeal. Permission was granted.

The Court adopted a wide interpretation and held that a patent holder may be restricted from exercising his intellectual property rights in circumstances which differ from those identified in Magill and *IMS*. In doing so, the summary judgment widens the instances in which compulsory licensing may be granted and narrows the requirement for a new product and exclusion of all competition. One should treat such approach with caution, taking into account the impact it may have on investment in innovation. Also note Case T–201/04 *Microsoft v Commission* (page 173 below).

The Court considered the potential effect US jurisprudence may have on the scope of abuse. It made reference to the opinion of Advocate-General Jacobs in *Oscar Bronner v Mediaprint* where the AG referred to the increasing similarities between the doctrine of essential facilities as applied in the United States and the practice of the European Commission (paras 45–51, AG opinion)

Microsoft Corp v Commission	**Article 82 EC**
Case T–201/04	Abuse
CFI, [2007] 5 CMLR 11	Refusal to Supply

Facts

An appeal on Commission Decision Comp/C–3/37.792 in which the Commission found Microsoft to have infringed Article 82 EC by refusing to supply interoperability information to its competitors and by tying its Windows Media Player to its operating system. (On tying see page 176 below.) The Commission found Microsoft's refusal to supply to infringe Article 82(b) EC by limiting technical development to the prejudice of consumers. The Commission ordered Microsoft to license on reasonable and non-discriminatory terms the relevant interoperability information to its competitors. It noted that, on balance, the possible negative impact of an order to supply on Microsoft's incentives to innovate is outweighed by its positive impact on the level of innovation of the whole industry (including Microsoft). Microsoft appealed the decision and argued, among other things, that refusal to supply interoperability information cannot constitute an abuse of a dominant position within the meaning of Article 82 EC because (i) the information is protected by intellectual property rights (or constitutes trade secrets), and (ii) the criteria established in the case-law which determine when an undertaking in a dominant position can be required to grant a license to a third party are not satisfied in this case.

Held

It follows from the Magill, *IMS Health* and *Bronner* judgments that a refusal by a dominant undertaking 'to license a third party to use a product covered by an intellectual property right cannot in itself constitute an abuse of a dominant position within the meaning of Article 82 EC. It is only in exceptional circumstances that the exercise of the exclusive right by the owner of the intellectual property right may give rise to such an abuse.' (paras 331, 131–331)

'It also follows from that case-law that the following circumstances, in particular, must be considered to be exceptional: – in the first place, the refusal relates to a product or service indispensable to the exercise of a particular activity on a neighboring market; – in the second place, the refusal is of such a kind as to exclude any effective competition on that neighboring market; – in the third place, the refusal prevents the appearance of a new product for which there is potential consumer demand.' (para 332)

Indispensability

The Commission was right to conclude that in order to be able to compete viably with Windows workgroup server operating systems, competitors' operating systems must be able to interoperate with the Windows domain architecture on an equal footing with those Windows systems. The Commission did not err in its analysis when it found that the information concerning the interoperability with the Windows domain architecture was indispensable. (paras 369–436)

Elimination of all effective competition

'In the contested decision, the Commission considered whether the refusal at issue gave rise to a "risk" of the elimination of competition on the work group server operating systems market. Microsoft contends that that criterion is not sufficiently strict, since according to the case-law on the exercise of an intellectual property right the Commission must demonstrate that the refusal to license an intellectual property right to a third party is "likely to eliminate all competition", or, in other words, that there is a "high probability" that the conduct in question will have such a result. The Court finds that Microsoft's complaint is purely one of terminology and is wholly irrelevant. The expressions "risk of elimination of competition" and "likely to eliminate competition" are used without distinction by the Community judicature to reflect the same idea, namely that Article 82 EC does not apply only from the time when there is no more, or practically no more, competition on the market. If the Commission were required to wait until competitors were eliminated from the market, or until their elimination was sufficiently imminent, before being able to take action under Article 82 EC, that would clearly run counter to the objective of that provision, which is to maintain undistorted competition in the common market and, in particular, to safeguard the competition that still exists on the relevant market. In this case, the Commission had all the more reason to apply Article 82 EC before the elimination of competition on the work group server operating systems market had become a reality because that market is characterised by significant network effects and because the elimination of competition would therefore be difficult to reverse. ... Nor is it necessary to demonstrate that all competition on the market would be eliminated. What matters, for the purpose of establishing an infringement of Article 82 EC, is that the refusal at issue is liable to, or is likely to, eliminate all effective competition on the market. It must be made clear that the fact that the competitors of the dominant undertaking retain a marginal presence in certain niches on the market cannot suffice to substantiate the existence of such competition.' (paras 560–63)

Preventing the appearance of a new product

'It must be emphasised that the fact that the applicant's conduct prevents the appearance of a new product on the market falls to be considered under Article 82(b) EC, which prohibits abusive practices which consist in "limiting production, markets or technical developments to the ... prejudice of consumers".' (para 643)

'The circumstance relating to the appearance of a new product, as envisaged in Magill and *IMS Health* ... cannot be the only parameter which determines whether a refusal to license an intellectual property right is capable of causing prejudice to consumers within the meaning of Article 82(b) EC. As that provision states, such prejudice may arise where there is a limitation not only of production or markets, but also of technical development.' (para 647)

'It was on that last hypothesis that the Commission based its finding in the contested decision. Thus, the Commission considered that Microsoft's refusal to supply the relevant information limited technical development to the prejudice of consumers within the meaning of Article 82(b) EC (recitals 693 to 701 and 782 to the contested decision) and it rejected Microsoft's assertion that it had not been demonstrated that its refusal caused prejudice to consumers (recitals 702 to 708 to the contested decision).' (para 648)

'The Court finds that the Commission's findings at the recitals referred to in the preceding paragraph are not manifestly incorrect.' (para 649)

'Thus, the contested decision rests on the concept that, once the obstacle represented for Microsoft's competitors by the insufficient degree of interoperability with the Windows domain architecture has been removed, those competitors will be able to offer work group server operating systems which, far from merely reproducing the Windows systems already on the market, will be distinguished from those systems with respect to parameters which consumers consider important ...' (para 656)

'It must be borne in mind, in that regard, that Microsoft's competitors would not be able to clone or reproduce its products solely by having access to the interoperability information covered by the contested decision. Apart from the fact that Microsoft itself acknowledges in its pleadings that the remedy prescribed by Article 5 of the contested decision would not allow such a result to be achieved ... it is appropriate to repeat that the information at issue does not extend to implementation details or to other features of Microsoft's source code. ... The Court also notes that the protocols whose specifications Microsoft is required to disclose in application of the contested decision represent only a minimum part of the entire set of protocols implemented in Windows work group server operating systems.' (para 657)

'Nor would Microsoft's competitors have any interest in merely reproducing Windows work group server operating systems. Once they are able to use the information communicated to them to develop systems that are sufficiently interoperable with the Windows domain architecture, they will have no other choice, if they wish to take advantage of a competitive advantage over Microsoft and maintain a profitable presence on the market, than to differentiate their products from Microsoft's products with respect to certain parameters and certain features. It must be borne in mind that, as the Commission explains at recitals 719 to 721 to the contested decision, the implementation of specifications is a difficult task which requires significant investment in money and time.' (para 658)

Microsoft's assertion that its refusal did not cause prejudice to consumers is unfounded. 'It is settled case-law that Article 82 EC covers not only practices which may prejudice consumers directly but also those which indirectly prejudice them by impairing an effective competitive structure (Case 85/76 *Hoffmann-La Roche v Commission* [1979] ECR 461, paragraph 125, and *Irish Sugar v Commission*, paragraph 229 above, paragraph 232). In this case, Microsoft impaired the effective competitive structure on the work group server operating systems market by acquiring a significant market share on that market.' (paras 664, 660–5)

The absence of objective justification

Microsoft relied as justification for its conduct solely on the fact that the technology concerned was covered by intellectual property rights. This argument cannot be accepted. The protection of the technology by intellectual property rights cannot constitute objective justification within the meaning of Magill and *IMS Health*. Microsoft did not sufficiently establish that if it were required to disclose the interoperability information that would have a significant negative impact on its incentives to innovate. (paras 688–711)

Comment

The judgment focuses narrowly on the facts of the case and adopts, at least in terms of form, the court's traditional consideration of exceptional circumstances when analysing a refusal to licence intellectual property rights.

However, in terms of substance, the Court held that the circumstances relating to the appearance of a new product, as envisaged in Magill and *IMS Health*, 'cannot be the only parameter which determines whether a refusal to license an intellectual property right is capable of causing prejudice to consumers within the meaning of Article 82(b) EC.' (para 647) It thus used Article 82(b) to 'import' innovation into the equation. This 'internal' expansion tips the balance of the carefully crafted list of exceptional circumstances in the Magill and *IMS* cases and lowers the threshold for finding of an abusive refusal to licence.

Note the CFI's findings in para 664 where as part of the assessment of consumer harm, the CFI held that Microsoft impaired competition by acquiring a significant market share. This statement controversially treats the mere attainment of significant market share as anticompetitive and stands at odds with an effects-based approach.

In its Discussion Paper on the Application of Article 82 of the Treaty to Exclusionary Abuses (December 2005), the Commission states that that refusal to licence should not impair customer's ability to benefit from innovation brought about by the dominant undertaking competitors. (para 240) The departure from the relative narrow grounds of 'essentiality' into the more obscure world of 'innovation' raise difficult questions as to the requisite level and nature of innovation. How meaningful should it be? The Microsoft case is illustrative in this respect. Here, the Commission argued that 'it follows from paragraph 49 of *IMS Health* … that a "new product" is a product which does not limit itself essentially to duplicating the products already offered on the market by the owner of the copyright. It is sufficient, therefore, that the product concerned contains substantial elements that result from the licensee's own efforts.' (para 631, CFI judgment). On appeal, the CFI did not comment directly on this statement.

With respect to objective justification, the CFI made it clear that protection of the technology by intellectual property rights cannot constitute objective justification. The Court explained that if the mere fact of holding intellectual property rights could in itself constitute objective justification for the refusal to grant a licence, the refusal to license could never be considered to constitute an infringement of Article 82 EC even though in Magill and *IMS Health* the Court of Justice specifically stated the contrary. (para 690)

Tetra Pak International SA v Commission	**Article 82 EC**
Case C–333/94 P	Abuse
ECJ, [1996] ECR I–5951, [1997] 4 CMLR 662	Tying & Bundling

Facts

Tetra Pak International SA (Tetra Pak) specialises in equipment for the packaging of liquid or semi-liquid food products in cartons. The Commission found Tetra Pak to have abused its dominant position by, among other things, tying the sales of machinery for packaging with the sales of cartons, and by engaging in predatory pricing (IV/31.043 – *Tetra Pak II*). The CFI dismissed Tetra Pak's application for annulment of the Commission's decision. Tetra Pak appealed to the ECJ asking it to quash the CFI judgment. On the issue of tying and bundling Tetra Pak submitted that the CFI erred when it held that the tied sales of cartons and filling machines were contrary to Article 82 EC in circumstances where there was a natural link between the two.

Held (on tying and bundling)

'Tetra Pak interprets [Article 82(d) EC] as prohibiting only the practice of making the conclusion of contracts dependent on acceptance of additional services which, by nature or according to commercial usage, have no link with the subject-matter of the contracts.' (para 35)

'It must be noted, first, that the Court of First Instance explicitly rejected the argument put forward by Tetra Pak to show the existence of a natural link between the machines and the cartons. In paragraph 82 of the judgment under appeal, it found: "consideration of commercial usage does not support the conclusion that the machinery for packaging a product is indivisible from the cartons. For a considerable time there have been independent manufacturers who specialize in the manufacture of non-aseptic cartons designed for use in machines manufactured by other concerns and who do not manufacture machinery themselves". That assessment, itself based on commercial usage, rules out the existence of the natural link claimed by Tetra Pak by stating that other manufacturers can produce cartons for use in Tetra Pak's machines. With regard to aseptic cartons, the Court of First Instance found, at paragraph 83 of its judgment, that "any independent producer is quite free, as far as Community competition law is concerned, to manufacture consumables intended for use in equipment manufactured by others, unless in doing so it infringes a competitor's intellectual property right". It also noted, at paragraph 138, rejecting the argument based on the alleged natural link, that it was not for Tetra Pak to impose certain measures on its own initiative on the basis of technical considerations or considerations relating to product liability, protection of public health and protection of its reputation. Those factors, taken as a whole, show that the Court of First Instance considered that Tetra Pak was not alone in being able to manufacture cartons for use in its machines.' (para 36)

'It must, moreover, be stressed that the list of abusive practices set out in the second paragraph of [Article 82 EC] is not exhaustive. Consequently, even where tied sales of two products are in accordance with commercial usage or there is a natural link between the two products in question, such sales may still constitute abuse within the meaning of [Article 82 EC] unless they are objectively justified. The reasoning of the Court of First Instance in paragraph 137 of its judgment is not therefore in any way defective.' (para 37)

Comment

Note that abusive tying may be established even when the tied sales of two products is in accordance with commercial usage or there is a natural link between the two products in question, such sale may constitute an abuse unless it is objectively justified. (para 37)

In Case T–30/89 *Hilti AG v Commission*, the Commission accused Hilti of abusing its dominant position by tying the sale of nails to the sale of cartridge strips, a practice that excluded competitors from the market and was aimed at increasing Hilti's market power. On appeal the CFI rejected Hilti's argument that its practice was objectively justifiable. (See detailed analysis on page 182 below.)

Microsoft Corp v Commission	**Article 82 EC**
Case T–201/04	Abuse
CFI, [2007] 5 CMLR 11	Tying & Bundling

Facts

An appeal on Commission Decision Comp/C–3/37.792 in which the Commission found Microsoft to have infringed Article 82 EC by refusing to supply interoperability information to its competitors and by bundling its Windows Media Player with its operating system (on refusal to supply, see page 173 above). The Commission found that Microsoft had abused its market power by bundling its Windows Media Player with its Windows operating system. This conduct enabled Microsoft to anticompetitively expand its position of market power and to significantly weaken competition on the media player market by foreclosing this market and artificially reducing the incentives of media companies, software developers and content providers to develop competing media players. The Commission ordered Microsoft to provide a version of its operating system without the Windows Media Player. Microsoft appealed the decision. On appeal the CFI held that the Commission's analysis of the constituent elements of bundling was correct. The Commission was right to base its finding that there was abusive tying in the present case on the following factors (Commission Decision, Recital 794): (1) the tying and tied products are two separate products; (2) the undertaking concerned is dominant in the market for the tying product; (3) the undertaking concerned does not give customers a choice to obtain the tying product without the tied product; and (4) the practice in question forecloses competition. (paras 842–59)

Held

'It must be borne in mind that the list of abusive practices set out in the second paragraph of Article 82 EC is not exhaustive and that the practices mentioned there are merely examples of abuse of a dominant position. … It follows that bundling by an undertaking in a dominant position may also infringe Article 82 EC where it does not correspond to the example given in Article 82(d) EC. Accordingly, in order to establish the existence of abusive bundling, the Commission was correct to rely in the contested decision on Article 82 EC in its entirety and not exclusively on Article 82(d) EC.' (paras 860, 861)

The existence of two separate products

'Microsoft contends, in substance, that media functionality is not a separate product from the Windows client PC operating system but forms an integral part of that system. As a result, what is at issue is a single product, namely the Windows client PC operating system, which is constantly evolving. In Microsoft's submission, customers expect that any client PC operating system will have the functionalities which they perceive as essential, including audio and video functionalities, and that those functionalities will be constantly updated.' (para 912)

The IT and communications industry is an industry in constant and rapid evolution. In such an industry what initially appear to be separate products may subsequently be regarded as forming a single product, both from the technological aspect and from the aspect of the competition rules. The Court must assess whether the Commission was correct to find two separate products at the period of the investigation. (paras 913–16)

The distinctness of products for the purpose of an analysis under Article 82 EC has to be assessed by reference to customer demand. In the absence of independent demand for the allegedly tied product, there can be no question of separate products and no abusive tying. (paras 917–21)

According to the Community case-law on bundling, complementary products can constitute separate products for the purposes of Article 82 EC. It is possible that customers will wish to obtain the client PC operating systems and application software together, but from different sources. For example, the fact that most client PC users want their client PC operating system to come with word-processing software does not transform those separate products into a single product for the purposes of Article 82 EC. (paras 922–3)

The Commission correctly observed at recital 807 to the contested decision, that there exists a demand for client PC operating systems. That fact is not disputed by Microsoft. In addition, 'a series of factors based on the nature and technical features of the products concerned, the facts observed on the market, the history of the development of the products concerned and also Microsoft's commercial practice demonstrate the existence of separate consumer demand for streaming media players.' (paras 925, 924–33)

'… The fact that tying takes the form of the technical integration of one product in another does not have the consequence that, for the purpose of assessing its impact on the market, that integration cannot be qualified as the bundling of two separate products.' (para 935)

'Furthermore, Microsoft's argument that the integration of Windows Media Player in the Windows operating system was dictated by technical reasons is scarcely credible in the light of the content of certain of its own internal communications … it follows from Mr Bay's email of 3 January 1999 to Mr Gates … that the integration of Windows Media Player in Windows was primarily designed to make Windows Media Player more competitive with RealPlayer by presenting it as a constituent part of Windows and not as application software that might be compared with RealPlayer.' (para 937)

'Microsoft cannot rely on the fact that vendors of competing client PC operating systems also bundle those systems with a streaming media player. On the one hand, Microsoft has not adduced any evidence that such bundling was already carried out by its competitors at the time when the abusive bundling commenced. On the other hand, moreover, it is clear that the commercial conduct of those competitors, far from invalidating the Commission's argument, corroborates it. … in any event, it is settled case-law that even when the tying of two products is consistent with commercial usage or when there is a natural link between the two products in question, it may none the less constitute abuse within the meaning of Article 82 EC, unless it is objectively justified (Case C–333/94 P *Tetra Pak II* … paragraph 37).' (paras 941–2)

The Commission was correct to find that client PC operating systems and streaming media players constituted separate products. (para 944)

Dominance in the market for the tying product

It is common ground that Microsoft has a dominant position on the market for the tying product, namely client PC operating systems. (para 870)

Consumers are unable to choose to obtain the tying product without the tied product

'Microsoft contends, in essence, that the fact that it integrated Windows Media Player in the Windows client PC operating system does not entail any coercion or supplementary obligation within the meaning of Article 82(d) EC. In support of its argument, it emphasizes … that customers pay nothing extra for the media functionality of Windows; [and] that they are not obliged to use that functionality; and, in the third place, that they are not prevented from installing and using competitors' media players.' (para 960)

'The Court observes that it cannot be disputed that, in consequence of the impugned conduct, consumers are unable to acquire the Windows client PC operating system without simultaneously acquiring Windows Media Player, which means (see paragraph 864 above) that the condition that the conclusion of contracts is made subject to acceptance of supplementary obligations must be considered to be satisfied.' (para 961)

The foreclosure of competition

'As indicated at recital 841 to the contested decision, the Commission considered that, in light of the specific circumstances of the present case, it could not merely assume, as it normally does in cases of abusive tying, that the tying of a specific product and a dominant product has by its nature a foreclosure effect. The Commission therefore examined more closely the actual effects which the bundling had already had on the streaming media player market and also the way in which that market was likely to evolve.' (para 868)

'Microsoft claims, in substance, that the Commission has failed to prove that the integration of Windows Media Player in the Windows client PC operating system involved foreclosure of competition, so that the fourth constituent element of abusive tying ... is not fulfilled in this case.' (para 1031)

The Commission was correct in its analysis of foreclosure. It is clear that owing to the bundling, Windows Media Player enjoyed an unparalleled presence on client PCs throughout the world, because it thereby automatically achieved a level of market penetration corresponding to that of the Windows client PC operating system. No third-party media player could achieve such a level of market penetration. As Windows Media Player cannot be removed by users from the package consisting of Windows and Windows Media Player, the third-party media player could never be the only media player on the client PC. The pre installed Media Player thus make users less likely to use alternative media players as they already have an application which delivers media streaming and playback functionality. In addition, the presence of several media players on the same client PC creates a risk of confusion on the part of users and an increase in customer support and testing costs. (paras 1037–59)

The Commission was correct to find that 'the market for streaming media players is characterised by significant indirect network effects or, to use the expression employed by Mr Gates, on the existence of a "positive feedback loop". ... That expression describes the phenomenon where, the greater the number of users of a given software platform, the more there will be invested in developing products compatible with that platform, which, in turn reinforces the popularity of that platform with users. The Court considers that the Commission was correct to find that such a phenomenon existed in the present case and to find that it was on the basis of the percentages of installation and use of media players that content providers and software developers chose the technology for which they would develop their own products ...' (paras 1061–2)

The absence of objective justification

Microsoft has not demonstrated the existence of any objective justification for the abusive bundling of Windows Media Player with the Windows client PC operating system. The Court rejects Microsoft's argument that the integration of media functionality in Windows is indispensable in order for software developers and internet site creators to be able to continue to benefit from the significant advantages offered by the 'stable and well-defined' Windows platform. In its decision the Commission did not interfere with Microsoft's business model in so far as that model includes the integration of a streaming media player in its client PC operating system. The Commission expressly states that Microsoft retains the right to offer a bundle of the Windows client PC operating system and Windows Media Player as long as at the same time a version of that system without Windows Media Player is available. Additionally, Microsoft's argument that the removal of media functionality from the system would undermine standardisation, and create problems to the detriment of consumers, software and Internet site developers, cannot be accepted. (paras 1144–67)

Comment

The Court acknowledged the rapid evolution of the industry and the possibility that, with time, separate products may be regarded as forming a single product. Note that the finding of two product markets was considered at the point of time when the Commission took its decision.

Note that although the Court did not engage in a detailed analysis of consumer harm, it took notice of the impact of bundling and market foreclosure on consumer choice.

The code removal remedy, under which Microsoft was ordered to offer an unbundled version, came under criticism from the US Department of Justice which argued that it went beyond what was necessary or appropriate to protect consumers and risked protecting competitors, rather then competition.

Irish Sugar v Commission	**Article 82 EC**
Case T–228/97	Objective Justification
CFI, [1999] ECR II–2969, [1999] 5 CMLR 1300	Price Alignment

Facts

Irish Sugar plc, the sole processor of sugar beet and the principal supplier of sugar in Ireland, was fined by the Commission for infringing Article 82 EC. The Commission's decision identified seven individual abuses by Irish Sugar on the market in granulated sugar intended for retail and for industry in Ireland. Irish sugar was found to have abused its dominant position by granting special rebates to certain retailers established in the border area between Ireland and Northern Ireland. This practice aimed to reduce the imports of cheaper retail packets from Northern Ireland into Ireland and was unrelated to objective economic factors such as the sales volume of the customers. According to the Commission, this practice amounted to abusive selective or discriminatory pricing and meant that Irish Sugar had been applying dissimilar conditions to equivalent transactions with other trading parties, thereby placing those who did not qualify for the rebate at a competitive disadvantage. Irish Sugar appealed to the CFI for the annulment of the decision. On appeal, it contested these finding and argued that its practice was aimed at meeting the competition and was defensive in nature. Accordingly, the practice was aimed at preventing Irish Sugar from losing part of its customer base and its turnover. Moreover, the practice aimed to face the competition where it manifested itself, using the limited means available to Irish Sugar at the time. Accordingly, due to financial difficulties, Irish Sugar was financially unable to cut prices on a national scale.

Held

'… the applicant cannot rely on the insufficiency of the financial resources at its disposal at the time to justify the selective and discriminatory granting of those border rebates and thereby escape the application of [Article 82 EC], without making a dead letter of the prohibition contained in that article. The circumstances in which an undertaking in a dominant position may be led to react to the limited competition which exists on the market, especially where that undertaking holds more than 88% of the market as in this case, form part of the competitive process which [Article 82 EC] is precisely designed to protect. Moreover, the applicant has several times underlined the high level of retail sale prices in Ireland, explaining it by the influence of the high level of the guaranteed intervention price in the context of the common organisation of the market in sugar.' (para 186)

'… the defensive nature of the practice complained of in this case cannot alter the fact that it constitutes an abuse for the purposes of [Article 82(c) EC].' (para 187)

'In this case, the applicant has been unable to establish an objective economic justification for the rebates. They were given to certain customers in the retail sugar market by reference solely to their exposure to competition resulting from cheap imports from another Member State and, in this case, by reference to their being established along the border with Northern Ireland. It also appears, according to the applicant's own statements, that it was able to practise such price rebates owing to the particular position it held on the Irish market. Thus it states that it was unable to practice such rebates over the whole of Irish territory owing to the financial losses it was making at the time. It follows that, by the applicant's own admission, its economic capacity to offer rebates in the region along the border with Northern Ireland depended on the stability of its prices in other regions, which amounts to recognition that it financed those rebates by means of its sales in the rest of the Irish territory. By conducting itself in that way, the applicant abused its dominant position in the retail sugar market in Ireland, by preventing the development of free competition on that market and distorting its structures, in relation to both purchasers and consumers. The latter were not able to benefit, outside the region along the border with Northern Ireland, from the price reductions caused by the imports of sugar from Northern Ireland.' (para 188)

'Thus, even if the existence of a dominant position does not deprive an undertaking placed in that position of the right to protect its own commercial interests when they are threatened … the protection of the commercial position of an undertaking in a dominant position with the characteristics of that of the applicant at the time in question must, at the very least, in order to be lawful, be based on criteria of economic efficiency and consistent with the interests of consumers. In this case, the applicant has not shown that those conditions were fulfilled.' (para 189)

Comment

The Court held that the protection of commercial interests must, at the very least, in order to be lawful, be based on criteria of economic efficiency and consistent with the interests of consumers. (para 189)

Note the ECJ judgement in Case 27/76 *United Brands v Commission* where in paragraphs 189–192 the court held that although the existence of a dominant position does not deprive the dominant undertaking of the right to protect its own commercial interests when they are attacked, such protection is not tolerated when its actual purpose is to strengthen the dominant position and abuse it. The protective action must be proportionate to the threat, taking into account the economic strength of the undertakings confronting each other.

See also Case T–83/91 *Tetra Pak International SA v Commission* [1994] ECR II–755, where the CFI rejected Tetra Pak's claims of objective justification on the basis of public health. The Court assessed these arguments in light of the principles enshrined in the *Hilti* judgment. It concluded that the protection of public health may be guaranteed by other means rather then tying of Tetra Pak's products, and added that in any event the remedy must lie in appropriate legislation or regulations, and not in rules adopted unilaterally by manufacturers, which would amount to prohibiting independent manufacturers from conducting the essential part of their business. (paras 83–5, 138)

See case T–201/04 *Microsoft Corp v Commission* (pages 173 and 177 above) where the CFI rejected Microsoft's argument that the fact that the technology concerned was covered by intellectual property rights justified its refusal to licence. The CFI also rejected Microsoft's claim that the bundling of Windows Media Player with the Windows client PC operating system was objectively justified as it was indispensable in order for software developers and Internet site creators to be able to continue to benefit from the significant advantages offered by the 'stable and well-defined' Windows platform.

The Commission's discussion paper on the application of Article 82 of the Treaty to exclusionary abuses, reviews the possible defence claims in case of finding of abuse. These include the objective necessity defence, the meeting competition defence and the efficiency defence. (paras 77–92)

Hilti AG v Commission	**Article 82 EC**
Case T–30/89	Objective Justification
CFI, [1991] ECR II–1439, [1992] 4 CMLR 16	

Facts

The Commission fined Hilti AG for the abuse of its dominant position in the market for nail guns and for the nails and cartridge strips for those guns. The abusive behaviour included the tying of the sale of nails to the sale of cartridge strips, a practice that excluded competitors from the market and was aimed at increasing Hilti's market power. (IV/30.787 and 31.488 – *Eurofix-Bauco v Hilti*)

Hilti appealed to the CFI and argued that, among other things, the tying of the sale of nails to cartridge strips was objectively justifiable on grounds of safety. Hilti claimed that deficiencies in nails produced elsewhere rendered them incompatible with Hilti's nail guns. Additionally, it argued that the tying was justified by Hili's duty of care as a manufacturer. (paras 102–07)

Held (on objective justification)

Hilti's argument that its actions stem out of safety concerns cannot be accepted. 'It is common ground that at no time during the period in question did Hilti approach the competent United Kingdom authorities for a ruling that the use of the interveners' nails in Hilti tools was dangerous'. (paras 115, 115–17)

There are laws in the United Kingdom which attach penalties to the sale of dangerous products and to the use of misleading claims as to the characteristics of any product. 'In those circumstances it is clearly not the task of an undertaking in a dominant position to take steps on its own initiative to eliminate products which, rightly or wrongly, it regards as dangerous or at least as inferior in quality to its own products.' (para 118)

'It must further be held in this connection that the effectiveness of the Community rules on competition would be jeopardized if the interpretation by an undertaking of the laws of the various Member States regarding product liability were to take precedence over those rules. Hilti's argument based on its alleged duty of care cannot therefore be upheld.' (para 119)

Comment

In its submission to the Court the Commission referred to the ECJ judgments in Case 193/83 *Windsurfing International v Commission*, [1986] ECR 611, and Case 226/84 *British Leyland v Commission*, [1986] ECR 3263. According to the Commission both cases show that 'abuse' within the meaning of Article 82 cannot be justified by considerations of product safety and reliability. (para 109)

Also note the Commission's analysis in its decision (IV/30.787 and 31.488 – *Eurofix-Bauco v Hilti* [1988] OJ L 65/19) relating to Hilti's claims for objective justification. There, the Commission considered at length Hilti's claims that its practices were the results of concerns as to the reliability, operation and safety of nail guns, nails and cartridge strips. The Commission concluded that Hilti's actions reflected 'a commercial interest in stopping the penetration of the market of non-Hilti consumables since the main profit from [nail guns, nails and cartridge strips] originates from the sale of consumables, not from the sale of nail guns. This is without prejudice to the possibility that Hilti had a genuine concern about safety and reliability.' (para 90)

An appeal by Hilti to the ECJ was dismissed. See Case C–53/92 P *Hilti v Commission* [1994] ECR I–667, paragraphs 11–16.

Irish Sugar v Commission	**Article 82 EC**
Case T–228/97	Effect on Trade
CFI, [1999] ECR II–2969, [1999] 5 CMLR 1300	

'... It should also be remembered that, to be capable of affecting trade between Member States, it is not necessary to demonstrate that the conduct complained of actually affected trade between Member States in a discernible way; it is sufficient to establish that the conduct is capable of having that effect. As regards abusive practices envisaged by [Article 82 EC], in order to assess whether trade between Member States is capable of being discernibly affected by the abuse of a dominant position, account must be taken of the consequences which result for the actual structure of competition in the common market...' (para 170)

Nederlandsche Banden Industrie Michelin v Commission	**Article 82 EC**
Case 322/81	Effect on Trade
ECJ, [1983] ECR 3461, [1985] 1 CMLR 282	

'It has not been denied in this case that important patterns of trade exist as a result of the establishment of competitors of significant size in other Member States. The effects of the discount system on the chances of Michelin NV's competitors of obtaining access to the Netherlands market have already been examined in the context of the examination of the abusive nature of Michelin NV's conduct. It must also be remembered that [Article 82 EC] does not require it to be proved that the abusive conduct has in fact appreciably affected trade between Member States but that it is capable of having that effect.' (para 104)

RTE & ITP v Commission (The Magill case)	**Article 82 EC**
Joined Cases C–241, 242/91P	Effect on Trade
ECJ, [1995] ECR I–743, [1995] 4 CMLR 718	

'In this case, the Court of First Instance found that the applicant had excluded all potential competitors on the geographical market consisting of one Member State (Ireland) and part of another Member State (Northern Ireland) and had thus modified the structure of competition on that market, thereby affecting potential commercial exchanges between Ireland and the United Kingdom. From this the Court of First Instance drew the proper conclusion that the condition that trade between Member States must be affected had been satisfied.' (para 70)

Compagnie Maritime Belge v Commission	**Article 82 EC**
Case T–24/93	Effect on Trade
ECJ, [1996] ECR II–1201	

'It should first be recalled that it has been consistently held that, in order that an agreement between under-takings, or moreover an abuse of a dominant position, may affect trade between Member States, it must be possible to foresee with a sufficient degree of probability and on the basis of objective factors of law or fact that it may have an influence, direct or indirect, actual or potential, on the pattern of trade between Member States, such as might prejudice the realization of the aim of a single market in all the Member States (Case C–250/92 DLG [1994] ECR I–5641, paragraph 54). Accordingly, it is not specifically necessary that the conduct in question should in fact have substantially affected trade between Member States. It is sufficient to establish that the conduct is capable of having such an effect (see, as regards [Article 82 EC], Joined Cases C–241/91 P and C–242/91 P *RTE and ITP v Commission* [1995] ECR I–743, paragraph 69, and, as regards [Article 81 EC], Case T–29/92 *SPO and others v Commission* [1995] ECR II–289).' (para 201)

English Welsh & Scottish Railway Limited v E.ON UK plc	**Article 82 EC**
2006 FOLIO 1338	Nullity and Severance
High Court of Justice Queen's Bench Division, [2007] EWHC 599	

Facts

English Welsh & Scottish Railway Limited (EWS) is an operator of bulk rail freight services. The defendant (E.ON) is in the business of electricity generation. The two parties entered into a Coal Carriage Agreement (CCA) under which E.ON was obliged to use EWS to carry all the coal required to be moved to one of a number of specified power stations from one of a number of specified locations, subject to certain exclusions.

Following a complaint by third parties, the UK Office of Rail Regulation (ORR) issued a decision in which it found EWS to have abused its dominant position by foreclosing the 'coal haulage by rail market' through, among other things, maintaining exclusionary terms in its CCA. The ORR directed that, within 30 days, EWS and, as appropriate, the other parties to each of the contracts in question, remove or modify the exclusionary terms from the contracts in existence so as to remove their exclusionary effect and/or in the event that any new contracts are concluded to exclude from those contracts any terms capable of achieving the same or similar exclusionary effect to those identified as abusive.

EWS wrote to E.ON maintaining that the effect of the ORR's decision was to render the entire CCA void. On the other hand, E.ON took the view that the CCA would continue to bind EWS even if the exclusionary terms were removed. The dispute between the two companies reached the Commercial Court.

Held (Mr Justice Field)

'The Directions are somewhat infelicitously worded, but in my judgement, construed against the background of the ORR's findings in respect of the exclusionary terms and giving the word "remove" its ordinary and natural meaning, their meaning is clear. If the parties have not within 30 days agreed modifications to the exclusionary terms which remove their exclusionary effect, the parties must remove the terms from the CCA. There is no question of the parties being directed to agree to remove the terms: absent compliant modifications in the time prescribed, the terms are to go, full stop ...' (para 25)

'I agree with Mr Turner's submission [for the Intervener ORR] that given: (i) the ORR's findings; (ii) Article 1.3 of Council Regulation 1/2003 ; and (iii) the direct effect of Article 82 , the exclusionary terms were illegal as a matter of public law from the moment the CCA was executed. And from 1st March 2000, when Chapter II of the Act came into effect, the exclusionary terms were doubly illegal for being in breach of the Chapter II prohibition. The consequence is that from the time the CCA was executed the exclusionary terms have been void. The Directions to remove the terms are an administrative measure to ensure that the CCA is brought within the law.' (para 26)

'Where terms are void at common law for being in restraint of trade or by reason of Article 81 EC and the Chapter I prohibition, the courts apply the doctrine of severance to determine if the offending terms can be severed from the contract leaving the residue to continue to operate as an enforceable contract; see e.g. *Crehan v Courage Limited*; *Byrne v Inntreprenneur Beer Supply Co Ltd* [1999] EuLR 834 at 896. In my judgement, exactly the same approach applies where a term or terms of a contract are void by reason of being in breach of Article 82 and the Chapter II prohibition. It is thus not a question of whether the contract is frustrated but whether the test for severance as formulated in the cases has been satisfied.' (para 27)

'The Court of Appeal in *Crehan v Courage* rehearsed various formulations of the severance test propounded over the years without identifying which if any was to be preferred. These included: (i) whether the invalid restraint formed the whole or substantially the whole consideration for the promise; (ii) whether the contract would be so changed in its character as not to be the sort of contract that the parties intended to enter at all; (iii) whether what was unenforceable was part of the main purpose and substance, or whether the deletion altered entirely the scope and intention of the agreement or, on the contrary, left the rest of the agreement a reasonable arrangement between the parties; (iv) whether it would disappoint the main purposes of one of the main parties; and (v) whether the agreement was in substance an agreement for an invalid restraint.' (para 28)

'Mr Sharpe [QC for E.ON] conceded that if the doctrine of severance applied, the CCA without the exclusionary terms would be of a fundamentally different nature. In my judgement this concession was well made. Accordingly, subject to the true effect of clause 34 of the CCA, there can be no severance of the exclusionary terms and the whole contract is void and unenforceable. As to this latter point, the Court of Appeal in *Richard Ground Ltd v (GB) Ltd* [1997] EuLR 277 upheld the finding of the first instance judge that a clause in substantially similar words to clause 34 was ineffective to allow severance where the resulting contract would not be the sort of contract that the parties intended to enter at all. Unsurprisingly, Mr Sharpe accepted that in the light of this decision clause 34 did not allow for severance where the common law test was not satisfied.' (para 29)

'For the reasons given above, EWS is entitled to a declaration the substance of which is that the effect of the ORR's Decision issued on 17 November 2006 and the Directions contained therein is that clauses 4.2, 4.3, 5.4 and 6.1 of the CCA have from the inception of the contract been void and since those clauses cannot be severed the whole of the CCA is void and unenforceable.' (para 30)

Comment

The judge made two clear statements on the outcome of Article 82 infringement: (1) a provision in an agreement that is in breach of Article 82 EC is illegal and void. In such instance the nullity takes effect from the moment the agreement is executed; (2) when a provision in breach of Article 82 EC cannot be severed from the rest of the contract without fundamentally changing its nature, the whole contract is void and unenforceable.

In the absence of a clear statement on the matter from the European courts, this decision provides a valuable indication that agreements that infringe Article 82 EC will not be enforceable.

6

Collective Dominance

The concept of collective dominance was developed under both Article 82 EC and the European Merger Regulation (Council Regulation (EC) No 139/2004 on the control of concentrations between undertakings, [2004] OJ L 24/1).

Article 82 EC

Article 82 EC targets the 'abuse by one or more undertakings of a dominant position'. Collective dominance, i.e. a dominant position held by a number of undertakings, may be established when two or more undertakings present themselves or act together from an economic point of view, as a collective entity. Their joint policies or activities subsequently enable them together, to behave to a considerable extent independently of their competitors, customers and consumers.

To establish collective dominance one needs to do more than recycle the facts constituting an infringement of Article 81 EC (Case T–68/89). Collective dominance may arise when the economic links between undertakings result in joint policies or activities (Case C–395/96 P) even if those are not identical (Case T–228/97). It may be established even in the absence of an agreement or of other links in law, through links between the undertakings which lead them to present themselves as a collective entity on the market or on the basis of an economic assessment of the structure of the market in question. In Case C–395/96 P *Compagnie Maritime Belge Transports v Commission* the ECJ held that 'A dominant position may be held by two or more economic entities legally independent of each other, provided that from an economic point of view they present themselves or act together on a particular market as a collective entity.' (para 36) This statement reflects the understanding that in some instances market conditions would give rise to collective dominance even absent structural links between the undertakings.

In its Discussion Paper on the Application of Article 82 of the Treaty to Exclusionary Abuses, the Commission made references to the possibility of establishing collective dominance in an oligopolistic market. (paras 43–50) This area of law and economics has been developed mostly under the ECMR, although as evident from the ECJ judgment in Compagnie Maritime Belge and the Commission discussion paper, it is also relevant to the analysis of collective dominance under Article 82 EC. Of particular relevance to Article 82 EC analysis is the CFI judgment in Case T–464/04 *Impala v Commission* in which the court considered the evidence necessary to establish an existing collective dominant position.

The European Merger Regulation (ECMR)

Whereas the analysis under Article 82 EC is by its nature an ex-post analysis, the appraisal of concentrations under the ECMR is an ex-ante one. In the context of collective dominance, this difference in analysis means that cases dealing with collective dominance under the ECMR are primarily concerned with establishing that market characteristics following the merger transaction would give rise to a position of collective dominance. As indicated above, unique in this respect is Case T–464/04 *IMPALA v Commission* which concerns not only the creation of a collective dominant position but also the determination of the existence of a collective dominant position. Another difference in analysis between the two is that whereas Article 82 EC condemns the abuse of a collective dominant position (and not the position in itself), the ECMR condemns the creation or strengthening of the collective dominant position.

C–68/94 etc	*French Republic and others v Commission*	194
T–102/96	*Gencor v Commission*	195
T–324/99	*Airtours plc v Commission*	196
T–464/04	*IMPALA v Commission*	198

On collective dominance under the ECMR, also note the Commission's Guidelines on the Assessment of Horizontal Mergers under the Council Regulation on the Control of Concentrations between Undertakings. (paras 39–57, [2004] OJ 31/5)

Concerted Practice vis-à-vis Tacit Collusion

As evident from the case-law, tight oligopolistic markets may at times by their structure enable undertakings to sustain joint policies without communicating with each other. This phenomena, often referred to by economists as 'tacit collusion', may materialise in oligopolistic markets when (1) the market is transparent and thus enables undertakings to monitor each other's activities, and (2) undertakings are capable of punishing deviators from the tacit agreement and (3) competitive constraints do not jeopardise the implementation of the common strategy. (Case T–324/99, T–464/04 above) Tacit collusion receives different treatment under the different legal instruments:

- ECMR: the creation or strengthening of a collective dominant position (through tacit collusion) which significantly impedes effective competition is prohibited.
- Article 82 EC: a collective dominant position (either as the result of tacit collusion or due to connecting links between the companies) is only condemned if the undertakings abuse it.
- Article 81 EC: parallel behaviour which is a rational reaction by the undertakings to market characteristics and does not result from concerted practice or agreement is not condemned. Parallel behaviour may amount to strong evidence of concerted practice when it leads to conditions of competition that do not respond to the market characteristics. See Case 48/69 *Imperial Chemical Industries (ICI) v Commission* (*Dyestuffs*), page 45 above.

Società Italiana Vetro SpA and others v Commission
Joined Cases T–68, 77, 78/89 (Italian flat glass)
CFI, [1992] ECR II–1403, [1992] 5 CMLR 302

Collective Dominance
Article 82 EC

Facts

An appeal on the Commission's decision in which it found that three Italian flat-glass producers had formed a cartel agreement contrary to Article 81 EC. The Commission also found the practice to have infringed Article 82 EC. The Commission asserted that the three undertakings, as participants in a tight oligopoly, enjoyed a degree of independence from competitive pressures that enabled them to impede the maintenance of effective competition, notably by not having to take account of the behaviour of the other market participants. (point 78) It concluded that the undertakings presented themselves on the market as a single entity and not as individuals (point 79) and that their conduct constituted an abuse of a collective dominant position, because it restricted the consumers' ability to choose sources of supply, limited market outlets and distorted competition within the common market. On appeal, the CFI considered, among other things, the Commission's finding of a collective dominant position.

Held

'The Court notes that the very words of the first paragraph of [Article 82 EC] provide that "one or more undertakings" may abuse a dominant position. It has consistently been held, as indeed all the parties acknowledge, that the concept of agreement or concerted practice between undertakings does not cover agreements or concerted practices among undertakings belonging to the same group if the undertakings form an economic unit (see, for example, the judgment in Case 15/74 *Centrafarm*, [[1974] ECR 1147], paragraph 41). It follows that when [Article 81] refers to agreements or concerted practices between "undertakings", it is referring to relations between two or more economic entities which are capable of competing with one another.' (para 357)

'The Court considers that there is no legal or economic reason to suppose that the term "undertaking" in [Article 82 EC] has a different meaning from the one given to it in the context of [Article 81 EC]. There is nothing, in principle, to prevent two or more independent economic entities from being, on a specific market, united by such economic links that, by virtue of that fact, together they hold a dominant position vis-a-vis the other operators on the same market. This could be the case, for example, where two or more independent undertakings jointly have, through agreements or licences, a technological lead affording them the power to behave to an appreciable extent independently of their competitors, their customers and ultimately of their consumers (judgment of the Court in *Hoffmann-La Roche*, [[1979] ECR 461], paragraphs 38 and 48).' (para 358)

'The Court finds support for that interpretation in the wording of Article 8 of Council Regulation (EEC) No 4056/86 of 22 December 1986 laying down detailed rules for the application of [Articles 81 and 82 EC] to maritime transport (Official Journal L 378, p 4). Article 8(2) provides that the conduct of a liner conference benefiting from an exemption from a prohibition laid down by [Article 81(1) EC] may have effects which are incompatible with [Article 82 EC]. A request by a conference to be exempted from the prohibition laid down by [Article 81(1) EC] necessarily presupposes an agreement between two or more independent economic undertakings.' (para 359)

'However, it should be pointed out that for the purposes of establishing an infringement of [Article 82 EC], it is not sufficient, as the Commission's agent claimed at the hearing, to "recycle" the facts constituting an infringement of [Article 81 EC], deducing from them the finding that the parties to an agreement or to an unlawful practice jointly hold a substantial share of the market, that by virtue of that fact alone they hold a collective dominant position, and that their unlawful behaviour constitutes an abuse of that collective dominant position. Amongst other considerations, a finding of a dominant position, which is in any case not in itself a matter of reproach, presupposes that the market in question has been defined (judgment of the

Court of Justice in Case 6/72 Continental Can, [[1973] ECR 215], paragraph 32 Case 322/81 *Michelin v Commission* [1983] ECR 3461, paragraph 57). The Court must therefore examine, firstly, the analysis of the market made in the decision and, secondly, the circumstances relied on in support of the finding of a collective dominant position.' (para 360)

'With regard to the definition of the market, the Court recalls that the section of the factual part of the decision entitled "The market" (points 2 to 17) is almost entirely descriptive and that, moreover, it contains a number of errors, omissions and uncertainties which have already been examined by the Court. The Court also recalls that the findings made by the Commission concerning relations between the three producers, and concerning relations between, on the one hand, the three producers, and on the other hand, the wholesalers on the non-automotive market and the manufacturers on the automotive market, are in many respects insufficiently supported. Finally, the Court points out that in the section of the legal part devoted to "The relevant market" (points 76 to 77) the decision adds nothing from the factual point of view to what was stated previously.' (para 361)

'It must therefore be determined whether the analysis of the market made in points 76 and points 77 of the decision is sufficiently well-founded and, moreover, whether that analysis is sufficient in itself to prove, as the Commission claims, that the appropriate market for the purposes of the application of [Article 82 EC] is, as regards the product, the flat-glass market in general and, from the geographical point of view, Italy.' (para 362)

The Commission analysis of the flat-glass market was lacking in this case. The Commission did not provide sufficient explanation as to why it considered it appropriate to divide its assessment of the undertakings' behaviour in relation, respectively, to the automotive market and the non-automotive market, while claiming that for the purposes of applying Article 82 EC, the flat-glass market must be considered to be a single market. 'However, the Court need not give a definitive ruling on the question whether the inadequate analysis that the Commission considered it appropriate to devote to the definition of the market is supported by satisfactory evidence, since the Commission stated ... that the sentence which appears in the sixth paragraph of point 79 of the decision, "the undertakings present themselves on the market as a single entity and not as individuals", constituted an essential element of its position with regard to the application of [Article 82 EC], and that it was for the Commission to substantiate it. It is evident from all the foregoing that the Commission has far from substantiated that statement.' (paras 365, 363–5)

'It follows that, even supposing that the circumstances of the present case lend themselves to application of the concept of "collective dominant position" (in the sense of a position of dominance held by a number of independent undertakings), the Commission has not adduced the necessary proof. The Commission has not even attempted to gather the information necessary to weigh up the economic power of the three producers against that of Fiat, which could cancel each other out.' (para 366)

Comment

The CFI held that collective dominance cannot be established by merely recycling the facts constituting an infringement of Article 81 EC and deducing from them the finding that the parties to an agreement or to an unlawful practice jointly hold a substantial share of the market. (para 360)

The Commission was criticised for its analysis of the relations between the undertakings, its market definition, and its finding that together the undertakings held a collective dominant position.

In Case C–393/92 *Municipality of Almelo and others v NV Energiebedrijf Ijsselmij*, [1994] ECR I–1477, the ECJ referred to the possibility of finding a group of undertakings to collectively occupy a dominant position. It held that 'in order for such a collective dominant position to exist, the undertakings in the group must be linked in such a way that they adopt the same conduct on the market'. (para 42) For a similar statement see also Case C–140/94 etc *DIP SpA v Comune di Bassano del Grappa*, [1996] 4 CMLR 157, [1995] ECR I–3257, para 26.

Note the development of the concept in Case C–395/96 etc, page 191 below.

Compagnie Maritime Belge Transports v Commission	**Collective Dominance**
Case C–395/96 P & C–396/96 P	Article 82 EC
ECJ, [2000] ECR I–1365, [2000] 4 CMLR 1076	Horizontal Links

Facts

Compagnie Maritime Belge Transports SA (CMB) was found by the Commission to have abused a collective dominant position that it held with other undertakings. Together, the companies formed the membership of a liner conference and implemented a cooperation agreement which aimed, through selective price cuts, to drive an independent competitor out of the market (a practice known as 'fighting ships'). The companies were also found to have infringed Article 81 EC by entering into a non-competition agreement. The CFI dismissed an application by CMB to annul the Commission's decision. CMB appealed to the ECJ, contesting, among other things, the conclusion that it held jointly with the other members of the liner conference a collective dominant position.

Held

'A dominant position may be held by two or more economic entities legally independent of each other, provided that from an economic point of view they present themselves or act together on a particular market as a collective entity.' (para 36)

'… A finding that two or more undertakings hold a collective dominant position must, in principle, proceed upon an economic assessment of the position on the relevant market of the undertakings concerned, prior to any examination of the question whether those undertakings have abused their position on the market.' (para 37)

The finding of abuse of a collective dominant position includes three elements. First, it is necessary to establish whether the undertakings concerned together constitute a collective entity vis-a-vis their competitors, their trading partners and consumers on a particular market. Secondly, where such collective entity is established, the following question is whether that entity holds a dominant position. Lastly, as under Article 82 EC the finding of collective dominance is not in itself grounds for criticism, one should further question whether the collective entity abused its dominant position. (paras 37–9)

'In order to establish the existence of a collective entity as defined above, it is necessary to examine the economic links or factors which give rise to a connection between the undertakings concerned (see, inter alia, Case C–393/92 *Almelo* [1994] ECR I–1477, paragraph 43, and Joined Cases C–68/94 and C–30/95 *France and Others v Commission* [1998] ECR I–1375, paragraph 221).' (para 41)

'In particular, it must be ascertained whether economic links exist between the undertakings concerned which enable them to act together independently of their competitors, their customers and consumers (see *Michelin*, cited above).' (para 42)

'The mere fact that two or more undertakings are linked by an agreement, a decision of associations of undertakings or a concerted practice within the meaning of [Article 81(1) EC] does not, of itself, constitute a sufficient basis for such a finding.' (para 43)

'On the other hand, an agreement, decision or concerted practice (whether or not covered by an exemption under [Article 81(3) EC]) may undoubtedly, where it is implemented, result in the undertakings concerned being so linked as to their conduct on a particular market that they present themselves on that market as a collective entity vis-a-vis their competitors, their trading partners and consumers.' (para 44)

'The existence of an agreement or of other links in law is not indispensable to a finding of a collective dominant position; such a finding may be based on other connecting factors and would depend on an economic assessment and, in particular, on an assessment of the structure of the market in question.' (para 45)

By its very nature and in the light of its objectives, a liner conference can be characterised as an entity which presents itself as a collective vis-B-vis both users and competitors. 'That in no way prejudges the question whether, in a given situation, a liner conference holds a dominant position on a particular market or, a fortiori, has abused that position ...' (paras 49, 46–51)

The ECJ found the liner conference in question to hold a collective dominant position and to abuse it.

Comment

The existence of a collective dominant position flows from the nature and terms of an agreement or concerted practice between undertakings, from the way in which they are implemented and, consequently, from the links or factors which give rise to a connection between undertakings.

The judgment provides a clear indication that collective dominance may be found when the undertakings operate as a collective entity even in the absence of the existence of an agreement or of other links in law. The judgment paved the way to findings of collective dominance in later cases which are based on tacit collusion (see in particular the CFI judgment in *Airtours v Commission* on page 196 below (ECMR)).

Accordingly, under Article 82 EC when market characteristics give rise to tacit collusion, collective dominance may be established without the existence of an agreement or of other links in law (on the conditions to establish tacit collusion see *Airtours v Commission* on page 196 below). On the other hand, when the market does not give rise to tacit collusion, collective dominance can only be established if sufficient links between the undertakings are present. In this respect note Case C–309/99 *Wouters and others v Algemene Raad van de Nederlandse Orde van Advocaten* [2002] ECR I–1577, [2002] 4 CMLR 27, in which the ECJ held that 'the legal profession is not concentrated to any significant degree. It is highly heterogenous and is characterised by a high degree of internal competition. In the absence of sufficient structural links between them, members of the Bar cannot be regarded as occupying a collective dominant position for the purposes of [Article 82 EC] ...' (para 114)

In paragraph 41 the ECJ made references to previous decisions of collective dominance under both Article 82 EC and the European Merger Regulation (ECMR). It therefore considered the concept to be the same under the two regulatory instruments. Under both provisions, examination of the economic links or factors which give rise to a connection between the undertakings concerned, is required, in order to establish collective dominance. Note, however, the differences between the ex-post analysis under Article 82 EC which condemns the abuse of a dominant (or collective dominant) position, and the ex-ante analysis under the ECMR which condemns significant impediment to effective competition, in particular, as the result of the creation or strengthening of a dominant (or collective dominant) position.

In paragraph 41 the Court referred to Cases C–68/94 and C–30/95 *France and others v Commission* [1998] ECR I–1375. There in paragraph 221, the ECJ held with respect to collective dominance under the ECMR that 'in the case of an alleged collective dominant position, the Commission is therefore obliged to assess, using a prospective analysis of the reference market, whether the concentration which has been referred to it, leads to a situation in which effective competition in the relevant market is significantly impeded by the undertakings involved in the concentration and one or more other undertakings which together, in particular because of correlative factors which exist between them, are able to adopt a common policy on the market and act to a considerable extent independently of their competitors, their customers, and also of consumers.'

Irish Sugar plc v Commission	**Collective Dominance**
Case T–228/97	Article 82 EC
CFI, [1999] ECR II–2969, [1999] 5 CMLR 1300	

Facts

Irish Sugar, the sole processor of sugar beet and the principal supplier of sugar in Ireland, was fined by the Commission for infringing Article 82 EC. The Commission found Irish Sugar to hold a collective dominant position together with the distributor of its products, Sugar Distributors Ltd (SDL). Irish Sugar appealed to the CFI and contested, among other things, the Commission's finding of a joint dominant position with SDL.

Held

'A joint dominant position consists in a number of undertakings being able together, in particular because of factors giving rise to a connection between them, to adopt a common policy on the market and act to a considerable extent independently of their competitors, their customers, and ultimately consumers.' (para 46)

The existence of economic independence between two entities does not prevent them from holding a joint dominant position. The mere independence of the economic entities in question is not sufficient to remove the possibility of their holding a joint dominant position. (para 49)

In this case the Commission identified connecting factors between Irish Sugar and SDL which show that the two economic entities had the power to adopt a common market policy. These connecting factors include, among other things, Irish Sugar's shareholding in SDL's parent company (SDH), its representation on the boards of SDH and SDL, the direct economic ties between SDL and Irish sugar, and the latter's financing of all consumer promotions and rebates offered by SDL to its customers. (paras 50–58)

The fact that the Irish Sugar and SDL are in a vertical commercial relationship does not affect the finding of joint dominant position. The case-law does not contain anything to support a claim that the concept of a joint dominant position is inapplicable to two or more undertakings in a vertical commercial relationship. As pointed out by the Commission, it cannot be accepted that undertakings in a vertical relationship, without however being integrated to the extent of constituting one and the same undertaking, should be able abusively to exploit a joint dominant position. (paras 61–3)

'Whilst the existence of a joint dominant position may be deduced from the position which the economic entities concerned together hold on the market in question, the abuse does not necessarily have to be the action of all the undertakings in question. It only has to be capable of being identified as one of the manifestations of such a joint dominant position being held. Therefore, undertakings occupying a joint dominant position may engage in joint or individual abusive conduct. It is enough for that abusive conduct to relate to the exploitation of the joint dominant position which the undertakings hold in the market.' (para 66)

Comment

The decision is interesting as it confirms the Commission's position that collective dominance may exist in a vertical setting. (para 62)

In paragraph 66 the CFI held that an abuse of the collective dominant position may be the result even if an action was taken by one of the companies and not the collective entity as a whole. Accordingly, the requirement that undertakings would present themselves on the market as a single entity does not infer identical conduct on the market in every respect. Interestingly, and somewhat controversially, the Court held that it is the abusive behaviour which may be carried out by one of the companies and not the collective entity.

In its investigation the Commission accepted Irish Sugar's argument that it did not control the management of SDL, despite holding 51 per cent of SDH's capital. In the absence of control, the Commission was unable to treat the two companies as one economic entity. However the links between the companies, although falling short of control, sufficed to establish collective dominance.

French Republic and others v Commission	Collective Dominance
Case C–68/94 & 30/95 (Kali und Salz)	ECMR
ECJ, [1998] ECR I–1375, [1998] 4 CMLR 829	

Facts

An appeal on a Commission's decision in which it approved, subject to conditions, a concentration between Kali und Salz AG and Mitteldeutsche Kali AG (Case No IV/M308). The decision was contested by the French government, which sought its annulment on the grounds, among other things, that the Commission erred in its analysis of collective dominance. On appeal the ECJ annulled the Commission's decision but confirmed in principle the application of the ECMR to collective dominance.

Held

'In the case of an alleged collective dominant position, the Commission is … obliged to assess, using a prospective analysis of the reference market, whether the concentration which has been referred to it leads to a situation in which effective competition in the relevant market is significantly impeded by the undertakings involved in the concentration and one or more other undertakings which together, in particular because of correlative factors which exist between them, are able to adopt a common policy on the market and act to a considerable extent independently of their competitors, their customers, and also of consumers.' (para 221)

'Such an approach warrants close examination in particular of the circumstances which, in each individual case, are relevant for assessing the effects of the concentration on competition in the reference market.' (para 222)

In the present case the Commission relied for its decision on a cluster of structural links which were found to be not as tight or as conclusive as it sought to make out. In addition its conclusions on the level of competition in the market post-merger were not sufficiently well founded. Subsequently, the Commission failed to establish to the necessary legal standard that the concentration would give rise to a collective dominant position. (paras 225–50)

Comment

The judgment refers to the existence of certain links as a precondition for collective dominance. However, in subsequent cases it was held that the reference to structural links was by way of example and did not lay down a requirement that such links must exist in order for a finding of collective dominance to be made. In *Gencor v Commission* the Court clarified the lose periphery of the term 'links' (see paras 273–6)

In paragraph 221 the Court refers to the ability of the companies to adopt a common policy on the market. Note the similarity in approach to the analysis under Article 82 EC. See in particular paragraph 41, Case C–395/96 etc *Compagnie Maritime Belge Transports v Commission* (page 191 above)

The combined market share of the collective entity in this case was approximately 60 per cent. The ECJ held that such a market share 'cannot of itself point conclusively to the existence of a collective dominant position on the part of those undertakings.' (para 226) The Akzo presumption is therefore not applicable in cases of collective dominance (Case C–62/86 *AKZO Chemie BV v Commission*, page 131 above). Also note the CFI judgment in Case T–102/96 *Gencor Ltd v Commission* (page 195 below) where the Court held that 'in the context of an oligopoly, the fact that the parties to the oligopoly hold large market shares does not necessarily have the same significance, compared to the analysis of an individual dominant position, with regard to the opportunities for those parties, as a group, to act to a considerable extent independently of their competitors, their customers and, ultimately, of consumers. Nevertheless, particularly in the case of a duopoly, a large market share is, in the absence of evidence to the contrary, likewise a strong indication of the existence of a collective dominant position.' (para 206)

Gencor Ltd v Commission
Case T–102/96
CFI, [1999] ECR II–753, [1999] 4 CMLR 971

Collective Dominance
ECMR

Facts

Gencor, a company incorporated under South African law, and Lonrho Plc (Lonrho), a company incorporated under English law, proposed to acquire joint control of Impala Platinum Holdings Ltd (Implats), a company incorporated under South African law. The transaction was cleared by the South African Competition Board. The European Commission also reviewed the transaction, and raised concerns as to its impact on the common market. Subsequently, the Commission blocked the concentration on the ground that it would lead to the creation of a collective dominant position in the world platinum and rhodium market. (Case IV/M619) On appeal Gencor unsuccessfully argued, among other things, that the Commission wrongly found that the concentration would create a collective dominant position.

Held

Although the ECMR lacks express reference to the concept of collective dominance, Article 2 ECMR is interpreted as including this concept and therefore applies the ECMR both to the creation or strengthening of individual and collective dominant positions (paras 124–36)

The finding of structural links is not indispensable for the establishment of collective dominance. Reference to such links in the flat-glass case (Joined Cases T–68/89 etc, *Società Italiana Vetro SpA and others v Commission*) was by way of example and did not compel that such links must exist in order for a finding of collective dominance to be made. (paras 273–5)

'Furthermore, there is no reason whatsoever in legal or economic terms to exclude from the notion of economic links the relationship of interdependence existing between the parties to a tight oligopoly within which, in a market with the appropriate characteristics, in particular in terms of market concentration, transparency and product homogeneity, those parties are in a position to anticipate one another's behaviour and are therefore strongly encouraged to align their conduct in the market, in particular in such a way as to maximise their joint profits by restricting production with a view to increasing prices. In such a context, each trader is aware that highly competitive action on its part designed to increase its market share (for example a price cut) would provoke identical action by the others, so that it would derive no benefit from its initiative. All the traders would thus be affected by the reduction in price levels.' (para 276)

'That conclusion is all the more pertinent with regard to the control of concentrations, whose objective is to prevent anti-competitive market structures from arising or being strengthened. Those structures may result from the existence of economic links in the strict sense argued by the applicant or from market structures of an oligopolistic kind where each undertaking may become aware of common interests and, in particular, cause prices to increase without having to enter into an agreement or resort to a concerted practice.' (para 277)

'The Commission was entitled to conclude, relying on the envisaged alteration in the structure of the market and on the similarity of the costs of Amplats and Implats/LPD, that the proposed transaction would create a collective dominant position and lead in actual fact to a duopoly constituted by those two undertakings.' (para 279)

Comment

Note the CFI comments on the interdependence between undertakings in a tight oligipolistic market.

Note that in this case the transaction would have led to the creation of a duopoly in the market. Contrast with Airtours/First Choice where the concentration would have reduced the number of players in the market from four to three (page 196 below).

Airtours plc v Commission	**Collective Dominance**
Case T–342/99	ECMR
CFI, [2002] ECR II–2585, [2002] 5 CMLR 7	

Facts

An appeal on the Commission's decision in Case IV/M1524 *Airtours/First Choice* in which the Commission blocked a take over by Airtours plc, a UK tour operator and supplier of package holidays, of First Choice plc, one of Airtours' competitors. The Commission found that the transaction would give rise to a collective dominant position in the United Kingdom short-haul foreign package-holiday market, as a result of which competition would be significantly impeded in the common market. Airtours appealed to the CFI, alleging, among other things, that the Commission erred in its finding of a collective dominant position. It argued that in the past the market has been operating competitively as a benign oligopoly and that the Commission failed to prove that the merger would have reduced the three remaining undertakings' incentive to compete. Additionally, it claimed that in any event, the absence of retaliatory measures and the low barriers to entry and expansion in the market would curtail any attempt to collude.

Held

'A collective dominant position significantly impeding effective competition in the common market or a substantial part of it may … arise as the result of a concentration where, in view of the actual characteristics of the relevant market and of the alteration in its structure that the transaction would entail, the latter would make each member of the dominant oligopoly, as it becomes aware of common interests, consider it possible, economically rational, and hence preferable, to adopt on a lasting basis a common policy on the market with the aim of selling at above competitive prices, without having to enter into an agreement or resort to a concerted practice within the meaning of Article 81 EC … and without any actual or potential competitors, let alone customers or consumers, being able to react effectively.' (para 61)

'Three conditions are necessary for a finding of collective dominance as defined:

– First, each member of the dominant oligopoly must have the ability to know how the other members are behaving in order to monitor whether or not they are adopting the common policy. As the Commission specifically acknowledges, it is not enough for each member of the dominant oligopoly to be aware that interdependent market conduct is profitable for all of them but each member must also have a means of knowing whether the other operators are adopting the same strategy and whether they are maintaining it. There must, therefore, be sufficient market transparency for all members of the dominant oligopoly to be aware, sufficiently precisely and quickly, of the way in which the other members' market conduct is evolving;

– Secondly, the situation of tacit co-ordination must be sustainable over time, that is to say, there must be an incentive not to depart from the common policy on the market. As the Commission observes, it is only if all the members of the dominant oligopoly maintain the parallel conduct that all can benefit. The notion of retaliation in respect of conduct deviating from the common policy is thus inherent in this condition. In this instance, the parties concur that, for a situation of collective dominance to be viable, there must be adequate deterrents to ensure that there is a long-term incentive in not departing from the common policy, which means that each member of the dominant oligopoly must be aware that highly competitive action on its part designed to increase its market share would provoke identical action by the others, so that it would derive no benefit from its initiative (see, to that effect, *Gencor v EC Commission*);

– Thirdly, to prove the existence of a collective dominant position to the requisite legal standard, the Commission must also establish that the foreseeable reaction of current and future competitors, as well as of consumers, would not jeopardise the results expected from the common policy.' (para 62)

'The prospective analysis which the Commission has to carry out in its review of concentrations involving collective dominance calls for close examination in particular of the circumstances which, in each individual case, are relevant for assessing the effects of the concentration on competition in the reference market ... Where the Commission takes the view that a merger should be prohibited because it will create a situation of collective dominance, it is incumbent upon it to produce convincing evidence thereof. The evidence must concern, in particular, factors playing a significant role in the assessment of whether a situation of collective dominance exists, such as, for example, the lack of effective competition between the operators alleged to be members of the dominant oligopoly and the weakness of any competitive pressure that might be exerted by other operators.' (para 63)

The Commission's assessment of the market characteristics in this case was incomplete and incorrect. It reached inaccurate conclusions on the level of competition, the likelihood for growth, the capacity constraints, the degree of market transparency and the existence of a credible retaliatory mechanism. (paras 66–293)

Consequently, the Commission's decision 'is vitiated by a series of errors of assessment as to factors fundamental to any assessment of whether a collective dominant position might be created. It follows that the Commission prohibited the transaction without having proven to the requisite legal standard that the concentration would give rise to a collective dominant position of the three major tour operators, of such a kind as significantly to impede effective competition in the relevant market.' (para 294)

Comment

The judgment provides an important contribution to the development of the collective dominance doctrine. While continuing the approach adopted in *Gencor v Commission*, it distills the concept of collective dominance and clarifies its realm. In the judgment the CFI brought the notion of collective dominance generally in line with the economic concept of tacit collusion. The latter rests on a three-part test under in which the undertakings involved are capable of (i) reaching a tacit agreement, (ii) detecting breaches and (iii) punishing deviations from the agreement. This alignment brought to an end the somewhat blurred distinction between unilateral and coordinated effects as was evident from the Commission's decision.

In paragraph 54 of its decision, the Commission argued that 'it is not a necessary condition of collective dominance for the oligopolists always to behave as if there were one or more explicit agreements'. The CFI rejected the Commission's reliance on the unilateral behaviour of the single undertaking as an indicator for collective dominance. In doing so, it clearly limited the scope of collective dominance to cases involving coordinated effects.

The CFI held that in order to determine whether a collective dominant position would be created following the merger, the Commission should have considered the pre-merger level of competition. In holding so, the Court rejected the Commission's approach that it should only consider the existing market conditions when it suspects a strengthening of a collective dominant position, but not the creation of one. In paragraph 82 the Court held that 'the level of competition obtaining in the relevant market at the time when the transaction is notified is a decisive factor in establishing whether a collective dominant position has been created.'

Also note the CFI's comments as to the standard of proof necessary in a prospective analysis of collective dominance and the need to produce 'convincing evidence'. (paras 63, 294)

The Horizontal Merger Guidelines, published by the Commission in 2004, largely reflect the criteria set in this judgment (see paras 39–57 Guidelines on the Assessment of Horizontal Mergers under the Council Regulation on the Control of Concentrations between Undertakings [2004] OJ C31).

IMPALA v Commission	**Collective Dominance**
Case T–464/04	ECMR
CFI, [2006] ECR II–2289, [2006] 5 CMLR 19	

Facts

An appeal on the Commission's decision in Case Comp/M3333 Sony/BMG, in which the Commission cleared the transaction between Sony and BMG (the second and fifth biggest record companies in the world), which reduced the number of players in the recorded industry market from five to four. In its decision the Commission considered whether the transaction would strengthen a pre-existing collective dominant position in the market, but concluded that there was not sufficient evidence that such position exists or will be created. On appeal, the Independent Music Publishers and Labels Association (IMPALA) contested these conclusions and asked the Court to annul the Commission's decision which cleared the transaction.

The CFI reviewed the Commission's analysis of both the pre-existing collective dominance and the creation of collective dominance.

Held

Pre-existing collective dominance

'In *Airtours v Commission* … paragraph 62, the Court of First Instance held … that the three following conditions must be satisfied in order for collective dominance as defined to be created. First, the market must be sufficiently transparent for the undertakings which coordinate their conduct to be able to monitor sufficiently whether the rules of coordination are being observed. Second, the discipline requires that there be a form of deterrent mechanism in the event of deviant conduct. Third, the reactions of undertakings which do not participate in the coordination, such as current or future competitors, and also the reactions of customers, should not be able to jeopardise the results expected from the coordination.' (para 247)

'It follows from the case-law of the Court of Justice (*Kali und Salz* … paragraph 222) and of the Court of First Instance (*Airtours v Commission* … paragraph 63) that the prospective analysis which the Commission is required to carry out in the context of the control of concentrations, in the case of collective dominance, requires close examination of, in particular, the circumstances which, in each individual case, are relevant for assessing the effects of the concentration on competition in the reference market and that the Commission must provide solid evidence.' (para 248)

'It must be observed that, as is apparent from the very wording of those judgments, that case-law was developed in the context of the assessment of the risk that a concentration would create a collective dominant position and not, as in the context of the first part of the present plea, of the determination of the existence of a collective dominant position.' (para 249)

'The determination of the existence of a collective dominant position must be supported by a series of elements of established facts, past or present, which show that there is a significant impediment of competition on the market owing to the power acquired by certain undertakings to adopt together the same course of conduct on that market, to a significant extent, independently of their competitors, their customers and consumers.' (para 250)

'It follows that, in the context of the assessment of the existence of a collective dominant position, although the three conditions defined by the Court of First Instance in *Airtours v Commission* … which were inferred from a theoretical analysis of the concept of a collective dominant position, are indeed also necessary, they may, however, in the appropriate circumstances, be established indirectly on the basis of what may be a very mixed series of indicia and items of evidence relating to the signs, manifestations and phenomena inherent in the presence of a collective dominant position.' (para 251)

'Thus, in particular, close alignment of prices over a long period, especially if they are above a competitive level, together with other factors typical of a collective dominant position, might, in the absence of an alternative reasonable explanation, suffice to demonstrate the existence of a collective dominant position, even where there is no firm direct evidence of strong market transparency, as such transparency may be presumed in such circumstances.' (para 252)

'It follows that, in the present case, the alignment of prices, both gross and net, over the last six years, even though the products are not the same (each disc having a different content), and also the fact that they were maintained at such a stable level, and at a level seen as high in spite of a significant fall in demand, together with other factors (power of the undertakings in an oligopoly situation, stability of market shares, etc.), as established by the Commission in the Decision, might, in the absence of an alternative explanation, suggest, or constitute an indication, that the alignment of prices is not the result of the normal play of effective competition and that the market is sufficiently transparent in that it allowed tacit price coordination.' (para 253)

'However, as the applicant has based its line of argument on an incorrect application of the various conditions that must be satisfied in order for there to be a collective dominant position, as defined in *Airtours v Commission* … and, in particular, the condition relating to market transparency, rather than on the theory that a finding of a common policy over a long period, together with the presence of a series of other factors characteristic of a collective dominant position, might, in certain circumstances and in the absence of an alternative explanation, suffice to demonstrate the existence of a dominant position, as opposed to the creation of such a position, without its being necessary positively to establish market transparency, the Court will confine itself, in its examination of the pleas in law put forward, to ascertaining that the Decision properly applied the conditions defined in *Airtours v Commission* …' (para 254)

The Commission's findings concerning the transparency of the market are vitiated by a manifest error of assessment in that they do not rest on an examination of all the relevant data that must be taken into consideration and are not capable of supporting the conclusion that the market is not sufficiently transparent to permit a collective dominant position. (paras 278–459)

As for the assessment of a retaliation mechanism, it follows from the case-law that in order for collective dominance to be viable, there must be adequate deterrents to ensure that there is a long-term incentive in not departing from the common policy. 'The mere existence of effective deterrent mechanisms is sufficient, in principle, since if the members of the oligopoly conform to the common policy, there is no need to resort to the exercise of a sanction. As the applicant observes, moreover, the most effective deterrent is that which has not been used.' (para 466)

As this plea relates to 'the finding of the existence of a collective dominant position, and not to its creation, it might be considered that the condition relating to retaliation may consist, not, as was the case in *Airtours v Commission* … in ascertaining the mere existence of retaliatory measures, but in examining whether there have been any breaches of the common course of conduct which have not been followed by retaliatory measures …' (para 468)

'Two cumulative elements must be satisfied in order for the fact that no retaliatory measures have been employed to be taken to mean that the condition relating to retaliation is not satisfied, namely proof of deviation from the common course of conduct, without which there is no need to consider the use of retaliatory measures, and then actual proof of the absence of retaliatory measures. However, it must be stated that on neither of these aspects is the necessary proof set out in the Decision.' (para 469)

The Commission's assertion that the markets for recorded music are not sufficiently transparent to permit a collective dominant position is vitiated by a manifest error of assessment. Its analysis in respect of retaliation is vitiated by an error of law. Decision annulled. The Court none the less considers it necessary, in the interest of completeness, to examine the second plea relating to the creation of a collective dominant position. (paras 470–81)

The creation of a collective dominant position

'It must be borne in mind that when the Commission examines the risk that a collective dominant position will be created, it must "assess, using a prospective analysis of the reference market, whether the concentration which has been referred to it, leads to a situation in which effective competition in the relevant market is significantly impeded by the undertakings involved in the concentration and one or more other undertakings which together, in particular because of factors giving rise to a connection between them, are able to adopt a common policy on the market and act to a considerable extent independently of their competitors, their customers, and [ultimately] of consumers" ...' (para 522)

The Commission's appraisal of the transaction was 'extremely succinct' (para 525) and its observation of the market 'superficial' and 'purely formal' (para 528). This level of analysis does not satisfy the Commission's obligation to carry out a prospective and detailed appraisal. (paras 523–9)

The Commission's analysis of transparency failed to assess how the reduction of number of albums to be monitored and the increased transparency in discounts will permit the development of a collective dominant position. (paras 530–33) The Commission also erred in its assessment of the retaliatory measures. The Commission concentrated not on ascertaining the existence of effective deterrent mechanisms but on seeking evidence that retaliatory measures had been employed in the past. That approach constitutes a misinterpretation of the conditions set out in *Airtours v Commission*, since that examination must be based on a prospective analysis. 'As the assessment of the risk of the creation of a collective dominant position is not, by definition, based on the existence of a prior common policy, the criterion relating to the absence of retaliatory measures in the past is wholly irrelevant.' (para 537)

Comment

This is the first time the CFI annulled in its entirety a Commission decision to approve a concentration.

With respect to the creation of a collective dominant position, the Court repeated the principles laid down in *Airtours v Commission* (page 195 above). Its criticism of the Commission's prospective analysis as being extremely succinct, superficial and purely formal sends a clear signal as to the depth of analysis and use of evidence required to establish collective dominance under the ECMR.

With respect to establishing the existence of a collective dominant position the judgment lays down a new modified test. The new test lowers the threshold for establishing a pre-existing collective dominant position through the use of indirect analysis. In doing so it widens the *Airtours* criteria by finding that collective dominance may be established indirectly on the basis of mixed series of indicia and items of evidence relating to the signs, manifestations and phenomena inherent in the presence of a collective dominance. (para 252)

Note that the Court's comments on establishing the existence of a collective dominant position under the ECMR have particular relevance to ex-post analysis under Article 82 EC.

As part of its investigation of the Sony/BMG transaction and before clearing it, the Commission issued a statement of objection in which it objected the transaction on the bases that it would create or strengthen a collective dominant position. The CFI was critical of the Commission's inability to explain its departure from its finding in the statement of objections and its clearance of the transaction. In its decision the Court seemed to take a novel approach to the role of the 'statement of objections' issued by the Commission. It held that the finding set out in the decision must be compatible with the finding of facts made in the statement of objections. Accordingly, these findings, although only being preliminary and set in a preparatory document, may limit the Commission's ability to adopt a final decision which is incompatible with them.

Following the CFI decision and the annulment of the Commission's decision, the parties re-notified the joint venture to the Commission. In its new assessment of the transaction the Commission was able to take into account current market conditions and to evaluate the actual impact of the transaction on the market following its original clearance decision in year 2004. This meant that the Commission was not limited to a prospective analysis and could examine the present effects of the transaction. In October 2007, at the end of an in-depth investigation, the Commission cleared the transaction without conditions.

7

Enforcement – The National Court

Regulatory Background

The enforcement of competition law in the national courts is primarily governed by the procedural rules of each of the Member States. At the European Community level, of major importance is Council Regulation (EC) No 1/2003 on the Implementation of the Rules on Competition Laid Down in Articles 81 and 82 of the Treaty, [2003] OJ L1/1. In addition, the cooperation between the Commission and the courts of the EU Member States is addressed in the 'Commission Notice on the cooperation between the Commission and the courts of the EU Member States in the application of Articles 81 and 82 EC', [2004] OJ C 101/54.

Direct Effect of Articles 81 and 82 EC

Articles 81 and 82 EC produce direct effects in relations between individuals, and create rights for the individuals concerned which the national courts must safeguard.

See also summary references to:

Relationship between Articles 81 EC and 82 EC and the National Competition Laws

Article 3, Regulation 1/2003 stipulates that:

'[1] Where the competition authorities of the Member States or national courts apply national competition law to agreements, decisions by associations of undertakings or concerted practices within the meaning of Article 81(1) of the Treaty which may affect trade between Member States within the meaning of that provision, they shall also apply Article 81 of the Treaty to such agreements, decisions or concerted practices. Where the competition authorities of the Member States or national courts apply national competition law to any abuse prohibited by Article 82 of the Treaty, they shall also apply Article 82 of the Treaty.

'[2] The application of national competition law may not lead to the prohibition of agreements, decisions by associations of undertakings or concerted practices which may affect trade between Member States but which do not restrict competition within the meaning of Article 81(1) of the Treaty, or which fulfil the conditions of Article 81(3) of the Treaty or which are covered by a Regulation for the application of Article 81(3) of the Treaty. Member States shall not under this Regulation be precluded from adopting and applying on their territory stricter national laws which prohibit or sanction unilateral conduct engaged in by undertakings.

'[3] Without prejudice to general principles and other provisions of Community law, paragraphs 1 and 2 do not apply when the competition authorities and the courts of the Member States apply national merger control laws nor do they preclude the application of provisions of national law that predominantly pursue an objective different from that pursued by Articles 81 and 82 of the Treaty.'

Actions for Damages

Competition law may be used in the national court in one of two ways, either as a shield or as a sword. The use of competition law as a sword commonly involves 'actions for injunctive relief' or 'claims for damages'.

Actions for damages for loss suffered as a result of an infringement of Articles 81 or 82 EC are commonly divided into two categories, each carrying a different 'public value'. The first category includes 'follow-on' damage actions. These originate from a public investigation and use the authorities' decision to support the claim for compensation in court. By doing so, private parties overcome part of the risk and costs associated with litigating a competition case as they rely on the already exercised investigative power of the public authority to substantiate the claim. The second category concerns 'stand-alone' damage actions. These by their nature are more complex as they require the claimant to prove not only causation and damage but also the violation of competition law.

The European right to sue in damages in competition law cases was recognised in the seminal case of *Courage v Crehan* (C–453/99). On this case and others, see:

C–453/99	*Courage Ltd v Bernard Crehan*	207
C–295/04	*Vincenzo Manfredi v Lloyd Adriatico Assicurazioni*	209
C–242/95	*GT–Link A/S v De Danske Statsbaner*	210

See also summary reference to:

HC05C00468	*Devenish Nutrition Limited v Sanofi-Aventis SA (France)*	209

The Measure of Damages

Damages may be set at compensatory levels or include exemplary or punitive elements. In the absence of Community provisions on this point, each Member State may establish different rules to govern the level of damages (C–295/04). Under Community law, compensation in damages includes the award of interest. Some may argue that this brings the level of single damages in Europe (including interest) closer to the treble damages in the United States (which exclude interest).

C-295/04	*Vincenzo Manfredi v Lloyd Adriatico Assicurazioni*	209
CH 1998 C801	*Bernard Crehan v Inntrepreneur Pub Company and another*	211

See also summary references to:

HC05C00468	*Devenish Nutrition Limited v Sanofi-Aventis SA (France)*	209
C–271/91	*M Helen Marshall v Southampton and others*	211

Euro Defence

Articles 81 and 82 EC may be used as part of a defence claim, most commonly through the application of the civil sanction of nullity of Article 81(2) EC against claims for breach of contract. Such claims, often referred to as the 'Euro Defence', have, on occasion, been sceptically assessed by the courts which feared that they are used as a general escape route for those wishing to avoid bad bargains.

See also summary references to:

Early Disposal of Competition Claims

Domestic procedural rules may allow for motions to strike out claims due to unlikelihood for success or lack of reasonable grounds. Motions may, for example, be based on the existence of block exemptions or the inexistence of an undertaking that would be subjected to the competition rules. See:

Burden and Standard of Proof in Competition Cases

Article 2, Regulation 1/2003 stipulates that 'In any national or Community proceedings for the application of Articles 81 and 82 of the Treaty, the burden of proving an infringement of Article 81(1) or of Article 82 of the Treaty shall rest on the party or the authority alleging the infringement. The undertaking or association of undertakings claiming the benefit of Article 81(3) of the Treaty shall bear the burden of proving that the conditions of that paragraph are fulfilled.'

Whereas the burden of proof in all Member States is identical, the standard of proof in the different jurisdictions varies and may, for example, be based on 'balance of probabilities' or 'winning the conviction of the court'. The claimant's evidentiary burden may be alleviated to compensate for the difficulty in establishing a claim. See for example:

Standing and Passing on Defence

Community law is silent on the use of the 'passing on defence' in competition cases, leaving this area to be governed by the laws of each of the European Member States. On the closely related question of standing of indirect purchasers, the ECJ held that any individual can rely on a breach of Article 81(1) EC before a national court and claim compensation for the harm suffered where there is a causal relationship between that harm and the prohibited agreement or practice. See:

Uniform Application of Competition Laws

Article 16(1) of Regulation 1/2003 stipulates that 'when national courts rule on agreements, decisions or practices under Article 81 or Article 82 EC which are already the subject of a Commission decision, they cannot take decisions running counter to the decision adopted by the Commission'. The provision echoes the case law in this area:

See also summary references to:

Cooperation between National Courts and Commission

Article 10 EC establishes the duty of loyal cooperation between the Commission and the Member States. This duty governs also the cooperation between the Commission and the national courts in competition cases. The extent of cooperation between the national courts and Commission is detailed in Regulation 1/2003 and in the 'Commission Notice on the Cooperation between the Commission and the Courts of the EU Member States in the Application of Articles 81 and 82 EC', [2004] OJ C 101/54. On the cooperation between national courts and Commission, and information disclosures between them, see:

See also summary references to:

Jurisdiction

The jurisdiction of the national court to hear cases is largely governed by Council Regulation 44/2001 (which replaced the Brussels Convention). Under the Regulation 'persons domiciled in a Member State shall, whatever their nationality, be sued in the courts of that Member State' (Article 2). Special jurisdiction may be established in matters relating to a contract, in the courts for the place of performance of the obligation in question (Article 5(1)). In matters relating to tort, delict or quasi-delict, jurisdiction may be established in the courts for the place where the harmful event occurred or may occur (Article 5(3)). Additionally, a person domiciled in a Member State may also be sued where he is one of a number of co-defendants, in the courts of the place where any one of them is domiciled, provided the claims are so closely connected that it is expedient to hear and determine them together to avoid the risk of irreconcilable judgments arising from separate proceedings. (Article 6(1)). On the interpretation of Council Regulation 44/2001 see:

Note also the 1980 Rome Convention on the law applicable to contractual obligations (OJ 1998 C27/34) and the Commission's proposal for a Regulation on the law applicable to non-contractual obligations (known as the Rome II Regulation) (COM(2003) 427 final).

On questions of jurisdiction involving the extraterritorial application of competition laws, see Chapter 10 below.

The Underdevelopment of Private Enforcement in Europe

The use of competition law in national courts may generate public value by supplementing public enforcement of competition law and enhancing its deterrent effect. As such, it has an important role in sustaining a competitive economy by harnessing the private parties' economic interests to ensure the full effectiveness of competition rules. In addition to its supplementary role to public enforcement, private enforcement promotes the individual rights of parties by providing a channel for corrective justice through compensation and injunctive relief. In doing so it complements the public system and safeguards the rights of private individuals in their relations with one another.

The introduction of Council Regulation (EC) No 1/2003 led to a turning point in the division of powers and responsibilities between the Commission, national courts and national competition authorities. The Regulation decentralised the enforcement of competition law in the Community, while strengthening the Commission's investigation powers. In the context of private enforcement, noteworthy are the provisions in Article 1 which provide for the full and direct application of Articles 81 and 82 EC at national level, and the provisions in Article 3 which govern the relationship between national and EC competition laws. Also noteworthy are the provisions in Article 15 which refer to the cooperation between national courts and the Commission, and those in Article 16 which ensure a uniform application of Community competition laws. Despite the removal of some of the obstacles to private enforcement, following the coming into force of Council Regulation (EC) No 1/2003, the modernisation package did not lead to a meaningful surge in competition litigation.

Two main publications shed light on the obstacles which hamper private enforcement in Europe.

The Ashurst Study, published in August 2004, provided a detailed account of the state of private litigation in Europe at the time and identified the main obstacles and possible ways to overcome them (The Ashurst Study on Claims for Damages in Case of Infringement of EC Competition Rules, 31 August 2004). It portrayed a gloomy picture of the state of damage actions in Europe and described it as one of 'astonishing diversity and total underdevelopment'.

In December 2005, the Commission initiated a consultation process following the publication of a *Green Paper* and *Staff Working Paper on Antitrust Damages Actions* (Green Paper, Damage Actions for Breach of the EC Antitrust Rules. COM(2005) 672 final; Commission Staff Working Paper – Annex to the Green Paper, published on 19 December 2005). In these papers the Commission highlighted the significance it attributes to the development of private enforcement as a means to promote vigorous competition. The papers focus on damage actions, outlining the main obstacles to these actions and the range of options that may be used to resolve them. The papers stimulated a wide-ranging debate on the obstacles to, and future of, private enforcement.

The papers and the submissions which followed are available on the European Commission website: http://ec.europa.eu/comm/competition/index_en.html

Another noteworthy publication at national level is the Office of Fair Trading Recommendations on Private Actions in Competition Law (OFT 916). Published in November 2007, this publication aims to facilitate private competition law actions in the UK. The paper focuses, among other things, on representative actions on behalf of consumers and businesses, costs and funding arrangements and the interface between private enforcement and the leniency programme.

Belgische Radio en Televisie v SV SABAM and NV Fonior (BRT I)	**Private Enforcement**
Case 127/73	Direct Effect
ECJ, [1974] ECR 51	

Facts

Reference for a preliminary ruling from the Tribunal de Première Instance of Brussels concerning the interpretation of Articles 82 and 86 EC. Before the ECJ considered the reference it had to deal with an appeal by SABAM against the order for reference. SABAM argued that since the Commission had initiated proceedings in respect to SABAM, the national court lacked competence under Article 9(3) of Regulation 17/62 and should have stayed the proceedings until the Commission had given its decision.

Held

The competence of the national court to apply the provisions of Community law derives from the direct effect of those provisions. (para 15)

'As the prohibitions of [Articles 81(1) and 82 EC] tend by their very nature to produce direct effects in relations between individuals, these Articles create direct rights in respect of the individuals concerned which the national courts must safeguard.' (para 16)

'To deny, by virtue of the aforementioned Article 9, the national courts' jurisdiction to afford this safeguard, would mean depriving individuals of rights which they hold under the Treaty itself.' (para 17)

The fact that the expression 'authorities of the Member States' appearing in Article 9(3) of Regulation 17/62 includes, in certain Member States, courts especially entrusted with the task of applying domestic legislation on competition or that of ensuring the legality of that application by the administrative authorities cannot exempt a court, before which the direct effect of Articles 81 and 82 is pleaded, from giving judgment. (paras 18–20)

Nevertheless if the Commission initiates a procedure the court may, if it considers it necessary for reasons of legal certainty, stay the proceedings before it while awaiting the outcome of the Commission's action. (para 21)

Comment

Note the ECJ judgment in C–282/95 P *Guérin Automobiles v Commission*, [1997] ECR I–1503, [1997] 5 CMLR 447, in which it held that 'it must also be noted that any undertaking which considers that it has suffered damage as a result of restrictive practices may rely before the national courts, particularly where the Commission decides not to act on a complaint, on the rights conferred on it by [Articles 81(1) and 82 EC], which produce direct effect in relations between individuals.' (para 39)

See similarly the ECJ in C–234/89 *Stergios Delimitis v Henninger Bräu AG*, [1991] ECR I–935, [1992] 5 CMLR 210, and in C–453/99 *Courage Ltd v Bernard Crehan*, [2001] ECR I–6297, [2001] 5 CMLR 28: '... it should be borne in mind that the Court has held that [Article 81(1) of the Treaty and Article 82 of the EC Treaty] produce direct effects in relations between individuals and create rights for the individuals concerned which the national courts must safeguard ...' (para 23).

Courage Ltd v Bernard Crehan	**Private Enforcement**
Case C–453/99	Right to Damages
ECJ, [2001] ECR I–6297, [2001] 5 CMLR 28	Article 81 EC

Facts

Mr Crehan, a tenant in two Inntrepreneur pubs was obliged, as part of his lease agreement, to purchase most of his beer from the brewer, Courage. Courage sued Crehan in the English High Court for unpaid debt. Crehan, as part of his defence, contested the lawfulness of the beer tie arrangements and claimed that these infringed Article 81 EC. In addition, Crehan launched a counterclaim for damages arguing, in essence, that the failure of his business and his inability to pay the debts originated from the tie arrangements. His damage claim was bared by an English law according to which a party to an illegal agreement is not allowed to claim damages from the other party. When the case reached the English Court of Appeal, the court referred it to the ECJ, asking, among other things, whether the provision in English law which bars Mr Crehan from claiming damages is compatible with Community law. The ECJ commented on the existence of the Community right to damages.

Held

Articles 81 and 82 EC produce direct effects in relations between individuals and create rights for the individuals concerned which the national courts must safeguard. Article 81 EC constitutes a fundamental provision which is essential for the accomplishment of the tasks entrusted to the Community and, in particular, for the functioning of the internal market. The principle of automatic nullity in Article 81(2) EC can be relied on by anyone, and the courts are bound by it once the conditions for the application of Article 81(1) are met and so long as the agreement concerned does not justify the grant of an exemption under Article 81(3) EC. (paras 19–23)

'It follows from the foregoing considerations that any individual can rely on a breach of [Article 81(1) EC] before a national court even where he is a party to a contract that is liable to restrict or distort competition within the meaning of that provision.' (para 24)

'As regards the possibility of seeking compensation for loss caused by a contract or by conduct liable to restrict or distort competition, it should be remembered from the outset that, in accordance with settled case-law, the national courts whose task it is to apply the provisions of Community law in areas within their jurisdiction must ensure that those rules take full effect and must protect the rights which they confer on individuals (see inter alia the judgments in Case 106/77 *Simmenthal* [1978] ECR 629, paragraph 16, and in Case C–213/89 *Factortame* [1990] ECR I–2433, paragraph 19). (para 25)

'The full effectiveness of [Article 81 EC] and, in particular, the practical effect of the prohibition laid down in [Article 81(1)] would be put at risk if it were not open to any individual to claim damages for loss caused to him by a contract or by conduct liable to restrict or distort competition.' (para 26)

'Indeed, the existence of such a right strengthens the working of the Community competition rules and discourages agreements or practices, which are frequently covert, which are liable to restrict or distort competition. From that point of view, actions for damages before the national courts can make a significant contribution to the maintenance of effective competition in the Community.' (para 27)

'There should not therefore be any absolute bar to such an action being brought by a party to a contract which would be held to violate the competition rules.' (para 28)

'However, in the absence of Community rules governing the matter, it is for the domestic legal system of each Member State to designate the courts and tribunals having jurisdiction and to lay down the detailed procedural rules governing actions for safeguarding rights which individuals derive directly from Community law, provided that such rules are not less favourable than those governing similar domestic actions (principle of equivalence) and that they do not render practically impossible or excessively difficult the exercise of rights conferred by Community law (principle of effectiveness) (see Case C–261/95 *Palmisani* [1997] ECR I–4025, paragraph 27).' (para 29)

Provided that the principles of equivalence and effectiveness are respected, the Community right in damages is subjected both to national rules of unjust enrichment and rules which bar an undertaking that bares significant responsibility for the distortion of competition the right to obtain damages from the other contracting party. In that regard, the court should take into account the economic and legal context in which the parties find themselves and the respective bargaining power and conduct of the two parties to the contract. (paras 30–32)

'In particular, it is for the national court to ascertain whether the party who claims to have suffered loss through concluding a contract that is liable to restrict or distort competition found himself in a markedly weaker position than the other party, such as seriously to compromise or even eliminate his freedom to negotiate the terms of the contract and his capacity to avoid the loss or reduce its extent, in particular by availing himself in good time of all the legal remedies available to him.' (para 33)

'Referring to the judgments in Case 23/67 *Brasserie de Haecht* [1967] ECR 127 and Case C–234/89 *Delimitis* [1991] ECR I–935, paragraphs 14 to 26, the Commission and the United Kingdom Government also rightly point out that a contract might prove to be contrary to [Article 81(1) EC] for the sole reason that it is part of a network of similar contracts which have a cumulative effect on competition. In such a case, the party contracting with the person controlling the network cannot bear significant responsibility for the breach of [Article 81 EC], particularly where in practice the terms of the contract were imposed on him by the party controlling the network.' (para 34)

'Having regard to all the foregoing considerations, the questions referred are to be answered as follows:
– a party to a contract liable to restrict or distort competition within the meaning of [Article 81 EC] can rely on the breach of that article to obtain relief from the other contracting party;
– [Article 81 EC] precludes a rule of national law under which a party to a contract liable to restrict or distort competition within the meaning of that provision is barred from claiming damages for loss caused by performance of that contract on the sole ground that the claimant is a party to that contract;
– Community law does not preclude a rule of national law barring a party to a contract liable to restrict or distort competition from relying on his own unlawful actions to obtain damages where it is established that that party bears significant responsibility for the distortion of competition.' (para 35)

Comment

Reflecting on the scope of the 'significant responsibility' benchmark Advocate General Mischo commented that the responsibility to be borne is clearly significant if a party is equally responsible for the distortion of competition. On the other hand the responsibility borne is negligible if the party is in a weaker position than the other party such that it was not genuinely free to choose the terms of the contract. (paras 71–8)

In paragraph 24 the Court held that 'any individual can rely on a breach of [Article 81(1) EC] before a national court'. See also Case 127/73 BRT v SABAM, [1974] ECR 51, paragraph 16, and Case C–282/95 P *Guérin Automobiles v Commission*, [1997] ECR I–1503, para 39, where the court held that 'any undertaking which considers that it has suffered damage as a result of restrictive practices may rely before the national courts, particularly where the Commission decides not to act on a complaint, on the rights conferred on it by [Articles 81(1) and 82 EC]'. These statements support the view that both direct and indirect purchasers have standing in court. On standing and passing on defence, see also the Commission Green Paper and Staff Working Paper on antitrust damages actions

Note AG Jacobs opinion in Case C–264/01 *AOK Bundesverband*, where he stated his opinion that the reasoning of the Courage judgment was applicable to injunctive relief as well (para 104).

Vincenzo Manfredi v Lloyd Adriatico Assicurazioni	**Private Enforcement**
Joined Cases C–295–298/04	Right to Damages
ECJ, [2006] ECR I–6619, [2006] 5 CMLR 17	The Measure of Damages

Facts

The Italian court referred to the ECJ several questions on the interpretation of Article 81 EC which arose in connection with claims against insurance companies for the repayment of excessive premiums. In its judgments the ECJ reaffirmed, among other things, that the European right in damages extends to third parties, and commented on the availability of punitive damages in competition cases.

Held

The principle of invalidity in Article 81(2) EC 'can be relied on by anyone, and the courts are bound by it once the conditions for the application of Article 81(1) EC are met and so long as the agreement concerned does not justify the grant of an exemption under Article 81(3) EC. … Since the invalidity referred to in Article 81(2) EC is absolute, an agreement which is null and void by virtue of this provision has no effect as between the contracting parties and cannot be invoked against third parties…' (paras 56–7)

The full effectiveness of Article 81 would be put at risk if it were not open to any individual to claim damages for loss caused to him by a contract or by conduct liable to restrict or distort competition. 'It follows that any individual can claim compensation for the harm suffered where there is a causal relationship between that harm and an agreement or practice prohibited under Article 81 EC.' (paras 60–1)

'As to the award of damages and the possibility of an award of punitive damages, in the absence of Community rules governing the matter, it is for the domestic legal system of each Member State to set the criteria for determining the extent of the damages, provided that the principles of equivalence and effectiveness are observed.' (para 92)

'… In accordance with the principle of equivalence, if it is possible to award specific damages, such as exemplary or punitive damages, in domestic actions similar to actions founded on the Community competition rules, it must also be possible to award such damages in actions founded on Community rules. However, Community law does not prevent national courts from taking steps to ensure that the protection of the rights guaranteed by Community law does not entail the unjust enrichment of those who enjoy them. Secondly, it follows from the principle of effectiveness … that injured persons must be able to seek compensation not only for actual loss (damnum emergens) but also for loss of profit (lucrum cessans) plus interest.' (paras 99–100)

Comment

'Article 81 EC produces direct effects in relations between individuals and directly creates rights in respect of the individuals concerned which the national courts must safeguard. That includes the right, for individuals, to be protected from the harmful effects which an agreement which is automatically void may create. The individuals who can benefit from such protection are, of course, primarily third parties, that is to say consumers and competitors who are adversely affected by a prohibited agreement.' (Opinion of AG Mischo in *Courage Ltd v Bernard Crehan*, paras 37, 38)

In *Devenish Nutrition Limited v Sanofi-Aventis SA* [2007] EWHC 2394 (Ch), the High Court of Justice ruled that claimants in a follow-on claim for damages, who suffered loss as a result of cartel activity, are not entitled to exemplary damages 'in a case in which the defendants have already been fined (or had fines imposed and then reduced or commuted) by the European Commission'. (para 52)

GT-Link A/S v De Danske Statsbaner (DSB)	**Private Enforcement**
Case C–242/95	Right to Damages
ECJ, [1997] ECR I–4449, [1997] 5 CMLR 601	Article 82 EC

Facts

The case was referred to the ECJ from the Danish court which asked, among other things, whether under Article 82 EC the state-owned railway company which operated a harbour was liable to compensate a ferry operator which was arguably subjected to abusive charges for the use of the port. The ECJ clarified the duty of a dominant undertaking to compensate those who were abused by its practices.

Held

'It is for the domestic legal order of each Member State to lay down the detailed procedural rules, including those relating to the burden of proof, governing actions for safeguarding rights which individuals derive from the direct effect of [Article 82 EC], provided that such rules are not less favourable than those governing similar domestic actions and do not render virtually impossible or excessively difficult the exercise of rights conferred by Community law.' (para 27, paras 22–7)

'[W]here a public undertaking which owns and operates a commercial port occupies a dominant position in a substantial part of the common market, it is contrary to [Article 81(1) EC] in conjunction with [Article 82 EC] for that undertaking to levy port duties of an unreasonable amount pursuant to regulations adopted by the Member State to which it is answerable or for it to exempt from payment of those duties its own ferry services and, reciprocally, some of its trading partners' ferry services, in so far as such exemptions entail the application of dissimilar conditions to equivalent services. It is for the national court to determine whether, having regard to the level of the duties and the economic value of the services supplied, the amount of duty is actually unfair. It is also for the national court to determine whether exempting its own ferry services, and reciprocally those of some of its trading partners, from payment of duties in fact amounts to the application of dissimilar conditions to equivalent services.' (para 46, paras 28–46)

Comment

The ECJ reaffirmed that Article 82 EC has direct effect and confers on individuals rights which the national court must protect. It further established that national procedural rules concerning the burden of proving the conditions of Article 82 EC should not 'render virtually impossible or excessively difficult the exercise of rights conferred by community law'.

Note also Advocate General Jacobs' opinion (Joint Opinion, [1997] ECR I–4085) in which he stated with respect to a reimbursement of a levy contrary to Article 82 EC that 'It is settled law that [Article 82 EC] creates direct rights in respect of the individuals concerned, which the national court must safeguard. [Case 127/73, *BRT v SABAM*, [1974] ECR 313] The principle set out above will accordingly apply: it is for the domestic legal system of the Member State concerned to determine the conditions governing actions to defend those rights, subject to the requirements of equivalence with actions to defend rights deriving from domestic law and of effectiveness, namely that it must be possible in fact to recover.' (para 176)

The judgment focused on a public undertaking, yet it arguably establishes a more general rule, applicable to any undertaking, that a requirement of proof which would make it impossible or excessively difficult to prove a breach of Article 82 EC is incompatible with Community law.

Bernard Crehan v Inntrepreneur Pub Company and another
CH 1998 C801
English High Court, [2004] EWCA Civ 637

Private Enforcement
The Award of Interest

Facts

Following the ECJ decision in Case C–453/99 *Courage Ltd v Bernard Crehan*, the Crehan case was remitted to the English High Court for a full trial and was heard in 2003. Mr Justice Park dismissed Mr Crehan's damages claim, finding that Crehan had failed to establish that the Inntrepreneur beer ties were in breach of Article 81 EC. In his judgment he did, however, make reference to the quantification of damages and the award of interest.

Held

'I accept that the normal rule [under English Law] is that damages are assessed at the date of loss, not at the date of judgment, and that it is assumed that interest will compensate the claimant for the passage of time between the time when he suffered his loss and the time when he gets judgment in respect of it. However, I believe the legal position to be that that is not an invariable rule of law, and that if the justice of the case requires damages to be measured at the date of judgment the court may award damages on that basis instead. This can arise, for example, in times of high inflation when interest would not be any form of acceptable compensation. In my judgment, if Mr Crehan was entitled to damages at all (which, for the reason which I have given earlier, turning on Delimitis condition 1, he is not), damages measured at 4 March 1993 (The Cock Inn) and 27 September 1993 (The Phoenix) plus interest would not be adequate compensation. Any profits which he would have made on a free of tie basis by then would have been modest at best. In this context I refer to my earlier observations to the effect that, although I think on balance that Mr Crehan would have survived if he had been free of tie from the outset on both pubs, it would have been a close run thing. The early years of his occupation of the pubs were always going to be tight in terms of profitability. The financial benefits to him if all had gone well would not have arisen in the first two years, but only in later years when he had got through the early expenditures and had been able to build up the trades of the pubs. Similarly, although the two leases would have had some capital value in 1993 if everything had progressed well, the values would not have approached those which might have been expected ten years or so later …' (para 267)

'I therefore consider that in this case the measure of damages should be ascertained at the time of judgment, not at the two dates in 1993 when Mr Crehan had to give up the agreements for lease of his two pubs …' (para 268)

Comment

Both the interest rate and the point in time from which interest is awarded affect the level of compensation. Had the court chosen an earlier point in time, such as the date of the infringement or injury, it would have awarded higher compensation, allegedly beyond real value. Such an award would have departed from the compensatory basis and resulted in a punitive one. On the possible approaches to compensation see: Commission Green Paper, Damage Actions for Breach of the EC Antitrust Rules. COM(2005) 672 final; Commission Staff Working paper – Annex to the Green Paper, published on 19 December 2005

Note Case C–271/91 *M Helen Marshall v Southampton and others*, [1993] ECR I–4367, [1993] 3 CMLR 293, where the ECJ considered the award of interest in a case concerning a claim for compensation for damages sustained by Ms Marshall as a result of her dismissal by the Authority. With respect to the award of interest the court held that the 'full compensation for the loss and damage sustained as a result of discriminatory dismissal cannot leave out of account factors, such as the effluxion of time, which may in fact reduce its value. The award of interest, in accordance with the applicable national rules, must therefore be regarded as an essential component of compensation for the purposes of restoring real equality of treatment.' (para 31)

Intel Corporation v Via Technologies Inc	**Private Enforcement**
Case Nos A3/2002/1380, A3/2002/1381	Euro Defence
English Court of Appeal, [2002] EWCA Civ 1905	Summary Judgment

Facts

Two patent infringement actions brought by Intel Corporation (Intel) in the patent court against Via Technologies (Via), alleging that Via infringed five of Intel's patents. Via's defence in the patent court (High Court of Justice Chancery Division) was based on, among other things, the claim that Intel's actions infringed Articles 81 and 82 EC. Intel applied for a summary judgment.

In his summary judgment, Lawrence Collins J, commented on the approach toward the 'Euro Defence' in intellectual property cases, saying that 'the ease with which a defence based on Article 81 or 82 may be generated on the basis of vague or imprecise allegations makes it necessary to scrutinise them with some care in order to avoid defences with no merit at all going to a lengthy trial with expert economic evidence. ... I would add that, although the burden of proof on the party asserting conduct to be unlawful under Articles 81 and 82 may be the normal civil standard, the penal consequences of those provisions re-enforce the need for careful scrutiny.' (para 90)

Lawrence Collins J considered two claims made by Via, namely that bringing these infringement proceedings was an abuse by Intel of the exercise of intellectual property rights and that the terms under which Intel was prepared to grant a licence would create an infringement of Article 81(1) EC. He then awarded Intel summary judgment on the competition issues and gave Via permission to appeal only on one part of his decision. Via appealed the decision, seeking, among other things, permission to appeal on all parts. On appeal the Court considered whether the defences under Articles 81 and 82 EC were ones for which Via had real prospects of success. The Court upheld the defence claims.

Held (on Euro Defence and Summary Judgment)

The tests to be satisfied if summary judgment is to be given under CPR Rule 24.2 are 'that Via has no real prospect of succeeding on the Euro-defence and there is no other compelling reason why that Euro-defence should be disposed of at a trial. A real prospect is to be contrasted with one which is fanciful, *Swain v Hillman* [2001] 1 AER 91. A Euro-defence which is likely at some stage to be the subject matter of a reference is likely also to be one which for that reason should only be disposed of at a trial. In most cases it is not necessary or appropriate to refer the point to the European Court before all the relevant facts have been ascertained by the national court.' (para 35)

'In paragraph 90 of his judgment Lawrence Collins J referred to the fact that what he described as Euro-defences are not in some special category but do demand careful scrutiny so as to avoid defences without merit going to what is likely to be a long and expensive trial. He also noted that cases involving Articles 81 and 82 often raise questions of mixed law and fact which are not suitable for summary determination. I would endorse both those propositions, but I would add two notes of caution. First, until the patent issues ... have been determined, the extent of the exclusivity conferred by the patents in suit on Intel and of the inhibition imposed on Via, as a consequence, is unknown. Both will depend on which claims in which patents are valid. Second, where it can be seen that the jurisprudence of the European Court of Justice is in the course of development it is dangerous to assume that it is beyond argument with real prospect of success that the existing case law will not be extended or modified so as to encompass the defence being advanced.' (para 32)

Comment

This case was part of a series of lawsuits and counter lawsuits launched by both parties and involving 27 patents. In 2003 the parties reached a settlement agreement under which all pending claims were dismissed.

Sportswear SpA v Stonestyle Ltd	**Private Enforcement**
Case No A3 2005/2316	Euro Defence
Court of Appeal, (Civ Div), [2006] EWCA Civ 380	Early Disposal of Claim

Facts

As part of a trade mark dispute at the lower court, the court struck out of the defence a number of paragraphs in which the defendants sought to allege that the plaintiffs were parties to agreements which infringe Article 81 EC and that for this reason they were not entitled to enforce their trade mark rights. The defendants appealed the lower court decision arguing that the court was wrong to strike out the paragraphs.

Held (on Euro defence and the order to strike out)

One of the main points which led to the order to strike out was the lack of sufficient nexus between the breach of Article 81 EC and the plaintiffs' claim. Even if proven, for a breach of Article 81 EC to be relevant to the claim, there must be a sufficient nexus between the two. 'A breach of the Article may give rise to various consequences, including a claim for damages, but the fact that two undertakings are parties to such an agreement does not of itself debar either of them from enforcing intellectual property rights.' (paras 29, 30)

The judge was wrong to conclude that the defence was bound to fail, on the basis that there was no arguable case of an adequate nexus between the anticompetitive agreement alleged and the plaintiffs' claim. The points are sufficiently arguable for it to be wrong to strike these paragraphs out of the defence. (para71)

Comment

While on appeal, the main claims at the lower court proceeded to trial. This created a sense of urgency as once the paragraphs in question were reinstated the issues at trial expanded considerably. On this point Lloyd LJ commented: 'I recognise the importance of the point in relation to litigation which is near to trial and, as I understand it, currently estimated for a hearing lasting three days. The introduction of an Art 81 defence will add to the burden on the respondents by way of disclosure, may give rise to a need for expert evidence, and may therefore drive up the costs of the litigation, and delay its resolution significantly. To hold, as I would, that the paragraphs ought not to have been struck out will mean that the trial has to be adjourned. Assuming that the remaining pleading deficiencies can be cured, it will be desirable for the future case management of the claim to address and, so far as possible, confine the additional preparation that will be necessary, by way of disclosure and evidence.' (para 72)

Note Longmore LJ's skeptical comment on the use of a Euro Defence: 'Undoubtedly it would be convenient if it were possible to hold that the Art 81 issue could only be used as a sword rather than a shield so that competition issues could not be used to muddy the waters of (here) a comparatively straightforward trade mark dispute. But convenience is not always the same as justice and I have been, a little reluctantly, persuaded that it is arguable that European Community law does not invariably allow trade mark issues and anti-competition issues to be compartmentalised and separated from one another. It may turn out at trial that the defendant will be able to rely on S 12(2) of the Trade Marks Act 1994 to defeat the claimant's claim but, as my Lord has said in para 71 above, it is not possible to be sure that the defendant's position will not be stronger if it can also establish a breach of Art 81. That is something which, in my view, the European case law, at any rate arguably, entitles the defendant to do.' (para 76)

Note also the sceptical approach in *Oakdale (Richmond) Ltd v National Westminster Bank Plc* [1997] ECC 130, where the Court held that: 'It is, in my view, necessary for a domestic court, faced at an interlocutory stage with ingenious arguments based on [Article 81 EC], to take care that it does not do injustice to the other party by too ready an acceptance of the submission that those arguments cannot properly be evaluated until trial in circumstances in which … reliance on the EC Treaty is no more than a pretext for the non payment of a debt …' (para 60)

Aalborg Portland and others v Commission	**Private Enforcement**
Joined cases C–204, 5, 11, 13, 17, 19/00	Burden of Proof
ECJ, [2004] ECR I–123, [2005] 4 CMLR 4	

Facts

An appeal against the CFI judgment in *Cimenteries CBR and others v Commission* in which the CFI confirmed parts of the infringements found in Commission Decision Cases IV/33.126 and 33.322 (Cement). In its decision the Commission found a large number of undertakings and associations active in the European cement market to have infringed Article 81 EC by entering into anticompetitive agreements and concerted practices. On appeal, the ECJ referred to, among other things, the burden of proof in competition cases.

Held (on the establishment of the liability of the undertakings)

According to Regulation 1/2003 on the implementation of the rules on competition laid down in Articles 81 and 82 of the Treaty, 'it should be for the party or the authority alleging an infringement of the competition rules to prove the existence thereof and it should be for the undertaking or association of undertakings invoking the benefit of a defence against a finding of an infringement to demonstrate that the conditions for applying such defence are satisfied, so that the authority will then have to resort to other evidence.' (para 78)

'Although according to those principles the legal burden of proof is borne either by the Commission or by the undertaking or association concerned, the factual evidence on which a party relies may be of such a kind as to require the other party to provide an explanation or justification, failing which it is permissible to conclude that the burden of proof has been discharged.' (para 79)

'According to settled case-law, it is sufficient for the Commission to show that the undertaking concerned participated in meetings at which anti-competitive agreements were concluded, without manifestly opposing them, to prove to the requisite standard that the undertaking participated in the cartel. Where participation in such meetings has been established, it is for that undertaking to put forward evidence to establish that its participation in those meetings was without any anti-competitive intention by demonstrating that it had indicated to its competitors that it was participating in those meetings in a spirit that was different from theirs (see Case C–199/92 P *Hüls v Commission* [1999] ECR I–4287, paragraph 155, and Case C–49/92 P *Commission v Anic* [1999] ECR I–4125, paragraph 96).' (para 81)

'The principles established in the case-law cited at paragraph 81 of this judgment also apply to participation in the implementation of a single agreement. In order to establish that an undertaking has participated in such an agreement, the Commission must show that the undertaking intended to contribute by its own conduct to the common objectives pursued by all the participants and that it was aware of the actual conduct planned or put into effect by other undertakings in pursuit of the same objectives or that it could reasonably have foreseen it and that it was prepared to take the risk (*Commission v Anic*, paragraph 87).' (para 83)

Comment

The alleviation of the claimant's evidentiary burden is justified when information asymmetry prevents the plaintiff from accessing information that is in the control of the defendant.

In paragraph 79 the ECJ indicated that presenting factual evidence indicating an infringement of competition law may shift the burden to the defendant who will have to provide an explanation or justification to prove that the factual evidence does not constitute an infringement of competition law.

Whereas the burden of proof in all European Member States is identical, the standard of proof in the different jurisdictions varies and may, for example, be based on 'balance of probabilities' or 'winning the conviction of the court'.

Masterfoods Ltd v HB Ice Cream Ltd	**Private Enforcement**
Case C–344/98	Uniform Application of Competition Laws
ECJ, [2000] ECR I–11369, [2001] 4 CMLR 14	

Facts

A reference for a preliminary ruling from the Supreme Court in Ireland. The case concerned an exclusivity clause contained in agreements for the supply of freezer cabinets concluded between HB Ice Cream Ltd (HB) and retailers of impulse ice-cream. In parallel with the Irish court proceedings, Masterfoods lodged a complaint with the Commission against HB. Following an investigation, the Commission concluded that the exclusivity provisions in the agreement and HB's inducement of retailers in Ireland to enter into the agreements infringed Articles 81 and 82 EC (Case Nos IV/34.073, IV/34.395 and IV/35.436 *Van den Bergh Foods Limited*). HB appealed the decision to the CFI.

The Supreme Court decided to stay the proceedings and to refer the case to the ECJ for a preliminary ruling on several questions. The Court asked whether, among other things, the obligation of sincere cooperation with the Commission requires the Supreme Court to stay the instant proceedings pending the disposal of the appeal on the Commission's decision to the CFI and any subsequent appeal to the ECJ.

Held

Under the fourth paragraph of Article 249 of the Treaty of Rome (previously 189) a decision adopted by the Commission 'shall be binding in its entirety upon those to whom it is addressed.' (para 50)

'The Court has held, in paragraph 47 of *Delimitis*, that in order not to breach the general principle of legal certainty, national courts must, when ruling on agreements or practices which may subsequently be the subject of a decision by the Commission, avoid giving decisions which would conflict with a decision contemplated by the Commission in the implementation of [Articles 81 and 82 EC].' (para 51)

'It is even more important that when national courts rule on agreements or practices which are already the subject of a Commission decision they cannot take decisions running counter to that of the Commission, even if the latter's decision conflicts with a decision given by a national court of first instance.' (para 52)

If a national court has doubts as to the validity or interpretation of an act of a Community institution it may, or must, in accordance with Article 234 of the Treaty, refer a question to the ECJ for a preliminary ruling. (para 54)

If, as here in the main proceedings, the addressee of a Commission decision has, within the period prescribed in the fifth paragraph of Article 230 of the Treaty of Rome (previously 173), brought an action for annulment of that decision, 'it is for the national court to decide whether to stay proceedings until a definitive decision has been given in the action for annulment or in order to refer a question to the Court for a preliminary ruling.' (para 55)

'It should be borne in mind, in that connection, that application of the Community competition rules is based on an obligation of sincere cooperation between the national courts, on the one hand, and the Commission and the Community Courts, on the other, in the context of which each acts on the basis of the role assigned to it by the Treaty.' (para 56)

'When the outcome of the dispute before the national court depends on the validity of the Commission decision, it follows from the obligation of sincere cooperation that the national court should, in order to avoid reaching a decision that runs counter to that of the Commission, stay its proceedings pending final judgment in the action for annulment by the Community Courts, unless it considers that, in the circumstances of the case, a reference to the Court of Justice for a preliminary ruling on the validity of the Commission decision is warranted.' (para 57)

'If a national court stays proceedings, it is incumbent on it to examine whether it is necessary to order interim measures in order to safeguard the interests of the parties pending final judgment.' (para 58)

'In this case it appears from the order for reference that the maintenance in force of the permanent injunction granted by the High Court restraining Masterfoods from inducing retailers to store its products in freezers belonging to HB depends on the validity of Decision 98/531. It therefore follows from the obligation of sincere cooperation that the national court should stay proceedings pending final judgment in the action for annulment by the Community Courts unless it considers that, in the circumstances of the case, a reference to the Court of Justice for a preliminary ruling on the validity of the Commission decision is warranted.' (para 59)

'The answer to Question 1 must therefore be that, where a national court is ruling on an agreement or practice, the compatibility of which with [Articles 81(1) and 82 EC] is already the subject of a Commission decision, it cannot take a decision running counter to that of the Commission, even if the latter's decision conflicts with a decision given by a national court of first instance. If the addressee of the Commission decision has, within the period prescribed in the fifth paragraph of Article 173 of the Treaty, brought an action for annulment of that decision, it is for the national court to decide whether to stay proceedings pending final judgment in that action for annulment or in order to refer a question to the Court for a preliminary ruling.' (para 60)

Comment

Article 16(1) of Regulation 1/2003 codifies the principles laid down in the decision and states that that 'When national courts rule on agreements, decisions or practices under Article 81 or Article 82 of the Treaty which are already the subject of a Commission decision, they cannot take decisions running counter to the decision adopted by the Commission. They must also avoid giving decisions which would conflict with a decision contemplated by the Commission in proceedings it has initiated. To that effect, the national court may assess whether it is necessary to stay its proceedings. This obligation is without prejudice to the rights and obligations under Article 234 of the Treaty.'

The principle in Article 16(1) has been extended in some jurisdictions to cover decisions of national competition authorities. (See, for example, the German 'Gesetz gegen Wettbewerbsbeschränkungen', Section 33(4))

Note Recital 22, Regulation 1/2003, which adds in respect to the need to avoid conflicting decisions that 'Commitment decisions adopted by the Commission do not affect the power of the courts and the competition authorities of the Member States to apply Articles 81 and 82 of the Treaty.'

Note Advocate General Cosmas' opinion, which clarifies that such a risk of inconsistent decisions will not arise 'where the legal and factual context of the case being examined by the Commission is not completely identical to that before the national courts. The Commission's decision may provide important indications as to the appropriate way to interpret [Articles 81(1) and 82 EC], but in this case there is no risk, from a purely legal point of view, of the adoption of conflicting decisions …' (para 16)

Also note Case C–234/89 *Stergios Delimitis v Henninger Bräu AG*, [1991] ECR I–935, [1992] 5 CMLR 210, in which the ECJ held that 'Account should here be taken of the risk of national courts taking decisions which conflict with those taken or envisaged by the Commission in the implementation of [Articles 81(1) and 82, and also of Article 81(3) EC]. Such conflicting decisions would be contrary to the general principle of legal certainty and must, therefore, be avoided when national courts give decisions on agreements or practices which may subsequently be the subject of a decision by the Commission.' (para 34)

Also note Case C–552/03 *Unilever Bestfoods (Ireland) Ltd v Commission*, [2006] 5 CMLR 27, where the ECJ held that 'the Community Courts cannot be bound by a finding of a national court that an exclusivity clause is compatible with Community law.' (para 128)

Inntrepreneur Pub Company (CPC) and others v Crehan	**Private Enforcement**
House of Lords (English Court), [2006] UKHL 38	Uniform Application
	Binding Effect

Facts

Following the ECJ decision in Case C–453/99 *Courage Ltd v Bernard Crehan*, the case was remitted to the English High Court for a full trial and was heard in 2003. The High Court considered the damage claim but found that in this case the beer tie agreement did not make it difficult for competitors to enter the market and therefore did not infringe Article 81 EC. The High Court distinguished between the case at issue and an earlier Commission finding which concerned similar beer tie arrangements, on the grounds that the case involved different parties and different arrangements. Crehan appealed the decision to the Court of Appeal, arguing that the High Court was bound to accept the Commission's factual conclusions on similar beer tie agreements. The case reached the House of Lords, which considered the extent to which the Commission's factual assessment of the UK beer market binds the national court.

Held (Lord Hoffmann)

Article 16, Regulation 1/2003 stipulates that 'When national courts rule on agreements, decisions or practices under article 81 or article 82 of the Treaty which are already the subject of a Commission decision, they cannot take decisions running counter to the decision adopted by the Commission. They must also avoid giving decisions which would conflict with a decision contemplated by the Commission in proceedings it has initiated. To that effect, the national court may assess whether it is necessary to stay its proceedings. This obligation is without prejudice to the rights and obligations under article 234 of the Treaty.' (para 63)

'This article makes it clear that a relevant conflict exists only when the "agreements, decisions or practices" ruled on by the national court have been or are about to be the subject of a Commission decision. It does not apply to other agreements, decisions or practices in the same market.' (para 64)

The national court cannot depart from a Commission decision which concerns the same subject matters and the same parties. However, the duty to avoid conflicting decisions, as stated by the Court of Justice in the two leading cases of *Delimitis* and *Masterfoods*, has no application to the present case as the Commission decision concerns a different subject matter arising between different parties. The Commission decision in this case therefore does bind the national court but provides important and persuasive evidence. (paras 14–74)

Comment

Some may argue that the House of Lords merely acknowledged the legal position as reflected in Regulation 1/2003. Others may see the judgment as cementing a new balancing point which requires less conformity between courts and the Commission. On a practical level claimants who seek to rely on a Commission decision in comparable circumstances risk having the national court reject the Commission's analysis. Subsequently, parties may have to adduce evidence beyond the Commission's decision to support its finding. The limited reliance on the Commission's analysis might also lead to inconsistency in national courts' findings related to similar agreements in the same market. Such potential inconsistency may impact on legal and business certainty lessening the motivation to launch an 'indirect' follow-on claim in the first place.

On the uniform application of competition laws see also page 215 above.

Postbank NV v Commission	**Private Enforcement**
Case T–353/94	Information Disclosure
CFI, [1996] ECR II–921, [1997] 4 CMLR 33	Business Secrets

Facts

The case concerned the use of documents from an administrative procedure before the Commission, in legal proceedings at the national court. The Commission disclosed to third parties a complete version of a statement of objections which it issued during its investigation into the legality of a payment and transfer agreement. The information was disclosed on condition that it would be used only in preparation for the hearing to which the third parties were invited but not 'for any other purpose, especially in legal proceedings'. The third parties who were involved in a legal dispute which reached the Amsterdam Regional Court of Appeal asked the Commission to allow them to produce the version of the statement of objections and the minutes of the hearing to the national court. In their request they noted that the Commission had no power to prohibit them from producing those documents in national legal proceedings. The Commission agreed to their request, stating that the restriction it imposed concerning the 'use in national legal proceedings of the version of the statement of objections appeared unfounded and are therefore inoperative'. Postbank NV asked the Commission to reverse its decision as it was contrary to Community law. The Commission refused and Postbank NV appealed for the annulment of the Commission decision.

Held

The principle of sincere cooperation as laid down in Article 10 of the Treaty (previously Article 5) requires the 'Community institutions, and above all the Commission, which is entrusted with the task of ensuring application of the provisions of the Treaty, to give active assistance to any national judicial authority dealing with an infringement of Community rules. That assistance, which takes various forms, may, where appropriate, consist in disclosing to the national courts documents acquired by the institutions in the discharge of their duties.' (para 64)

'In proceedings for the application of the Community competition rules, this principle implies in particular, as held by the Court of Justice, that the national court is entitled to seek information from the Commission on the state of any procedure which the Commission may have set in motion and to obtain from that institution such economic and legal information as it may be able to supply to it (Case C–234/89 *Delimitis* [1991] ECR I–935, paragraph 53, and Joined Cases C–319/93, C–40/94 and C–224/94 *Dijkstra and others* [1995] ECR I–4471, paragraph 36).' (para 65)

'As far as the rights of the defence of Postbank in the national proceedings are concerned, it must be pointed out that even if production by one of the parties to those proceedings of documents containing the abovementioned information is capable of weakening the position of the undertakings to which the information relates, it is nevertheless for the national court to guarantee, on the basis of national rules of procedure, that the rights of defence of such undertakings are protected. In that connection, in a case for example like this one, the national court may inter alia take account of the provisional nature of the opinion expressed by the Commission in the statement of objections and of the possibility of suspending the national proceedings pending adoption by the Commission of a final position. The allegedly harmful effect of transmitting certain documents to the national courts certainly cannot therefore justify an outright prohibition by the Commission of such transmission.' (para 72)

The applicants also argue that the statement of objections contained business secrets and therefore could only be disclosed to third parties after they would have been informed of the disclosure and given an opportunity to object to it. Accordingly, they contested that failing to do so infringed Article 287 of the Treaty (formerly 214) and Article 20(2) of Regulation No 17, which prohibit disclosure outside the procedure for the application of competition law initiated by the Commission and, consequently, to the transmission to national courts of information covered by professional secrecy. (paras 78, 79)

'[Article 287] of the Treaty applies to "information of the kind covered by professional secrecy". It applies in particular to "information about undertakings, their business relations or their cost components". It thus expressly refers to information which, in principle, falls, by reason of its content, within the category of business secrets, as defined by the Court of Justice (Case 53/85 *Akzo Chemie v Commission* [1986] ECR 1965).' (para 86)

Article 287 cannot be interpreted as meaning that, by virtue of its obligation to observe professional secrecy, the Commission is required to prohibit undertakings from producing, in national court, documents received in the procedure before the Commission which contain confidential information and business secrets. Such an interpretation might compromise cooperation between the national judicial authorities and the Community institutions, as provided for by Article 10 of the Treaty, and above all detract from the right of economic agents to effective judicial protection. More specifically, in a case like this one, it would deprive certain undertakings of the protection, afforded by national courts, of the rights conferred on them by virtue of the direct effect of Articles 81 and 82 EC. (para 89, paras 87–9)

'It follows that, in this case, the Commission failed in its obligation of professional secrecy by not giving Postbank an opportunity to state its view on the production in legal proceedings of the documents in question and by failing to take any measure designed to protect the confidentiality of the information or business secrets of which, for their part, the banks concerned requested protection.' (para 96)

Comment

Although the case surrounded the provisions of Regulation 17/62, which is no longer in force, the Court's comments on the duty of loyal cooperation are based on the Treaty provisions and are just as relevant under Regulation 1/2003.

Article 15(1), Regulation 1/2003 stipulates that 'In proceedings for the application of Article 81 or Article 82 of the Treaty, courts of the Member States may ask the Commission to transmit to them information in its possession or its opinion on questions concerning the application of the Community competition rules.'

Note the Commission's Notice on Cooperation between Commission and the Courts of the Member States which contains a section (paras 21–6) on the Commission's duty to transmit information to national courts.

In Case C–234/89 *Stergios Delimitis v Henninger Bräu AG*, [1991] ECR I–935, [1992] 5 CMLR 210, the ECJ held that 'It should be noted in this context that it is always open to a national court, within the limits of the applicable national procedural rules and subject to [Article 287] of the Treaty, to seek information from the Commission on the state of any procedure which the Commission may have set in motion and as to the likelihood of its giving an official ruling on the agreement at issue. … Under the same conditions, the national court may contact the Commission where the concrete application of [Article 81(1) or 81 EC] raises particular difficulties, in order to obtain the economic and legal information which that institution can supply to it. Under [Article 10 of the Treaty], the Commission is bound by a duty of sincere cooperation with the judicial authorities of the Member State, who are responsible for ensuring that Community law is applied and respected in the national legal system.' (para 53)

With respect to business secrets note that Article 287 of the Treaty stipulates that: 'The members of the institutions of the Community, the members of committees, and the officials and other servants of the Community shall be required, even after their duties have ceased, not to disclose information of the kind covered by the obligation of professional secrecy, in particular information about undertakings, their business relations or their cost components.'

Note that 'the Commission may justify a refusal to produce documents to a national judicial authority on legitimate grounds connected with the protection of the rights of third parties or where the disclosure of this information would be capable of interfering with the functioning and independence of the Community, in particular by jeopardizing the accomplishment of the tasks entrusted to it.' (Case C–2/88 *JJ Zwartveld and others*, para 11, [1990] ECR I–4405)

Sandisk Corporation v Koninklijke Philips Electronics NV	**Private Enforcement**
Case HC06C03489	Jurisdiction
English High Court of Justice, [2007] EWHC 332 (Ch)	Regulation No 44/2001

Facts

A claim for relief made by SanDisk (a US corporation) in respect of an alleged abuse of a dominant position by several companies and patentees in the market for the licensing of patents essential to the production, sale and importation into the EEA of MP3 players and MP3-compliant memory cards. The defendants, who were based in Italy, the Netherlands, France and Germany, agued that the English court had no jurisdiction to consider the claims raised by SanDisk.

Held

'The question whether and in what circumstances the English court has jurisdiction is to be determined according to the provisions of the Council Regulation (EC) 44/2001 ("the Brussels Regulation"). The basic rule, as is well-known, is that a defendant is to be sued in the courts of the Member State where that person is domiciled (Article 2). The exceptions provided for by Sections 2 to 7 of Chapter II of the Brussels Regulation constitute the only exceptions to this rule; and, so far as this case is concerned, the only relevant rule is the special jurisdiction conferred by Article 5. Before embarking on this analysis, it is worth noting that Sisvel, against whom the greatest complaint is made, can certainly and without any doubt be sued in Italy, and there is little question that the Patentees could be joined to such proceedings under Article 6(1) which provides that a person domiciled in a Member State may also be sued, where he is one of a number of defendants, in the courts for the place where any one of them is domiciled, provided the claims are so closely connected that it is expedient to hear and determine them together to avoid the risk of irreconcilable judgments resulting from separate proceedings. Because none of the Defendants are domiciled in England and Wales (see Article 60), this possibility is not open to SanDisk in this jurisdiction, who must establish that a special jurisdiction is available. The only arguable head of jurisdiction is found in Article 5(3), which provides that: A person domiciled in a Member State may, in another Member State, be sued: … 3. in matters relating to tort, delict or quasi-delict, in the courts for the place where the harmful event occurred or may occur.' (para 12)

'If the court is to have substantive jurisdiction by virtue of Article 5(3), the harmful act either must have occurred or may occur within England and Wales. The expression "matters relating to tort, delict or quasi-delict" have an autonomous meaning and must be regarded as an independent concept covering all actions which seek to establish the liability of the defendant and which are not related to a contract within the meaning of Article 5(1). The special jurisdictions enumerated in Articles 5 and 6 of the Brussels Regulation constitute derogations from the principle that jurisdiction is vested in the courts of the state where the defendant is domiciled, and as such must be interpreted restrictively. (See generally Case 189/87 *Kalfelis* [1988] ECR 5565). The idea of "place" also has the autonomous meaning that it embraces both the place where the damage occurred and the place of the event giving rise to it – see Case 21/76 *Bier v Mines de Potasse d'Alsace SA* [1976] ECR 1735. The option conferred on a claimant by Bier's case is not as wide as it may at first appear, since in general any claimant will suffer loss at its place of business caused to it by a harmful act committed abroad. To permit the court of the place of business of the claimant assuming juris-diction in every such case and so weakening or entirely subverting the basic jurisdictional principle of Article 2 of the regulation, to which Article 5 is, as I have indicated, an exception, it is settled that the "place of damage" connotes the place where the physical damage is done or the recoverable economic loss is actually suffered. In Case C–220/88 *Dumez* [1990] ECR I–49, the Court of Justice said this (paragraph 20): "It follows from foregoing considerations that although, by virtue of a previous judgment of the court (in [*Bier*] …), the expression "place where the harmful event occurred" contained in Article 5(3) of the Convention may refer to the place where the damage occurred, the latter concept can be understood only as indicating the place where the event giving rise to the damage, and entailing tortious, delictual or quasi-delictual liability, directly produced its harmful effects upon the person who is the immediate victim of that event.' (para 20)

'An interesting illustration of the principle is to be found in Case C–364/93 *Marinari* [1995] ECR I–2738 , in which Mr Marinari had presented promissory bank notes to the value of US $752,500,000 to the Manchester branch of Lloyds Bank, whose staff refused to return them to him. Mr Marinari sued Lloyds Bank, domiciled in England and Wales, in the Tribunale di Pisa for compensation. He failed, the court ruling that the term "place where the harmful event occurred" in Article 5(3) of the [Brussels Regulation] does not, on a proper interpretation, cover the place where the victim claims to have suffered financial damage following upon initial damage arising and suffered by him in another Member State. In paragraph 14 of the judgment, the court said this: "Whilst it has thus been recognised that the term 'place where the harmful event occurred' within the meaning of Article 5(3) of the [Brussels Regulation] may cover both the place where the damage occurred and the place of the event giving rise to it, that term cannot be construed so extensively as to encompass any place where the adverse consequences can be felt of an event which has already caused damage actually arising elsewhere."'(para 21)

'Finally, the present case is concerned with acts which are themselves difficult to localise. Thus, assuming that the offer of an objectionable licence is rightly characterised as an abuse of a dominant position, where does the offer take place? The letter may be written in one jurisdiction and received in another. It seems to be settled that, at least in two obvious cases in which a tortious act is not complete until a statement has been both made and understood, the relevant location is that where the statement was made. In the case of defamation, the place of the harmful act was held to be the place where the statement was put into circulation, the place of receipt being the place where immediate damage arose: see Case C–68/93 *Shevill* [1995] ECR I–415, paragraph 24 of the judgment. It follows from Shevill that while all damages will be recoverable in the jurisdiction where the harmful event originated, damages for the jurisdiction in which injury to reputation is suffered will determine the extent of damage in that jurisdiction only …' (para 22)

In order for the court to possess the exceptional jurisdiction pursuant to Article 5(3) of the Brussels Regulation in the present case, it must be satisfied that either the event setting the tort in motion was in England and Wales or, alternatively, that the claimant must show that it is the immediate victim of that abuse suffering direct harm in England and Wales. In this case damages as a result of the alleged abuse accrue to SanDisk in Delaware and not to its two subsidiaries within the UK. Consequently, the alleged abuses cannot, even if established, give rise to jurisdiction under Article 5(3) in England and Wales. (paras 25–41)

According to the claimant, the English court has jurisdiction since the enforcement of patent rights by the defendant may be regarded as an abusive and anticompetitive activity throughout Europe, including the UK, which led to a loss suffered by SanDisk throughout the EU and immediate damage is suffered in every country. This argument may establish jurisdiction both under Article 5(3) and under Article 31 which permits applications for provisional, including protective, measures even if, under the Regulation, the courts of another Member State have jurisdiction as to the substance of the matter. However, Article 31 must be interpreted strictly, given that it is an exception to the basic system of jurisdiction established by the Brussels Regulation (Case C–104/03 *St Paul Dairy* [2005] ILPR 416). The granting of provisional or protective measures on the basis of Article 31 depends upon identifying a connection between the subject-matter of the provisional or protective measures sought, on the one hand, and this jurisdiction on the other. In the present case there is no such connection and therefore jurisdiction does not exist under Article 31. (paras 42–55)

Comment

The attempt to secure an interim relief failed due to the lack of a real connecting link between the subject matter of the interim measure and the jurisdiction of the court.

'The rules of jurisdiction must be highly predictable and founded on the principle that jurisdiction is generally based on the defendant's domicile, and jurisdiction must always be available on this ground save in a few well-defined situations in which the subject-matter of the litigation or the autonomy of the parties warrants a different linking factor. … In addition to the defendant's domicile, there should be alternative grounds of jurisdiction based on a close link between the court and the action or in order to facilitate the sound administration of justice.' (Recitals 11, 12, Council Regulation (EC) 44/2001)

Color Drack GmbH v Lexx International Vertriebs GmbH	**Private Enforcement**
Case C–386/05	Jurisdiction
ECJ, [2007] ILPr 35	Regulation No 44/2001

Facts

Reference for a preliminary ruling from the Oberster Gerichtshof (Austrian Court) concerning the interpretation of the first indent of Article 5(1)(b) of Council Regulation (EC) No 44/2001. The dispute in the main proceedings concerned the performance of a contract for the sale of goods under which Lexx International Vertriebs GmbH (Lexx), a company established in Germany, undertook to deliver goods to various retailers of Color Drack GmbH in Austria. Following Lexx's failure to perform some of its obligations under the agreement, Color Drack GmbH brought an action for payment before the Austrian court within whose jurisdiction its registered office is located. That court accepted jurisdiction on the basis of the first indent of Article 5(1)(b) of Regulation No 44/2001. Following an appeal by Lexx, the appeal court set aside that judgment on the ground that the first instance court did not have jurisdiction. It took the view that a single linking place, as provided for in the first indent of Article 5(1)(b) of Regulation No 44/2001, could not be determined where there were several places of delivery not only in the area of that court's jurisdiction but at different places in Austria. Color Drack appealed the decision to the Oberster Gerichtshof, which considered that an interpretation of the first indent of Article 5(1)(b) of Regulation No 44/2001 is necessary in order to resolve the question of the jurisdiction. The court stayed the proceedings and referred the case to the ECJ asking whether the first indent of Article 5(1)(b) of Regulation No 44/2001 applies in the case of a sale of goods involving several places of delivery within a single Member State and, if so, whether, where the claim relates to all those deliveries, the plaintiff may sue the defendant in the court of the place of delivery of its choice.

Held

'As a preliminary point, it must be stated that the considerations that follow apply solely to the case where there are several places of delivery within a single Member State and are without prejudice to the answer to be given where there are several places of delivery in a number of Member States.' (para 16)

The wording of the first indent of Article 5(1)(b) of Regulation No 44/2001 does not refer expressly to a case such as that to which the question relates. The Article must therefore be interpreted in the light of the origins, objectives and scheme of that regulation. (paras 17, 18)

Regulation No 44/2001 seeks to unify the rules of conflict of jurisdiction in civil and commercial matters and to strengthen the legal protection of persons established in the Community, by enabling the plaintiff to identify easily the court in which he may sue and the defendant reasonably to foresee before which court he may be sued. (paras 19, 20)

The principal rule in the Regulation that 'jurisdiction is generally based on the defendant's domicile is complemented, in Article 5(1), by a rule of special jurisdiction in matters relating to a contract. The reason for that rule, which reflects an objective of proximity, is the existence of a close link between the contract and the court called upon to hear and determine the case. Under that rule the defendant may also be sued in the court for the place of performance of the obligation in question, since that court is presumed to have a close link to the contract.' (paras 21–3)

'Pursuant to the first indent of Article 5(1)(b) of that regulation, the place of performance of the obligation in question is the place in a Member State where, under the contract, the goods were delivered or should have been delivered. In the context of Regulation No 44/2001, contrary to Lexx's submissions, that rule of special jurisdiction in matters relating to a contract establishes the place of delivery as the autonomous linking factor to apply to all claims founded on one and the same contract for the sale of goods rather than merely to the claims founded on the obligation of delivery itself.' (paras 25, 26)

The first indent of Article 5(1)(b) of the regulation must be regarded as applying whether there is one place of delivery or several. 'By providing for a single court to have jurisdiction and a single linking factor, the Community legislature did not intend generally to exclude cases where a number of courts may have jurisdiction nor those where the existence of that linking factor can be established in different places.' (paras 28, 29)

The first indent of Article 5(1)(b) of Regulation No 44/2001 is applicable where there are several places of delivery within a single Member State. This applicability complies with the Regulation's objective of predictability as parties to the contract can easily and reasonably foresee before which Member State's courts they can bring their dispute. Additionally, it complies with the objective of proximity underlying the rules of special jurisdiction in matters relating to a contract. (paras 31–6)

'With regard, secondly, to the question whether, where there are several places of delivery within a single Member State and the claim relates to all those deliveries, the plaintiff may sue the defendant in the court for the place of delivery of its choice on the basis of the first indent of Article 5(1)(b) of Regulation No 44/2001, it is necessary to point out that one court must have jurisdiction to hear all the claims arising out of the contract.' (para 38)

'In that regard, it is appropriate to take into consideration the origins of the provision under consideration. By that provision, the Community legislature intended, in respect of sales contracts, expressly to break with the earlier solution under which the place of performance was determined, for each of the obligations in question, in accordance with the private international rules of the court seised of the dispute. By designating autonomously as the place of performance' the place where the obligation which characterises the contract is to be performed, the Community legislature sought to centralise at its place of performance jurisdiction over disputes concerning all the contractual obligations and to determine sole jurisdiction for all claims arising out of the contract.' (para 39)

'In that regard it is necessary to take account of the fact that the special jurisdiction under the first indent of Article 5(1)(b) of Regulation No 44/2001 is warranted, in principle, by the existence of a particularly close linking factor between the contract and the court called upon to hear the litigation, with a view to the efficient organisation of the proceedings. It follows that, where there are several places of delivery of the goods, "place of delivery" must be understood, for the purposes of application of the provision under consideration, as the place with the closest linking factor between the contract and the court having jurisdiction. In such a case, the point of closest linking factor will, as a general rule, be at the place of the principal delivery, which must be determined on the basis of economic criteria.' (para 40)

'If it is not possible to determine the principal place of delivery, each of the places of delivery has a sufficiently close link of proximity to the material elements of the dispute and, accordingly, a significant link as regards jurisdiction. In such a case, the plaintiff may sue the defendant in the court for the place of delivery of its choice on the basis of the first indent of Article 5(1)(b) of Regulation No 44/2001.' (para 42)

Comment

Note Advocate General Bot's opinion in which he took a different view on the determination of the competent court among those in whose territorial jurisdictions deliveries were made. (AG Bot opinion, 15 February 2007, paras 95–116, 130)

8

Enforcement – The European Commission

Regulatory Framework

The enforcement of competition law by the European Commission is primarily governed by Council Regulation (EC) No 1/2003 on the Implementation of the Rules on Competition Laid Down in Articles 81 and 82 of the Treaty (2004 OJ L 1/1).

Several regulations, notices and guidelines provide details on different aspects of the Commission's enforcement of competition law. See in particular:

- Commission Regulation (EC) No 773/2004 of 7 April 2004 relating to the Conduct of Proceedings by the Commission Pursuant to Articles 81 and 82 of the EC Treaty (2004 OJ L 123/18).
- Commission Notice on the Handling of Complaints by the Commission under Articles 81 and 82 of the EC Treaty (2004 OJ C 101/65).
- Commission Notice on the Rules for Access to the Commission File in Cases Pursuant to Articles 81 and 82 of the EC Treaty, Articles 53, 54 and 57 of the EEA Agreement and Council Regulation (EC) No 139/2004 (2005 OJ C 325/7).
- Commission Notice on Immunity from Fines and Reduction of Fines in Cartel Cases (2006 OJ C 298/17).
- Commission Notice on Cooperation within the Network of Competition Authorities (2004 OJ C 101/43).
- Commission Notice on Informal Guidance Relating to Novel Questions Concerning Articles 81 and 82 of the EC Treaty that Arise in Individual Cases (guidance letters) (2004 OJ C 101/78).
- Guidelines on the Method of Setting fines Imposed Pursuant to Article 23(2)(a) of Regulation No 1/2003 (2006 OJ C 210/2).

Inspection Powers

Article 20, Regulation 1/2003 lays down the Commission's powers of inspection and authorises Commission officials to enter any premises, examine books and other records relating to business, and demand from members of staff explanations on facts and documents relating to the subject matter of the inspection. Undertakings are required to submit to the inspection ordered by a decision of the Commission. Failure to do so results in the imposition of fines as provided in Articles 23 and 24 of Regulation 1/2003. In the event that undertakings refuse to submit to an inspection as ordered, such inspection will be conducted with the assistance of the relevant Member State's enforcement authorities in accordance with national laws and when necessary following an authorisation of the judicial authority.

Article 21, Regulation 1/2003 widens the Commission's inspection powers to private premises. Subject to the authorisation of the national judicial authority, the Commission may be empowered to conduct an inspection of private premises, land and means of transport. Such inspection targets business records and other documents linked to the anticompetitive cartels that are kept in the homes of the directors, managers and other members of staff.

On the Commission inspection powers, see:

See also summary references to:

Request for Information

Articles 18, Regulation 1/2003 sets the Commission's power to request undertakings 'to provide all necessary information'. A request for information may take the form of a 'simple request' or 'decision'. Both types of requests result in penalties where information supplied is found to be incorrect or misleading. On the Commission's power to require the disclosure of documents in connection with a request for information, see:

Statement of Objections and Access to File

Where the Commission considers on the basis of the information in its possession that a competition infringement has occurred, it will inform the parties concerned in writing of the objections raised against them. The parties will reply in written submissions to the objections raised by the Commission. The Commission shall grant access to the file to the parties to whom it has addressed a statement of objections. The right of access to the file shall not extend to business secrets, other confidential information and internal documents of the Commission or of the competition authorities of the Member States (Articles 10–17, Regulation 773/2004). On statement of objections and access to file, see:

See also summary references to:

Professional Secrecy

Article 28, Regulation 1/2003 stipulates that information collected under the Commission's powers of investigation and inspection shall only be used for the purpose for which it was acquired. The Commission and the competition authorities of the Member States shall not disclose information acquired or exchanged by them of the kind covered by the obligation of professional secrecy. Article 16, Regulation 773/2004 provides further guidance on the identification and protection of confidential information. Also note generally Article 287 EC, which deals with the non-disclosure of information of the kind covered by the obligation of professional secrecy. On professional secrecy, see:

See also summary references to:

Limited Right against Self-incrimination

The Commission is empowered to take statements and interview natural and legal persons who consent to be interviewed for the purpose of collecting information relating to the subject-matter of an investigation. When complying with a decision of the Commission, undertakings have a right of silence only to the extent that they would be compelled to provide answers which might involve an admission on their part of existence of an agreement which it is incumbent upon the Commission to prove. However, undertakings are obliged to answer factual questions and to provide documents, even if this information may be used to establish against them, or against another undertaking, the existence of an infringement (Recital 23, Regulation 1/2003). Note also Articles 3 and 4, Regulation 773/2004, which deal with the Commission's power to take statements and ask questions during inspections. On the limited right against self incrimination, see:

See also summary references to:

Professional Legal Privilege

European Community law recognises the protection of written communications between lawyer and client. However, under European Community law such protection does not apply to communications with in-house counsel.

See also summary references to:

Interim Measures

Article 8, Regulation 1/2003 codifies the Commission's power to order interim measures in cases of urgency due to the risk of serious and irreparable damage to competition.

Finding and Termination of Infringement – Remedies

Article 7, Regulation 1/2003 sets the Commission's powers to find and terminate an infringement of Articles 81 or 82 EC. The Commission is empowered for that purpose to impose behavioural or structural remedies which are proportionate to the infringement committed and necessary to bring the infringement effectively to an end. Structural remedies will be imposed where there is no equally effective behavioural remedy, or where an equally effective behavioural remedy is more burdensome for the undertaking concerned. Note that structural remedies would only be proportionate where there is a substantial risk of a lasting or repeated infringement that derives from the very structure of the undertaking (Recital 12, Regulation 1/2003).

The Commission may order the termination of abuse under Article 82 EC. Such decision may include an order to do certain acts which have been wrongfully withheld as well as prohibiting the continuation of certain actions (Case 6/73).

The Commission may order the termination of an anticompetitive agreement under Article 81 EC but does not have the power to order a party to enter into contractual relations following such infringement (Case T–24/90):

T–24/90	*Automec Srl v Commission* (Automec II)	250

See also summary references to:

6/73	*Istituto Chemioterapico Italiano SpA and others v Commission*	250

Commitments

Article 9, Regulation 1/2003 stipulates that 'Where the Commission intends to adopt a decision requiring that an infringement be brought to an end and the undertakings concerned offer commitments to meet the concerns expressed to them by the Commission in its preliminary assessment, the Commission may by decision make those commitments binding on the undertakings. Such a decision may be adopted for a specified period and shall conclude that there are no longer grounds for action by the Commission.' Commitment decisions are not appropriate in cases where the Commission intends to impose a fine. See, for example, the following decisions:

COMP/38.173	*FA Premier League*	251
COMP/39.116	*Coca Cola*	251

Informal Guidance and Finding of Inapplicability

Where cases give rise to uncertainty because they present novel or unresolved questions for the application of Articles 81 and 82, individual undertakings may obtain informal guidance from the Commission (Recital 38, Regulation 1/2003). The procedure concerning such guidance is laid down in the Commission Notice on Informal Guidance (2004 OJ C 101/78).

The Commission, acting on its own initiative, may by decision find that Article 81 of the Treaty is not applicable to an agreement, a decision by an association of undertakings or a concerted practice, when the Community public interest relating to the application of Articles 81 and 82 of the Treaty so requires (Article 10, Regulation 1/2003).

Fines

Regulation 1/2003 sets the financial penalty in cases of intentional or negligent infringement of Articles 81 and 82 EC. In general, the fine shall not exceed 10 per cent of the undertaking's total turnover in the preceding business year. On 28 June 2006, the Commission adopted revised guidelines on the method of setting fines in cases of infringement of Articles 81 and 82 EC. The Guidelines introduce new methodology for the calculation of fines within the limits set by Regulation 1/2003, [2006] OJ C–210/2. More generally on the setting of fines, see:

Leniency Programme

The European leniency programme was hailed as being tremendously successful, and generated the vast majority of cartel investigations and decisions in Europe. A 'third generation' of the leniency notice entered into force in December 2006. See Commission Notice on Immunity from Fines and Reduction of Fines in Cartel Cases (2006 OJ C 298/17).

Note that the European Community has yet to adopt a one-stop-shop Community-wide leniency programme. A proposed Euro-wide leniency programme is still in its infancy.

Settlement Procedure for Cartels

In October 2007 the European Commission launched a public consultation on a proposed legislative package to introduce settlement procedures for cartels. The package consists of a draft Commission Notice and a draft Commission Regulation amending Commission Regulation (EC) No 773/2004 of 7 April 2004. The new procedure would enable the Commission to reach a settlement agreement with parties that acknowledge their participation in a cartel violating Article 81 of the EC and agree to a faster and simplified procedure.

The proposed legislative package is available on the European Commission website:

http://ec.europa.eu/comm/competition/index_en.html

Cooperation with National Competition Authorities

Article 5, Regulation 1/2003 set the powers of the competition authorities of the Member States. Articles 11 and 12, Regulation 1/2003 set the framework for the cooperation and exchange of information between the Commission and the competition authorities of the Member States. The cooperation framework is further elaborated upon in the Commission Notice on Cooperation within the Network of Competition Authorities.

Hoechst AG v Commission	**Public Enforcement**
Case 46/87	Inspection Powers
ECJ, [1989] ECR 2859, [1991] 4 CMLR 410	Article 8(1) ECHR

Facts

The Commission suspected that several producers and suppliers of PVC and polyethylene in the Community fixed prices and delivery quotas for those products. As part of its investigation into this alleged cartel activity, the Commission reached a decision to carry out an investigation (under Article 14(3) Regulation 17/62) into several of the undertakings involved, one of them being Hoechst AG. When the Commission's officials arrived at Hoechst AG offices, they were refused entry on the ground that the inspection constituted an unlawful search. Following two additional failed attempts to enter the premises, the Commission adopted a decision in which it imposed a periodic penalty payment on Hoechst AG. The Commission's inspection took place two months later, on 2 and 3 April 1987, following the issue of a search warrant by the national court. Hoechst AG brought an action to declare, among other things, that the Commission decision of investigation under Article 14(3) Regulation 17/62 was void.

Held

Article 14, Regulation 17/62 cannot be interpreted in a way that gives rise to results which are incompatible with the general principles of Community law and in particular with fundamental rights. (para 12)

'The Court has consistently held that fundamental rights are an integral part of the general principles of law the observance of which the Court ensures, in accordance with constitutional traditions common to the Member States, and the international treaties on which the Member States have collaborated or of which they are signatories (see, in particular, the judgment of 14 May 1974 in Case 4/73 *Nold v Commission* [1974] ECR 491). The European Convention for the Protection of Human Rights and Fundamental Freedoms of 4 November 1950 (hereinafter referred to as "the European Convention on Human Rights") is of particular significance in that regard (see, in particular, the judgment of 15 May 1986 in Case 222/84 *Johnston v Chief Constable of the Royal Ulster Constabulary* [1986] ECR 1651).' (para 13)

In interpreting Article 14 of Regulation 17/62 regard must be had in particular to the rights of defence. This is a fundamental principle that has been stressed on numerous occasions in the Court's decisions. In Case 322/81 *Michelin v Commission* [1983] ECR 3461, paragraph 7, 'the Court pointed out that the rights of the defence must be observed in administrative procedures which may lead to the imposition of penalties. But it is also necessary to prevent those rights from being irremediably impaired during preliminary inquiry procedures including, in particular, investigations which may be decisive in providing evidence of the unlawful nature of conduct engaged in by undertakings for which they may be liable.' (paras 14, 15)

'Consequently, although certain rights of the defence relate only to the contentious proceedings which follow the delivery of the statement of objections, other rights, such as the right to legal representation and the privileged nature of correspondence between lawyer and client (recognized by the Court in the judgment of 18 May 1982 in Case 155/79 *AM & S v Commission* [1982] ECR 1575) must be respected as from the preliminary-inquiry stage.' (para 16)

'Since the applicant has also relied on the requirements stemming from the fundamental right to the inviolability of the home, it should be observed that, although the existence of such a right must be recognized in the Community legal order as a principle common to the laws of the Member States in regard to the private dwellings of natural persons, the same is not true in regard to undertakings, because there are not inconsiderable divergences between the legal systems of the Member States in regard to the nature and degree of protection afforded to business premises against intervention by the public authorities.' (para 17)

'No other inference is to be drawn from Article 8(1) of the European Convention on Human Rights which provides that: "Everyone has the right to respect for his private and family life, his home and his correspondence". The protective scope of that article is concerned with the development of man's personal freedom and may not therefore be extended to business premises. Furthermore, it should be noted that there is no case-law of the European Court of Human Rights on that subject.' (para 18)

'None the less, in all the legal systems of the Member States, any intervention by the public authorities in the sphere of private activities of any person, whether natural or legal, must have a legal basis and be justified on the grounds laid down by law, and, consequently, those systems provide, albeit in different forms, protection against arbitrary or disproportionate intervention. The need for such protection must be recognized as a general principle of Community law. In that regard, it should be pointed out that the Court has held that it has the power to determine whether measures of investigation taken by the Commission under the ECSC Treaty are excessive (judgment of 14 December 1962 in Joined Cases 5 to 11 and 13 to 15/62 *San Michele and others v Commission* [1962] ECR 449).' (para 19)

The nature and scope of the Commission's powers of investigation under Article 14, Regulation 17/62 should therefore be considered in the light of the general principles set out above. The purpose of Regulation 17/62 to enable the Commission to carry out its duty under the Treaty of ensuring that the rules on competition are applied in the common market, and the list of powers conferred on the Commission's officials by Article 14, show that the scope of investigations may be very wide. (paras 20–26)

'The right to enter any premises, land and means of transport of undertakings is of particular importance inasmuch as it is intended to permit the Commission to obtain evidence of infringements of the competition rules in the places in which such evidence is normally to be found, that is to say, on the business premises of undertakings. That right of access would serve no useful purpose if the Commission's officials could do no more than ask for documents or files which they could identify precisely in advance. On the contrary, such a right implies the power to search for various items of information which are not already known or fully identified. Without such a power, it would be impossible for the Commission to obtain the information necessary to carry out the investigation if the undertakings concerned refused to cooperate or adopted an obstructive attitude.' (paras 26–7)

The Commission's wide powers of investigation are subject to conditions serving to ensure that the rights of the undertakings concerned are respected. 'In that regard, it should be noted first that the Commission is required to specify the subject-matter and purpose of the investigation. That obligation is a fundamental requirement not merely in order to show that the investigation to be carried out on the premises of the undertakings concerned is justified, but also to enable those undertakings to assess the scope of their duty to cooperate while at the same time safeguarding the rights of the defence.' (paras 28–9)

The Commission's investigation powers vary according to the procedure the Commission has chosen, the attitude of the undertakings concerned and the intervention of the national authorities. Investigations can be carried out with the cooperation of the undertakings concerned, either voluntarily, where there is a written authorisation, or by virtue of an obligation arising under a decision ordering an investigation. In the absence of cooperation, the Commission may conduct investigation with the assistance of the national authorities, subject to the relevant procedural guarantees laid down by national law. (paras 30–36)

In this case the Commission decision does not exceed its powers under regulation 17/62 as it merely requires the applicant 'to permit officials authorized by the Commission to enter its premises during normal office hours, to produce for inspection and to permit copies to be made of business documents related to the subject-matter of the enquiry which are requested by the said officials and to provide immediately any explanations which those officials may seek'. (para 36)

Comment

The application of Article 8(1) of the European Convention for the Protection of Human Rights and Fundamental Freedoms (4 Nov 1950) was also considered in Case 136/79 *National Panasonic (UK) Limited v Commission*. See extract of this case in the comment on page 234 below.

Roquette Frères v Directeur Général de la Concurrence	**Public Enforcement**
Case C–94/00	Inspection Powers
ECJ, [2002] ECR I–9011, [2003] 4 CMLR 1	Authorisation – The National Court

Facts

The Commission adopted, on the basis of Article 14(3) of Regulation 17/62, a decision ordering Roquette Frères to submit to an investigation concerning its possible participation in agreements and/or concerted practices that may have constituted an infringement of Article 81 EC. As a precautionary measure the Commission requested the French Government to take the necessary steps to ensure that, in the event of opposition by Roquette Frères to the investigation, the national authorities would provide assistance. To provide such assistance, an authorisation of the French court was applied for and granted. Following the Commission's inspection, in which Roquette Frères cooperated, Roquette Frères appealed against the French court's authorisation order, asserting that it was not open to the court to order entry onto private premises without first satisfying itself that there were reasonable grounds for suspecting the existence of anticompetitive practices such as to justify the grant of coercive powers. On appeal, the French Cour de cassation referred to the ECJ under Article 234 EC questions concerning the scope of the review which may need to be undertaken by a national court having jurisdiction under domestic law to authorise entry onto the premises of undertakings suspected of having infringed competition rules.

Held

The national court, when considering the matter, 'may not substitute its own assessment of the need for the investigations ordered for that of the Commission, the lawfulness of whose assessments of fact and law is subject only to review by the Community judicature (*Hoechst*, paragraph 35).' (paras 39, 60)

'The review carried out by the competent national court, which must concern itself only with the coercive measures applied for, may not go beyond an examination, as required by Community law, to establish that the coercive measures in question are not arbitrary and that they are proportionate to the subject-matter of the investigation.' (para 40)

'When conducting its review to ensure that there is nothing arbitrary about a coercive measure designed to permit implementation of an investigation ordered by the Commission, the competent national court is required, in essence, to satisfy itself that there exist reasonable grounds for suspecting an infringement of the competition rules by the undertaking concerned.' (para 54)

The similarity in the nature of that review and the review which the Community judicature may be called upon to carry out for the purposes of ensuring that the investigation decision itself is in no way arbitrary, (that is to say, that it has not been adopted in the absence of facts capable of justifying the investigation), must not obscure the distinction between the objectives which those two types of review respectively seek to attain. (paras 55, 56)

'For the purposes of enabling the competent national court to satisfy itself that the coercive measures sought are not arbitrary, the Commission is required to provide that court with explanations showing, in a properly substantiated manner, that the Commission is in possession of information and evidence providing reasonable grounds for suspecting infringement of the competition rules by the undertaking concerned.' (para 61)

'On the other hand, the competent national court may not demand that it be provided with the information and evidence in the Commission's file on which the latter's suspicions are based.' (para 62)

In that regard, it is necessary to take into consideration the obligation of the Member States, to ensure that the Commission's action is effective. To ensure effective prevention of anticompetitive practices it is of crucial importance to allow the Commission to guarantee the anonymity of certain of its sources of information by not revealing certain information from its file. Similarly, in cases involving parallel investigations carried out simultaneously in more than one Member State, a duty to reveal the information in the file may have a detrimental effect on the effectiveness of the investigation. (paras 63–6)

'In the context of the allocation of competences in terms of Article 234 EC, it is in principle for the competent national court to assess whether, in a given case, the explanations referred to in paragraph 61 of this judgment have been properly provided and to carry out, on that basis, the review which it is required to undertake under Community law. In addition, where the national court is called upon to rule on a request for assistance submitted by the Commission pursuant to Article 14(6) of Regulation No 17, it must pay even greater heed to that allocation of competences, inasmuch as a reference for a preliminary ruling – unless made, as in the present case, after the investigations have been carried out – is apt to delay the decision of that court and may bring the request for assistance into the public domain, thereby creating a risk that the Commission's action may be paralysed and that any subsequent investigation may serve no useful purpose.' (para 67)

As regards the main proceedings in the present case, the Commission gave a very precise account of the suspicions harboured by it with regard to Roquette Frères. 'Although the Commission has not indicated the nature of the evidence on which its suspicions are based … the mere fact that no such indication is given cannot suffice to cast doubt on the existence of reasonable grounds for those suspicions where, as in the main proceedings, the detailed account of the information held by the Commission concerning the specific subject-matter of the suspected cartel is such as to enable the competent national court to establish a firm basis for its conclusion that the Commission does indeed possess such evidence.' (paras 68–9)

'As regards the need to verify that the coercive measures are proportionate to the subject-matter of the investigation ordered by the Commission, it should be noted that this involves establishing that such measures are appropriate to ensure that the investigation can be carried out. … It is for the Commission to provide the competent national court with the explanations needed by that court to satisfy itself that, if the Commission were unable to obtain, as a precautionary measure, the requisite assistance in order to overcome any opposition on the part of the undertaking, it would be impossible, or very difficult, to establish the facts amounting to the infringement.' (paras 71–5)

It is in principle for the Commission to decide whether particular information is necessary to enable it to bring to light an infringement of the competition rules. 'Even if it already has evidence, or indeed proof, of the existence of an infringement, the Commission may legitimately take the view that it is necessary to order further investigations enabling it to better define the scope of the infringement, to determine its duration or to identify the circle of undertakings involved.' (paras 77–8)

However, the national court may refuse to grant the coercive measures applied for 'where the suspected impairment of competition is so minimal, the extent of the likely involvement of the undertaking concerned so limited, or the evidence sought so peripheral, that the intervention in the sphere of the private activities of a legal person which a search using law-enforcement authorities entails, necessarily appears manifestly disproportionate and intolerable in the light of the objectives pursued by the investigation.' (para 80)

Community law requires the Commission to ensure that the national court has at its disposal the information that it needs in order to carry out the review that it is required to undertake. In that regard, the information supplied by the Commission must in principle include: a description of the essential features of the suspected infringement, explanations concerning the manner in which the undertaking at which the coercive measures are aimed is thought to be involved in the infringement in question; detailed explanations showing that the Commission possesses solid factual information and evidence providing grounds for suspecting such infringement on the part of the undertaking concerned; indication of the evidence sought, of the matters to which the investigation must relate and of the powers conferred on the Community investigators; and in the event that the assistance is requested by the Commission as a precautionary measure, explanations enabling the national court to satisfy itself that, if authorisation for the coercive measures were not granted on precautionary grounds, it would be impossible, or very difficult, to establish the facts amounting to the infringement. (paras 90–6, 99)

Comment

Regulation No 17/62 was replaced by Regulation 1/2003. Article 21(8), Regulation 1/2003 codifies the *Roquette Frères* finding and stipulates that 'Where authorisation as referred to in paragraph 7 is applied for, the national judicial authority shall control that the Commission decision is authentic and that the coercive measures envisaged are neither arbitrary nor excessive having regard to the subject matter of the inspection. In its control of the proportionality of the coercive measures, the national judicial authority may ask the Commission, directly or through the Member State competition authority, for detailed explanations in particular on the grounds the Commission has for suspecting infringement of Articles 81 and 82 of the Treaty, as well as on the seriousness of the suspected infringement and on the nature of the involvement of the undertaking concerned. However, the national judicial authority may not call into question the necessity for the inspection nor demand that it be provided with the information in the Commission's file. The lawfulness of the Commission decision shall be subject to review only by the Court of Justice.'

Note the ECJ's reference in paragraph 67 which concerns the allocation of competences in terms of a preliminary ruling under Article 234 EC and the need to avoid unnecessary delay in ruling which may paralyse the Commission's action.

Note AG Mischo's opinion and his review of the case-law of the European Court of Human Rights (paras 29–41).

In Case 46/87 *Hoechst AG v Commission*, [1989] ECR 2859, [1991] 4 CMLR 410, the ECJ held that 'The Commission must make sure that the competent body under national law has all that it needs to exercise its own supervisory powers. It should be pointed out that that body, whether judicial or otherwise, cannot in this respect substitute its own assessment of the need for the investigations ordered for that of the Commission's, the lawfulness of whose assessments of fact and law is subject only to review by the Court of Justice. On the other hand, it is within the powers of the national body, after satisfying itself that the decision ordering the investigation is authentic, to consider whether the measures of constraint envisaged are arbitrary or excessive having regard to the subject-matter of the investigation and to ensure that the rules of national law are complied with in the application of those measures.' (para 35)

Note Case 136/79 *National Panasonic (UK) Limited v Commission*, [1980] ECR 2033, [1980] 3 CMLR 169, in which National Panasonic challenged the validity of a Commission inspection in which competition officials arrived at its offices and, after handing a Commission decision to the directors of the company, carried out an inspection without awaiting the arrival of the company's solicitor, leaving the premises with copies of several documents and notes made during the investigation. National Panasonic applied for the annulment of the Commission's decision concerning the investigation and for the return of the documents taken from its premises. The Court held that it must be borne in mind in that the investigations carried out by the Commission are intended to enable it to gather the necessary documentary evidence to check the actual existence and scope of a given factual and legal situation concerning which the Commission already possesses certain information which it could have obtained from various sources, the undertakings not necessarily being one of them. (paras 13, 21) The Commission is not required to communicate with the undertakings before reaching a decision ordering an investigation. (paras 17 2) The Court also referred to the application of Article 8(1) of the European Convention for the Protection of Human Rights and Fundamental Freedoms (paras 17 2). It noted that 'Article 8(2) of the European convention, in so far as it applies to legal persons, whilst stating the principle that public authorities should not interfere with the exercise of the rights referred to in Article 8(1), acknowledges that such interference is permissible to the extent to which it "is in accordance with the law and is necessary in a democratic society in the interests of national security, public safety or the economic well-being of the country, for the prevention of disorder or crime, for the protection of health or morals, or for the protection of the rights and freedom of others".' (para 19) The Court dismissed the application.

Orkem v Commission	**Public Enforcement**
Case 374/87	Request for Information
ECJ, [1989] ECR 3283, [1991] 4 CMLR 502	

Facts

An action by Orkem SA for the annulment of a Commission decision which required it to reply to questions set out in a request for information issued by the Commission. Orkem SA argued, among other things, that the request in question (under Article 11, Regulation 17/62) was unlawful and lacked proportionality as it aimed to obtain documents which the Commission could only obtain under its powers of investigation (Article 14, Regulation 17/62).

Held

'It must be stated, with respect to the Commission's right to require the disclosure of documents in connection with a request for information, that Articles 11 and 14 of Regulation No 17 establish two entirely independent procedures. The fact that an investigation under Article 14 has already taken place cannot in any way diminish the powers of investigation available to the Commission under Article 11. No consideration of a procedural nature inherent in Regulation No 17 thus prevents the Commission from requiring, for the purposes of a request for information, the disclosure of documents of which it was unable to take a copy or extract when carrying out a previous investigation.' (para 14)

'With regard to the necessity of the information requested, it must be borne in mind that Regulation No 17 confers on the Commission wide powers to make investigations and to obtain information by providing in the eighth recital in its preamble that the Commission must be empowered, throughout the common market, to require such information to be supplied and to undertake such investigations as are necessary to bring to light infringements of [Articles 81 and 82 EC]. As the Court held in its judgment of 18 May 1982 in Case 155/79 *AM & S Europe Limited v Commission* [1982] ECR 1575, it is for the Commission to decide, for the purposes of an investigation under Article 14, whether particular information is necessary to enable it to bring to light an infringement of the competition rules. Even if it already has evidence, or indeed proof, of the existence of an infringement, the Commission may legitimately take the view that it is necessary to request further information to enable it better to define the scope of the infringement, to determine its duration or to identify the circle of undertakings involved.' (para 15)

'In the present case it does not appear that the information requested falls outside those limits or exceeds what might be regarded as necessary in the light of the purpose of the investigation.' (para 16)

Comment

Regulation 16/72 was replaced by Regulation 1/2003. The latter enables the Commission to obtain information through various means; Article 18, Regulation 1/2003 sets the Commission's power to request undertakings 'to provide all necessary information'. A request for information may take the form of a 'simple request' or a 'decision'. Both types of requests result in penalties where information supplied is found to be incorrect or misleading. The Commission may also obtain information while inspecting the undertakings premises. (Articles 20 and 21, Regulation 1/2003)

The fact that an inspection under Articles 20 and 21, Regulation 1/2003 has already taken place does not diminish the powers of investigation available to the Commission under other provisions, such as Article Articles 18, Regulation 1/2003.

Hercules Chemicals NV v Commission	**Public Enforcement**
Case C–51/92 P	Statement of Objections
ECJ, [1999] ECR I–4235, [1999] 5 CMLR 976	Access to File

Facts

The case emerged out of the Commission's *Polypropylene* decision, in which it found that Hercules Chemicals NV (Hercules) had infringed Article 81 EC by taking part in anticompetitive agreements and concerted practices with other producers of polypropylene (IV/31.149 – *Polypropylene* (OJ 1986 L 230/1)). On appeal, an action for the annulment of the decision was dismissed by the CFI (Case T–7/89 *Hercules Chemicals v Commission* [1991] ECR II–1711). Hercules appealed to the ECJ, arguing, among other things, that the CFI erred when it did not examine whether the Commission's refusal to allow Hercules to access the replies of the other producers to the statement of objections constituted an infringement of the rights of defence.

Held

'… Access to the file in competition cases is intended in particular to enable the addressees of statements of objections to acquaint themselves with the evidence in the Commission's file so that on the basis of that evidence they can express their views effectively on the conclusions reached by the Commission in its statement of objections (Case 322/81 *Michelin v Commission*, [1983] ECR 3461, paragraph 7; Case 85/76 *Hoffmann-La Roche v Commission* [1979] ECR 461, paragraphs 9 and 11; Case C–310/93 P *BPB Industries and British Gypsum v Commission* [1995] ECR I–865, paragraph 21; and Case C–185/95 P *Baustahlgewebe v Commission* [1998] ECR I–8417, paragraph 89).' (para 75)

'In the case of a decision concerning infringement of the competition rules applicable to undertakings and imposing fines or penalty payments, breach of those general principles of Community law in the procedure prior to the adoption of the decision can, in principle, cause the decision to be annulled if the rights of defence of the undertaking concerned have been infringed.' (para 77)

'In such a case, the infringement committed is not remedied by the mere fact that access was made possible at a later stage, in particular during the judicial proceedings relating to an action in which annulment of the contested decision is sought.' (para 78)

However, such an infringement does not bring about the annulment of the decision in question unless the undertaking concerned shows that it could have used the documents to which it was denied access for its defence. The undertaking does not have to show that if it had used the documents, the Commission decision would have been different in content, but only that it would have been able to use those documents for its defence. (paras 79–81)

Hercules did not establish that the fact that it was not able to apprise itself the replies of the other producers to the statement of objections, before the Decision was adopted, had infringed its rights of defence. (para 81)

Comment

The statement of objections sets all the essential facts upon which the Commission is relying at that stage of the procedure. The Commission final decision is not necessarily required to be a replica of the Commission's statement of objections, since the statement of objections is a preparatory document containing assessments of fact and of law which are purely provisional in nature. See paragraph 67, Joint Cases C–204/00 etc *Aalborg Portland and others v Commission* (page 235 below), paragraph 70, Joined Cases 142/84 etc *BAT and Reynolds v Commission*, [1987] ECR 4487, and paragraph 14, Joined Cases 100/80 etc *Musique Diffusion Française and others v Commission*, [1983] ECR 1825.

Aalborg Portland and others v Commission	**Public Enforcement**
Joined cases C–204, 5, 11, 13, 17, 19/00	Statement of Objections
ECJ, [2004] ECR I–123, [2005] 4 CMLR 4	Access to File

Facts

An appeal against the CFI judgment in *Cimenteries CBR and others v Commission* in which the CFI confirmed parts of the infringements found against the appellants in Commission Decision IV/33.126 and 33.322 'Cement'. In its decision the Commission found a large number of undertakings and associations active in the European cement market to have infringed Article 81 EC by entering into anticompetitive agreements and concerted practices. In its decision the ECJ referred to, among other things, the right of access to the file.

Held (on the right of access to the file)

'... the right of access to the file means that the Commission must give the undertaking concerned the opportunity to examine all the documents in the investigation file which may be relevant for its defence (see, to that effect, Case T–30/91 *Solvay v Commission* [1995] ECR II–1775, paragraph 81, and Case C–199/99 P *Corus UK v Commission* [2003] ECR I–11177, paragraphs 125 to 128). Those documents include both incriminating evidence and exculpatory evidence, save where the business secrets of other undertakings, the internal documents of the Commission or other confidential information are involved (see Case 85/76 *Hoffmann-La Roche v Commission* [1979] ECR 461, paragraphs 9 and 11; Case C–51/92 P *Hercules Chemicals v Commission* [1999] ECR I–4235, paragraph 75; and Joined Cases C–238/99 P, C 244/99 P, C–245/99 P, C–247/99 P, C–250/99 P to C–252/99 P and C–254/99 P *Limburgse Vinyl Maatschappij and others v Commission* [2002] ECR I–8375, paragraph 315).' (para 68)

'It may be that the undertaking draws the Commission's attention to documents capable of providing a different economic explanation for the overall economic assessment carried out by the Commission, in particular those describing the relevant market and the importance and the conduct of the undertakings acting on that market (see, to that effect, *Solvay v Commission*, cited above, paragraphs 76 and 77).' (para 69)

'The European Court of Human Rights has none the less held that, just like observance of the other procedural safeguards enshrined in Article 6(1) of the ECHR, compliance with the adversarial principle relates only to judicial proceedings before a "tribunal" and that there is no general, abstract principle that the parties must in all instances have the opportunity to attend the interviews carried out or to receive copies of all the documents taken into account in the case of other persons (see, to that effect, Euro Court HR, the *Kerojärvi v Finland* judgment of 19 July 1995, Series A No 322, 42, and the *Mantovanelli v France* judgment of 18 March 1997, Reports of Judgments and Decisions 1997 I, 33).' (para 70)

'The failure to communicate a document constitutes a breach of the rights of the defence only if the undertaking concerned shows, first, that the Commission relied on that document to support its objection concerning the existence of an infringement (see, to that effect, Case 322/81 *Michelin v Commission* [1983] ECR 3461, paragraphs 7 and 9) and, second, that the objection could be proved only by reference to that document (see Case 107/82 *AEG v Commission* [1983] ECR 3151, paragraphs 24 to 30, and *Solvay v Commission*, cited above, paragraph 58).' (para 71)

'If there were other documentary evidence of which the parties were aware during the administrative procedure, that specifically supported the Commission's findings, the fact that an incriminating document not communicated to the person concerned was inadmissible as evidence would not affect the validity of the objections upheld in the contested decision (see, to that effect, *Musique Diffusion Française and others v Commission*, cited above, paragraph 30, and *Solvay v Commission*, cited above, paragraph 58).' (para 72)

'It is thus for the undertaking concerned to show that the result at which the Commission arrived in its decision would have been different if a document which was not communicated to that undertaking and on which the Commission relied to make a finding of infringement against it had to be disallowed as evidence. On the other hand, where an exculpatory document has not been communicated, the undertaking concerned must only establish that its non-disclosure was able to influence, to its disadvantage, the course of the proceedings and the content of the decision of the Commission.' (paras 73, 74).

'It is sufficient for the undertaking to show that it would have been able to use the exculpatory documents in its defence (see *Hercules Chemicals v Commission*, paragraph 81, and *Limburgse Vinyl Maatschappij and others v Commission*, paragraph 318), in the sense that, had it been able to rely on them during the administrative procedure, it would have been able to put forward evidence which did not agree with the findings made by the Commission at that stage and would therefore have been able to have some influence on the Commission's assessment in any decision it adopted, at least as regards the gravity and duration of the conduct of which it was accused and, accordingly, the level of the fine (see, to that effect, *Solvay v Commission*, paragraph 98). (para 75)

'The possibility that a document which was not disclosed might have influenced the course of the proceedings and the content of the Commission's decision can be established only if a provisional examination of certain evidence shows that the documents not disclosed might in the light of that evidence have had a significance which ought not to have been disregarded (see *Solvay v Commission*, paragraph 68).' (para 76)

'In the context of that provisional analysis, it is for the Court of First Instance alone to assess the value which should be attached to the evidence produced to it (see order of 17 September 1996 in Case C–19/95 P *San Marco v Commission* [1996] ECR I–4435, paragraph 40). As stated at paragraph 49 of this judgment, its assessment of the facts does not, provided the evidence is not distorted, constitute a question of law which is subject, as such, to review by the Court of Justice.' (para 77)

Comment

In Case T–30/91 *Solvay SA v Commission*, [1995] ECR II–1775, [1996] 5 CMLR 57, the CFI held that where difficult and complex economic appraisals are to be made, the Commission must give the advisers of the undertaking concerned the opportunity to examine documents which may be relevant so that their probative value for the defence can be assessed. In this respect, it cannot be for the Commission alone to decide which documents are of use for the defence. If the Commission were to do so, the rights of defence which the applicant enjoys during the administrative procedure would be excessively restricted in relation to the powers of the Commission, which would then act as both the authority notifying the objections and the deciding authority, while having more detailed knowledge of the case-file than the defence. (paras 81, 83) 'That is particularly true where parallel conduct is concerned, which is characterised by a set of actions that are prima facie neutral, where documents may just as easily be interpreted in a way favourable to the undertakings concerned as in an unfavourable way. The Court considers that in such circumstances any error made by the Commission's officials in categorising as "neutral" a given document which, as an item of irrelevant evidence, will not then be disclosed to the undertakings, must not be allowed to impair their defence. The opposite view, for which the Commission contends, would mean that such an error could not be discovered in time, before adoption of the Commission's decision, except in the exceptional case where the undertakings concerned cooperated spontaneously, which would present unacceptable risks for the sound administration of justice.' (para 82)

AKZO Chemie BV and AKZO Chemie UK Ltd v Commission	**Public Enforcement**
Case 53/85	Professional Secrecy
ECJ, [1986] ECR 1965, [1987] 1 CMLR 231	

Facts

The Commission investigated allegations that Akzo abused its dominant position by engaging in a pricing policy aimed at eliminating its competitor, ECS, from the flour additives market (see page 135 for a description of the abuse). As part of the administrative procedure the Commission disclosed documents it obtained through the investigation to ECS, so the latter could prepare for the hearing in the case. Akzo informed the Commission that several of the documents involved were subjected to protection as business secrets. The Commission took the view that it was for it to decide whether the documents in questions were confidential or not and released to ECS some of the documents flagged by Akzo as confidential. Akzo objected the disclosure and brought an action for a declaration that the Commission's decision to transmit confidential documents to ECS was void.

Held

'[Article 287 EC] requires the officials and other servants of the institutions of the Community not to disclose information in their possession of the kind covered by the obligation of professional secrecy. Article 20 of Regulation No 17/62, which implements that provision in regard to the rules applicable to undertakings, contains in paragraph (2) a special provision worded as follows: "without prejudice to the provisions of Articles 19 and 21, the Commission and the competent authorities of the Member States, their officials and other servants shall not disclose information acquired by them as a result of the application of this Regulation and of the kind covered by the obligation of professional secrecy."' (para 26)

'The provisions of Articles 19 and 21, the application of which is thus reserved, deal with the Commission's obligations in regard to hearings and the publication of Decisions. It follows that the obligation of professional secrecy laid down in Article 20(2) is mitigated in regard to third parties on whom Article 19(2) confers the right to be heard, that is to say in regard, in particular, to a third party who has made a complaint. The Commission may communicate to such a party certain information covered by the obligation of professional secrecy in so far as it is necessary to do so for the proper conduct of the investigation.' (para 27)

'However, that power does not apply to all documents of the kind covered by the obligation of professional secrecy. Article 19(3) which provides for the publication of notices prior to the granting of negative clearance or exemptions, and Article 21 which provides for the publication of certain Decisions, both require the Commission to have regard to the legitimate interest of undertakings in the protection of their business secrets. Business secrets are thus afforded very special protection. Although they deal with particular situations, those provisions must be regarded as the expression of a general principle which applies during the course of the administrative procedure. It follows that a third party who has submitted a complaint may not in any circumstances be given access to documents containing business secrets. Any other solution would lead to the unacceptable consequence that an undertaking might be inspired to lodge a complaint with the Commission solely in order to gain access to its competitors' business secrets.' (para 28)

'It is undoubtedly for the Commission to assess whether or not a particular document contains business secrets. After giving an undertaking an opportunity to state its views, the Commission is required to adopt a Decision in that connection which contains an adequate statement of the reasons on which it is based and which must be notified to the undertaking concerned. Having regard to the extremely serious damage which could result from improper communication of documents to a competitor, the Commission must, before implementing its Decision, give the undertaking an opportunity to bring an action before the court with a view to having the assessments made reviewed by it and to preventing disclosure of the documents in question.' (para 29)

'In this case, the Commission gave the undertaking concerned an opportunity to make its position known and adopted a Decision containing an adequate statement of the reasons on which it was based and concerning both the confidential nature of the documents at issue and the possibility of communicating them. At the same time, however, by an act which cannot be severed from that Decision, the Commission decided to hand over the documents to the third party who had made the complaint even before it notified its findings to that undertaking. It thus made it impossible for the undertaking to avail itself of the means of redress provided by Article 173 in conjunction with Article 185 of the Treaty with a view to preventing the implementation of a contested Decision.' (para 30)

'That being the case, the Decision which the Commission notified to the applicant by letter of 18 December 1984 must be declared void without there being any need to determine whether the documents communicated to the intervener did in fact contain business secrets.' (para 31)

Comment

In Case 85/76 *Hoffmann-La Roche & Co AG v Commission*, [1979] ECR 461, [1979] 3 CMLR 211, the ECJ commented that 'the said Article 20 by providing undertakings, from whom information has been obtained, with a guarantee that their interests which are closely connected with observance of professional secrecy, are not jeopardized, enables the Commission to collect on the widest possible scale the requisite data for the fulfilment of the task conferred upon it by [Articles 81 and 82 EC] without the undertakings being able to prevent it from doing so, but it does not nevertheless allow it to use, to the detriment of the undertakings involved in a proceeding referred to in Regulation No 17, facts, circumstances or documents which it cannot in its view disclose if such a refusal of disclosure adversely affects that undertaking's opportunity to make known effectively its views on the truth or implications of those circumstances, on those documents or again on the conclusions drawn by the Commission from them.' (para 14)

In Case C–36/92 *SEP v Commission*, [1994] ECR I–1911, the ECJ held that when the Commission is obliged under Article 10 of Regulation 17/62 to transmit documents to the competent authorities of the Member States, that obligation may be limited by the general principle of the right of undertakings to protection of their business secrets. When an undertaking raises before the Commission the confidential nature of a document as against the competent national authorities, it is for the Commission to judge whether or not a particular document contains business secrets. The undertaking should have an opportunity to state its views before the Commission reaches a decision on the matter. If the Commission wishes to transmit a document to the national authorities notwithstanding the claim that that document is of a confidential nature with respect to those authorities, it must, before implementing its decision, give the undertaking an opportunity to bring an action before the Court with a view to having the assessments made reviewed by it and to preventing the contested disclosure.

Regulation 17/62 was replaced by Regulation 1/2003. Article 28(2), Regulation 1/2003 stipulates that 'the Commission and the competition authorities of the Member States ... shall not disclose information acquired or exchanged by them pursuant to this Regulation and of the kind covered by the obligation of professional secrecy.' Also note Article 16, Regulation 773/2004, which provides further guidance on the identification and protection of confidential information.

Also note Recital 16, Regulation 1/2003, which states that the exchange of information and the use of such information in evidence should be allowed between the members of the European Competition Network even where the information is confidential.

Orkem v Commission
Case 374/87
ECJ, [1989] ECR 3283, [1991] 4 CMLR 502

Public Enforcement
Rights of the Defence
Self-incrimination

Facts

An action by Orkem SA for the annulment of a Commission decision which required it to reply to questions set out in a request for information issued by the Commission. Orkem SA argued that, among other things, the request in question breached its rights of defence as it compelled it to incriminate itself by confessing to an infringement of the competition rules and to inform against other undertakings.

Held

Regulation 17/62 conferred on the Commission wide powers of investigation and imposed on undertakings the obligation to cooperate actively in the investigative measures. This obligation implies that the undertaking must make available to the Commission all information relating to the subject-matter of the investigation. The Regulation does not give an undertaking under investigation any right to evade the investigation on the ground that the results thereof might provide evidence of an infringement by it of the competition rules. (paras 20–27)

In the absence of any right to remain silent expressly embodied in Regulation 17/62, it is appropriate to consider the general principles of Community law, of which fundamental rights form an integral part. 'In general, the laws of the Member States grant the right not to give evidence against oneself only to a natural person charged with an offence in criminal proceedings. A comparative analysis of national law does not therefore indicate the existence of such a principle, common to the laws of the Member States, which may be relied upon by legal persons in relation to infringements in the economic sphere, in particular infringements of competition law.' (paras 28, 29)

'As far as Article 6 of the European Convention is concerned, although it may be relied upon by an undertaking subject to an investigation relating to competition law, it must be observed that neither the wording of that article nor the decisions of the European Court of Human Rights indicate that it upholds the right not to give evidence against oneself.' (para 30)

'Article 14 of the International Covenant, which upholds, in addition to the presumption of innocence, the right (in paragraph 3(g)) not to give evidence against oneself or to confess guilt, relates only to persons accused of a criminal offence in court proceedings and thus has no bearing on investigations in the field of competition law.' (para 31)

'It is necessary, however, to consider whether certain limitations on the Commission's powers of investigation are implied by the need to safeguard the rights of the defence which the Court has held to be a fundamental principle of the Community legal order (judgment of 9 November 1983 in Case 322/82 *Michelin v Commission* [1983] ECR 3461, paragraph 7).' (para 32)

'In that connection, the Court observed recently, in its judgment of 21 September 1989 in Joined Cases 46/87 and 227/88 *Hoechst v Commission* [1989] ECR 2859, paragraph 15, that whilst it is true that the rights of the defence must be observed in administrative procedures which may lead to the imposition of penalties, it is necessary to prevent those rights from being irremediably impaired during preliminary inquiry procedures which may be decisive in providing evidence of the unlawful nature of conduct engaged in by undertakings and for which they may be liable. Consequently, although certain rights of the defence relate only to contentious proceedings which follow the delivery of the statement of objections, other rights must be respected even during the preliminary inquiry.' (para 33)

'Accordingly, whilst the Commission is entitled, in order to preserve the useful effect of Article 11(2) and (5) of Regulation No 17, to compel an undertaking to provide all necessary information concerning such facts as may be known to it and to disclose to it, if necessary, such documents relating thereto as are in its possession, even if the latter may be used to establish, against it or another undertaking, the existence of anti-competitive conduct, it may not, by means of a decision calling for information, undermine the rights of defence of the undertaking concerned.' (para 34)

'Thus, the Commission may not compel an undertaking to provide it with answers which might involve an admission on its part of the existence of an infringement which it is incumbent upon the Commission to prove.' (para 35)

Comment

In Case T–34/93 *Société Générale v Commission*, [1995] ECR II–545, [1996] 4 CMLR 665, the CFI held that 'whilst the Commission is entitled, in order to preserve the effectiveness of Article 11(2) and (5) of Regulation No 17, to compel an undertaking to provide all necessary information, even if that information may be used to establish, against it or another undertaking, the existence of anti-competitive conduct, it may not, by means of a request for information, undermine the rights of defence of the undertaking concerned and compel it to provide answers which might involve an admission on its part of the existence of an infringement which it is incumbent on the Commission to prove (*Orkem*, paragraphs 34 and 35, and Case 27/88 *Solvay v Commission* [1989] ECR 3355, summary publication).' (para 74)

In Case C–238/99 etc *Limburgse Vinyl Maatschappij NV and others v Commission*, [2002] ECR I–8375, [2003] 4 CMLR 10, the ECJ considered possible infringement of the privilege against self-incrimination. It referred to the *Orkem* judgment and held that 'the *Orkem* judgment thus acknowledged as one of the general principles of Community law, of which fundamental rights are an integral part and in the light of which all Community laws must be interpreted, the right of undertakings not to be compelled by the Commission, under Article 11 of Regulation No 17, to admit their participation in an infringement (see *Orkem*, paragraphs 28, 38 in fine and 39). The protection of that right means that, in the event of a dispute as to the scope of a question, it must be determined whether an answer from the undertaking to which the question is addressed is in fact equivalent to the admission of an infringement, such as to undermine the rights of the defence.' (para 273) 'The parties agree that, since *Orkem*, there have been further developments in the case-law of the European Court of Human Rights which the Community judicature must take into account when interpreting the fundamental rights, as introduced by the judgment in *Funke* [Series A No 256 A], on which the appellants rely, and the judgments of 17 December 1996 in *Saunders v United Kingdom* (Reports of Judgments and Decisions 1996–VI, p 2044) and of 3 May 2001 in *JB v Switzerland* (not yet published in the Reports of Judgments and Decisions).' (para 274) 'However, both the *Orkem* judgment and the recent case-law of the European Court of Human Rights require, first, the exercise of coercion against the suspect in order to obtain information from him and, second, establishment of the existence of an actual interference with the right which they define.' (para 275) 'Examined in the light of that finding and the specific circumstances of the present case, the ground of appeal alleging infringement of the privilege against self-incrimination does not permit annulment of the contested judgment on the basis of the developments in the case-law of the European Court of Human Rights.' (para 276)

Regulation 17/62 was replaced by Regulation 1/2003. Recital 23, Regulation 1/2003 stipulates that: When complying with a decision of the Commission, undertakings cannot be forced to admit that they have committed an infringement, but they are in any event obliged to answer factual questions and to provide documents, even if this information may be used to establish against them or against another undertaking the existence of an infringement.' Recital 37, Regulation 1/2003 adds that 'this Regulation respects the fundamental rights and observes the principles recognised in particular by the Charter of Fundamental Rights of the European Union. Accordingly, this Regulation should be interpreted and applied with respect to those rights and principles.'

On the distinction between factual questions and admission, see further page 243 below.

Mannesmannröhren-Werke AG v EC Commission	**Public Enforcement**
Case T–112/98	Right of Defence
CFI, [2001] ECR II–729, [2001] 5 CMLR 1	Self-incrimination

Facts

The applicant Mannesmannröhren-Werke AG (MW) refused to reply to a request for information made by the Commission under Article 11 of Regulation 17/62. The request for information was made as part of an investigation with respect to the applicant and other producers of steel tubes, in the course of which the Commission carried out inspections on the premises of the undertakings involved. The Commission rejected MW's argument that it was not obliged to provide the information and adopted a decision imposing a fine on MW if it failed to provide the information. MW applied for annulment of the Commission's decision.

Held

There is no absolute right to silence in competition proceedings.

The Commission's power of investigation during a preliminary investigation is limited insofar as it cannot undermine the right of defence. Such limitation does not give rise to an absolute right to silence, but to a partial right to silence to the extent that an undertaking would not be compelled to provide answers which might involve an admission of the existence of an infringement. (paras 59–69)

MW was obliged to respond to questions of a purely factual nature and to provide the Commission with details of meetings between steel tube producers. MW was not obliged to respond to questions which did not concern exclusively factual information and might have compelled it to admit its participation in an unlawful agreement. (paras 70–3)

Answering purely factual questions cannot be regarded as undermining the right of defence as the undertaking is free to put forward its own interpretation as to the meaning of the documents produced by it. (para 78)

The contested decision was annulled in so far as it obliged MW to answer questions which might involve it in admitting that it was a party to an anticompetitive agreement.

Comment

Recital 23 of Regulation 1/2003 reasserts the above principle and states that when complying with a decision of the Commission requiring information 'undertakings cannot be forced to admit that they have committed an infringement, but they are in any event obliged to answer factual questions and to provide documents, even if this information may be used to establish against them or against another undertaking the existence of an infringement'.

The European Court of Human Rights recognised a right to remain silent in criminal cases (see additional discussion in *Orkem*, page 241 above). Consequently, the use by National Competition Authorities of information gathered under the partial right to silence rule in Regulation 1/2003 would be limited in cases involving criminal proceedings. Note Recital 37 of Regulation 1/2003, which states that the Regulation should be interpreted and applied with due regard being given to fundamental rights and principles recognised in particular by the Charter of Fundamental Rights of the European Union.

Note Case C–301/04 P *Commission v SGL Carbon* [2006] ECR I–5915, in which the ECJ held that an undertaking is subject to an obligation to cooperate actively with the Commission. Accordingly, it must make available to the Commission all information relating to the subject matter of the investigation (para 40).

AM&S Europe Limited v Commission   **Public Enforcement**
Case 155/79   Legal Privilege
ECJ, [1982] ECR 1575, [1982] 2 CMLR 264

Facts

Commission officials arrived at the offices of AM&S to conduct an unannounced investigation under Article 14, Regulation 17/62. Following two days of inspections, the officials seized a number of documents and left a written request, asking AM&S to provide additional documents. AM&S supplied some, but not all, of the documents required, arguing that these were protected by legal privilege. The Commission adopted a decision requiring AM&S to produce for examination all the documents for which legal privilege was claimed (Commission Decision 79/760/EEC). AM&S lodged an application to declare the decision void.

Held

Articles 11 and 14 of Regulation 17/62 provide that the Commission may obtain information and undertake the necessary investigation in order to bring to an end an infringement of community competition laws. Article 14(1) in particular empowers the Commission to require production of business records, that is to say, documents concerning the market activities of the undertaking, in particular as regards compliance with those rules. Written communications between lawyer and client fall, in so far as they have a bearing on such activities, within the category of documents referred to in Articles 11 and 14. (paras 15–7)

'However, the above rules do not exclude the possibility of recognizing, subject to certain conditions, that certain business records are of a confidential nature. Community law, which derives from not only the economic but also the legal interpenetration of the Member States, must take into account the principles and concepts common to the laws of those states concerning the observance of confidentiality, in particular, as regards certain communications between lawyer and client. That confidentiality serves the requirements, the importance of which is recognized in all of the Member States, that any person must be able, without constraint, to consult a lawyer whose profession entails the giving of independent legal advice to all those in need of it.' (para 18)

'As far as the protection of written communications between lawyer and client is concerned, it is apparent from the legal systems of the Member States that, although the principle of such protection is generally recognized, its scope and the criteria for applying it vary. Whilst in some of the Member States the protection against disclosure afforded to written communications between lawyer and client is based principally on a recognition of the very nature of the legal profession, inasmuch as it contributes towards the maintenance of the rule of law, in other Member States the same protection is justified by the more specific requirement (which, moreover, is also recognized in the first-mentioned states) that the rights of the defence must be respected.' (paras 19–20)

'Apart from these differences, however, there are to be found in the national laws of the Member States common criteria inasmuch as those laws protect, in similar circumstances, the confidentiality of written communications between lawyer and client provided that, on the one hand, such communications are made for the purposes and in the interests of the client's rights of defence and, on the other hand, they emanate from independent lawyers, that is to say, lawyers who are not bound to the client by a relationship of employment. (para 21)

'Viewed in that context Regulation No 17 must be interpreted as protecting, in its turn, the confidentiality of written communications between lawyer and client subject to those two conditions, and thus incorporating such elements of that protection as are common to the laws of the Member States. (para 22)

'As far as the first of those two conditions is concerned, in Regulation No 17 itself, in particular in the eleventh recital in its preamble and in the provisions contained in Article 19, care is taken to ensure that the rights of the defence may be exercised to the full, and the protection of the confidentiality of written communications between lawyer and client is an essential corollary to those rights. In those circumstances, such protection must, if it is to be effective, be recognized as covering all written communications exchanged after the initiation of the administrative procedure under Regulation No 17 which may lead to a Decision on the application of [Articles 81 and 82 EC] or to a Decision imposing a pecuniary sanction on the undertaking. It must also be possible to extend it to earlier written communications which have a relationship to the subject-matter of that procedure.' (para 23)

'As regards the second condition, it should be stated that the requirement as to the position and status as an independent lawyer, which must be fulfilled by the legal adviser from whom the written communications which may be protected emanate, is based on a conception of the lawyer's role as collaborating in the administration of justice by the courts and as being required to provide, in full independence, and in the overriding interests of that cause, such legal assistance as the client needs. The counterpart of that protection lies in the rules of professional ethics and discipline which are laid down and enforced in the general interest by institutions endowed with the requisite powers for that purpose. Such a conception reflects the legal traditions common to the Member States and is also to be found in legal order of the Community, as is demonstrated by Article 17 of the protocols on the statutes of the Court of Justice of the EEC and the EAEC, and also by Article 20 of the protocol on the statute of the Court of Justice of the ECSC.' (para 24)

The protection to written communications between lawyer and client must apply without distinction to any lawyer entitled to practice his profession in one of the Member States, regardless of the Member State in which the client lives. (para 25)

'In view of all these factors it must therefore be concluded that although Regulation No 17, and in particular Article 14 thereof, interpreted in the light of its wording, structure and aims, and having regard to the laws of the Member States, empowers the Commission to require, in the course of an investigation within the meaning of that Article, production of the business documents the disclosure of which it considers necessary, including written communications between lawyer and client, for proceedings in respect of any infringements of [Articles 81 and 82 EC], that power is, however, subject to a restriction imposed by the need to protect confidentiality, on the conditions defined above, and provided that the communications in question are exchanged between an independent lawyer, that is to say one who is not bound to his client by a relationship of employment, and his client.' (para 27)

If an undertaking which refuses, on the ground that it is entitled to protection of the confidentiality of information, to produce, written communications between itself and its lawyer, it must nevertheless provide the Commission with relevant material of such a nature as to demonstrate that the communications fulfil the conditions for being granted legal protection as defined above, although it is not bound to reveal the contents of the communications in question. Where the Commission is not satisfied that such evidence has been supplied, the solution of disputes as to the application of the protection of the confidentiality of written communications between lawyer and client may be sought only at Community level. In that case it is for the Commission to order, production of the communications in question and, if necessary, to impose on the undertaking fines or periodic penalty payments for the undertaking's refusal to supply such evidence. The undertaking will then be able to bring an action against the decision under Article 242 EC. Such an action does not have suspensory effect yet the interests of the undertaking concerned are safeguarded by the possibility which exists under Articles 242 and 243 EC, as well as under Article 83 of the rules of procedure of the Court, of obtaining an order suspending the application of the Decision which has been taken, or any other interim measure. (paras 29–32)

Comment

See the Hilti judgment on page 246 below and the Akzo judgment of 17 September 2007, on page 247 below.

Hilti AG v Commission	**Public Enforcement**
Case T–30/89	Legal Privilege
CFI, [1990] ECR II–163, [1990] 4 CMLR 602	Independent lawyer/In-house counsel

Facts

Hilti AG brought an action for the annulment of a Commission Decision relating to a proceeding under Article 82 EC (IV/30.787 *Eurofix-Bauco v Hilti*). Two other undertakings, Bauco (UK) Ltd and Profix Distribution Ltd, were granted leave to intervene in the case in support of the Commission's decision. Hilti AG requested that certain documents in its submission be treated, vis-à-vis the interveners, as confidential. With respect to a few of the documents it argued that they were covered by legal professional privilege and should be treated as confidential. It submitted that the documents should not be disclosed to the interveners, even though, vis-à-vis the Commission, it waived that privilege.

Held

'The Court of Justice has held (Case 155/79 AM&S v Commission) that Regulation No 17 must be interpreted as protecting the confidentiality of written communications between lawyer and client provided that, on the one hand, such communications are made for the purposes and in the interests of the client's right of defence and, on the other hand, they emanate from independent lawyers, that is to say, lawyers who are not bound to the client by a relationship of employment. In the same judgment the Court of Justice held that that protection must, in the administrative procedure before the Commission, be recognized as covering all written communications exchanged after the initiation of the administrative procedure which may lead to a decision on the application of [Articles 81 and 82 EC] or to a decision imposing a pecuniary sanction on the undertaking. The Court of Justice further held that that protection must be extended to earlier written communications which have a relationship to the subject-matter of that procedure.' (para 13)

'In this case the letter in point is one sent to the applicant by an independent lawyer, after the initiation of the administrative procedure before the Commission, for the purposes and in the interests of the applicant's right of defence that letter must accordingly be regarded as confidential within the meaning of Article 93(4) of the Rules of Procedure. It follows that the applicant's request must be allowed.' (para 14)

With respect to additional documents for which confidential treatment is requested, these include internal notes distributed within the undertaking which reported the content of advice received from external legal advisers. Such legal advice would be covered by the principle of the protection of confidentiality. The principle of the protection of written communications between lawyer and client extends also to the internal notes which are confined to reporting the text or the content of those communications. (paras 15–18)

Comment

In Case IV/35.733 *Volkswagen AG and others*, [1998] 5 CMLR 33, the Commission commented in its decision that 'pursuant to Article 14(1) [Regulation 17/62] the Commission may in the course of an investigation examine the undertaking's business records. "Business Records" are those which relate to the activity of the undertakings on the relevant market. Written communication between lawyer and client are in this respect "records" in the meaning of Article 14. Regulation 17 protects the confidentiality of written communications between lawyer and client, but only on condition that, on the one hand, such communications are made for the purpose and in the interest of the client's rights of defence and, on the other hand, they emanate from independent lawyers, that is to say lawyers who are not bound to the client by a relationship of employment.' (para 199)

In Case IV/30.809 *Re John Deere Tractors*, [1985] 2 CMLR 554, the Commission used as evidence communication between the company and its in house counsel to establish that the undertakings knew that the conduct was contrary to EC and national competition law. (para 21) 'Deere's own in-house counsel expressed doubts as to legitimacy of such device.' (para 27)

Akzo Nobel Chemicals and Akcros Chemicals Ltd v Commission	**Public Enforcement**
Joined Cases T–125/03 and T–253/03	Legal Privilege
CFI, [2007] CILL 2513	In-house Counsel

Facts

The Commission conducted an investigation regarding possible infringements of Community competition law by Akzo Nobel and Akcros Chemicals. During the investigation the Commission raided Akzo's offices and obtained various documents in accordance with its investigative powers under Article 14(3), Regulation 17/62. Akzo claimed that some of the documents were protected by professional privilege. Some of the documents included internal communications for the purpose of obtaining external legal advice on competition maters. These were placed in sealed envelops titled 'Set A'. Another group of documents, classified as 'Set B', included email correspondences between Akzo's in-house counsel (titled 'competition law coordinator') who was a registered attorney at the Dutch bar, and the General Manager of Akcros Chemicals. The 'Set B' documents were not sealed in an envelope, as the Commission was of the opinion that they did not benefit from legal privilege. Akzo claimed that both sets of documents were protected by professional privilege. Following a Commission decision, in which it indicated that it intended to read the 'Set A' documents the undertakings applied for interim measures seeking suspension of the operation of the decision. The president of the CFI granted a preliminary order requiring the Commission to deposit the 'Set A' documents at the registry of the CFI. Both the Commission and Akzo/Akcros appealed the president's order.

Held

'… if an undertaking which is the subject of an investigation under Article 14 of Regulation No 17 refuses, by claiming protection under [legal professional privilege], to produce, as part of the business records demanded by the Commission, written communications between itself and its lawyer, it must nevertheless provide the Commission officials with relevant material which demonstrates that the communications fulfill the conditions for the grant of legal protection, while not being bound to disclose their contents. … where the Commission considers that such evidence has not been provided, it must, pursuant to Article 14(3) of Regulation No 17, order production of the communications in question and, if necessary, impose on the undertaking fines or periodic penalty payments under that regulation as a penalty for the undertaking's refusal either to supply such additional evidence as the Commission considers necessary or to produce the documents whose confidentiality, in the Commission's view, is not protected in law (*AM&S*, paragraphs 29 to 31). The undertaking under investigation may subsequently bring an action for the annulment of such a Commission decision, where appropriate, coupled with a request for interim relief pursuant to Articles 242 EC and 243 EC (see, to that effect, *AM&S*, paragraph 32).' (para 79)

'In a significant number of cases, a mere cursory look by the Commission officials at the general layout, heading, title or other superficial features of the document will enable them to confirm the accuracy of the reasons invoked by the undertaking and to determine whether the document at issue was confidential, when deciding whether to put it aside. Nevertheless, on certain occasions, there would be a risk that, even with a cursory look at the document, in spite of the superficial nature of their examination, the Commission officials would gain access to information covered by legal professional privilege. That may be so, in particular, if the confidentiality of the document in question is not clear from external indications.' (para 81)

'As stated in paragraph 79 above, it is clear from AM & S that the undertaking concerned is not bound to reveal their contents when presenting the Commission officials with relevant material of such a nature as to demonstrate that the documents fulfill the conditions for being granted legal protection (paragraph 29 of the judgment). Accordingly, the Court concludes that an undertaking subject to an investigation under Article 14(3) of Regulation No 17 is entitled to refuse to allow the Commission officials to take even a cursory look at one or more specific documents which it claims to be covered by [legal professional privilege], provided that the undertaking considers that such a cursory look is impossible without revealing the content of those documents and that it gives the Commission officials appropriate reasons for its view.' (para 82)

Where the Commission and the undertakings are not in agreement as to the confidential nature of the document, the Commission officials may place a copy of the document in a sealed envelope and then remove it with a view to a subsequent resolution of the dispute. This procedure enables risks of a breach of legal professional privilege to be avoided while at the same time enabling the Commission to retain a certain control over the documents forming the subject-matter of the investigation. In any event, the Commission must not read the contents of the document before it has adopted a decision allowing the undertaking concerned to refer the matter to the CFI, and, if appropriate, to make an application for interim relief. Having regard to the particular nature of the principle of legal professional privilege, the purpose of which is both to guarantee the full exercise of individuals' rights of defence and to safeguard the requirement that any person must be able, without constraint, to consult his lawyer, the Court considers that the fact that the Commission reads the content of a confidential document is in itself a breach of this principle. Protection under legal professional privilege requires the Commission, once it has adopted its decision rejecting a request under that head, not to read the content of the documents in question until it has given the undertaking concerned the opportunity to refer the matter to the CFI. (paras 83–7)

'In those circumstances, the Court considers that the Commission forced the applicants to accept the cursory look at the disputed documents, even though, as regards the two copies of the typewritten memorandum in Set A and the handwritten notes in Set B, the applicants' representatives claimed, and provided supporting justification, that such an examination would require the contents of those documents to be disclosed. The Court would point out that a cursory look at the documents was unlikely to allow the Commission officials to assess whether they were confidential without at the same time giving them the opportunity to read their content. Accordingly, the Court concludes that the Commission infringed the procedure for protection under legal professional privilege in this regard.' (para 95)

'... according to the judgment in AM&S, Regulation No 17 is to be interpreted as protecting the confidentiality of communications between lawyer and client provided that (i) such communications are made for the purposes of the exercise of the client's rights of defence and (ii) they emanate from independent lawyers (paragraphs 21, 22 and 27 of the judgment). As far as the first of those two conditions is concerned, such protection must, if it is to be effective, be recognised as covering as a matter of law all written communications exchanged after the initiation of the administrative procedure under the regulation which may lead to a decision on the application of Articles 81 EC and 82 EC or to a decision imposing a pecuniary sanction on the undertaking. That protection can also extend to earlier written communications which have a relationship to the subject-matter of that procedure (AM & S, paragraph 23). In the order in Hilti v Commission, it was held that legal professional privilege must, in view of its purpose, be regarded as extending also to the internal notes circulated within an undertaking which are confined to reporting the text or the content of communications with independent lawyers containing legal advice (paragraphs 13 and 16 to 18 of the order).' (para 117)

In the present case, 'the Set A documents do not by themselves constitute written communications with an independent lawyer or an internal note reporting the content of a communication with such a lawyer. Nor do the applicants submit that those documents were prepared in order to be sent physically to an independent lawyer. Accordingly, it must be held that those documents do not formally come within the categories of documents expressly identified in the abovementioned case-law.' (para 118)

The applicants claim that the documents must be recognised as being covered by legal professional privilege since, in their view, they were drawn up, for the particular purpose of seeking legal advice. (para 119)

Legal professional privilege meets the need to ensure that every person must be able, without constraint, to consult a lawyer whose profession entails the giving of independent legal advice to all those in need of it. So that a person may effectively consult a lawyer without constraint, it may be necessary, in certain circumstances, for the client to prepare working documents or summaries and gather information which will be used by the lawyer. Such preparatory documents, even if they were not exchanged with a lawyer or were not created for the purpose of being sent physically to a lawyer, may none the less be covered by legal professional privilege, provided that they were drawn up exclusively for the purpose of seeking legal advice from a lawyer in exercise of the rights of the defence. The mere fact that a document has been discussed with a lawyer is not sufficient to give it such protection. (paras 120–24)

However, in this case the applicants did not prove that the two copies of the memorandum constituting the Set A documents were prepared exclusively for the purposes of seeking legal advice from a lawyer in exercise of the rights of the defence. The documents are therefore not protected under legal professional privilege. (paras 125–35)

With respect to the protection afforded to communications with in-house lawyers, the Court of Justice in *AM&S* expressly held that the protection accorded to legal professional privilege under Community law, only applies to the extent that the lawyer is independent, that is to say, not bound to his client by a relationship of employment (paragraphs 21, 22 and 27 of the *AM&S* judgment). (para 166)

'It follows that the Court expressly excluded communications with in-house lawyers, that is, legal advisers bound to their clients by a relationship of employment, from protection under LPP. It must also be pointed out that the Court reached a conscious decision on that exception, given that the issue had been debated at length during the proceeding and that Advocate General Sir Gordon Slynn had expressly proposed in his Opinion for that judgment that where a lawyer bound by an employment contract remains a member of the profession and subject to its discipline and ethics, he should be treated in the same way as independent lawyers (Opinion of Advocate General Sir Gordon Slynn in *AM&S*, p 1655).' (para 167)

'… an examination of the laws of the Member States shows that, even though it is the case, as the applicants and certain interveners submit, that specific recognition of the role of in-house lawyers and the protection of communications with such lawyers under [legal professional privilege] is relatively more common today than when the judgment in AM & S was handed down, it is not possible, nevertheless, to identify tendencies which are uniform or have clear majority support in that regard in the laws of the Member States.' (para 170)

The fact that the correspondence in this case was protected under national laws does not mean that Community law should also afford such protection. This is especially the case when taking into account the uniform application of the Commission's powers in the common market. (para 176)

Comment

The CFI clarified that legal professional privilege does not extend to communications with in-house lawyers.

Arguably, the modernisation of European competition law and the emphasis on self-assessment by undertakings increase the reliance on legal advice and may justify legal privilege for in-house communications, to increase the effectiveness of in house lawyers. However in paragraphs 172 and 173 the Court noted that the issues linked to self-assessment are not directly relevant to legal professional privilege. The Court added that 'such exercises of self-assessment and strategy definition may be conducted by an outside lawyer in full cooperation with the relevant departments of the undertaking, including its internal legal department. In that context, communications between in-house lawyers and outside lawyers are in principle protected under LPP, provided that they are made for the purpose of the undertaking's exercise of the rights of defence. It is therefore clear that the personal scope of that protection, as laid down in *AM&S*, is not a real obstacle preventing undertakings from seeking the legal advice they need and does not prevent their in-house lawyers from taking part in self-assessment exercises or strategy definition.' (para 173)

Note the position in the UK where the High Court held that in-house lawyers 'are regarded by the law as in every respect in the same position as those who practice on their own account. The only difference is that they act for one client only, and not for several clients. They must uphold the same standards of honour and of etiquette. They are subject to the same duties to their client and to the court …' *Alfred Crompton Amusement Machines Ltd v Customs and Excise Commissioners* (No 2) [1972] 2 WLR 835.

In its judgment the CFI criticised the Commission for forcing the undertakings to give a cursory glance at the documents. See para 95.

Automec Srl v Commission	**Public Enforcement**
Case T–24/90	Termination of Infringement
CFI, [1992] ECR II–2223, [1992] 5 CMLR 431	

Facts

Automec Srl was in contractual relations with BMW Italia SpA which were due to expire on 31 December 1984. Prior to the expiry of the contract between the two companies, BMW Italia informed Automec of its intention not to renew the agreement. Automec brought proceedings before the Italian national court claiming that it was wrongly excluded from the distribution network, but its action was dismissed. It then made application to the Commission under Article 3(2) of Regulation 17/62, claiming that BMW Italia and BMW AG infringed Article 81 EC by refusing to continue supplying it with BMW vehicles and spare parts and preventing it from using BMW trademarks. Automec requested the Commission to order BMW Italia and BMW AG to bring the alleged infringement to an end and to resume deliveries. The Commission decided not to open an investigation on the matter, among other things, on the basis that even if the distribution agreement used by BMW was contrary to Article 81 EC, it could at most find that there was an infringement and that the agreement was therefore void. However, under Article 81 EC the Commission has no power of injunction which would allow it to require BMW to deliver, in the circumstances of this case, its own products. Automec appealed to the CFI for the annulment of the decision.

Held

'As freedom of contract must remain the rule, the Commission cannot in principle be considered to have, among the powers to issue orders which are available to it for the purpose of bringing to an end infringements of [Article 81(1) EC], the power to order a party to enter into contractual relations, since in general the Commission has suitable remedies at its disposal for the purpose of requiring an undertaking to terminate an infringement.' (para 51)

'In particular, there cannot be held to be any justification for such a restriction on freedom of contract where several remedies exist for bringing an infringement to an end. This is true of infringements of [Article 81(1) EC] arising out of the application of a distribution system. Such infringements can also be eliminated by the abandonment or amendment of the distribution system. Consequently, the Commission undoubtedly has the power to find that an infringement exists and to order the parties concerned to bring it to an end, but it is not for the Commission to impose upon the parties its own choice from among all the various potential courses of action which are in conformity with the Treaty.' (para 52)

The Commission has been entrusted with an extensive and general supervisory and regulatory task in the field of competition. It is consistent with its obligations under Community law for it to apply different degrees of priority to the cases submitted to it. A decision to close the file on a complaint will only be taken following a careful factual and legal examination of the particulars brought to its notice by the complainant. (paras 55–98)

Comment

Contrast with the Commission's powers under Article 82 EC to bring an abuse to an end. Such decision 'may include an order to do certain acts or provide certain advantages which have been wrongfully withheld as well as prohibiting the continuation of certain action, practices or situations which are contrary to the Treaty …' Case 6/73 *Istituto Chemioterapico Italiano SpA and Commercial Solvents Corporation v Commission* (para 45, [1974] ECR 223, [1974] 1 CMLR 309).

Joint selling of the media rights to FA Premier League	Public Enforcement
COMP/C–2/38.173	Commitments
European Commission, C (2006) 868 final	Article 9, Regulation 1/2003

On June 2001 the Commission opened an investigation, under Regulation 17/62, into the arrangements surrounding the FA Premier League competition. In a statement of objection issued in December 2002, the Commission concluded that the horizontal joint-selling arrangements put in place by the football clubs in the Premier League for exploitation of media rights to Premier League matches infringed Article 81 EC. The Commission was concerned that the joint-selling agreement deprived media operators and British football fans of choice, led to higher prices and reduced innovation. In July 2003 the FA Premier League introduced changes to the arrangements surrounding the sale of media rights and supplemented these with a set of commitments in December 2003 which included a commitment that no single broadcaster would be allowed to buy all of the packages of live match rights from 2007 onward. These commitments were later amended and clarified following discussions with the Commission. The amended commitments provided, among other things, for more television, mobile and internet rights to be made available and ensured that these would be sold in an open and competitive bidding process subject to scrutiny by an independent Trustee. On March 2006 the FA Premier League confirmed that the commitments it submitted are to be treated as commitments under Article 9, Regulation 1/2003 (which replaced Regulation 17/62). Subsequently, the Commission adopted a decision making these commitments binding upon the FA Premier League until 30 June 2013 and finding that there are no longer grounds for action by the Commission. The Commission could impose a fine amounting to 10 per cent of the FA Premier League's total worldwide turnover if it breaks its commitments without having to prove any violation of the EC Treaty's competition rules. The decision does not bind national competition authorities or national courts.

Coca-Cola	Public Enforcement
COMP/A.39.116/B2	Commitments
European Commission, [2005] OJ L 253/21	Article 9, Regulation 1/2003

The commitment decision was adopted pursuant to Article 9(1) of Council Regulation 1/2003. The procedure concerned the conduct by the Coca-Cola Company and its three major bottlers in the supply of carbonated soft drinks. In a preliminary assessment, the Commission expressed concerns that practices by the undertakings, including exclusivity-related requirements, growth and target rebates, infringed Article 82 EC. In order to resolve these concerns the undertakings offered a range of commitments which were formally accepted by the Commission and made binding until 31 December 2010. The Commission could impose a fine amounting to 10 per cent of Coca-Cola total worldwide turnover if Coca-Cola breaks its commitments. In the commitments the undertakings agreed, among other things, to refrain from exclusivity arrangements, target or growth rebates and tying. In addition Coca-Cola committed that where it provides a free cooler to a retailer and there is no other chilled beverage capacity in the outlet to which the consumer has a direct access, it will free at least 20 per cent of the space in the cooler provided by Coca-Cola for the display and sales of competing products.

Musique Diffusion Française SA v Commission	**Public Enforcement**
Case 100/80	Fines
ECJ, [1983] ECR 1825, [1983] 3 CMLR 221	

'… the Commission's power to impose fines on undertakings which, intentionally or negligently, commit an infringement of the provisions of [Articles 81(1) or 82 EC] is one of the means conferred on the Commission in order to enable it to carry out the task of supervision conferred on it by Community law. That task certainly includes the duty to investigate and punish individual infringements, but it also encompasses the duty to pursue a general policy designed to apply, in competition matters, the principles laid down by the Treaty and to guide the conduct of undertakings in the light of those principles.' (para 105)

'… in assessing the gravity of an infringement for the purpose of fixing the amount of the fine, the Commission must take into consideration not only the particular circumstances of the case but also the context in which the infringement occurs and must ensure that its action has the necessary deterrent effect, especially as regards those types of infringement which are particularly harmful to the attainment of the objectives of the Community.' (para 106)

'From that point of view, the Commission was right to classify as very serious infringements; prohibitions on exports and imports seeking artificially to maintain price differences between the markets of the various Member States. Such prohibitions jeopardize the freedom of intra-Community trade, which is a fundamental principle of the Treaty, and they prevent the attainment of one of its objectives, namely the creation of a single market.' (para 107)

'It was also open to the Commission to have regard to the fact that practices of this nature, although they were established as being unlawful at the outset of Community competition policy, are still relatively frequent on account of the profit that certain of the undertakings concerned are able to derive from them and, consequently, it was open to the Commission to consider that it was appropriate to raise the level of fines so as to reinforce their deterrent effect.' (para 108)

'For the same reasons, the fact that the Commission, in the past, imposed fines of a certain level for certain types of infringement does not mean that it is estopped from raising that level within the limits indicated in Regulation no 17 if that is necessary to ensure the implementation of Community competition policy. On the contrary, the proper application of the Community competition rules requires that the Commission may at any time adjust the level of fines to the needs of that policy.' (para 109)

Dansk Rørindustri A/S and others v Commission	**Public Enforcement**
Joined Cases C–189, 202, 205–208, 213/02 P	Fines
ECJ, [2005] ECR I–5425, [2005] 5 CMLR 17	

'The supervisory task conferred on the Commission by [Articles 81(1) and 82 EC] not only includes the duty to investigate and punish individual infringements but also encompasses the duty to pursue a general policy designed to apply, in competition matters, the principles laid down by the Treaty and to guide the conduct of undertakings in the light of those principles (see *Musique Diffusion Française and others v Commission*, paragraph 105).' (para 170)

'… traders cannot have a legitimate expectation that an existing situation which is capable of being altered by the Commission in the exercise of its discretionary power will be maintained (Case C–350/88 *Delacre and others v Commission* [1990] ECR I–395, paragraph 33 and the case-law cited).' (para 171)

'That principle clearly applies in the field of competition policy, which is characterised by a wide discretion on the part of the Commission, in particular as regards the determination of the amount of fines.' (para 172)

9

Competition Law and the State

Article 10, Treaty of Rome

Article 10 EC stipulates that 'Member States shall take all appropriate measures, whether general or particular, to ensure fulfilment of the obligations arising out of this Treaty or resulting from action taken by the institutions of the Community. They shall facilitate the achievement of the Community's tasks. They shall abstain from any measure which could jeopardise the attainment of the objectives of this Treaty'

Although Articles 81 and 82 EC are concerned solely with the conduct of undertakings and not with laws emanating from Member States, those articles, read in conjunction with Article 10 EC, require Member States not to introduce or maintain in force measures that may render ineffective the competition rules applicable to undertakings.

In particular, a Member State may infringe Articles 10 EC and Article 81 EC where it requires, favours or reinforces the effects of agreements or measures contrary to Article 81, or where it divests its own rules by delegating to private economic operators responsibility for taking decisions affecting the economic sphere.

See also summary references to:

Article 86(1), Treaty of Rome

Article 86(1) EC stipulates that 'In the case of public undertakings and undertakings to which Member States grant special or exclusive rights, Member States shall neither enact nor maintain in force any measure contrary to the rules contained in this Treaty, in particular to those rules provided for in Article 12 and Articles 81 to 89.'

See also summary references to:

Article 86(2), Treaty of Rome

Article 86(2) EC stipulates that 'Undertakings entrusted with the operation of services of general economic interest or having the character of a revenue-producing monopoly shall be subject to the rules contained in this Treaty, in particular to the rules on competition, insofar as the application of such rules does not obstruct the performance, in law or in fact, of the particular tasks assigned to them. The development of trade must not be affected to such an extent as would be contrary to the interests of the Community.'

Article 86(3), Treaty of Rome

'The Commission shall ensure the application of the provisions of this Article and shall, where necessary, address appropriate directives or decisions to Member States.'

State Bodies Subject to the Same Laws as Private Undertakings

The concept of 'undertakings' is central to identifying the addressees of competition law provisions. A state body may be subjected to competition law provisions when it engages in economic activity and subsequently is classified as an undertaking. See further discussion on this point in Chapter 1 above.

Federico Cipolla v Rosaria Fazari	**Competition Law and the State**
Joined Cases C–94/04 and C–202/04	Article 10 EC
ECJ, [2006] ECR I–11421, [2007] 4 CMLR 8	

Facts

References for a preliminary ruling under Article 234 EC from the Italian Corte d'appello di Torino and the Tribunale di Roma. Both references emerged from proceedings between lawyers and their respective clients in respect of the payment of fees. In both procedures the national court queried, among other things, whether Articles 10 EC, 81 EC and 82 EC preclude a Member State from adopting a legislative measure which approves, on the basis of a draft produced by a professional body of lawyers, a scale fixing a minimum fee for members of the legal profession. The scale at issue did not allow derogation in respect of either services reserved to those members or those such as out-of-court services which may also be provided by any other economic operator not subject to that scale.

Held

Although Articles 81 EC and 82 EC are concerned solely with the conduct of undertakings and not with laws emanating from Member States, those articles, read in conjunction with Article 10 EC, require Member States not to introduce or maintain in force measures, even of a legislative or regulatory nature, which may render ineffective the competition rules applicable to undertakings. 'The Court has held, in particular, that Articles 10 EC and 81 EC are infringed where a Member State requires or encourages the adoption of agreements, decisions or concerted practices contrary to Article 81 EC or reinforces their effects, or where it divests its own rules of the character of legislation by delegating to private economic operators responsibility for taking decisions affecting the economic sphere.' (paras 46–7)

The fact that a Member State requires a professional body of lawyers to produce a draft scale of fees does not, in the circumstances specific to these cases, appear to establish that that State has divested the scale finally adopted of its character of legislation by delegating to lawyers responsibility for taking decisions concerning them. According to the regulation in question the Italian State retains its power to make decisions of last resort or to review implementation of that scale. Additionally, the draft scale is not binding and is subjected to the Minister of Justice's approval. Moreover, in certain exceptional circumstances the Court may depart from the maximum and minimum limits fixed in the scale. (paras 48–51)

Consequently, the Italian State cannot be said to have delegated to private economic operators responsibility for taking decisions affecting the economic sphere, which would have the effect of depriving the provisions of the character of legislation. Additionally, in those circumstances nor is the Italian State open to the criticism that it required or encouraged the adoption of agreements, decisions or concerted practices contrary to Article 81 EC or reinforced their effects. (paras 52–3)

Comment

In its decision the Court relied on the earlier case of *Manuele Arduino* (Case C–35/99, [2002] ECR I–1529, [2002] 4 CMLR 25) which concerned similar circumstances. There the court held that '[Articles 10 and 81 EC] do not preclude a Member State from adopting a law or regulation which approves, on the basis of a draft produced by a professional body of members of the Bar, a tariff fixing minimum and maximum fees for members of the profession, where that State measure forms part of a procedure such as that laid down in the Italian legislation.' (para 44)

In his Opinion, (Joined Cases C–94/04 and C–202/04) AG Poiares Maduro provided a clear overview of the joint application of Articles 10 and 81 EC. See in particular the following extracts from the opinion:

'31. … According to case-law, [Articles 10 and 81 EC] are regarded as having been infringed only in two cases: where a Member State requires or favours the adoption of agreements, decisions or concerted practices contrary to Article 81 EC or reinforces their effects, [Case C–198/01 CIF [2003] ECR I–8055, paragraph 46] or where that State divests its own rules of the character of legislation by delegating to private economic operators responsibility for taking decisions affecting the economic sphere. [Case 136/86 *Aubert* [1987] ECR 4789, paragraph 23 and Case C–35/96 *Commission v Italy* [1998] I–3851; C–35/99 *Arduino*, paragraph 35, and Order of 17 February 2005 in Case C–250/03 *Mauri* [2005] ECR I–1267, paragraph 30].'

'32. There is a clear difference between the two cases. In the first case an agreement between undertakings is in existence before the State measure which validates or reinforces it. The State's liability arises from the fact that it aggravates by its action conduct that is already anticompetitive. In the second case, in which the State delegates its authority to private entities, undertakings adopt a decision which is then codified in a legislative measure. Application of Articles 10 EC and 81 EC is therefore designed to prevent a measure's form alone making it subject to competition law. In my view, that means that the concept of delegation must be interpreted in a substantive way by requiring an assessment of the decision-making process leading to the adoption of the State legislation. The following cases are covered by the concept of substantive delegation: first, delegation by the State to a private entity of the right to adopt a measure and, second, delegation of official authority to a private entity to review the decision-making process leading to the adoption of a legislative measure. A State may be regarded as having delegated its authority where its intervention is limited to the formal adoption of a measure, even though public interest requires the way in which the decisions are adopted to be taken into account. To define the concept of "delegation" as covering both those cases strengthens the requirement for consistency to which State action is subject. That principle of consistency ensures that whilst the State is acting in the public interest its intervention is subject to political and democratic review procedures, and if it delegates the pursuit of certain objectives to private operators it must make them subject to the competition rules which constitute the procedures for supervising power within the market. However, the State cannot delegate certain powers to private market operators whilst exempting them from application of the competition rules. This extended interpretation of delegation ensures that exclusion of the application of the rules of competition law is due to submission to the public interest and not to appropriation of public authority by private interests.'

'33. This is why the case-law cited above must certainly be construed as meaning that it is necessary to be aware what aims the State is pursuing in order to determine when its action may be made subject to competition law. It is necessary to establish whether legislative action by the State is dominated by a concern to protect the public interest or, on the other hand, whether the degree to which private interests are being taken into account is likely to alter the overriding objective of the State measure, which is therefore to protect those interests. Involvement of private operators in the legislative process, at the stage at which a rule is proposed, or by their presence within a body responsible for drafting that rule, is likely to have a determining influence on the content of the rule. The danger is that a legislative provision might have the sole purpose of protecting certain private interests from the elements of competition, to the detriment of the public interest.'

'34. There is no doubt that there is no justification for making every State measure subject to Articles 10 EC and 81 EC. The concerns expressed in their Opinions by Advocates General Jacobs and Leger in *Pavlov and others* and *Arduino*, respectively, are not along those lines, but follow closely the case-law. They set out two criteria for determining whether State measures are in fact under the control of private operators. In their view, the measure in question does not constitute an infringement of Articles 10 EC and 81 EC, first, if its adoption is justified by pursuit of a legitimate public interest and, secondly, if Member States actively supervise the involvement of private operators in the decision-making process. Those criteria are intended to establish to what extent the State is supervising delegation to private operators. Although the criteria set out are intended to be cumulative, it seems to me that the public interest criterion covers the other criterion too. It is even liable to lead the Court to assess all measures likely to reduce competition. This is perhaps the reason why the Court rejected the adoption of such a criterion.'

'35. However, in my view, the concerns underlying the Advocate Generals' suggestions are valid. It seems to me that current case-law allows them to be answered. … Doubts remain, however, as to the way in which this criterion is assessed by the Court, in particular as regards the effectiveness of the supervision exercised by the State, since formal control of the nature of the measure would appear to be inadequate …'

CIF v Autorità Garante della Concorrenza e del Mercato	**Competition Law and the State**
Case C–198/01	Article 10 EC
ECJ, [2003] ECR I–8055, [2003] 5 CMLR 16	Penalties for Infringement

Facts

Reference under Article 234 EC which originated from proceedings in the Italian court in which Consorzio Industrie Fiammiferi (CIF), the Italian consortium of domestic match manufacturers, challenges a decision of the Italian national competition authority which declared the legislation establishing and governing the CIF contrary to Articles 10 EC and 81 EC and found that CIF and the undertakings comprising it infringed Article 81 EC through the allocation of production quotas.

Held

'… although Articles 81 EC and 82 EC are, in themselves, concerned solely with the conduct of undertakings and not with laws or regulations emanating from Member States, those articles, read in conjunction with Article 10 EC, which lays down a duty to cooperate, none the less require the Member States not to introduce or maintain in force measures, even of a legislative or regulatory nature, which may render ineffective the competition rules applicable to undertakings (see Case 13/77 *GB-Inno-BM* [1977] ECR 2115, paragraph 31; Case 267/86 *Van Eycke* [1988] ECR 4769, paragraph 16; Case C–185/91 *Reiff* [1993] ECR I–5801, paragraph 14; Case C–153/93 *Delta Schiffahrts-und Speditionsgesellschaft* [1994] ECR I–2517, paragraph 14; Case C–96/94 *Centro Servizi Spediporto* [1995] ECR I–2883, paragraph 20; and Case C–35/99 *Arduino* [2002] ECR I–1529, paragraph 34).' (para 45)

'The Court has held in particular that Articles 10 EC and 81 EC are infringed where a Member State requires or favours the adoption of agreements, decisions or concerted practices contrary to Article 81 EC or reinforces their effects, or where it divests its own rules of the character of legislation by delegating to private economic operators responsibility for taking decisions affecting the economic sphere (see *Van Eycke*, paragraph 16; *Reiff*, paragraph 14; *Delta Schiffahrts- und Speditionsgesellschaft*, paragraph 14; *Centro Servizi Spediporto*, paragraph 21; and *Arduino*, paragraph 35).' (para 46)

'Moreover, since the Treaty of Maastricht entered into force, the EC Treaty has expressly provided that in the context of their economic policy the activities of the Member States must observe the principle of an open market economy with free competition (see Articles 3a(1) and 102a of the EC Treaty (now Article 4(1) EC and Article 98 EC)).' (para 47)

The duty to disapply national legislation which contravenes EC law applies to national courts and other organs of the State, including administrative authorities. Article 81 EC in conjunction with Article 10 EC, 'imposes a duty on Member States to refrain from introducing measures contrary to the Community competition rules, those rules would be rendered less effective if, in the course of an investigation under Article 81 EC into the conduct of undertakings, the authority were not able to declare a national measure contrary to the combined provisions of Articles 10 EC and 81 EC and if, consequently, it failed to disapply it.' (paras 49–50)

However, with respect to the penalties which may be imposed on the undertakings concerned, 'if the general Community-law principle of legal certainty is not to be violated, the duty of national competition authorities to disapply such an anti-competitive law cannot expose the undertakings concerned to any penalties, either criminal or administrative, in respect of past conduct where the conduct was required by the law concerned. … Once the national competition authority's decision, finding an infringement of Article 81 EC and disapplying such an anti-competitive national law, becomes definitive … the decision becomes binding on the undertakings concerned. From that time onwards the undertakings can no longer claim that they are obliged by that law to act in breach of the Community competition rules. Their future conduct is therefore liable to be penalised.' (paras 52–5)

The national competition authority may impose penalties on the undertakings concerned in respect of past conduct where the conduct was merely facilitated or encouraged by the national legislation. The level of the penalty in this case may be assessed in the light of the national legal framework, which is a mitigating factor. (paras 56–8)

'… it is for the referring court to assess whether national legislation such as that at issue in the main proceedings, under which competence to fix the retail selling prices of a product is delegated to a ministry and power to allocate production between undertakings is entrusted to a consortium to which the relevant producers are obliged to belong, may be regarded, for the purposes of Article 81(1) EC, as precluding those undertakings from engaging in autonomous conduct which remains capable of preventing, restricting or distorting competition.' (paras 80, 59–80)

Comment

Articles 10 EC and 81 EC are infringed where a Member State (1) requires or (2) favours the adoption of agreements, decisions or concerted practices contrary to Article 81 EC or (3) reinforces their effects. The appraisal of reinforcement of effects is comprised of two stages: first the Court needs to ascertain the prior existence of agreements, decisions or concerted practices of that kind to which the legislation refers to. Secondly, the Court needs to assess whether the national regulation has the purpose or the effect of reinforcing the effects of such agreements, decisions and concerted practices.

In Case 311/85 *Vzw Vereniging van Vlaamse Reisbureaus v Vzw Sociale Dienst van de Plaatselijke en Gewestelijke Overheidsdiensten*, [1987] ECR 3801, [1989] 4 CMLR 213, the ECJ was asked to provide a preliminary ruling on the lawfulness of the statutory prohibition on granting of certain rebates by Belgian travel agencies. The ECJ considered whether the legislation in question requires or favours the conclusion of agreements contrary to Article 81 EC or reinforces their effects. First the ECJ ascertained that in the travel business there was a network of restrictive agreements contrary to Article 81 EC, both between the travel agents themselves and between travel agents and tour operators, the purpose or effect of which was to compel travel agents to observe the travel prices set by tour operators and subsequently restrict competition. Secondly, the ECJ considered whether the national legislation was capable of reinforcing the effects of agreements concluded between travel agents and tour operators. The ECJ concluded that this was the case.

In Case C–2/91 *Criminal proceedings against Wolf W Meng*, [1993] ECR I–5751, the ECJ was asked by the Higher Regional Court in Berlin to clarify the obligation of the State under Articles 10 and 81 EC. The case concerned insurance regulations preventing insurance intermediaries from transferring to their clients all or part of the commission paid to them by insurance companies. Mr Meng, a professional financial adviser, was subjected to a fine for infringement of these regulations and challenged, on appeal, their lawfulness under Articles 10 and 81 EC. The ECJ observed that 'the German rules on insurance neither require nor favour the conclusion of any unlawful agreement, decision or concerted practice by insurance intermediaries, since the prohibition which they lay down is a self-contained one.' (para 15) The Court then proceeded to determine whether the rules have the effect of reinforcing an anticompetitive agreement. The rules at issue were not preceded by any agreement in the sectors to which they relate. The Court held that it is not relevant that agreements to prohibit transfers of commission existed in other sectors of insurance, to which the legislation does not apply. 'Rules applicable to a particular branch of insurance cannot be regarded as reinforcing the effects of a pre-existing agreement, decision or concerted practice unless they simply reproduce the elements of an agreement, decision or concerted practice between economic agents in that sector.' (para 20)

Klaus Höfner and Fritz Elser v Macrotron GmbH	**Competition Law and the State**
Case C–41/90	Article 86(1) EC
ECJ, [1991] ECR I–1979, [1993] 4 CMLR 306	Article 86(2) EC

Facts

The dispute surrounded a recruitment contract concluded between recruitment consultants Hofner and Elser, on the one hand, and Macrotron, on the other. As required by the contract, Hofner and Elser presented Macrotron with a candidate for the post of sales director. However, Macrotron decided not to appoint that candidate and refused to pay the fees stipulated in the contract. Hofner and Elser commenced proceedings against Macrotron before the Munich Regional Court but the court dismissed their claim. On appeal to the Munich Higher Regional Court, the court considered that the contract at issue could be void as it infringed a national regulation which entrusted, subject to certain derogations, the 'Federal Office for Employment' with an exclusive right of employment procurement in Germany. The court referred the case to the ECJ, asking about, among other things, the interpretation of Article 86 EC and the legality of the national regulation.

Held

Employment procurement activity is an economic activity which is not necessarily carried out by public entities. A public employment agency such as the 'Federal Office for Employment' engaged in the business of employment procurement is an undertaking within the meaning of Articles 81 and 82 EC. (paras 20–23)

'… a public employment agency which is entrusted, under the legislation of a Member State, with the operation of services of general economic interest … remains subject to the competition rules pursuant to [Article 86 (2) EC] unless and to the extent to which it is shown that their application is incompatible with the discharge of its duties (see judgment in Case 155/73 *Sacchi* [1974] ECR 409).' (para 24)

'As regards the manner in which a public employment agency enjoying an exclusive right of employment procurement conducts itself in relation to executive recruitment undertaken by private recruitment consultancy companies, it must be stated that the application of [Article 82 EC] cannot obstruct the performance of the particular task assigned to that agency in so far as the latter is manifestly not in a position to satisfy demand in that area of the market and in fact allows its exclusive rights to be encroached on by those companies.' (para 25)

'Whilst it is true that [Article 82] concerns undertakings and may be applied within the limits laid down by [Article 86(2)] to public undertakings or undertakings vested with exclusive rights or specific rights, the fact nevertheless remains that the Treaty requires the Member States not to take or maintain in force measures which could destroy the effectiveness of that provision (see judgment in Case 13/77 *Inno* [1977] ECR 2115, paragraphs 31 and 32). [Article 86(1)] in fact provides that the Member States are not to enact or maintain in force, in the case of public undertakings and the undertakings to which they grant special or exclusive rights, any measure contrary to the rules contained in the Treaty, in particular those provided for in [Articles 81 to 89].' (para 26)

'Consequently, any measure adopted by a Member State which maintains in force a statutory provision that creates a situation in which a public employment agency cannot avoid infringing [Article 82 EC] is incompatible with the rules of the Treaty.' (para 27)

'It must be remembered, first, that an undertaking vested with a legal monopoly may be regarded as occupying a dominant position within the meaning of [Article 82 EC] (see judgment in Case 311/84 CBEM [1985] 3261) and that the territory of a Member State, to which that monopoly extends, may constitute a substantial part of the common market (judgment in Case 322/81 *Michelin* [1983] ECR 3461, paragraph 28).' (para 28)

'Secondly, the simple fact of creating a dominant position of that kind by granting an exclusive right within the meaning of [Article 86(1) EC] is not as such incompatible with Article 82 of the Treaty (see Case 311/84

CBEM, ... paragraph 17). A Member State is in breach of the prohibition contained in those two provisions only if the undertaking in question, merely by exercising the exclusive right granted to it, cannot avoid abusing its dominant position.' (para 29)

'Pursuant to [Article 82(b) EC], such an abuse may in particular consist in limiting the provision of a service, to the prejudice of those seeking to avail themselves of it.' (para 30)

'A Member State creates a situation in which the provision of a service is limited when the undertaking to which it grants an exclusive right extending to executive recruitment activities is manifestly not in a position to satisfy the demand prevailing on the market for activities of that kind and when the effective pursuit of such activities by private companies is rendered impossible by the maintenance in force of a statutory provision under which such activities are prohibited and non-observance of that prohibition renders the contracts concerned void.' (para 31)

'It must be observed, thirdly, that the responsibility imposed on a Member State by virtue of [Articles 82 and 86(1) EC] is engaged only if the abusive conduct on the part of the agency concerned is liable to affect trade between Member States ...' (para 32)

A Member State which has conferred an exclusive right to carry on that activity upon the public employment agency is in breach of Article 86(1) EC where it creates a situation in which that agency cannot avoid infringing Article 82 EC. That is the case, in particular, where: (1) the exclusive right extends to executive recruitment activities; (2) the public employment agency which enjoys exclusivity is incapable of satisfying demand for such activities, and (3) the pursuit of those activities by private recruitment consultants is rendered impossible by the statutory provision, and (4) the activities in question may extend to the nationals or to the territory of other Member States. (paras 27–34)

Comment

The analysis comprises of two stages. First the existence of an undertaking is ascertained, and following this, the public nature of the undertaking is assessed (finding public undertakings or undertakings to which Member States granted special or exclusive rights).

The concept of 'public undertaking' was referred to by the ECJ in Case 188/80 etc *French Republic, Italian Republic and the UK v Commission*, [1982] ECR 2545, [1982] 3 CMLR 144. There, the ECJ dismissed applications to declare void the directive on the transparency of financial relations between Member States and public undertakings that was adopted by the Commission on the basis of Article 86(3) EC. The Court upheld the definition of public undertaking in the directive, which encompasses 'any undertaking over which the public authorities may exercise directly or indirectly a dominant influence by virtue of their ownership of it, their financial participation therein or the rules which govern it. A dominant influence is to be presumed when the public authorities directly or indirectly hold the major part of the undertakings' subscribed capital, control the majority of the votes, or can appoint more than half of the members of its administrative, managerial or supervisory body.' Note, however, that the ECJ considered that the object of the definition in the directive's provision is not to define the concept of public undertakings as it appears in Article 86 EC, 'but to establish the necessary criteria to delimit the group of undertakings whose financial relations with the public authorities are to be subject to the duty laid down by the Directive to supply information.' (para 24)

The analysis of Article 86(1), which addresses the Member State, and Article 86(2) EC, which addresses the undertaking, is closely linked in this case as the public authority was both a 'public undertaking' within the meaning of Article 86(1) EC, and an 'undertaking entrusted with the operation of services of general economic interest' within the meaning of Article 86(2) EC.

The conferral of exclusive rights may lead to infringement when other surrounding factors make abuse inevitable. Note AG Jacobs opinion and comment on the criteria for establishing abuse. (paras 42–50)

ERT and others v DEP and others	**Competition Law and the State**
Case C–260/89	Article 86(1) EC
ECJ, [1991] ECR I–2925, [1994] 4 CMLR 540	Article 86(2) EC

Facts

A reference for a preliminary ruling from the Thessaloniki Regional Court. The case concerned the exclusive rights granted by the Greek State to Elliniki Radiophonia Tileorassi (ERT), a Greek radio and television undertaking, to organise, exploit and develop radio and television. These exclusive rights were infringed by Dimotiki Etairia Pliroforissis (DEP) and the Mayor of Thessaloniki, which set up a television station. ERT brought summary proceedings before the Thessaloniki Regional Court against the two. In court, the defendants relied on the provisions of Community law and the European Convention on Human Rights. The Greek court stayed the proceedings and referred to the ECJ several questions on the lawfulness of the television monopoly.

Held

'In Case C–155/73 *Sacchi* [1974] ECR 409, paragraph 14, the Court held that nothing in the Treaty prevents Member States, for considerations of a non-economic nature relating to the public interest, from removing radio and television broadcasts from the field of competition by conferring on one or more establishments an exclusive right to carry them out.' (para 10)

'Nevertheless, it follows from [Article 86(1) and (2) EC] that the manner in which the monopoly is organized or exercised may infringe the rules of the Treaty, in particular those relating to the free movement of goods, the freedom to provide services and the rules on competition.' (para 11)

'The reply to the national court must therefore be that Community law does not prevent the granting of a television monopoly for considerations of a non-economic nature relating to the public interest. However, the manner in which such a monopoly is organized and exercised must not infringe the provisions of the Treaty on the free movement of goods and services or the rules on competition.' (para 12)

'The independent conduct of an undertaking must be considered with regard to the provisions of the Treaty applicable to undertakings, such as, in particular, [Articles 81, 82 and 86(2)].' (para 28)

Article 82 EC may be applicable in this case as an undertaking which has a statutory monopoly may be regarded as having a dominant position within the meaning of Article 82 EC. Although Article 82 EC does not prohibit monopolies as such, it nevertheless prohibits their abusive conduct. (paras 30–32)

'... [Article 86(1) EC] prohibits the granting of an exclusive right to transmit and an exclusive right to retransmit television broadcasts to a single undertaking, where those rights are liable to create a situation in which that undertaking is led to infringe [Article 82 EC] by virtue of a discriminatory broadcasting policy which favours its own programmes, unless the application of [Article 82 EC] obstructs the performance of the particular tasks entrusted to it.' (paras 38, 34–8)

Comment

Note the difference between this case and *Höfner v Macrotron*. Whereas in *Höfner v Macrotron* (page 259 above) the abuse was inevitable due to the incapability of satisfying demand, in *ERT v DEP* the ECJ held that 'the manner in which the monopoly is organized or exercised may infringe the rules of the Treaty'. (para 11) This finding led the court to reach the conclusion in paragraph 38. See also Case C–179/90 *Merci v Siderurgica Gabrielli SpA*, page 262 below.

Merci v Siderurgica Gabrielli SpA	**Competition Law and the State**
Case C–179/90	Article 86(1) EC
ECJ, [1991] ECR I–5889, [1994] 4 CMLR 422	Conferral of Exclusive Rights

Facts

The questions arose in the course of proceedings in the Italian Tribunale di Genova where Siderurgica Gabrielli SpA (Siderurgica) demanded compensation from Merci Convenzionali Porto di Genova SpA (Merci) for the damage it had suffered as a result of delays in the unloading of goods in the port of Genoa. In Italy, the loading and trans-shipment of goods in ports was governed by the 'Navigation Code' and reserved by it to dock-work companies whose workers were of Italian nationality. Merci enjoyed the exclusive right to organise dock work in the Port of Genoa. On reference to the ECJ, the Italian court asked, among other things, whether Article 86(1) EC precludes rules of a Member State which confer on an undertaking established in that State, the exclusive right to organise dock work and require it, for the performance of such work, to have recourse to a dock-work company formed exclusively of nationals.

Held

'… a dock-work undertaking enjoying the exclusive right to organize dock work for third parties, as well as a dock-work company having the exclusive right to perform dock work, must be regarded as undertakings to which exclusive rights have been granted by the State within the meaning of [Article 86 (1) EC].' (para 9)

'… as to the existence of exclusive rights, it should be stated first that with regard to the interpretation of [Article 82 EC] the Court has consistently held that an undertaking having a statutory monopoly over a substantial part of the common market may be regarded as having a dominant position within the meaning of [Article 86 EC] (see the judgments in Case C–41/90 *Höfner and Elser v Macrotron* [1991] ECR I–1979, paragraph 28 Case C–260/89 *ERT v DEP* [1991] ECR I–2925, paragraph 31).' (para 14)

The simple fact of creating a dominant position by granting exclusive rights within the meaning of Article 86(1) EC is not as such incompatible with Article 82 EC. However, a Member State is in breach of those two provisions if the undertaking in question, merely by exercising the exclusive rights granted to it, cannot avoid abusing its dominant position or when such rights are liable to create a situation such that it is induced to commit such abuses. (paras 16–17)

It appears that in this case the undertakings enjoying exclusive rights in accordance with the national rules are, as a result, 'induced either to demand payment for services which have not been requested, to charge disproportionate prices, to refuse to have recourse to modern technology, which involves an increase in the cost of the operations and a prolongation of the time required for their performance, or to grant price reductions to certain consumers and at the same time to offset such reductions by an increase in the charges to other consumers.' (para 19)

Comment

Similarly to *ERT v DEP* (page 261 above), the court focused on the inability of the undertaking to avoid abusing its dominant position merely by exercising the exclusive rights granted to it (paras 16–17). This extension to the judgment in *Höfner v Macrotron* widens the application of Article 86 EC and makes it more likely that the conferral of exclusive rights would lead to a conclusion of potential infringement of competition rules.

RTT v GB-Inno-BM SA	**Competition Law and the State**
Case C–18/88	Article 86(1) EC
ECJ, [1991] ECR I–5941	

Facts

A dispute between RTT and GB-Inno-BM (GB) in the Brussels Commercial Court. Under Belgian law RTT was granted an exclusive right to supply and approve equipment connected to the national telephone network. It claimed in court that GB, which sold non-approved telephones, infringed this exclusive right. In its defence, GB contested the legality of the legislation granting RTT the exclusive right. The national court referred the case to the ECJ, asking it to assess the legality of the legislation.

Held

'… RTT has the power to grant or withhold authorization to connect telephone equipment to the network, the power to lay down the technical standards to be met by that equipment, and the power to check whether the equipment not produced by it, is in conformity with the specifications that it has laid down.' (para 15)

'… the fact that an undertaking holding a monopoly in the market for the establishment and operation of the network, without any objective necessity, reserves to itself a neighbouring but separate market, in this case the market for the importation, marketing, connection, commissioning and maintenance of equipment for connection to the said network, thereby eliminating all competition from other undertakings, constitutes an infringement of [Article 82 EC]' (para 19)

'However, [Article 82 EC] applies only to anti-competitive conduct engaged in by undertakings on their own initiative … not to measures adopted by States. As regards measures adopted by States, it is [Article 86(1) EC] that applies. Under that provision, Member States must not, by laws, regulations or administrative measures, put public undertakings and undertakings to which they grant special or exclusive rights in a position which the said undertakings could not themselves attain by their own conduct without infringing [Article 82].' (para 20)

'Accordingly, where the extension of the dominant position of a public undertaking or undertaking to which the State has granted special or exclusive rights results from a State measure, such a measure constitutes an infringement of [Article 86] in conjunction with [Article 82 EC].' (para 21)

'… it is the extension of the monopoly in the establishment and operation of the telephone network to the market in telephone equipment, without any objective justification, which is prohibited as such by [Article 82 EC], or by [Article 86(1) EC] in conjunction with [Article 82 EC], where that extension results from a measure adopted by a State.' (para 24)

RTT's monopoly is intended to make a public telephone network available to users, and constitutes a service of general economic interest within the meaning of Article 86(2) EC. However the restriction of competition on the market in telephone equipment cannot be regarded as justified by a task of a public service of general economic interest within the meaning of Article 86(2). (paras 16, 22)

Comment

In paragraph 24 the Court held that it was the extension of the monopoly, rather than a potential abusive action by RTT, which infringed the competition provisions. The State was not allowed to leverage RTT's dominant position from the telephone network to the market in telephone equipment.

Criminal proceedings against Paul Corbeau	**Competition Law and the State**
Case C–320/91	Article 86(1) EC
ECJ, [1993] ECR I–2533, [1995] 4 CMLR 621	Article 86(2) EC

Facts

Mr Corbeau provided, within the City of Liège, Belgium, a service consisting of mail collection and distribution. He was charged in court with infringing Belgian legislation which conferred on the 'Regie des Postes' an exclusive right to collect and distribute mail. In a preliminary reference the Belgian Tribunal Correctionnel de Liège asked the ECJ, among other things, whether the Belgian legislation establishing the postal monopoly is contrary to Article 86 EC.

Held

A body such as the 'Regie des Postes' which has been granted exclusive rights to collect and distribute mail must be regarded as an undertaking to which the Member State concerned has granted exclusive rights within the meaning of Article 86(1) EC. (para 8)

'… the Court has consistently held that an undertaking having a statutory monopoly over a substantial part of the common market may be regarded as having a dominant position within the meaning of [Article 82 EC] (see the judgments in Case C–179/90 *Merci Convenzionali Porto di Genova* [1991] ECR I–5889 at paragraph 14 and in Case C–18/88 *RTT v GB-Inno-BM* [1991] ECR I–5941 at paragraph 17).' (para 9)

'However, [Article 82 EC] applies only to anti-competitive conduct engaged in by undertakings on their own initiative, not to measures adopted by States (*RTT v GB-Inno-BM* judgment, paragraph 20).' (para 10)

'The Court has had occasion to state in this respect, that although the mere fact that a Member State has created a dominant position by the grant of exclusive rights, is not as such incompatible with [Article 82 EC], none the less requires the Member States not to adopt or maintain in force any measure which might deprive those provisions of their effectiveness (see the judgment in Case C–260/89 *ERT* [1991] ECR I–2925, paragraph 35).' (para 11)

'Thus [Article 86(1) EC] provides that in the case of public undertakings to which Member States grant special or exclusive rights, they are neither to enact nor to maintain in force any measure contrary to the rules contained in the Treaty with regard to competition.' (para 12)

'That provision must be read in conjunction with [Article 86(2) EC] which provides that undertakings entrusted with the operation of services of general economic interest are to be subject to the rules on competition in so far as the application of such rules does not obstruct the performance, in law or in fact, of the particular tasks assigned to them.' (para 13)

'That latter provision thus permits the Member States to confer on undertakings to which they entrust the operation of services of general economic interest, exclusive rights which may hinder the application of the rules of the Treaty on competition in so far as restrictions on competition, or even the exclusion of all competition, by other economic operators are necessary to ensure the performance of the particular tasks assigned to the undertakings possessed of the exclusive rights.' (para 14)

As regards the services at issue in the main proceedings, the 'Regie des Postes' is entrusted with a service of general economic interest. The question to be considered is therefore 'the extent to which a restriction on competition or even the exclusion of all competition from other economic operators is necessary in order to allow the holder of the exclusive right to perform its task of general interest and in particular to have the benefit of economically acceptable conditions'. (paras 15, 16)

'The starting point of such an examination must be the premise that the obligation on the part of the undertaking entrusted with that task to perform its services in conditions of economic equilibrium presupposes that it will be possible to offset less profitable sectors against the profitable sectors and hence justifies a restriction of competition from individual undertakings where the economically profitable sectors are concerned.' (para 17)

'Indeed, to authorize individual undertakings to compete with the holder of the exclusive rights in the sectors of their choice corresponding to those rights would make it possible for them to concentrate on the economically profitable operations and to offer more advantageous tariffs than those adopted by the holders of the exclusive rights since, unlike the latter, they are not bound for economic reasons to offset losses in the unprofitable sectors against profits in the more profitable sectors.' (para 18)

'However, the exclusion of competition is not justified as regards specific services dissociable from the service of general interest which meet special needs of economic operators and which call for certain additional services not offered by the traditional postal service, such as collection from the senders' address, greater speed or reliability of distribution or the possibility of changing the destination in the course of transit, in so far as such specific services, by their nature and the conditions in which they are offered, such as the geographical area in which they are provided, do not compromise the economic equilibrium of the service of general economic interest performed by the holder of the exclusive right.' (para 19)

'The answer to the questions referred to the Court … should therefore be that it is contrary to [Article 86 EC] for legislation of a Member State which confers on a body such as the Regie des Postes the exclusive right to collect, carry and distribute mail, to prohibit, under threat of criminal penalties, an economic operator established in that State from offering certain specific services dissociable from the service of general interest which meet the special needs of economic operators and call for certain additional services not offered by the traditional postal service, in so far as those services do not compromise the economic equilibrium of the service of general economic interest performed by the holder of the exclusive right. It is for the national court to consider whether the services in question in the main proceedings meet those criteria.' (para 21)

Comment

Note that in *Corbeau*, as well as in *RTT v GB-Inno-BM SA* (page 263 above), the ECJ applied Article 86(1) EC in conjunction with Article 82 EC directly to the Member State's action without separately requiring an undertaking's abuse.

It is possible to distinguish *Corbeau* from *RTT v GB-Inno-BM SA* on the basis that the former required a weaker link between Article 86(1) EC and the finding of abuse under Article 82 EC. *Corbeau* seems to suggest that in the circumstances of that case, the mere conferral of exclusive rights (i.e. creation of dominance) would lead to conclusion of infringement of the competition rules. Such wide interpretation, shifts the focus from Article 86(1) to Article 86(2) EC and in doing so also shifts the burden of proof.

Arguably, this shift would inevitably result in a widening of the protection offered by Article 86(2) EC in an attempt to counterbalance the harshness of Article 86(1) EC. In this respect note that in paragraph 17 the ECJ justified the restriction by the need to offset less profitable sectors against the profitable sectors. Note, however, the opinion Mr Advocate General Tesauro in which he proposes a less restrictive alternative, taking into account the possibility for the postal service to achieve financial equilibrium without harming the rapid delivery service through the creation of certain thresholds. (paras 18–19)

Corsica Ferries France SA v Gruppo Antichi Ormeggiatori del porto di Genova
Case C–266/96
ECJ, [1998] ECR I–3949, [1998] 5 CMLR 402

Competition Law and the State
Article 86(1) EC
Article 86(2) EC

Facts

Reference for preliminary ruling from the Tribunale di Genova, concerning proceedings in the Italian court between Corsica Ferries France SA (Corsica Ferries) and Gruppo Antichi Ormeggiatori del Porto di Genova Coop arl (Porto di Genova). In the proceedings Corsica Ferries requested the court to order Porto di Genova and other mooring providers to return fees it paid to them for mooring services. Corsica Ferries argued, among other things, that there was no legal cause for the payments it had made and that the payments had been imposed in breach of the competition rules. Porto di Genova and the other mooring providers operated under Italian legislation which granted them exclusive rights to provide mooring services. The ECJ considered, among other things, the compatibility of these provisions with Article 86 EC.

Held

The creation of a dominant position by granting exclusive rights is not in itself incompatible with Article 82 EC. However, a Member State is in breach of Articles 82 and 86 EC if the undertaking in question, while exercising the exclusive rights granted to it, is led to abuse its dominant position. 'It follows that a Member State may, without infringing [Article 82 EC], grant exclusive rights for the supply of mooring services in its ports to local mooring groups provided those groups do not abuse their dominant position or are not led necessarily to commit such an abuse.' (paras 41, 40–41)

In order to rebut the existence of abuse, the Genoa and La Spezia mooring groups rely on Article 86(2) EC and maintain that the tariffs applied are indispensable if a universal mooring service is to be maintained. It must therefore be considered whether the mooring service can be regarded as a service of general economic interest within the meaning Article 86(2) EC, which can only be achieved through the measures stipulated in the legislation. (paras 42–4)

Mooring operations in the circumstances surrounding this case 'are of general economic interest, such interest having special characteristics, in relation to those of other economic activities, which is capable of bringing them within the scope of [Article 86(2) EC]. Mooring groups are obliged to provide at any time and to any user a universal mooring service, for reasons of safety in port waters. At all events, the Italian Republic could properly have considered that it was necessary, on grounds of public security, to confer on local groups of operators the exclusive right to provide a universal mooring service.' (para 45)

'In those circumstances it is not incompatible with [Articles 82 and 86(1) EC] to include in the price of the service a component designed to cover the cost of maintaining the universal mooring service, inasmuch as it corresponds to the supplementary cost occasioned by the special characteristics of that service, and to lay down for that service different tariffs on the basis of the particular characteristics of each port. Consequently, since the mooring groups have in fact been entrusted by the Member State with managing a service of general economic interest within the meaning of [Article 86(2) EC] ... legislation such as that at issue does not constitute an infringement of [Article 82 EC], read in conjunction with [Article 86(1) EC].' (paras 46–7)

Comment

Universal services were referred to in the Commission's Green Paper on Services of General Interest (COM/2003/0270 final), as those who are 'made available at a specified quality to all consumers and users throughout the territory of a Member State, independently of geographical location, and, in the light of specific national conditions, at an affordable price. ... In a liberalised market environment, a universal service obligation guarantees that everybody has access to the service at an affordable price and that the service quality is maintained and, where necessary, improved.' (para 50)

Firma Ambulanz Glöckner v Landkreis Sudwestpfalz	**Competition Law and the State**
Case C–475/99	Article 86(1) EC
ECJ, [2001] ECR I–8089, [2002] 4 CMLR 21	Article 86(2) EC

Facts

Proceedings in the German court between 'Ambulanz Glockner', a private undertaking providing non-emergency ambulance services, and the administrative district Landkreis Sudwestpfalz (Landkreis). Under regional legislation (paragraph 18(3) of the Rettungsdienstgesetz 1991), the Landkreis can refuse authorisation for the provision of ambulance transport services if this would be likely to have an adverse effect on the general interest in the operation of an effective public ambulance service. The Landkreis refused the renewal of the authorisation for Ambulanz Glockner on the basis that other 'medical aid organisations' entrusted with the public ambulance service were not being fully exploited and were operating at a loss. Ambulanz Glockner challenged the decision in court. In a preliminary reference to the ECJ the compatibility of the regulation with Article 86 EC was considered.

Held

Entities such as 'medical aid organisations' providing emergency transport services are engaged in economic activity and may be treated as undertakings. The regulation in question reserves the patient transport services to these undertakings and confers on them special or exclusive right within the meaning of Article 86(1) EC. These rights affect the ability of other operators to exercise the same economic activity. (paras 18–25)

In order to assess whether the regulation is liable to create a situation in which 'medical aid organisations' are led to commit abuses of a dominant position, the national court needs to establish the existence of a dominant position and then that such position was abused, without any objective necessity. A Member State will be in breach of the prohibitions laid down in Articles 82 and 86 EC only if the undertaking in question, merely by exercising the special or exclusive rights conferred upon it, is led to abuse its dominant position or where such rights create a situation in which that undertaking is led to commit such abuses. (paras 30–42)

The regulation in question gave an advantage to 'medical aid organisations' that already had an exclusive right on the urgent transport market by also allowing them to provide non-emergency patient transport exclusively. The regulation therefore has the effect of limiting markets to the prejudice of consumers within the meaning of Article 82(b) EC. (para 43)

It is necessary to examine whether the regulation may be justified by the existence of a task of operating a service of general economic interest, within the meaning of Article 86(2) EC. The question to be determined is 'whether the restriction of competition is necessary to enable the holder of an exclusive right to perform its task of general interest in economically acceptable conditions. The Court has held that the starting point in making that determination must be the premise that the obligation, on the part of the undertaking entrusted with such a task, to perform its services in conditions of economic equilibrium presupposes that it will be possible to offset less profitable sectors against the profitable sectors and hence justifies a restriction of competition from individual undertakings in economically profitable sectors (*Corbeau*, paragraphs 16 and 17).' (paras 56, 57, 51–7)

'It is true that, in paragraph 19 of *Corbeau*, the Court held that the exclusion of competition is not justified in certain cases involving specific services, severable from the service of general interest in question, if those services do not compromise the economic equilibrium of the service of general economic interest performed by the holder of the exclusive rights.' (para 59)

'However, that is not the case with the two services now under consideration, for two reasons in particular. First, unlike the situation in *Corbeau*, the two types of service in question, traditionally assumed by the medical aid organisations, are so closely linked that it is difficult to sever the non-emergency transport services from the task of general economic interest constituted by the provision of the public ambulance service, with which they also have characteristics in common.' (para 60)

'Second, the extension of the medical aid organisations' exclusive rights to the non-emergency transport sector does indeed enable them to discharge their general-interest task of providing emergency transport in conditions of economic equilibrium. The possibility which would be open to private operators to concentrate, in the non-emergency sector, on more profitable journeys could affect the degree of economic viability of the service provided by the medical aid organisations and, consequently, jeopardise the quality and reliability of that service.' (para 61)

'However, as the Advocate General explains in point 188 of his Opinion, it is only if it were established that the medical aid organisations entrusted with the operation of the public ambulance service were manifestly unable to satisfy demand for emergency ambulance services and for patient transport at all times that the justification for extending their exclusive rights, based on the task of general interest, could not be accepted.' (para 62)

'It is for [the] national court to determine whether the medical aid organisations which occupy a dominant position on the markets in question are in fact able to satisfy demand and to fulfil not only their statutory obligation to provide the public emergency ambulance services in all situations and 24 hours a day but also to offer efficient patient transport services.' (para 64)

Consequently, the regulation is justified under Article 86(2) EC 'provided that it does not bar the grant of an authorisation to independent operators where it is established that the medical aid organisations entrusted with the operation of the public ambulance service are manifestly unable to satisfy demand in the area of emergency transport and patient transport services.' (para 65)

Comment

The term 'services of general economic interest' in Article 86(2) EC has been referred to in the Commission's 'Communication on services of general economic interest' ([2001] OJ C 17/4) as one 'which the Member States subject to specific public service obligations by virtue of a general interest criterion. This would tend to cover such things as transport networks, energy and communications' (Annex II). Also note the Commission's 2003 Green Paper and subsequent White Paper on Services of General Interest (COM/2003/0270).

In Case 66/86 *Ahmed Saeed Flugreisen and others v Zentrale zur Bekämpfung unlauteren Wettbewerbs*, [1989] ECR 803, the ECJ held that the approval by the public authority of agreements regarding airline tariffs which are contrary to Article 81 EC and do not benefit from exemption under Article 81(3) is contrary to Article 86(1) EC. The ECJ added that Article 86(2) EC may be applicable where air carriers are obliged by the public authorities to operate on routes that are not commercially viable but in which it is necessary to operate for reasons of the general interest. However, for this to be possible the national authorities responsible for the approval of tariffs and the courts to which disputes relating thereto are submitted must be able to determine the exact nature of the needs in question and their impact on the structure of the tariffs applied by the airlines in question. (paras 47–58)

Albany International BV v Stichting	**Competition Law and the State**
Bedrijfspensioenfonds Textielindustrie	Article 86(1) EC
Case C–67/96	Article 86(2) EC
ECJ, [1999] ECR I–5751, [2000] 4 CMLR 446	

Facts

A preliminary reference to the ECJ which originated in proceedings in the Netherlands Hoge Raad in which three undertakings challenged orders issued by the 'Netherlands sectoral pension funds' demanding payment of the contributions to their respective schemes. The ECJ was asked to appraise, among other things, whether the sectoral pension system in the Netherlands which includes compulsory affiliation to the pension funds infringes Article 86(1) EC in conjunction with Article 82 EC.

Held

'The decision of the public authorities to make affiliation to a sectoral pension fund compulsory … necessarily implies granting to that fund an exclusive right to collect and administer the contributions paid with a view to accruing pension rights. Such a fund must therefore be regarded as an undertaking to which exclusive rights have been granted by the public authorities, of the kind referred to in [Article 86(1) EC].' (para 90)

An undertaking which has a legal monopoly in a substantial part of the common market may be regarded as occupying a dominant position within the meaning of Article 82 EC. Subsequently, a sectoral pension fund which has an exclusive right to manage a supplementary pension scheme in an industrial sector in a Member State may be regarded as occupying a dominant position. (paras 91–2)

The creation of a dominant position by granting exclusive rights within the meaning of Article 86(1) EC is incompatible with Article 82 EC only when the undertaking in question, merely by exercising the exclusive rights granted to it, is led to abuse its dominant position or when such rights are liable to create a situation in which that undertaking is led to commit such abuses. In the present case the granting of an exclusive right conferred on the sectoral pension fund results in restriction of competition. (paras 93–7)

It is necessary to consider whether the exclusive right of the sectoral pension fund may be justified under Article 86(2) EC as a measure necessary for the performance of a particular social task of general interest with which that fund has been charged. Article 86(2) provides for derogations from the general rules of the Treaty and 'seeks to reconcile the Member States' interest in using certain undertakings, in particular in the public sector, as an instrument of economic or fiscal policy, with the Community's interest in ensuring compliance with the rules on competition and preservation of the unity of the common market.' (paras 103, 98–103)

The supplementary pension scheme at issue fulfils an essential social function within the Netherlands pensions system. The removal of the exclusive right conferred on the Fund might make it impossible for it to perform its tasks. The fund is therefore not precluded by Articles 82 and 86(1) EC. (paras 104–23)

Comment

The Court held that the granting of the exclusive right conferred on the sectoral pension fund resulted in restriction of competition. However, it did not explore how the undertaking in question, merely by exercising the exclusive rights granted to it, was led to abuse its dominant position. (paras 93–7) It is possible that the court omitted this examination since the exclusive right of the sectoral pension fund was held justified under Article 86(2) EC.

French Republic v Commission	**Competition Law and the State**
Case C–202/88	Article 86(3) EC
ECJ, [1991] ECR I–1223, [1992] 5 CMLR 552	Article 86(1) EC

Facts

Application brought by the French Republic for the partial annulment of Commission Directive 88/301/EEC of 16 May 1988 on 'competition in the markets in telecommunications terminal equipment' which was adopted on the basis of Article 86(3) EC.

Held

'Inasmuch as it makes it possible for the Commission to adopt directives, [Article 86(3) EC] empowers it to lay down general rules specifying the obligations arising from the Treaty which are binding on the Member States as regards the undertakings referred to in [Article 86(1) and (2)].' (para 14)

'… [Article 86(3) EC] empowers the Commission to specify in general terms the obligations arising under [Article 86(1) EC] by adopting directives. The Commission exercises that power where, without taking into consideration the particular situation existing in the various Member States, it defines in concrete terms the obligations imposed on them under the Treaty. In view of its very nature, such a power cannot be used to make a finding that a Member State has failed to fulfil a particular obligation under the Treaty.' (para 17)

With respect to the substantive provisions of the Directive:

Article 2 of the Directive relates to the abolition of special and exclusive rights regarding the importation, marketing and connection of terminal equipment and/or maintenance of such equipment. The Article deprives undertakings of the possibility of having their products purchased by consumers. Additionally, due to technical complexity an undertaking with exclusive rights might not be able to satisfy demand. This in turn would restrict consumer choice and interstate trade. The Article must therefore be declared void in so far as it requires the withdrawal of such rights. (paras 31–47)

With respect to the legality of Article 7 of the directive, this Article requires Member States to make it possible to terminate leasing or maintenance contracts which are subject to exclusive or special rights within a maximum notice period of one year. The Article aims at resolving the anticompetitive effects stemming from long-term contracts which prevented the introduction of free competition. However, there is no indication that that the conclusion of long-term contracts was compelled or encouraged by State regulations. Consequently, that Article falls outside the scope of Article 86(3) EC which confers powers on the Commission only in relation to State measures and not in relations to anticompetitive conduct engaged in by undertakings on their own initiative. Article 86(3) EC is therefore not an appropriate basis for dealing with the obstacles to competition created by the long-term contracts. (paras 53–7)

Comment

In the judgment the ECJ noted that the power of surveillance in Article 86(3) EC conferred on the Commission the power to specify obligations resulting from the Treaty. That provision is more specific than the powers of the Council acting under Article 95 EC or Article 83 EC. This finding allows the Commission to control the form and nature of the directives, in contracts to the Article 95 EC route which allows Member States to affect the scope and nature of the Directive. (see paras 23–5)

Article 86(3) EC and the power of surveillance provide the Commission with a valuable route to specify in general terms the obligations of Member States. As such it provides an effective alternative to the commencing of proceedings against the individual Member States under Article 226 EC.

10

Extraterritoriality

Principles of Extraterritoriality

In the field of competition law an infringement can have consequences within a given territory even though the conduct that caused that consequence occurred, and may have even been completed, elsewhere. In order to protect their domestic markets, competition agencies may extend their jurisdiction beyond the boundaries of their state and apply their national laws to activities that may have been cleared by the local jurisdiction in which they took place, but nevertheless affect competition within the former.

This concept of extraterritoriality departs from the traditional 'territoriality principle' under which a country has the power to make laws to affect conduct within its territory or to regulate conduct which although initiated in another jurisdiction, is completed within its territory.

The extension of the territoriality principle in competition cases commonly relies on two concepts. The first extends jurisdiction when it finds that the transaction had an 'effect' within its territory. The second is more restricted in nature and requires 'implementation' within its territory, as a condition for extraterritorial application of domestic laws.

The Effects Doctrine

The examination of effects was initially recognised by the Permanent Court of International Justice in the *Lotus* case, with regard to the extent of states' criminal jurisdiction over acts causing a collision in open sea (*France v Turkey*, 1927 Permanent Court of International Justice, Ser A, no 10). The Court found that international law does not contain a general prohibition on states to extend the application of their laws and the jurisdiction of their courts to persons, property and acts outside their territory. The Court developed the objective of the territorial principle into its variation of the effects principle and stated that 'offences ... which at the moment of commission are in the territory of another State, are nevertheless to be regarded as having been committed in the national territory, if one of the constituent elements of the offence, and more especially its effects, have taken place there'. (para IV)

The effects doctrine has been particularly significant in the United States' enforcement of Antitrust law. In *United States v Aluminum Co of America*, the US Second Circuit Court asserted that: 'Any state may impose liabilities, even upon persons not within its allegiance, for conduct outside its borders, which has consequences within its borders, which State reprehends; and these liabilities other States will ordinarily recognize.' *United States v Aluminum Company of America* (Aloca) 148 F 2d 416 (2 Cir 1945)

In following cases such as *Timberlane Lumber Co v Bank of America* (549 F 2d at 596, 613–14 (9th Cir 1976)) and *Metro Industries Inc v Sammi Corp* (82 F 3d 839 (9th Cir 1996)), the courts applied the effects doctrine in a more restrictive way and required that not only should there be a direct and substantial effect within the US, but also that the respective interests of the US should be weighed against the interests of other States involved. Other cases followed a more expansive approach as laid down by the Supreme Court in the case of *Hartford Fire Insurance Co v California* (*Hartford Fire Insurance Co v California* 113 S Ct 2891 (1993)).

These cases, although different in their tone and emphasis, share the notion that under certain conditions the finding of direct and substantial effects enables the assertion of US jurisdiction.

The Implementation Doctrine

The ECJ has taken a narrower approach and has refrained from a direct and clear adoption of the 'effects' doctrine. In its rulings, the ECJ preferred to limit itself to the extension of the territoriality principle.

In the *Wood Pulp* judgment, the ECJ held that jurisdiction under EC law exists over firms outside the Community if they implement a price-fixing agreement reached outside the EC by selling to purchasers within the Community. See:

89/95 etc	*A Ahlström Osakeyhtiö v Commission* (Wood Pulp)	273

The implementation doctrine has also been used as the jurisdictional benchmark for establishing control over cross-border merger transactions. In *Gencor Limited v Commission* the Court of First Instance made reference to the implementation principle as established in *Wood Pulp* before finding that the transaction can be subjected to the European Merger Regulation. See:

T–102/96	*Gencor Ltd v Commission*	275

See also summary references to:

IV/M.877	*Boeing/McDonnell Douglas*	276
COMP/M.2220	*General Electric/Honeywell*	276

Effects vis-à-vis Implementation

Although the effects and implementation doctrines rely on different principles of public international law, they do provide for a similar jurisdictional coverage. In other words, most anticompetitive activities would generate effects through implementation, thus satisfying both benchmarks. A noticeable activity which may results in 'effects' yet not 'implementation' is the one of boycott cartel, where undertakings refuse to supply goods to a territory, thus affecting competition without implementing the agreement in the foreign territory.

The Single Economic Entity Doctrine

Another doctrine that has been used to exert jurisdiction over foreign undertakings is the 'single economic entity' doctrine. This doctrine enables the extension of jurisdiction over corporations located outside the jurisdiction by treating the corporate group as a single economic unit and attributing the conduct of one of the group's members which is located in the jurisdiction to other members of the group based outside the jurisdiction. This doctrine is limited in scope and application, as it requires the presence of at least one of the group's undertaking in the domestic territory and the finding of a 'single economic entity'. See:

C–48/69	*Imperial Chemical Industries Ltd v Commission*	277

Also note the discussion in Chapter 1 on the concept of 'undertakings' and 'single economic entity'.

A Ahlström Osakeyhtiö and others v Commission (Wood Pulp)
Joined Cases 89, 104, 114, 116, 117 and 125 to 129/85
ECJ, [1988] ECR 5193, [1988] 4 CMLR 901

Extraterritoriality
Implementation Doctrine

Facts

In this case, the Commission had issued a decision against non-EC producers of wood pulp for various restrictive practices alleged to have restrained trade within the EC. A number of the producers had no subsidiaries or branches in the EC and one, KEA, was a US Webb–Pomerene export association. The Commission stated that Article 81 EC applies to restrictive practices which may affect trade between Member States even if the undertakings and associations which are parties to the restrictive practices are established outside the Community. The foreign defendants argued, among other things, that the Commission lacked jurisdiction over them because of their location outside the EC. The ECJ rejected their argument and held that jurisdiction under EC law exists over firms outside the Community if they implement price fixing reached outside the EC by selling to purchasers within the Community.

Held

'In so far as the submission concerning the infringement of [Article 81 EC] itself is concerned, it should be recalled that that provision prohibits all agreements between undertakings and concerted practices which may affect trade between Member States and which have as their object or effect the restriction of competition within the common market.' (para 11)

'It should be noted that the main sources of supply of wood pulp are outside the Community, in Canada, the United States, Sweden and Finland, and that the market therefore has global dimensions. Where wood pulp producers established in those countries sell directly to purchasers established in the Community and engage in price competition in order to win orders from those customers, that constitutes competition within the common market.' (para 12)

'It follows that where those producers concert on the prices to be charged to their customers in the Community and put that concertation into effect by selling at prices which are actually coordinated, they are taking part in concertation which has the object and effect of restricting competition within the common market within the meaning of [Article 81 EC].' (para 13)

'Accordingly, it must be concluded that by applying the competition rules in the Treaty in the circumstances of this case to undertakings whose registered offices are situated outside the Community, the Commission has not made an incorrect assessment of the territorial scope of [Article 81].' (para 14)

'The applicants have submitted that the decision is incompatible with public international law on the grounds that the application of the competition rules in this case was founded exclusively on the economic repercussions within the common market of conduct restricting competition which was adopted outside the Community.' (para 15)

'It should be observed that an infringement of [Article 81 EC], such as the conclusion of an agreement which has had the effect of restricting competition within the common market, consists of conduct made up of two elements, the formation of the agreement, decision or concerted practice and the implementation thereof. If the applicability of prohibitions laid down under competition law were made to depend on the place where the agreement, decision or concerted practice was formed, the result would obviously be to give undertakings an easy means of evading those prohibitions. The decisive factor is therefore the place where it is implemented.' (para 16)

'The producers in this case implemented their pricing agreement within the common market. It is immaterial in that respect whether or not they had recourse to subsidiaries, agents, sub-agents, or branches within the Community in order to make their contacts with purchasers within the Community.' (para 17)

'Accordingly the Community's jurisdiction to apply its competition rules to such conduct is covered by the territoriality principle as universally recognized in public international law.' (para 18)

'As regards the argument based on the infringement of the principle of non-interference, it should be pointed out that the applicants who are members of KEA have referred to a rule according to which, where two States have jurisdiction to lay down and enforce rules and the effect of those rules is that a person finds himself subject to contradictory orders as to the conduct he must adopt, each State is obliged to exercise its jurisdiction with moderation. The applicants have concluded that by disregarding that rule in applying its competition rules the Community has infringed the principle of non-interference.' (para 19)

'There is no need to enquire into the existence in international law of such a rule since it suffices to observe that the conditions for its application are in any event not satisfied. There is not, in this case, any contradiction between the conduct required by the United States and that required by the Community since the Webb Pomerene Act merely exempts the conclusion of export cartels from the application of United States anti-trust laws but does not require such cartels to be concluded.' (para 20)

'It should further be pointed out that the United States authorities raised no objections regarding any conflict of jurisdiction when consulted by the Commission pursuant to the OECD Council Recommendation of 25 October 1979 concerning Cooperation between Member Countries on Restrictive Business Practices affecting International Trade (Acts of the Organization, Vol 19, p 376).' (para 21)

'Accordingly it must be concluded that the Commission's decision is not contrary to [Article 81 EC] or to the rules of public international law relied on by the applicants.' (para 23)

Comment

By referring to the implementation of the agreement (and not to its formation) and by relying on the specific facts of the case, the ECJ was able to establish jurisdiction using an extension of the territoriality principle. Overall, although tailored narrowly to the facts of the case, *Wood Pulp* set the basic criteria for the extraterritorial application of EC competition law while defining the implementation of an agreement as the leading benchmark for jurisdiction.

The Court held that implementation is not dependant on the existence of 'subsidiaries, agents, sub-agents, or branches within the Community'. (para 17) The focus is therefore on the act of sale within the Community. Note in this respect the CFI judgment in Case T–102/96 *Gencor Ltd v Commission* (page 275 below) in which the court held that 'the implementation of an agreement is satisfied by mere sale within the Community'. (para 87)

After establishing the extraterritorial jurisdiction based on the implementation doctrine, the Court considered the possible infringement of the principle of non-interference. It held that there was no contradiction between the conduct required by the United States and that required by the Community since the Webb–Pomerene Act merely permits the conclusion of export cartels but does not require such cartels to be concluded. (paras 19–21)

In his opinion, Advocate General Darmon asserted that the wording of Article 81 EC offers general support for the applicability of EC competition law whenever anticompetitive effects have been produced within the territory of the Community. The Advocate General, supporting the adoption of the effects doctrine, took the view that it is 'neither the nationality nor the geographical location of the undertaking but the location of the anti-competitive effect which constitutes the criteria for the application of Community competition law'. (Opinion of the Advocate General (MM Darmon) [1988] 4 CMLR 901 at 916–37)

Gencor Ltd v Commission
Case T–102/96
CFI, [1999] ECR II–753, [1999] 4 CMLR 971

Facts

Gencor, a company incorporated under South African law, and Lonrho Plc (Lonrho), a company incorporated under English law, proposed to acquire joint control of Impala Platinum Holdings Ltd (Implats), a company incorporated under South African law. The transaction was cleared by the South African Competition Board. The European Commission also reviewed the transaction under the European Merger Regulation (ECMR) and was concerned with its impact on the common market. Following its investigation the Commission blocked the transaction on the ground that it would lead to the creation of a dominant duopoly position in the world platinum and rhodium market as a result of which effective competition would have been significantly impeded in the common market. On appeal to the CFI for annulment of the decision, Gencor argued, among other things, that the Commission lacked jurisdiction over the transaction at issue.

Held

In contrast to the Commission's view, the mere notification of a concentration to the Commission under the procedure in the ECMR does not imply a voluntary submission by the undertaking to the Commission's jurisdiction. Such notification stems from the severe financial penalties which may be imposed under the ECMR for failure to notify the Commission of the concentration. (para 76)

The ECMR applies to all Concentrations with a Community Dimension. Article 1 ECMR does not require that, in order for a Concentration to be regarded as having a Community Dimension, the undertakings in question must be established in the Community or that the production activities covered by the Concentration must be carried out within Community territory. (paras 78–86)

'According to *Wood Pulp*, the criterion as to the implementation of an agreement is satisfied by mere sale within the Community, irrespective of the location of the sources of supply and the production plant. It is not disputed that Gencor and Lonrho carried out sales in the Community before the concentration and would have continued to do so thereafter.' (para 87)

'Accordingly, the Commission did not err in its assessment of the territorial scope of the [ECMR] by applying it in this case to a proposed concentration notified by undertakings whose registered offices and mining and production operations are outside the Community.' (para 88)

It is necessary to consider whether the Commission's decision is compatible with principles of public international law. In this case the concentration would have altered the competitive structure within the common market since in would reduce the number of undertakings in the market from three to two. 'The implementation of the proposed concentration would have led to the merger not only of the parties' … operations in South Africa but also of their marketing operations throughout the world, particularly in the Community where Implats and LPD achieved significant sales.' (para 89)

Application of the Regulation is justified under public international law when it is foreseeable that a proposed concentration will have an immediate, substantial and foreseeable effect in the Community. These three criteria are satisfied in this case. (paras 90–101)

It is necessary to examine next whether the Community violated a principle of non-interference or the principle of proportionality in exercising its jurisdiction. In this case there was no conflict between the course of action required by the South African Government and that required by the Commission given that the South African competition authorities simply concluded that the concentration agreement did not give rise to any competition policy concerns, without requiring that such an agreement be entered into. (paras 102–05)

Comment

After establishing that the concentration had a Community dimension under the ECMR, the Court made references to the implementation doctrine and held that it is satisfied by a mere sale within the Community. Note that in practice, transactions which satisfy the requirement for concentration and Community dimension as set in the ECMR, will exhibit large turnover within the Community and thus satisfy the requirement for implementation. In other words, the ECMR jurisdictional threshold of concentration with a Community dimension encompasses the implementation threshold.

After referring to the implementation of the agreement, the CFI considered its effects in the common market. (paras 81–101) This section of the judgment created some ambiguity as to whether the CFI embraced the effects doctrine as a jurisdictional benchmark. This is not the case, as it is generally accepted that the CFI merely considered the compatibility of the decision with the international law principle of comity. Note that in practical terms, due to the level of Community turnover required to establish Community dimension, the ECMR jurisdictional threshold creates a strong nexus between the transaction and the common market and is likely to result not only in implementation but also in substantial and foreseeable effect.

The extraterritorial application of the ECMR became very common during the last merger wave. Two noticeable Commission Decisions that highlight the tension such long-arm jurisdiction may result in are the *Boeing/McDonnell Douglas* and *General Electric/Honeywell* transactions.

In *Boeing/McDonnell Douglas* (Case IV/M.877), the European Commission reviewed a transaction between two corporations based in the United States. Although neither Boeing nor McDonnell Douglas had any facilities or assets in the European Community, their Community-wide and worldwide turnover met the thresholds laid down in Article 1 ECMR and brought the transaction under the Commission's jurisdiction. Before the Commission withdrew its objections to the transaction, the merger triggered a debate on the Commission's authority to assess and block the transaction. Some critics suggested that the Commission's concerns were based purely on its protectionist interest in promoting Airbus, rejecting the Commission's claim that its investigation was conducted strictly on the basis of EU law. The tension between the EU and the US authorities increased, leading to President Clinton's announcement threatening that the matter could be taken to the World Trade Organization if the EU carried out its threat to declare the merger illegal. The clearance of the merger served to silence most of these critics, but nevertheless the case illustrated the possible political clashes due to extraterritorial application of merger analysis on significant transactions close to the heart of the home jurisdiction.

In the *General Electric/Honeywell* decision (Case COMP/M.2220), the European Commission prohibited the proposed $42 billion acquisition by General Electric Co (GE) of Honeywell Inc. The Commission asserted that the merger would have severely reduced competition in the aerospace industry by combining GE's strong position in the aircraft engine markets with Honeywell's similarly strong position in avionics and non-avionics systems. The importance of the *GE/Honeywell* decision lies in the fact that the Commission's decision followed an opposite conclusion by the US Department of Justice (DOJ), which cleared the merger earlier that year, requiring only minimal disposals. The DOJ Antitrust Division reached the conclusion that the merger, as modified by the remedies insisted upon, would have been procompetitive and beneficial to consumers. The DOJ concluded that the combined firm would offer better products and services at more attractive prices than either firm could do individually. In addition to the differences in the legal approach towards the transaction, the extraterritoriality resulted in political tension between the two jurisdictions. Similar to the *Boeing/McDonnell Douglas* case, this transaction drew attention to the possibility of implementing non-competitive considerations disguised by competition analysis. The Commission was subject to accusations that it implemented such considerations in its assessment. Commissioner Monti rejected these claims, asserting that 'this is a matter of law and economics, not politics'. The Commissioner added that 'the nationality of the companies and political considerations have played and will play no role in the examination of mergers in this case and in all others.' This statement by the Commission may also be seen as a response to increased political pressure from the US, attempting to persuade the Commission to relax its opposition.

Imperial Chemical Industries Ltd v Commission (Dyestuffs)	**Extraterritoriality**
Case 48/69	Economic Entity Doctrine
ECJ, [1972] ECR 619, [1972] CMLR 557	

Facts

An appeal on a Commission Decision in which it found seventeen producers of dyestuffs established within and outside the Common Market to have colluded with the aim of increasing the price of dyestuffs. In its decision the Commission asserted that Article 81 EC applies to all agreements or concerted practices which distort competition within the common market, regardless of the location of the undertakings involved. On appeal, the producers challenged the Commission's jurisdiction over undertakings based outside the Community.

Held

The increased prices at issue were put into effect within the common market. The actions for which the fine at issue has been imposed constitute practices carried on directly within that market. (paras 127, 128)

'By making use of its power to control its subsidiaries established in the Community, the applicant was able to ensure that its [d]ecision was implemented on that market.' (para 130)

'The applicant objects that this conduct is to be imputed to its subsidiaries and not to itself.' (para 131)

'The fact that a subsidiary has separate legal personality is not sufficient to exclude the possibility of imputing its conduct to the parent company.' (para 132)

'Such may be the case in particular where the subsidiary, although having separate legal personality, does not decide independently upon its own conduct on the market, but carries out, in all material respects, the instructions given to it by the parent company.' (para 133)

'Where a subsidiary does not enjoy real autonomy in determining its course of action in the market, the prohibitions set out in [Article 81(1) EC] may be considered inapplicable in the relationship between it and the parent company with which it forms one economic unit.' (para 134)

'In view of the unity of the group thus formed, the actions of the subsidiaries may in certain circumstances be attributed to the parent company.' (para 135)

In this case the applicant held the majority of the shares in the subsidiaries and was able to exercise decisive influence over the policy of the subsidiaries as regards selling prices in the common market. In fact the applicant used this power in relation to the three price increases in question. 'The formal separation between these companies, resulting from their separate legal personality, cannot outweigh the unity of their conduct on the market for the purposes of applying the rules on competition.' (paras 136–40)

Comment

In this case the ECJ had its first opportunity to rule on the extraterritorial application of competition law. The ECJ refrained from ruling directly on the existence or lack of existence of the effects doctrine under European law and relied on the economic-entity doctrine. The judgment was criticised as to the finding of a single economic entity, since it was supported by unsubstantial evidence. Note in this respect Chapter 1 and the conditions under which the separate legal personalities of companies give way to a finding of a single economic entity.

The Commission, supported by Advocate General Mayras, favoured the acceptance of the effects doctrine. It was claimed that substantial and foreseeable effects in the EU should trigger the extraterritorial application of Articles 81 and 82 EC.

Index

Introductory Note

References such as '178–9' indicate (not necessarily continuous) discussion of a topic across a range of pages. Key locations – where the term referenced is defined in a chapter introduction or highlighted in a case entry – are identified by bold type. Because the entire volume is about competition law, the use of this and related terms occurring constantly throughout (notably Articles 81 and 82 EC) as entry points has been minimized. Information will be found under the corresponding detailed topics